THE GOOD PARSI

· · · THE · · ·
GOOD PARSI

*The Fate
of a
Colonial Elite
in a
Postcolonial
Society*

· · ·

T. M. LUHRMANN

Harvard University Press
Cambridge, Massachusetts
London, England
1996

Design by Marianne Perlak

Library of Congress Cataloging-in-Publication Data

Luhrmann, T. M. (Tanya M.), 1959–
The good Parsi : the fate of a colonial elite in a
postcolonial society / T. M. Luhrmann.
p. cm.
Includes bibliographical references (p. 000) and index.
ISBN 0-674-35675-6 (cloth : alk. paper).
—ISBN 0-674-35676-4 (paper : alk. paper)
1. Parsees—Social conditions.
2. Parsees—History—20th century.
3. Parsees—Ethnic identity.
4. Elites (Social sciences)—India—Bombay.
5. Zoroastrianism—India—Bombay.
6. Bombay (India)—Social life and customs.
I. Title.
DS432.P3L85 1996
305.891′411—dc20
95-51967

CONTENTS

Preface *vii*

Prologue: Fateful Embraces   *1*

1   The Current Community   27

2   In the Beginning   63

3   The Power and the Glory   96

4   We Are Not What We Were   126

5   Uncomfortable Realities   158

6   On Postcolonial Identity   186

7   Anthropological Repositionings   223

Notes   245
Bibliography   289
Acknowledgments   313
Index   315

I arrived in Bombay in 1987 to study Parsi Zoroastrianism. I was then interested in theology, and particularly in the problem of illogic in monotheistic religions. God is absolutely good, powerful, and knowing, and yet human life is fraught with pain. How does the anthropologist understand this paradox? Or rather, what is its meaning for a religious community? Parsi Zoroastrianism, with its potential dualism of good and evil, seemed a prime arena for this exploration.

I spent nine months in Bombay in 1987–88. For the most part, the fieldwork was a kind of "appointment" anthropology, very different from my previous study of middle-class London magic. There, I joined groups, and the groups provided me with a kind of village square in which most of what I wanted to see took place. The Parsis, too, had lunches and dinner parties and lectures and conferences, but there was no exemplary small group for me to join. And so I met a great number of people individually. On a typical day I would spend part of the morning in the K. R. Cama Oriental Institute, reading through its remarkable collection of Parsiana. In the afternoon and evening, I would have two to three coffee meetings and a lecture or class. In this way I traveled slowly along a list of acquaintances with my notebook. Many people I came to know quite well; many I met only once or twice. Most were of the middle class, neither the richest nor the poorest. Still, I had tea with J. R. D. Tata—a kind man—and some other members of the elite; and I also met some of the community indigents.

The outcome of this one-on-one socializing was quite unexpected. First, I noticed that the use people made of their theological resources was remarkably varied. An individual's theological orientation told me more about his temperament and the chance circumstances of personal history than about his community's theological struggles; there was nothing substantive enough to form the meaty center of an ethnography. A second problem was that Parsis kept querulously complaining about other Parsis—particularly about young Parsis, and particularly about their young men—and I had an eerie, embarrassed sense that there was something wrong with that kind of complaint, that it didn't make sense, that it needed to be explained. After all, Parsis had been perhaps the most powerful, important communities in Bombay over the last few centuries, and despite urban pressures the community was still comfortably middle-class and eminent. Some time after I left Bombay in 1988, I began to wonder whether the criticism might be related to the experience of the colonial period and to the wrenching process of reorientation to a quite different political order.

I returned to Bombay for three months in 1990. Later, in 1992, I spent several weeks in the India Office Library in London to enhance the historical reading I had done in Bombay. Meanwhile, I got to know some of the southern California Parsis and attended a large Zoroastrian congress in Houston. In 1993, on leave and at work on another project in Boston, I met a Parsi woman I had known in Bombay and spent time with a number of the other Boston Parsis; in 1994 attended yet another large Zoroastrian congress. It seemed to me that the American-based Parsis were, generally speaking, concerned with very different problems than were the Bombay Parsis. They had begun the complex process of "repositioning" their community sensibility, and they seemed to lack the harsh self-criticism of the Bombay community living in the shadow of a glorious past.

And so the book evolved into a study of the inappropriateness of these self-critical claims, and a search for their origin. It argues, essentially, that Parsis appropriated the powerful side of the colonialist constructions of India and that it is the unintended consequence of that self-identification which now causes them such grief. British colonial self-representation depicted the colonizers as manly, rational, and progressive, as against effeminate, irrational, and backward Indians. As did many elite Indians, turn-of-the-century Parsis, at the height of their remarkable economic, political, and cultural achievements, represented themselves as manly and rational and progressive like the British, and unlike the rest of backward India. This is of course a broad interpretation and more pertinent to the socially ambitious middle-level Parsis than to great individuals, but the archives bear out the claim at least in part. Now, Parsis seem to be caught out by this power play, and by a slow lag time in adjusting their semiotics to the changed political order. At least some Parsis seem now more likely to describe Hindus—who have won the battle for political and economic domination—as aggressive and progressing; many Parsis seem to condemn themselves as effeminate, irrational, and backward. And perhaps, the book tentatively suggests, this phenomenon is not unique to Parsis but is shared in some respect by other elite, sophisticated people whose grandparents defined themselves through the values of the western colonizing culture and who now, as postcolonial subjects in a very different world, must reconstruct and reorient a quite complex sensibility.

It would be disingenuous to suggest that I went to India because Zoroastrianism, of all possible projects, uniquely attracted me. After I finished the project on middle-class London magic, it was quite plain to me that to sustain an identity and a salary as an anthropologist I would have to do some fieldwork in the exotic third world. As it transpired, Bombay reminded me far more of New York and its tired professionals than did London, where fieldwork consisted in my being witch and wizard and invoking ancestral spirits around a weathered altar. Irony seems to be not only a trope for modern cacophony but an experience of it. This feeling raised for me a question that I address at the end of the book. Anthropology is repositioning itself to adjust to very different modern polities. It may be that some of its self-criticisms, like those of the Bombay Parsis, are similarly epiphenomena of a rapidly changing culture. The best way to handle the criticism may be to recognize just how ephemeral they are, and to focus our gaze on shifting the discipline from a study of the exotic other to a study of culture in which the close-to-home is as important as the far away.

The Parsis will not like this book. Many of them, if they read it, will say that it is not true. Criticisms of the community are embarrassing and private, and in the public domain they are often denied. Yet other Parsis told me that I must write this book and not produce another sweetly polite book about the glorious past. I decided that for me to deny the present-day distress was to reenact the denial that had led the community into the cul-de-sac in the first place. I care for the Parsis as a people, for their stubborn tenaciousness and their belly laughs and their ancient, white-frocked priests. And I also care deeply for many individual Parsis. That is why I wanted to write something for them that would matter and that might help, because it hurt to see them damage themselves by their own words. It may be hard for them to see this as *agape,* an act of love, but in its own way, it is.

Once upon a time, on an uninhabited island on the shores of the Red Sea, there lived a Parsee from whose hat the rays of the sun were reflected in more-than-oriental splendour . . . And one day he took flour and water and currants and plums and sugar and things, and made himself one cake which was two feet across and three feet thick. . . . And the Rhinoceros upset the oil stove with his nose, and the cake rolled on the sand, and he spiked that cake on the end of his nose, and he ate it . . . Then the Parsee came down from his palm tree and put the stove on its legs and recited the following *sloka* which, if you have not heard, I will now proceed to relate:—

> Them that takes cakes
> Which the Parsee-man bakes
> Makes dreadful mistakes . . .

Five weeks later, there was a heatwave in the Red Sea, and everybody took off all the clothes they had. The Parsee took off his hat; but the Rhinoceros took off his skin and carried it over his shoulder as he came down to the beach to bathe . . . Presently the Parsee came by and found the skin, and he smiled one smile that ran all around his face two times . . . He took that skin, and he shook that skin, and he scrubbed that skin, and he rubbed that skin just as full of old, dry, stale, tickly cake-crumbs and some burned currants as ever it could *possibly* hold . . . From that day to this every rhinoceros has great folds in his skin [from scratching the cake crumbs] and a very bad temper, all on account of the cake crumbs inside . . .

Rudyard Kipling
"How the Rhinoceros Got His Skin,"
Just So Stories

One of my Parsi friends told me a story which she said Lord Inchcape had told to her aunt, Mrs. Ratan Cama, her mother's sister-in-law. They were on a ship together, and Inchcape told her that when he came to India he had been told that he could swear at Indians, say anything he liked, and they wouldn't respond. But he mustn't use bad language to a Parsi, he was told. He went to Calcutta, and after some time there, during which he constantly swore at the Indians, he sent for a file, and when it arrived he swore at the man who brought it. The man picked up a ruler and smacked it against the table. "Do not use that language to me," he said. "Take back your words, sir. You asked for a file, I have brought it." "Are you a Parsi?" Lord Inchcape asked. "What does that matter?" the clerk replied. "You asked for a file, and I brought it." And from that time on, Lord Inchcape said, he remembered not to swear at Parsis.

THE GOOD PARSI

FATEFUL
EMBRACES

• • • P R O L O G U E • • •

In the center of Bombay stands a decaying mansion. Fort House was built as the private residence of Sir Jamshetji Jeejeebhoy, a merchant, the first Indian baronet and one of the most esteemed of the much esteemed nineteenth-century Parsis. In its time it was one of the great town houses and commanded a spacious view of the *maidan,* the great field which opened on to the Arabian Sea. Now, buildings obscure the vista. Jeejeebhoy was widely respected by the British, and to many Parsis, even today, he represents the pinnacle of Parsi achievements and the success for which they strive. All that remains of his town house is a facade, the grand scrollwork cracked, a garden of weeds where the piano once stood. Gutted by fire and abandoned by commerce, the facade is an icon of a community in decline.

• • •

Modern Parsis are a tiny Indian community settled in Bombay. They are an old people who emigrated from Persia a thousand years ago, probably to preserve Zoroastrianism from Islam. They were remarkably successful during the Raj. But their success came at the cost of jettisoning their adopted Indian identity in favor of a western one. As a native colonial elite, Parsis were more westernized than most other Indian elites, and as displaced Persians, they committed themselves thoroughly to a non-Indian sensibility. Now they feel marginalized in a postcolonial world, with an aching sense of a loss of status, of cultural genius, of their historical moment.

They had adopted, as a community, the ideals of the English gentleman and his wife. They had worn his clothes, taken his language, emulated his habits, and educated their women in his culture. These days, as the larger political winds have shifted and the singularity of Parsi eminence has passed, they accuse themselves of being everything the English gentleman was not: traditional, backward, unsophisticated, above all unmanned. I see in this self-criticism a desperate attempt to locate a sense of control and mastery over a now unmanageable world, an embittered effort to defend pride against the anxiety of decline, rather than a realistic assessment.

Anthropology itself shares some of these traits. I worry that it might seem strange to compare the anthropological subject with the discipline of its researchers, but Michael Herzfeld has shown us that we can learn from this rhetorical ploy. And it seems to me that as a cautionary tale Parsi distress carries a lesson for an anthropology in flux. Modern anthropologists are oddly like Parsis, and they share with this stalwart but struggling community the capacity to harangue themselves into irrelevance. Like the Parsis, to the degree that they live within the historical constraints of their past ambitions, with nostalgia or with anger, they suffer; but in refashioning themselves to the new historical realities they flourish. At the end of this analysis, then, I intend to draw the parallel with the repositioning of anthropology in late-twentieth-century America.

◆　◆　◆

British India was a glorious, grand, and tragically poignant world which implicated its players in emotional commitments whose traces still mark the prosaic lives of their descendents. As figured in Kipling, and in novels and memoirs and letters home, for the British that India was a larger-than-life fantasy—"that extraordinary world of crows and dust sunsets"[1]—of elaborate dinner parties with rigid etiquette, of pig stickings and polo. "Dinner parties that started with anchovy paste (always) and ended seven courses later with little glass bowls full of water and hibiscus flowers to wash the fingers in; of cane chairs on club verandahs and damp sugar full of ants; of shining Indian rivers and beautiful women."[2] An 1898 memoir recalled: "There was light, vastness, beauty, pomp and true affection. All was not gold, however . . . Our bedrooms were really merely barns, no ceilings, the bare rafters, bare walls, no fastenings to the doors, the bathrooms very much like sculleries, the flowery terraces suspected of concealing snakes and most certainly harbouring myriads of insects most supremely troublesome . . . Still, those were minor evils. It was all a stageplay life, and we were enchanted with it."[3] This was a romantic world of splendor and realistic danger, with a pomp greater than most of its middle-class administrators would have experienced at home, and worries about insurrection, large animals, and disease that could not have been envisioned in England's damp predictability.[4]

Reading these accounts now, from the jaundiced late-twentieth century, it seems that the British must have seen in India the reality of their nursery fantasies: tigers behind the closet door and heroic deeds before dinner. Stories circulated of villagers who asked their administrators to kill marauding tigers and treated those men as virtual gods. Servants called their masters "Heaven-born." There were extravagant celebrations: the *durbar* organized in 1902 to celebrate Edward VII's coronation involved a special five-mile railway to convey people around the celebratory area.[5] There were games, fireworks, music, and a grand state entry, watched by a million people, in which maharajahs on elephants, vividly costumed soldiers, and state government officials slowly advanced to a central dais from which the coronation was announced.[6] There were also beggars and lepers. Cholera and cobra could strike without warning, leaving children orphans and adults childless within hours. In one decade of the mid-eighteenth century, over seventy percent of the East India Company employees in Calcutta died of illness (Moorhouse 1983:31). "Everything is so sudden in India, the sudden twilights, the sudden death. A man can be talking to you at breakfast and be dead in the afternoon—and this is one of the things you have to deal with."[7] And it was also for the British a land of enchantment, of mystery and romance, which travelers constantly compared to the Arabian Nights. "The fantastic traffic of this city, half Indian, half European, fascinated me today with the garish ebb and flow of its population, perhaps the most variegated in hue of the world."[8] "A bed of flowers gives you no conception of its brilliancy."[9] Pictures of the British in India reiterate the drama of these imperial lives: the Englishman, surrounded by natives, holding up the head of a tiger he has just slain, the Englishwoman on horseback against the Himalayan peaks, the lady seated on her oriental carpet and attended by sixteen servants, Colonel James Todd, agent of the East India Company, on a palanquined elephant as he went about his business.[10] The British were intensely drawn to this world of sexuality and spectacle and magic, but they were compelled, as well, to control it, to deny themselves its seductiveness and uncertainty. George Orwell's "Shooting an Elephant" is about the flip side of this nursery-play come true: the civil servant steps into the grandly authoritative role of his imperialism (the villagers demand that he shoot an elephant) and he feels himself to be an embarrassed fool.

These are of course the resonant imaginings of those in power who have accepted the moral rightness of their power and believe in it earnestly, no matter what more self-interested motives may have influenced them to assume their righteousness. They can then romanticize their sufferings—which were genuine enough—and take just pride in their achievements, which were opulent. There was, beyond the threshold of the white man's bungalow, another India, in which famines were a plague let loose by British land-tenure policies and taxes; in which nascent processes of class differentiation rigidified and widened under British rule; in which money drained out of the Indian people who were in many ways prevented from making it and accumulated in the colonizing country; in which racial humiliation was a regularity so common that it was, like grammar, invisible to its speakers until disrupted. Still, the great promise of the white man's curtained power was that it seemed to have a threshold over which the educated, the well-born, and the successful could pass. And because of this implied advantage, those who saw themselves as the most eligible were perhaps less likely to see the invisible barriers of racial difference, less likely to feel outrage on the part of fellow natives, more prone to dream of the just achievement of their desires to be "as-if" Englishmen, for it is not unnatural to see the world in the way that seems to suit you best.

The story of the Parsis is the agony of the long-delayed recognition of the emptiness of this promise. When native elites identified with the British, they saw in their gloves and carriages a civilizing mission that would bring to India the grace and authority of a morally superior power. Indians—elite Indians, anyway—would become players on the grand stage of western philosophical, artistic, and socioeconomic endeavor. Their views would matter and their opinions would be sought after. They would be recognized as equals in the hard-fought battle against poverty, neglect and discontent; more than equals, indeed, because the battle would take place in the land of their blood and their history, which the British could understand only at second remove. The Indians who fought the fight would be rewarded in the amphitheatre of the western world, applauded not only by the British but by the French, the Germans, even the Americans; and India, with the manpower of her masses and the brilliance demonstrated by her leaders, would rise again to greatness. But these impassioned imaginings in the end only embarrassed their Parsi dreamers. The despair of their experience lies in a double loss, for after Gandhi and Independence, they were deprived both of the moral rightness of the British ideal and of the hope that if they embodied that ideal, power—real power—would come to them in the end. In India, Parsi memory and Parsi selves emerge from these Anglophilic dreams and their destruction, and the struggles of recent generations to reconnect.

The Colonized Soul

Loss and a melancholy nostalgia pervade the discourse of colonialism, for the colonial relationship itself is about the loss of homeland, the loss of confidence, and the loss of selfhood. But the overwhelming theme in many powerful accounts of colonialism is the desire and the danger that emerge around the boundary of self and other—the intense attraction to difference, complicated by the power asymmetry that renders the colonizer guilty and denying and the colonized yearning and denied. Gender and sexuality weave around these political and social themes like dancing girls (perhaps *hjiras*) because the sexual encounter, in which women figure inevitably as weaker but alluring, becomes an explosive metaphor for the forbidden attraction across the barrier. "This is the story of a rape," Paul Scott famously says at the start of his monumental portrait of the end of the Raj. "The affair that began on the evening of August 9th, 1942, in Mayapore, ended with the spectacle of two nations in violent opposition, not for the first time nor as yet for the last, because they were still locked in an imperial embrace of such long standing and subtlety it was no longer possible for them to know whether they loved or hated one another, or what it was that held them together and seemed to have confused the image of their separate destinies" (1966:1). Above all this sexual metaphor is a colonialist vision, in which desire, power, fear, unease, and attraction commingle in a morally ambiguous allegory of political relations. India becomes a sensual woman whom the good British man must resist; India is a native man who lusts violently for a white woman; yet India is also the perfect romance, and its voluptuousness will release the passion of the stilted English body. The English novels of imperial India settle firmly on these themes: the horror of Aziz's supposed attempt on Adela Quested and the suppressed homosexual bond between Aziz and Fielding in *A Passage to India*; Hari Kumar and Daphne Manners and the criss-crossing liaisons throughout the Raj Quartet; Olivia's affair with the Nawab in R. P. Jhabvala's *Heat and Dust* and her grandniece's determination to bear an Indian-sired baby while Olivia herself had aborted one. And as a colonialist idiom, the symbolic coupling enters into the elite Indian's imaging of India, in Tagore's sensual, mystical, rural, womanly Indian landscape as opposed to a practical, sociable, rational, manly west; in the aristocratic heroine of Gita Mehta's *Raj,* determined to live according to her traditions but still during turbulent times drawn to the just, kind Englishman; in the desire and alienation across the racial barriers between two families in Amitav Ghosh's *Shadow Lines;* in Salman Rushie's Saladin with his Pamela, in love with her but also with the Nirad Chaudhuri dream of possessing Britishness.[11] One of the most popular elite rumors around Independence was that Nehru was sleeping with Edwina Mountbatten, India getting her own back after years of emasculation. And the sexuality is invariably about loss, for the merging is about the loss of bounded selfhood, and the merging is invariably denied, so that both in the desire and its denial there is poignancy, what Suleri calls perpetual longing and perpetual loss. Those real unions which did occur metamorphozed into the liminal no-man's land in which the halfbreeds lived their lives, guardians of the province-crossing trains which held together the country's sprawling vastness.

This fictional sexual encounter serves to recognize a process which changed each partner forever.[12] "This colonialism colonizes minds in addition to bodies and it releases forces within the colonized societies to alter their cultural priorities once for all" (Nandy 1983:xi). Nandy points out how profoundly colonialism is a matter of psychological transformation. In a colonial context, self-awareness emerges within a hierarchical culture in which colonizers must feel themselves superior to and different from the colonized, and the colonized must desire to have the colonizer's authority through identifying with the colonizer, despite the impossibility of surmounting the difference upon which colonial authority depends. The tragedy of Macaulay's plan to make Englishmen with brown skins was that it worked in part; while brown-skinned Englishmen were never acknowledged by the English as English, everything in their cultural experience had taught them that their hope for goodness and power lay only in their Englishness.

To understand colonial elites, we must first understand the wrenching process of self-transformation for the colonizers with whom they identified. Edmund Gosse said of Kipling that his work "produces in the reader a peculiar thrill, a voluptuous and agitating sentiment of intellectual uneasiness . . . It excites, disturbs and attracts me; I cannot throw off its disquieting influence." The psychohistorian Wurgaft who quotes these lines (1983:xi) argues that the British conceptualized Indians as childlike, feminine, and in need of rigid control, because it was the only way they could comfortably dominate a people who fascinated and allured them by being different. "At an intrapsychic level the British were unable to separate their possession of India and control of its population from an erotic involvement with native life" (Wurgaft 1983:74). The anguished colonizer in this nostalgic configuration is an insecure man who hates the colonized because they allow him to dominate them (they agonize his conscience), and at the same time he knows that he needs their weakness to make him feel strong. He is a tragic figure who despises himself for his Indianness—for he becomes in part Indian, in order to understand and to cope— and is desperately lonely for yet distanced from his English roots. The newly arrived young British officer, frightened by the non-Englishness of his supposed subjects, "must have felt once again abandoned, threatened and worthless [as he had done in public school], must have raged again at his blindness and impotence, and must have wondered whether the twin ropes of his sanity and authority would hold" (McClure 1980:17).

Kipling is seen, then and now, as the scribe of this fearful, desperately defensive man, yearning on the one hand to become a part of the hot, dusty land, and on the other hand, horrified at the very thought and determined to resist its pull.[13] "I could never make up my mind," mused Leonard Woolf, "whether Kipling had moulded his characters accurately on the image of Anglo-Indian society or whether we were moulding our characters accurately in the image of a Kipling story" (1961:46). There are many Kiplings: the multiply ironic author of *Plain Tales of the Hills*; of the more complex, but more evasive *Kim*; of the fantastic *Jungle Books*. But surely one of his most revealing and most allegorical stories is "Without Benefit of Clergy," in which a British civil servant falls in love with a beautiful Indian woman who bears his child, who "was taken away as many things are in India—suddenly, and without warning" (1987b:145). Ameera dies because she loves him too much to leave him when cholera enters the city. The man has lost all he cared for in the world, and yet can tell no one—because, of course, and particularly for a man in the civil service, their union is secret, illicit, and unacceptable. His landlord, in sympathy, offers to raze their house so that no one shall know where it stood. Ameera is the India of the British heroics of desire, a romance of enduring devotion and painful loss: India is loving, loyal, dependent, but also capriciously cruel. And in the end, India is stronger than the British civil servant, and she breaks his heart, although he loved her. There is a remarkable tone to the British memoirs of India—the wistful fondness one finds, for example, in the memories collected in the B.B.C.'s *Plain Tales from the Raj*. These memoirs have the nostalgia of torn letters to an impossible love.

Scholars now argue that to defend themselves against their desire and their pain, the British in India constructed both themselves and their natives as dyadic opposites, particularly around the categories of gender, age, and race. The British were hypermasculinized, scientific and progressive, a high step on the evolutionary ladder; the Indians were effeminate, childlike, primitive, and superstitious. This speculative psychology of the colonial relation—Nandy himself depicts it as a myth—is now accepted as a fair portrayal of the British conceptualization of empire and (ultimately) of the colonial elite's identification with the aggressor.[14] Inden takes to its furthest extreme the argument that the India understood in the British civil service, by western scholars of India, by the ordinary British citizen, and ultimately, by Indians, was an imaginary realm constructed to demonstrate the superiority of its western imperialist. India's caste system, her spirituality, her ancient little villages, her feminine seduction, were, he argues, essentializing characteristics imposed on her by the colonizers to resist the agency and independence of her Indians. Inden describes the British conception of Hinduism thus: "Hinduism is a *female* presence who is able, through her very amorphousness and absorptive powers, to baffle and perhaps even threaten Western rationality, clearly a male in this encounter. European reason penetrates the womb of Indian unreason but always at the risk of being engulfed by her" (1990:86). Even here—Inden is not psychologically oriented—the same psychological themes emerge: the colonizer is insecure, seeks to dominate to reassure himself, conceptualizes the colonized as feminine and thus (being well-defended) simultaneously finds "India" appropriately mastered, but emotionally overwhelming.

To the extent that colonial elites modeled themselves upon the colonizers, they absorbed these peculiar, defensive semiotics. There was among elite Indians what Nandy calls a "homology between the sexual and the political" (1983:6) and from it followed a cultural collusion, particularly with the nineteenth-century cultural elite, which saw the British as the agent of change, which accepted a masculinized ethos of aggressive but gentlemanly competition, and which took the existence of British domination as proof of the masculine superiority that elite Indians should emulate. Elite Indians, of whom Parsis are only one but a remarkable example, shaped their ideals and sensibilities and the ideals and sensibilities of their children upon the canons of English colonial culture: its literature, its sociability, its competitive athletics, its pianos and lace and fitted suits, but also its dismissal of their countrymen as effeminate, traditional, and lowly. In the attempt to create a monotheistic Hinduism and a martial Indianness, in the hot, unfamiliar suits demanded by the British government which then became the required business dress, in an education replete with Dickens and Wordsworth, nineteenth-century elites replayed this copycat enculturation. Nandy presents Gandhi (believably, although Gandhi's character seems so idiosyncratic that it is hard to accept that his traits were deliberately chosen) as a man whose shrewdness enabled him to see that inverting the standard categories—becoming a feminine, childlike, fundamentally passive leader—could be to his advantage. Indeed, it was the seemingly innocent, irrelevant, passive Dandi Salt March that became the sign, to the watching western world, that the British were undone.

The psychological vise of colonialism receives perhaps its starkest depiction in two classic texts of colonial anguish: Albert Memmi's *The Colonizer and the Colonized* (1965) and Frantz Fanon's *Black Skin, White Masks* (1967).[15] Both responded to a brilliant (if misguided) psychological portrait of colonialism, written in 1948 by Oscar Mannoni about the Malagasy revolt and its repression. From Mannoni's perspective, colonizer and colonized each came to colonialism with powerful psychological needs which the colonial relationship could satisfy. The native had lived in a world of mutually dependent adults under the care of authoritative elders, while the colonizers drawn to the colonial situation had feared dependence and sought proof of their competitively successful autonomy. The European with an inferiority complex needed someone to dominate, and the Malagasy with a dependency complex needed someone on whom to depend. *Prospero and Caliban* is an effortlessly superior text, rendered more confident by the unabashed authority of its times. What is perhaps more remarkable is that both Memmi and Fanon acknowledge the rightness of the description—but as consequent to colonialism, not as its cause.

"I was Tunisian, therefore colonized. I discovered that few aspects of my life and my personality were untouched by this fact" (Memmi 1965:vii). The colonizer, Memmi writes, is usually a mediocre man drawn to a world which guarantees his superiority, and he clings to his superiority by all the rationalizations he can muster. His fervent patriotism, for instance, justifies his presence abroad and helps him to ignore the fact that colonialism, with all its armies and administration, taxes his mother country more than it rewards her. And he devalues the colonized, whose inadequacy demonstrates the need for his presence, but who must exist for him to be there at all.

> [The colonizer] is fed up with his subject, who tortures his conscience and his life. He tries to dismiss him from his mind, to imagine the colony without the colonized . . . But the colonialist realizes that without the colonized, the colony would no longer have any meaning. This intolerable contradiction fills him with a rage, a loathing, always ready to be loosed on the colonized, the innocent yet inevitable reason for his drama. (Memmi 1965:67)

Our reading of this text must not be a search for the historical trail of the emotional lives of those on either side of the colonial divide; what we must look for is the psychological drama which Memmi envisions, combatants locked in a death grip in which neither is victorious and both are emotionally consumed and destroyed.

> In order for the colonizer to be the complete master, it is not enough for him to be so in actual fact, but he must also believe in its legitimacy. In order for that legitimacy to be complete, it is not enough for the colonized to be a slave, he must also accept this role. The bond between colonized and colonizer is thus destructive and creative. It destroys and re-creates the two partners of colonization into colonizer and colonized. (1965:89)

The colonized man must live confronted by the flagrant contradictions of the colonizer's conception of him: he is a frugal man without wants, but also a lazy good-for-nothing with insatiable greed; he is a coward who must be protected and a brute who must be controlled. All these characterizations emerge from the colonizer's need to justify his political and thus economic command. And this becomes the source of what truth there is in the "dependency complex."

Against this colonial drama, for Memmi, the colonized has no choice but to rebel. He first aspires to the colonizer's style and role. He models himself on the colonizer, aping his customs and yearning for his appearance. He loses his past; he learns the history of Cromwell but nothing of his own progenitors. He grows embarrassed by his mother tongue. "The first ambition of the colonized is to become equal to that splendid model [of the colonizer] and to resemble him to the point of disappearing in him" (1965:120). The colonized agrees, in Memmi's words, to destroy himself and become what he is not. But then he learns that in the end the colonizer will reject him anyway, and he is filled with shame and self-hatred (1965:121–22). Ultimately, he has no choice. "Revolt is the only way out of the colonial situation, and the colonizer realizes it sooner or later" (1965:127). Then the colonized individual will return to his own, unassimilated culture. He will reject European dress and the European tongue. He will stop eating European food and smoking European cigarettes. "Having penetrated the colonizer's experience to the highest limit, to the point of finding it unbelievable, [the colonized] withdraw to their own bases" (1965:136). And yet he remains still tortured, still living in a psyche defined by the colonizer, defined by what he is not. "So goes the drama of the man who is a product and victim of colonialism. He almost never succeeds in corresponding with himself."[16]

Frantz Fanon's vision focused more closely and psychoanalytically on the paradoxical striving of the colonized to be Other. "For the black man there is only one destiny. And it is white" (1967:10). The black man in the Antilles becomes more white as he renounces Creole and adopts French, as he understands Montesquieu and talks about the opera, when he wears European clothes and follows European customs, when he touches a white woman. But he is not white, and can never be, and will never grasp that for which he reaches. "The good and merciful God cannot be black. He is a white man with bright pink cheeks" (1967:51). The so-called dependency complex is a situational response to colonialism, Fanon argued, and to the tensions inherent in the colonial encounter. It is not an expression of inherent tendencies towards dependence that lurked in the Malagasy soul. "The reactions and the behavior patterns to which the arrival of the European in Madagascar gave rise were not tacked on to a pre-existing set . . . If, for instance, Martians undertook to colonize the earthmen—not to initiate them into Martian culture but to *colonize* them—we should be doubtful of the persistence of any earth personality" (1967:95). After colonization, he argues, the Malagasy man no longer exists *sui generis;* he can only be understood in relation to the white man. The urge to be white—and thus, to please and imitate the white man—only arises in the white man's presence: "If [the Malagasy is overwhelmed to such a degree by the wish to be white, it is because he lives in a society that makes his inferiority complex possible [here attributing the inferiority complex to the black man], in a society that derives its stability from the perpetuation of this complex, in a society that proclaims the superiority of one race (1965:100)." The terrible cost of colonialism is that in yearning to be like the white colonizer, the black colonized man comes to accept the white man's vision of the black man and so to hate himself.

In the tense psychodynamics of this imagined standoff, the colonized native becomes to the white colonizer what the colonizer hopes is Other: the stupid, lazy savage who justifies economic domination, but also the aggressive, sexual, rageful bad self.[17] Fanon wrote of "the bad instincts, of the darkness inherent in every ego, of the uncivilized savage, the Negro who slumbers in every white man." As a black Antillean, particularly to the extent that one identifies with the cultured white world, one recognizes one's own blackness only in what shames one. "One is a Negro to the degree to which one is wicked, sloppy, malicious, instinctual. Everything that is the opposite of these Negro modes of behavior is white" (1967:192). And so, perpetually, the black man is torn, rejecting himself to become white, only then to grasp a more terrible vision of his never-to-be-scrubbed-clean skin. "A Negro is forever in combat with his own image" (1967:194). In this envisioning, the problem in colonialism is not that one portion of a population is exploited and underfed; the problem is that the more accomplished the colonized become, the more like the colonizers they look, the more they come to hate themselves. And only through revolution can they come to claim themselves.

How do we read these power politics of the soul? Like the Parsis, Memmi and Fanon were members of colonial elites, and the story they tell is probably irrelevant to the poor laborers who never dreamed of joining the colonizers in their class. Memmi was a Tunisian Jew. "More or less privileged in comparison with the colonized masses, but . . . rejected . . . by the colonizing group" (Memmi 1965:xxi), the Tunisian Jews were undeniably natives in colonial French eyes, but many had enthusiastically embraced the whole of French culture. Some bore arms with the French in the streets of Algiers, and felt threatened when the colonial structure began to weaken. Fanon studied medicine in France, in Lyons; he attended lectures by Merleau-Ponty and others, read deeply in European philosophy, married a French woman, and traveled widely. He became politically active in the Algerian struggle and elsewhere in Africa. Like the Parsis, then, these men understood profoundly the urge to identify with the colonizers and the powerful pleasures at the top of colonialism's hierarchy. And like Memmi and Fanon, many sophisticated, elite Parsis also became more or less radical revolutionaries. Dadabhai Naoroji, Madame Cama, Pherozeshah Mehta: in different ways, to different degrees, many Parsis saw the paradox of British identification—the more clearly you identify, the more you will come to hate yourself—and turned to the Indian majority to find a sense of positive selfhood. Elite Parsis were instrumental in creating the Indian National Congress, in encouraging the investment of capital into nationalistic projects like steel and iron foundries, even in advocating the use of violence to free India from British clutches. But among the majority of

Parsis, few were radical. Few adopted even the external appearance of colonial rejection by identifying with Indian nationalism in donning Indian clothes, eating Indian food, and communicating through Indian customs. And so the Parsis become a particularly interesting example of a common colonial phenomenon, for the loss of their attachment has been particularly protracted.

However well the literary representations of Nandy, Memmi, Fanon, and others capture the "real" relationship of British imperialist and Indian native—most writing about India in English, from E. M. Forster to Gita Mehta, is about the complex interaction of the real and what we might call the fantasies of transference—contemporary Parsis, I suspect, are acting out a response to this psychosocial burden of the past, in which they originally identified with the British representations of colonial superiority and are now confronted with the loss of that attachment and the need to adapt to a political reality in which that past attachment is seen as distinctly double-edged. The important and interesting consequence of this need to adapt seems to be that modern Parsi culture speaks a discourse of decay, in which Parsis attack themselves as inadequate—inadequate as Englishmen, inadequate as Indians, inadequate as effective, socially appropriate human beings.

Postcolonial Parsi woes are not what I had intended to study. I arrived in Bombay in 1987 because I had been told that this tiny community held active debates over the proper understanding of evil and the source of sorrow. The project was to evaluate the meaning of different answers, within the same small theological community, to the general problem of why God should permit human pain. The idea grew directly out of my first project on witchcraft (Luhrmann 1989). There, the problem had been to understand the paradox of how rational people could believe in irrational beliefs; here, the problem was to understand the paradox of multiple answers to an insoluble problem in moral logic. But the more I talked to Parsis, the more I began to feel that I was learning less about culture and more about the infinite variety of the ways in which individuals rationalize, symbolize, deny, embrace, and otherwise come to terms with suffering. And what I began to notice, as the ethnography will unfold, was an insistent, reiterated complaint that the Parsis were not as they once were, that the Parsis had fallen, that the young Parsi men in particular were pathetic, spineless, cowardly, and impotent.

And yet Parsis had not, in fact, noticeably dropped in their socioeconomic status from the late nineteenth century, nor was there striking and incontrovertible evidence that their sons were indeed pathetic. It seemed to me that the most fruitful path toward understanding this critique was not to search diligently for specific ways in which the Parsis, and their young men in particular, *were* traditional, irrational, and above all effeminate. Instead, in the same manner that scholars have taken the feminization of the Orient as a trope for legitimizing political domination—and refused, in principle, to explore seriously the question of whether Hindus are "in fact" more effeminate than British men—I decided to approach this Parsi self-criticism as a cultural construction about something other than flesh-and-blood Parsis. The question, then, became an analysis of rhetorical inversion: why should Parsis, once self-described as hypermasculinized and British-identified, describe their sons as effeminate? The answer seemed to lie in the painful, convoluted consequences of the colonial identification with the colonizer.

The colonial experience has captured the anthropological and historical imagination because it raises the hard questions about identity that fascinate people who "go native" and then come back: the degree to which our capacity to reason, our capacity to see ourselves as others see us, is hampered by the smallness of our local world, the degree to which we choose our actions and our destinies, the degree to which we are other people. The scholarly approaches to these problems have vacillated on the question of how best to describe the ambivalent identities of these colonized others: as active, intentional, deliberately insurgent rebels, whether through the drama of Quit India or the everyday resistance of reluctant factory workers;[18] as passive victims constructed by the orientalist gaze;[19] as complexly neither free nor determined but caught in a Gramscian struggle within the language, politics, and conceptual frames established by that authority to which the subject is opposed.[20]

This book contributes to the theorizing of the colonized subjects by describing a process in which members of a particular group chose a course to advance a morally desirable end, and yet, through the slow weave of circumstances, they became caught within the sticky web of their own symbolism and have come to accuse themselves of moral weakness.[21] The Parsis appear to have chosen their adoption of British style, education, and political orientation.²² They accepted the colonial ideology of progress and moral superiority, of westernization as a means to advancement, and of the British as the agents of positive change. But while one can argue that their adoption of a westernized ideal was a choice—since there were, after all, other, and for some, like the Chettiars and Marwaris, equally successful economic and political options—the twentieth-century Parsis seem to have been caught out by their own history of self-representation. Under colonial rule, the attributes of the good Parsi became hierarchized, in part through the adoption of hierarchized British self-description: like the British colonizer, the good Parsi was more truthful, more pure, more charitable, more progressive, more rational, and more masculine than the Hindu-of-the-masses. Then power relations shifted dramatically. With the absence of the British as the clear tip of the pyramid of power, the self-ascribed position of best-of-all-the-rest no longer existed, and community discourse has shifted to an identification with that rest, from whom they had once distinguished themselves with a proud, superior distance. Now, in independent India, as the Parsis experience their community's decline from a state of former glory, they describe themselves with the critical condemnation the British would have used to describe Hindu others.

And so this is the story of what Bernard Williams might call bad moral luck: that because we judge our actions not solely on intentions but also on the uncertain outcomes of our acts, we can condemn ourselves for actions taken for the noblest ends. The Parsis flourished under colonial rule; and surely it would be unfair to criticize them for the honest hard work with which they secured for their children an admirable future. And yet when we look at the cluster of attributes which the Parsis readily articulate as salient to the idea of the "good Parsi," and in particular, at those adopted during the colonial period, we can see that the more recent schemes reverse the moral judgments of the successful nineteenth century. These two clusters must be related, because the contemporary criticism cannot be explained as a realistic assessment of the community. It has to be seen against the background of perceived loss of status from the nineteenth century, and as painful reminders that none of us see clearly the consequences of our choices, that uncertainty makes blind men of us all.

The Parsis' predicament is the dilemma of all those who gamble on history's outcomes and lose, and find themselves in a different, often inverted, symbolic position from the one they had chosen. This is the twist, for instance, of Ishiguro's *An Artist of the Floating World* (1986), whose protagonist grew impatient with the indulgent narcissism of the painter's world and boldly committed his services to a vision of a strong, powerful Japan. But Japan lost the war, and the men who inspired young soldiers to lose their lives were mercilessly condemned, and in postwar Japan the artist who had chosen what he thought was the high moral road before the war struggles with his damnation for iniquity after circumstances have changed. Parsis chose to be like the British and so adopted the common British understanding of the Indian world. They did not anticipate that when they lost the British, they would condemn themselves for being themselves the pathetic natives they had learned to see and despise with British eyes. They live now with an identification which had been emotionally gripping and, once lost, has plunged them into the emotional despondency of moral failure.

The important theoretical point is that the appearance—perhaps even more than the actuality—of a shift in power relations can cause a dramatic reversal in symbolic self-description. Parsis identified themselves with the symbolic discourse of colonial authority, and in the absence of that authority have applied the low-status end of the hierarchical symbolism to themselves. They have been trapped, as it were, by a colonial world view that has not yet (for Parsis in India, at any rate) adjusted to the change in power of the postcolonial era. They are struggling with the burden of a colonial symbolism which held that those identified with the mass of natives were emasculated. And while their dilemma—being a tiny community, neither Hindu nor Muslim—is idiosyncratic, it is only a variant of the more general problem of the colonial encounter: the asymmetrical power relationship in which the elites in particular try and fail, to cross the barrier that divides the colonizer from the colonized.

The Parsis are an unusual and in some ways extreme example of a colonial native elite. Because they tried to assimilate, and did not turn to revolution, they reveal the postcolonial consequences of their assimilation more powerfully than do most other colonial elites. But they are not unique. Since antiquity, as colonial powers have withdrawn like spent tides across the globe, they have left many pockets of Parsi-like elites, *compradors* whose authority and finances depended upon their affiliation with the local culture: the Christianized British in England when the Romans left, the *pieds noirs* in Algeria, Jews in Tunisia and elsewhere in the Middle East, Muslim communities in South India as Arab power waned, Indians in East and South Africa, perhaps soon Russians in the new polities of the former Soviet Union, elites in India and Africa and the Middle East who threw their identities and lot in with the foreign power and now find themselves feeble, eviscerated, deracinated even from their precolonial past. They suffer the bleak anxieties of Satyajit Ray's wan elites, with their old family houses and bloodless futures, the fate of Anita Desai's Calcutta Bohemians, searching for artist integrity amidst the shards of their family traditions, or the complex hatred Naipaul finds in postcolonial East Africa. It is hard to see clearly the sensibilities of these various elites, for anthropologists tend to want to give the world success stories, as Mead once remarked, and these postcolonial stories are more often sad. But there are echoes of Parsi experience in some anthropological and historical works.

The Krios (Creoles) of Sierra Leone, Black Englishmen as they were called, were not unlike the Parsis in the intensity of their identification with the British, their feelings of unique importance under colonial rule, and their sense of racial separation from their countrymen.[23] Like the Parsis, the Krios appear in nineteenth century photographs in stately English costume. They spoke English and rode in carriages and drank Scotch in the evening of the hot African sun. As relations worsened with the British in the late nineteenth century, one Krio response was not to criticize the Europeans but to attack themselves—a response aided by the belief that they were dying out.[24] Another response was a movement which suggested that it was a mistake to identify too closely with Europeans.[25] Gradually, in the 1930s, after the failure of an elite political organization to have much impact upon British policy, some Krios joined forces with Africans, whom they had once seen as socially quite different, and agitated for greater political power.[26] And yet after Independence the Krios retained their European ways and have had to come to terms with their growing irrelevance (as a community) to their countrymen. Wyse refers to their "emasculation" in 1939: he writes of their experience of losing commercial control over Freetown; remarks upon their hysterical reaction in 1947 when they realized that they had become a permanent minority in Sierra Leone instead of the heirs-apparent to the British; and concludes with the remark that "they should above all not feel guilty for sins they did not commit, but rather uphold and preserve all that is good in their culture"[27]—implying that relentless self-criticsm is for them an insistent and salient problem.[28]

In 1947 the titles of Japanese nobility were revoked, and the Emperor—who had renounced his own divine status one year earlier—met the aristocrats ceremoniously to say farewell. Takie Lebra's (1993) study of the declining Japanese aristocracy, or *kazoku,* opens with this story. While its parallels to the Parsi experience are not exact—these are not colonial compradors—the story describes an elite class whose authority and power are vitiated by political change. Postwar reforms like heavy taxation on estates, farmland redistribution, and the dissolution of family-based industrial and financial groups bankrupted many of them, and as Japan turned towards democracy, their status began to be something that could be achieved through education and wealth, rather than ascribed. Lebra avoids a portrait of the felt sense of decline, but she compares at one point the stereotypes of the "spiritless" *kazoku* woman and the "tough, vigorous" commoner, and she says of modern *kazoku* that they maintain a low, shadowed profile in modern Tokyo and joke about having become the "new commoners," *shinheimin,* outcasts.

And then there are the British themselves, the often middle middle-class men and women who came to make a life for themselves in Imperial India, and lived a life grander and more exotic than they could have done at home, and when Independence came, retired to cramped quarters in a country they might not have seen for thirty years. Sometimes they stayed on in India, pale reminders, watching their status and money and power dwindle until at last they too died. Paul Scott's *Staying on* (1977) opens in 1972 with the two last survivors of Pankot's permanent retired British residents. The memsahib says to her husband in the early pages of the novel: "You have no pride any longer. Don't interrupt. And because you have no pride neither of us does. We should have gone home" (1977:28). It is a depressing book. They lead tired, sad lives, no longer able to communicate with each other or with the world around them, difficult and quarrelsome, dismayed at the loss of status that came with Independence, crying at the petty politics over garden work waged by the Punjabi woman who holds the lease to their house and thus control over their lives. When the husband makes a disparaging remark about the food at an Indian-run restaurant, the wife thinks to herself that it is they who are the leftovers, while her husband later remarks unhappily that he no longer thinks of them as staying on, but hanging on. But perhaps the best examples of decline, though again without the colonial parallel, are the British aristocrats themselves, who in the 1870s were the wealthiest and most powerful people in Britain, and conscious of the rightness of so being. With the decline of the agricultural base of the European economy, and the emergence of a full-fledged industrial economy, those elites lost their hereditary power. Over the next hundred years, as their magisterial historian depicts, "the lords of the earth would become strangers in their own lands, the stars of the firmament would cease to shine with such unrivalled brilliance, and the makers of history would become, at last and at length, its victims" (Cannadine 1990:31).

The puzzle in making sense of Parsi self-criticism, and perhaps of the Krios, and of other ex-colonial elites whose self-condemnation is striking and enduring, is why the symbolic inversion should carry on so long. The Parsis and Krios do not suffer condemnation at the hands of others so much as in their own esteem, and the stagnant self-denigration has carried on for several generations. The chapters that follow provide the evidence for a British-identified model of a good Parsi and also for its inverse, a rasping, contrary, critical model of the inadequate Parsi. The evidence is rich with particularities which might explain why, in this community, the criticism runs so deep: the community's marginalized status in a country dominated by Hindus and Muslims; its dropping population and falling reproductive rate in a country of mushrooming millions; the entrepreneurial success of those defined as its competitors; its theological squabbles and the limitation of popular views of the religion; the shrinking availability of housing coupled with the unwillingness of young adults to give birth in their parents' home; the gradual diaspora; and other, specific, idiosyncratic features of community experience which help to explain how it is that the loss of the British could entail such a long-lasting commitment to the negative attributes ascribed by the British to those they defined themselves against.

And yet I think there is an explanation which is deeper and truer and more profound than the sum of the evidence, which roots the self-criticism in mingled loss and longing and in the anxious, guilty unease that the rosy past might seem tawdry in the cold moral light of the present. The Parsi experience of Independence was an experience of loss, no matter how much joy and optimism they found in freedom. As the British were forced out of India, the Parsis, however complicated their own emotional responses to the colonizers might have been, gave up the measure of goodness which was associated with the community's hour of greatness. They had, more or less as a community, identified with the British, and adopted their own self-representation using British colonial representation as a model. And the model was dishonored, although as a community the Parsis did not rebel against it, and many Parsis today are angrily embarrassed at their colonial complicity and their colonial nostalgia.

It *must* have been disappointing for the Parsis to see the British reviled by a massive political movement, to hear that things English—clothes, customs, aspirations—were bad, and perhaps to see that the British response to this attack was to leave. They struggled for fifty years with the idea of leaving, but they did leave. For at least one hundred years Parsis as a community had taken the British as their community ideal. They had encouraged their men to spend hours in "physical culture" and cricket to become as manly as the British; they had devoted significant amounts of time and money to English education; they had worn the hot, uncomfortable Victorian dress—crazy in the Bombay heat—because that was what the British did; they had gone to great lengths to separate themselves by breeding and origin not only from other Indian groups, but from India; they had travelled to London for holidays the way Muslims went to Mecca. They did this as a community, unlike the Muslims, Brahmins, or Gujaratis whose westernized elites were only a tiny fraction of their community. Poor, non-westernized Parsis were also part of the community, but in turn-of-the-century discourse they existed not as separate selves, alienated ways of being Parsis, but as Parsis who were not quite up to speed. The good Parsi, the esteemed and ideal Parsi, was almost English.

And in the thirties their identification had, as it were, been aborted. They were not going to become European, after all. They were going to become a tiny minority in a world of the Hindu masses whom they had tried so hard to see as Other. And this would happen just because the Hindus had renounced the British, and the British had withdrawn. For Parsis, the period from the thirties onward must have been confusing indeed. And it is not as if the community has even now a clear historical perspective on their colonial involvement. Jokes about colonial nostalgia are exceedingly common, as are pictures of English royalty, English objects, desire for things English; but also common is embarrassment at the longing for the past, anger at self-ascribed community superiority, hatred of Parsi self-congratulation, rage at those Parsis who feel a complacent, commonsense pride. Individual Parsis express a great jumble of varying emotions about their community. But there is no doubt that feelings about British involvement are contradictory and intense.

My deeper explanation for the endurance of Parsi self-criticism is that the self-attack becomes an attempt to master despair when both desire and separation are so profoundly conflicted. The intense, ambivalent attachment to the British encompasses the resentment of the British, the inappropriateness of British identification, and nevertheless the yearning for the glamorous merging into British identity, the knot/not at the center of the postcolonial encounter. My guess is that at the center of this tangled, awkward, self-abnegating knot lie guilt and shame: guilt at the desire to trespass and violate the colonizer's rules; guilt, as well, for the desire to so betray one's colonized compatriots; and shame for the public drama of status failure. This is the situation's emotional logic—not the feeling in each Parsi breast, but the burden of the collective pain which the collective discourse articulates. From the shameful guilt fired by the explosive combination of this knowledge and this longing follows the punishment of self-flagellation but also the possibility of redemption. Parsi self-criticism is an attempt to give suffering a name and a local habitation, an effort to control the aching pain of loss and hurt and embarrassment, by asserting that in these random historical eddies Parsis made mistakes which could be identified and righted. This attempt to master pain by naming it and assigning blame is the very oldest of our magical and therapeutic strategies. The paradoxically redemptive power of self-attack lies in its dual capacity to identify the hurt and at the same time to assert control: the hurt was not arbitrary, it is something we caused, it is something which, because we caused it, we can also resolve. Parsis lost their gamble with history, but in blaming themselves for their loss of status they resist the profoundly human truth that they are flotsam in the shifting tides of history. They maintain the illusions of their power at the same time that they name the intimacy of their pain.

In a famous essay Freud described intense self-criticism as the ego's attempt to cope with loss when the feelings of attachment were highly ambivalent—at least, disappointed—and the negative feelings are insufficiently acknowledged. Confronted with disappointment but unable to acknowledge the ambivalence of his feelings about the loss, the individual simultaneously internalizes the lost object and attacks himself severely. "In the clinical picture of melancholia, dissatisfaction with the self on moral grounds is by far the most outstanding feature" (1957:129). This meld of emotionally intense ambivalence and self-attack lies at the center of elite postcolonial experience. Certainly it is the emotional involvement both in the desire and the rejection, and the simultaneous condemnation of both, that produces the impasse. In the absence of other cultural options—Zoroastrians abroad, as I shall explain at the end, seem less caught in the inwardly curved horns of this dilemma—that emotional bind has left the community in this destructive state. Had they rebelled, revolted against the colonizer, adopted the route which Memmi and Fanon describe as the only way to break the self-destructive impasse, they could perhaps have freed themselves. But they did not, and the past remained unaltered. Caught within these contradictory tensions and attachments, avoiding powerlessness by taking responsibility for the fall, shamed for their trespass but yearning for their former glory, Bombay Parsis use the semiotics of the past to define the relationships of the present—because the past is still profoundly present.

Perhaps the ambivalent attachment so highlighted in the Parsis is shared by all partners in the colonial tango. Gandhi's homespun *khadi* did not restore the Indian elite to wholesome precolonial consciousness, nor did the elite's red double-decker buses and double-breasted suits signal their comfortable ease in consolidating the good qualities of the British with the virtues of Indianness. And while some Brown Sahibs, undaunted by postimperial cynicism, continue with their preference for imported Scotch, intensely contradictory feelings about the colonial legacy and (even more) the modern west plague the identity of (in particular) the Indian middle classes. In all these moments, it is those on the border who suffer, in their own minds condemned for crossing it by those they have joined and those they have abandoned. And possibly the way critical modernity will heal itself is when enough of us come to live on the border, on the exemplars of what Marcus and Fischer call the flux of culture, that the borders will seem less a place of self-destruction and more a haven for balanced self-creation.

The Historical Trail

1670 · Gerald Aungier, Governor of Bombay
[Parsis] are an industrious people and ingenious in trade, therein they totally employ themselves. There are at present few of them [in Bombay] but we expect a greater number of them, having gratified them in their desire to build a burying place for their dead on the island.[29]

1830 · Sir John Malcolm, Governor of Bombay
There is no body of natives in India so remarkable for their intelligence and enterprise as the Parsis. Bombay has owed its advancement in a great degree to this class.[30]

1884 · Karaka, *History of the Parsis*
[Parsis] . . . have shown themselves to be far in advance of the other races of the peninsula.[31]

. . . . .

With the advent of British power in India better and brighter days dawned for the [the Parsis]. With the rise of that power they have risen from poverty and oppression to security and wealth. Upon that power they depend.[32]

1905 · *The Parsi*
The close union of Europeans and Parsis is the finest thing that can happen to our races. . . . The complete Europeanization of the Parsis is now a mere matter of time.[33]

1906 · Earl of Lytton, Letter to Queen Victoria
The Parsees are, I think, among the very best of your Majesty's Indian subjects; and I wish your Majesty had more of them. They are a wonderfully thriving community wherever you find them. They have a genius for business, and rarely fail in it. I have not yet seen a

thin Parsi, and I doubt if I have seen a poor one. They seem all to be fat, rich, and thriving.[34]

1932 · Pithawalla, *The Young Zoroastrian*
Today the scale appears to turn the other way. The Parsis themselves are getting poorer day by day. They do not seem to stand the strain of racial competition, physical exertion and moral bankruptcy. One can but wholeheartedly wish that the Parsis possessed the Iranian glory even in a foreign land. Nothing but degeneration and demoralization appears to have set in among them.[35]

1933 · Markham, *A Report . . . on Problems Affecting the Parsee Community*
There seems to be a feeling, however, in certain quarters that the community has reached or passed its zenith.[36]

1940 · Desai, *Parsis and Eugenics*
Where have the great men of the last two centuries gone? . . . Are the Parsis deteriorating? How often that question is dinned into our ears and how often it is as vehemently affirmed as denied!.[37]

1944 · Letter to the editor, *Times of India*
Any sane member of the community who observes the present movements and doings of the Parsis will,—in spite of all his inborn enthusiasm, affirm that they, as a community, are deteriorating not only physically but also morally, economically, as well as socially and politically . . . For the last few years this communal depression of the Parsis is being openly admitted.[38]

1948 · Desai, *A Community at the Cross-Roads*
The broad facts that emerge from any consideration of the problem are that a deterioration in the moral fibre of the community has set in. We have an idle rich class, contributing little to the general well-being of the community beyond indiscriminate charity, and our poor are getting poorer and losing their self-respect.[39]

1949 · Wadia, *Parsis Ere the Shadows Thicken*
A small community like ours can escape the process of decadence and degeneration, if it has the art of rejuvenating itself from within . . . Our community, however, seems to have exhausted by this time

the chances of bringing to birth leaders who with courage and understanding can break the ever tightening grip of its dead past.[40]

1974 · Parsi quoted in interview in *Parsiana*
In British times, Parsis were the number one community. Now the English have lost their position as a world power, and we have lost ours. During those times, Parsis had initiative, integrity, grit and go. Today, they live on past glory, on their grandfather's money. . . .[41]

1989 · Letter to the editor, *Parsiana*
We Parsis get what we deserve. We ingrain in our children an attitude that the Western philosophy and way of life is the best, that Western values are to be copied and imitated, shrugging off respect for elders and for religious rituals.[42]

1991 · Pestonji, *The Daily*
As part of the post-Independence generation I have often been embarrassed by my [Parsi] compatriots' colonial hangovers and their insensitive jeering of Indian culture and customs.[43]

THE CURRENT COMMUNITY

I

Turn-of-the-Century Bombay

Imagine a great city, of over 800,000 souls, lying on the shores of a beautiful sea, sparkling in the sunshine, glorious in the monsoon, backed by grand mountains, with many a castellated peak nestling in palm groves, with hundreds of sea-going vessels anchored in its harbour, with two busy lines of railway piercing it, broad thoroughfares and grand buildings, with a most active and intelligent mercantile community, both European and native; with its lawns crowded day and night with pleasure and leisure seekers, and its brightness added to by the most brilliantly dressed ladies in the world, the Parsees. Imagine it if you can. I don't think you can. I have seen many great cities of the East, and I have not seen one that could touch Bombay.[1]

• • •

Bombay, says one of its literary men, "is a gritty, impossible, unforgettable place. It has child beggars, pavement sleepers and sprawling urban slums; noise, tangled traffic, skyscrapers, fashionable apartment blocks; the very poor, who have migrated from the villages in the surrounding regions to seek better fortune and the very rich—merchants, industrialists, film stars."[2] The city looks remarkably like Manhattan but is hotter, dirtier, safer, more disorderly, an even more schizoid enmeshment of financial power and poverty. Its elegant Victorian buildings are now old, their once light-colored facades corroding beneath sulphuric grime, the palms which thrust up past their walls giving them a Piranesi-like romantic decadence. I was told that there are more taxis in Bombay than in any other city in the world, and the traffic is more chaotic than any I have seen: dented red double-decker buses sway past bicycles, cars, and hand-drawn carts of fish and textiles along the city streets. There are twelve million people in the city. Nearly half of them live on the pavement or in the slums, squalid blots stretched across the island's width. In Dharhavi, the worst slum, supposedly the largest slum in Asia, the census found one person per square meter.[3] There are people everywhere, all the time; perhaps 1,500 arrive daily from the rural areas, attracted by the city's occupational opportunities. They sell tea, coconuts, comic books, socks, anything; one day I came across a street vendor offering only suitcase handles, his inventory of some one hundred styles spread along the pavement. Little boys jump on the trains and push through the crowds to sell *bindis* (small felt dots for the forehead), barrettes, hairbands, little snacks. Men sit on boxes beside piled green leaves making *paan,* a digestive snack of betel nut and spices. Women carry flat baskets of stumpy bananas on their heads, selling them two for a rupee. Sweepers sweep the broad roads with hand brooms. Billboards hang above the traffic to advertise butter, films, brightly colored *rasna* (soft) drinks. And despite its poor Bombay is a resolutely middle-class city, the business and financial capital of India, and home to the Parsis.

Parsis are now a tiny element in the bustling metropolis they helped to create. The skyscrapers that rise above the crowded streets are filled with businesses and law firms, housed in real estate as expensive as it is in New York City, in a city where the common worker's daily wage is somewhat over a dollar. Some of the largest, most prestigious firms are Parsi, but far more of them are not: Marwaris, Gujaratis, Sindhis, Jains, Bohras, Khojas are among the many different ethnicities who have grown wealthy by seizing the city's entrepreneurial possibilities. Bombay was built around a natural port, and unlike those of London and New York its shipping industry still flourishes. Other businesses include the largest textile market in the world, plastic products, electronic and electrical equipment. Bombay has the hotel called the best in India (the

Taj Mahal) and several of its competitors, and a glitzy, jetsetting social scene (not very Parsi) of film stars, movie moguls, business-men, socialites.[4] The city produces perhaps 500 feature films each year, far outstripping Hollywood, pandering to an immense audi-ence. Most of these films are *masala* (a spice mixture) films, so called because they have a predictable mix of heroes, villains, dancing, violence, and chaste sex scenes (the heroine sings her love to the hero as the skies open, and the thin soaked sari clings to her body). Their actors carry, if anything, more of a magical aura than do their American counterparts, and their presence adds to the glamour of the city.

Bombay did not impress its earliest visitors. In 1689 a traveller described it thus:

> The Unhealthfulness of the Water bears a just proportion to the Scarcity and meaness of the Diet, and both of them together with a bad Air, make a sudden end of many a poor Sailor and Souldier, who pay their lives for hopes of a Livelihood. Indeed, whether it be that the Air stagnates, or the stinking of the Fish which was used to be applied to the Roots of the Trees, instead of dung, or whatever other Cause it is which renders it so very unhealthful, 'tis certainly a mortal enemy to the lives of the Europeans. And as the Ancients gave the epithet of *Fortunate* to some islands in the West, because of their Delightfulness and Health; so the Modern may, in opposition to them, denominate this the *Unfortunate* one in the East, because of the Antipathy it bears to those two qualities.[5]

Yet in the nineteenth century, even until Independence, Bombay seems to have been one of the most pleasant cities in India. It was cosmopolitan; it also had a reputation as the most egalitarian of Indian cities, the city in which hierarchy was least important and in which interaction between native and colonist was most relaxed. For the most part this was because it was a merchant's town. The *Times* remarked in 1911, "in most parts of India the line of demar-cation between the Englishman and the Indian is sharply drawn. . . . In Bombay the line is so faint it must soon be extin-guished. Englishman and Indian, Parsi and Mahomedan, Jew and Hindu, meet in daily and intimate commercial dealing."[6] In the nineteenth century social relations seem to have been more com-fortable, taboos less rigid, in this city than in others. And it seems also to have been a beautiful city then: grand, graceful Victorian architecture, wide streets lined by swaying palm trees, a coastal drive called the Queen's Necklace because in the dark the lights which lined it shone like a string of pearls along the bay. At the end of the nineteenth century the city would have been dominated by the Victoria Terminus, a splendor of crenellated domes which was meant, when it was built by F. W. Stevens in 1878, to unite European and Oriental architectural style, and still enchants or appalls its modern visitors. Farther south, Bombay University, with its clocktower and columnal facade, its expansive cricket field, would have reminded the British of their own university past, and the sea frontage would have been lined with the elegant mansions built by the mercantilist rich. In 1908 an English visitor exclaimed:

> Of Bombay as a city, what can one say? Its sea-front looks bright and magnificent from the harbour . . . The principal commercial street would be a splendid thorough-fare in any European capital, and its warehouse, its bank, its insurance offices, need not fear comparison with the best of their kind at home . . . It is a brilliant city, brimful of interest in its native quarter, picturesque in its residential suburbs, with their wealth of colour and foliage.[7]

Like other colonial cities, Bombay reveals the complexity of the colonial relationship in its architecture. As you go north in the city, away from the orientalized grandeur of the British mansions, the world becomes markedly more Indian: the buildings are lower, more teeming with chai shops, street vendors and stalls. This is no accident: in all colonial cities, there was a British town and outside it a "native town" where the non-British lived and shopped. Here in north Bombay are the temples and the mosques, not the elegant clubs and *maidans* (open park-like spaces) of a once British and now governmental Bombay in the south. There is Crawford market, with freshly ground spices, boxes of choice mangoes packed in straw, and a meat market which I was told would (but did not) instantly convert me to a vegetarian diet. Just beyond lies Bhendi bazaar, the Muslim market, with its *salwar-kameez*—the long shirt and pant combination first introduced in north India and now worn mostly by young women—hanging in the breeze. There is the *chori* bazaar, the thieves' market, with its collection of antique and often British junk, and there is Lal bazaar, the red light district around Falklands Road, where young girls stand in what are called cages, barred bazaar shops in the Gujarati style. And beyond this one finds Mahim, and the first suburbs, and between them the great dark stretch of Dharhavi, densest and most difficult of all the slums.[8] Government officials have made concerted efforts to Indianize the still visibly colonial southern city. The street names have been aggressively altered in recent years: Hornby Road is now Dadabhai Naoroji Road, Flora Fountain, Hutatma Chowk. Very few people ever use the Indian names—the newcomer is left looking for a street address with no resemblance to the street sign. The blend of official Indian street sign and idiomatic English name is in some ways the most poignant marker of the city's past. Bombay is an Indian city by population and by much of its language, appearance, and style. But part of that Indian identity has Britain interwoven to its core. The Parsis are perhaps the best exemplars of that interweaving.

The tiny community of Bombay Parsis—around 54,000, with another 25,000 elsewhere in India, and perhaps another 40,000 across the globe—form a distinctive community in modern Bombay.[9] They often live in Parsi areas, they eat Parsi food, they often socialize primarily with Parsis; their faces look more angularly Iranian than Hindu. Their fire temples dot the city. There is a Parsi style of dress. The men wear suits, as most middle-class Indian men do. The women wear dresses from an older world, square tabs on sleeveless dresses or leg-of-mutton sleeves, awkward hourglasses from the fifties. They will wear saris for a social event, although not for work or a casual evening out, and treasured Parsi saris are elaborately embroidered Chinese silks acquired in nineteenth-century trade. Some of the younger women, particularly those who become angry at the community's supposed rejection of things Indian, wear *salwar-kameez*.

Most Parsis live in the southern or central once-colonial sections of the city. There are Parsis in the graceful Malabar Hills area, overlooking the financial district from a hill; in the Fort area, the old British section; along elegant Cuffe Parade, farther south. Less wealthy Parsis live around busy Grant Road north of the Fort area, and the poorer still in Tardeo. But these distinctions are increasingly less accurate as housing grows increasingly scarce, and one can find well-to-do Parsis in traditionally poor neighborhoods.[10] I hesitate to call this gentrifying: the young couple's residential choice is often determined by the Panchayat, the community administrative body which slowly doles out the apartments which it controls. And if upwardly mobile offspring inherit their parents' flat they often do not leave it, regardless of the neighborhood.

About a third of the community lives in "colonies," large enclosed areas with many buildings, often in central Bombay. Most of the colonies were built in the first third of the twentieth century as housing for the poor and middle class. Many of the descendents of the original owners of the flats have now reached well into the upper middle class, but the tenants do not leave, the leases passing down through the generations. You can see these complexes as you drive along the main streets of Bombay, imposing buildings streaked grey by the polluted rain and air, often with their own enclosed courtyards: self-contained, self-observant worlds. Now those worlds are aging, along with the community as a whole, and many within those complexes have failing sight. Nevertheless, little can be done in the community that is not observed by many others. It is in these small societies of several hundred people, their windows facing common ground, their entries and exits common knowledge, that many Parsis achieve adulthood.

Cusrow Baag (Cusrow colony) is the most famous and perhaps the wealthiest of all the colonies.[11] It sits midway down the Colaba causeway, a handsome complex with several hundred flats around an imposing fire temple, its arched entrance framed by two winged Persian bulls. On Sunday evenings in the premonsoon heat I occasionally dropped by the clubhouse at the back—they called it the pavilion—where the regulars would gather for their card games. A man I will call Burjor was inevitably there, a handsome man in his sixties. He had always lived in Cusrow Baag; his father had been given a flat and Burjor had lived there since birth, now with his wife, but no children. He owned a Maruti car, a sign of some prosperity, and for years he had run a farm on the other side of the bay until, he said, the difficulty of long distance management became too great. Now, he told me, he did what he liked, to take things easy, to sail, and to play gin rummy out by the pavilion in the evenings. The pavilion was a pleasant place to spend these heavy evenings, the yolk yellow of the buildings deepened by the setting sun, the assiduously watered grass before the building actually green, the walls draped with magenta bougainvillea—by the premonsoon months most unwatered areas had parched to brown. In the evening the pavilion became crowded with card players up on the porch, with the elderly in silent circles at the patio's edge and children running back and forth on the grass playing ball. It was a marked contrast to the chaos on the Colaba Causeway.

The colonies drive home, to the observer, an important Parsi demographic: one in five Bombay Parsis is over sixty-five. These enclosed worlds have children, but far more noticeably, they house the old. It was an elderly woman who first introduced me to the community, and who embodied so much that seemed Parsi: fading wealth, European-identified sophistication, and a sense of considerable distance from modern India. Pareen called for me in a chauffeur-driven car on my second day in Bombay, and as we sat on a bench on elegant Marine Drive, we mostly spoke about Paris. Her father was the youngest son of a successful trading family. Pareen was sent to an English boarding school until the family went to live in Paris. There, neither she nor her mother wore saris, but they continued to say their ancient prayers. They returned to Bombay five years later, in the thirties, and Pareen married a Parsi stockbroker. Now in her eighties, the world in which she was raised has disappeared. India is independent, the British long gone, and bands no longer play to the middle classes upon the maidan on Sunday evenings. Pareen was disillusioned about modern India and its promise of freedom and progress. "We liked Gandhi, we were proud of him. We wore his homespun cotton saris to join the *swadeshi* movement. Some of the Parsis did this but most were against it. We thought it was only natural that our people should rule us. My God, how we regret that now."

Not all the elderly, by any means, are well-to-do, and the community's extensive charities—established with the donations of wealthy merchants and industrialists in the nineteenth century—support many of them. I went one afternoon with Tehmina, a social worker in her twenties, to see some of her clients, and to learn about the community's very poor. We first went to the N. M. Petit Widow's *chawl* (tenement building), a Dickensian place with dark hallways, rats, no fans, and the abandoned elderly waiting out the remnant of their time. But the rooms were relatively large, if overfurnished with the kitchenware and tables and trunks that each widow seemed to have brought with her from her earlier home. All of the five or so rooms we visited had pictures of Zarathustra somewhere, along with Sai Baba (an Indian guru popular with Parsis), the Virgin Mary, and—less usual for Parsis—various Hindu deities. Tehmina's job was to give the widows jobs to help them earn some money. She said that some of the women in the *chawl* were demanding and difficult, and did not want to work. "Some," she said, "feel that they have a right to the charity, that it is their forefathers' money and why should it be kept from them?" To others Tehmina's institution had brought a sense of identity, she said, "because it gives them jobs instead of alms, maintaining their self-respect. One woman learnt to make wicks, and made 4000 rupees in the first two months." That woman lived in one of these dark crowded caverns, and proudly showed me how to twist the wool around the thread. She had lived with her son in Kethwadi (an area of Bombay) but there was no room for three, so she came to the *chawl*, she said, for she had nowhere else to go. This was a story with many permutations: far more than most Indian communities, Parsis adopt the English model of one nuclear family to an apartment, and go to considerable lengths to achieve it.

Even the poorer homes are often distinctively Parsi, and carry the memory of their days of colonial grandeur. Tiny flats in Andheri in north Bombay are stuffed with the accumulation of many generations, Chinese vases from Indo-Chinese trade perch on mahogany chests. Young people in Colaba, gradually selling the flats in the building the family owned three generations prior, retreat to their penthouses, crowding their grandparents' furniture into fewer rooms. Airy flats on wealthy Malabar Hill also hold the square, solid, responsible furniture of their Victorian past. Heavy rosewood screens, intricately carved, hide the watermarks monsoons have left behind. There are cabinets of English knickknacks with Staffordshire poodles on top. Polaroids of American grandchildren are tucked into the beveled edges of dark scrolled mirrors. Cabinets, endtables, escritoires, umbrella stands, pianos—once, a teak elevator—the dark wood is inherited from the nineteenth century wealth of industry and trade. A memoir recalls the early twentieth century:

> Our house was a strange blending of the East and the West. There was an odd assortment of things in the drawing room which had come from all over the world. Its floors were covered with Persian carpets. Its furniture was of heavy mahogany with but a few delicate pieces. Brassware, gathered from different parts of India, had also found its place in the drawing room. The servants polished the pieces continually with the zest and ceremony of a religious ritual.

> There was a piano at the far end of the room. Often I stood beside
> it wearing my Lord Fauntleroy suit and, as my aunt played, I sang
> "Rule Britannia!" Our English guests applauded.[12]

Always there are portraits of family: husbands and wives and
children, aunts and uncles, grandparents in Chinese silk saris and
stiff headgear, solemn, posed, sepia-tinted daguerrotypes. One
novel describes a rural Gujarat house, not too different from many
I saw in Bombay and particularly true of contemporary Parsis in
Gujarat:

> photographs on the walls, each bordered by an elaborate wooden
> frame, of *all* our relatives (which meant *all* the Parsis in Navsari; all
> Parsis in Navsari have photographs on their walls of all the Parsis in
> Navsari), single portraits, duos, trios, larger groups, at *navjotes*,
> weddings, standing like schoolchildren in single file along stoops,
> seated like prophets on chairs lining the walls in the sitting room,
> arranged in studios with dramatic jungle backdrops, the men wearing
> white ceremonial dress with high collars (satin *daglas*, cotton *daglis*),
> and ceremonial headgear *(paghris, fehtnas)*, the women covering
> their heads with their saris, gazing into the distance as if they had
> weightier matters to consider than photographs, the children with
> large round eyes as if they had something to hide . . . (Desai
> 1988:29)

And always on the wall or table there will be pictures of Zarathustra, eyes heavenward, a golden Christ-like glow around his head.
Then there will be pictures of Zoroastrian "saints": Dastur
Kookadaru, a nineteenth-century priest credited with magical,
mystical powers; Shah Jamshed, an Iranian king in a world so
prosperous that during his reign no one died; Shah Faredun, also
a great king, whose triumph over the evil Zohak is the central story
of the Shahnameh; Lohrasp, father of King Vishtasp, early convert,
so saintly that he renounced his kingship. In many households there
will also be pictures of the nineteenth-century Sai Baba of Shirdi,
and perhaps of Christ or Mary. "We respect all gods," the owner
of such pictures will explain.

On my second visit to Bombay I lived with a Parsi family in a
spacious sunny flat in southern Bombay. The solid walls were
painted light green, the furniture was square and sturdy, beautifully
made and inherited from earlier decades. Like many Parsis, Pervez

and Meher Contractor had married late, but nevertheless—unlike many Parsis—had had three children. He was eighty, she sixty five, and at 29 their youngest daughter, Marrukh, still lived in the house. One daughter had married out of the community and lived abroad with her husband, a wealthy doctor. Another married daughter sent her children over to the grandparents during the day; when I went out in the morning Meher would be reading to the smallest on her knee. Marrukh worked in a travel agency north of the city center. They are not an unusual middle-class Parsi family.

Like most Indians they rose early in the morning, although in Bombay one is not expected at work until ten. Marrukh would often go for a walk along Marine Drive, joining the portly businessmen in tennis whites for their morning constitutional. Meher would say her prayers before breakfast: she would come out to the living room, head covered, prayer book in hand, and would sit and stand for sometimes more than an hour, murmuring the ancient prayers in a singsong voice. Pervez prayed as well, and they both wore the *sudreh kusti*—a fine cotton shirt traditionally worn by all Zoroastrians—but prayer seemed less central to his life. Meher was more visibly religious, and when she switched on the light in the early evening she would put her hands together in *namaste*, honored greeting.[13] Marrukh neither wore the *sudreh kusti* nor often said her prayers; when she was young she had done so, she said, but now somehow it did not seem relevant. The granddaughter, however, imitated her grandmother.

Zoroastrianism is a solitary religion. The religious Parsi—and surprisingly many Parsis are religious, despite their westernization—has as his or her main responsibility the recitation of prayers in the ancient tongues, Avestan or Pahlavi. The most basic of them is the *kusti* prayer, said as the sacred cord worn around the waist of the *sudreh* is retied. It is a ritual supposedly performed at least five times during the day, but often done only once or twice (on rising or before bed) by those who perform it at all. Then there are other prayers, to honor the patron of an auspicious day[14] or to heal or help or even just to worship; there are prayer books, in English or Gujarati transliteration, out of which devotional Parsis will choose their texts. One can pray either at home or at the fire temple; some people go to the temple daily, others only once a year, some pray two hours each day, some who are still called very religious pray for five minutes a day. Zoroastrian prayer in Bombay is a private, hidden activity. There are occasional public rituals, for lifecycle events or even just thanksgiving (the *jashan*) where white-clothed priests sing the prayers in lowered monotones, and there is a sacred well in the city, close to a frenetic commuter rail station, where people gather to pray. But they pray alone. In the temple the priests are everpresent, saying prayers they have been paid to pray by hopeful Parsis, tending the sandalwood fires no layperson can ever approach. As a non-Parsi I was never allowed into the fire temple to verify that there were no sermons, no common prayers, no collective action, although I knew this to be the case.[15] And so to me the quintessence of the religion was Meher, head covered early in the morning, speaking under her breath a tongue she could not translate, yet which she devoutly believed to be spiritually powerful and good.

The family ate Parsi food. There were cornflakes, porridge, toast and eggs in the mornings; for tea, salty biscuits like hard French pastry, and sometimes cake. Food during the rest of the day was more Indian, but still there are distinctive Parsi dishes, the sort required at weddings and *navjotes* (the religious induction cere-mony, something like a bar mitzvah), often sweet and sour, more Persian than normal fare. Sometimes Parsi food simply meant west-ernized food. There was a Parsi restaurant in the center of town, near the institute which housed perhaps the best collection of Zoroastrian scholarship in the world. The Wayside Inn was a light-filled, cheerful place. There were square tables with red-checked tablecloths. A heavy wainscot held a collection of English porcelain decanters and a dark, plain screen shut the kitchen from the customer's view. The full lunch always began with soup and often ended with ice-cream or custard. Its main course would often be *dhansak* or else fried fish, with boiled vegetables and what the English call chips and the Americans french fries. *Dhansak* is a Parsi dish, quite delicious, in which *dhal* (lentils) and meat are cooked together. You could also order kidneys and onion, eggs, mutton chops, vegetable imitation cutlets and other items. It was a remarkably non-Hindu menu, yet not entirely English. At the Contractors, too, there would be *dhansak,* but more often food which looked Indian though not necessarily what a Hindu would serve, and it was eaten with bread and not *chappatis.*

These days seventy percent of the current community reads a daily English paper (Karkal 1984:46). Eighty percent are probably

fluent in English and more than half are probably more comfortable in English than in Parsi-Gujarati, the identified community
language. (In a recent survey, 44 percent of the elders and 52
percent of the youth said that they thought in English.)[16] One
woman explained to me with some shame that when she had been
young she could speak good Gujarati, *shud* Gujarati, not the corrupted, English-laden Parsi Gujarati of her community, and her
fellow Parsis laughed at her when she came to Bombay. *Banio
thayo,* they said: you have become a bania (the merchant caste
from Gujarat); you were not supposed to be like a member of an
Indian community. I heard a similar story several times. I myself
tried hard, like a good anthropologist, to learn Gujarati, but it was
difficult to master because most Bombay Parsis (certainly the middle class) used English as their dominant language, even at home.
The Contractors, for instance, spoke a colloquial Gujarati on the
telephone but spoke English more often. Marrukh rarely spoke
Gujarati to her parents. I more or less gave up trying to use the
language after Pervez Contractor's brother came to visit and after
listening to my book-learned efforts said, "you speak good Gujarati, the sentences are good. But why do you bother with all that
work when our English is better than our Gujarati anyway?" But
most of the very poor Parsis, and the Parsis in rural Gujarat, still
speak primarily in Parsi-Gujarati.[17]

The vast majority of the Indian Parsis live in Bombay, although
some can be found in Delhi, Calcutta, Madras, Hyderabad, and
many have spread in the diaspora abroad: Karachi, Britain, Hong
Kong, North America.[18] Many of those will be like the Bombay
Parsis: urbanized, middle-class, English-speaking, urbane. The Gujarati Parsis are different. Parsis landed first in Gujarat when they
came to India a thousand years ago, and in Navsari, Udwada,
Sanjan, and Surat there are still Parsi strongholds, with the most
sacred fire temples and holy sites. These Parsis will speak Gujarati
without a Parsi accent and without the idiomatic Parsi grammar,
and their streets seem like a collective memory of an earlier, ethnically purer, time. Navsari is a lively town, but Udwada, with the
holiest of all fire temples, is an abandoned, dusty relic of the past,
like a quiet setting in a Ray film. The temple's visitors take auto-
rickshaws from the train station some kilometers away. They drive
past tilled fields and arrive at a little town by the sea, with dirt
streets and an open well and a black sand beach where the local

Hindu children play cricket. There are no Parsi children in the town. Perhaps a hundred Parsis live there now, in grand, many-storied, wooden Victorian houses, perhaps one or two Parsis to a house. Many of them are in their eighties. There is no English-language school in town, nor white-collar work, and so whatever young Parsis were there have moved. Five thousand Hindus are said to live on the outskirts, in as much space as the hundred Parsis. Udwada is a strange, sad ghost town and it is about to be overrun.

In Bombay, the community as a whole is doing rather well. The figures are these: in a 1982 survey of the Parsis in Greater Bombay, 29 percent of the community lived in two rooms, and 27 percent in three (77 percent of the Greater Bombay population lived in one room).[19] The average household size was 3.67, compared to a wider Bombay figure of 5.07, and 49 percent of the Greater Bombay Parsis had hot water heaters; 82 percent gas cooking; 78 percent a refrigerator; 11 percent airconditioning; 21 percent cars; 59 percent television; 36 percent had telephones, a percentage considered high. Of the 20–39 year-old age group, 42 percent had completed only their Secondary School Certificate (the SSC, equivalent of an American high school degree); 44 percent more were also college graduates; 9 percent more had done some post-graduate work. 98 percent of the adult community was literate, compared to 65 percent of the Greater Bombay population. Of those who worked, 19 percent were in professional, technical or related fields, compared to 7 percent of the Greater Bombay population; 27 percent were in administrative positions, compared to 4 percent of the Greater Bombay population; and 20 percent held clerical posts, compared to 15 percent of the Greater Bombay population.[20] One third of the community—most of those that worked—earned more than two thousand rupees a month, the highest category listed in the survey.[21] These figures place the community well within the middle class.

Moreover, although the visibility of Parsis is perhaps less than it was some hundred years ago, the community's achievements are still remarkable.[22] It boasts a number of very eminent lawyers: one of India's most noted lawyers, once ambassador to the United States (Nani Palkhivala); the man said—by Parsis—to be Delhi's foremost lawyer (Farli Narriman); three members of the High Court of Bombay, with a most respected retired fourth (Sam Bharucha, Dinshaw Mehta, Sam Variawa, Bakhtawar Lentin); a leading authority on constitutional law (H M. Seervai); and others well-known in India (for example, Rustom Gagrat, Shiavax Vakil, Homi Ranina). Soli Sorabjee was recently India's Attorney General. J. R. D. Tata now heads the Tata Group of companies, one of the largest publicly owned companies in India, and Soli Godrej chairs the company which is often ranked as the largest privately owned company. Mehroo Bengalee is the Vice Chancellor of Bombay University. Sam Maneckshaw is India's one and only Field Marshall. Maneck Goiporia is the Chairman of the State Bank of India. Sorabji Pochkhanawalla was the Chairman of Central Bank. Noshir Wadia is the Chairman of Bombay Dyeing, a large firm. Sapurji Pallonji's buildings—he is an architect—are dotted across India, even the world. Homi Sethna is ex-chairman of the Atomic Energy Commission and principal secretary to the Government of India. There are many well-known doctors and medical specialists in positions of authority (Farrokh and Temtem Udwadia, brothers; Noshir Antia; Keki Mistry; Kekobad Modi; Aspi Golwalla; Keiki Mehta). In the arts there is the world-famous conductor Zubin Mehta (although he no longer lives in India), Asti Debo in Indian classical dance, with Rohinton Cama in Indian classical and modern dance; Phiroze Dastoor in Indian classical music. Sooni Taraporevala's first screenplay won the Camera D'Or award at Cannes and Pervez Meherwanji's first feature film won an award at Mannheim. In Bombay Parsi artists, playwrights, and poets are central to the artistic community and often carry international reputations (Gieve Patel, Cyrus Mistry, Vera Mehta, Adil Jussalwalla) and others—also with international reputations—are located elsewhere (Boman Desai, Keki Daruwalla, Rohinton Mistry, Farrokh Dhondy).[23]

It is very hard to acquire any firm grasp on the question of whether the Parsi standard of living and social status has declined over the last hundred years: the question has the same airy feel as whether the quality of American leisure time has altered during the same period. How do you contrast social status and living standard across such different worlds? And yet by the scant data from census returns and contemporary reports, the contrast between the greatness of the past and meanness of the present is less clear than is sometimes supposed. One might summarize the data on nineteenth-century Parsis as suggesting that some portion of that community was extremely wealthy and influential, that few Parsis starved, but that a substantial portion of the community was lower middle class—as it is today. Census data from 1872 suggest that as a community, the Parsis were not uniformly wealthy, and that while the visibility of the wealthiest members of the community may have decreased over time, community socioeconomic standing has not dramatically declined. In fact, it may have risen.[24]

Still, Parsi poverty is often assumed to have increased in contemporary Bombay, although not to destitution.[25] Most Parsis will explain that you will never see a Parsi begging, although some will say that now there is a Parsi begging at such-and-such a temple, it is so sad.[26] Indeed, some of the Parsis that remain in Gujarat are now very poor.[27] In Bombay, in 1982, 21 percent of the Parsi households surveyed reported an income of less than 300 rupees a month, and another 21 percent less than 800 rupees (the standard lower-middle-class income would have been around 2000 rupees a month in 1982). If the figures are accurate, some 42 percent of the community is very poor indeed. And yet most of these people live in subsidized housing with a nominal rent, or own their housing without a mortgage, and there is quite a high chance that these income figures are under-reported by a sizable margin.[28]

Parsi Ethos

Perhaps the most important point to be made about Parsi culture is that in many ways—in dress, in aesthetic and intellectual aspiration, in the westernized clubs and drinks and food, in torn loyalties to western and eastern style and in embarrassed ambivalence about the virtues of modern India—Parsis merely highlight the dilemmas and paradoxes of modern, elite, educated Indians. The Parsi people of course are unique. Their expressed unease about India probably runs deeper, their sense of marginality is probably more intense, the subtle style of Parsi sophistication and their unsubtle laughter is like nothing else. But in some broad, crude, general sense, the conflicts they experience and the ambivalence they express must be seen as emblematic of a middle-class, western-educated Indian sensibility in which things western are both deeply desirable and resented, in which glamour lies both in a commitment to India and in a multicontinental life. In these broad cultural currents, "India" and "the west" are complicated, shifting categories, whose primary meaning resides more in their opposition than their content. As the parade of material goods marches across an individual's life, his or her discourse about India may bear an uneasy connection to what appear to be the facts of their life. And this brings us to another point. The culture described here is particularly relevant to middle-class Parsis, as it is to middle-class Indians: the very poor cannot afford the club memberships and the concert subscriptions, and the very rich have possibilities which set them apart. These are the uncertainties of the well-taught and the comfortable. They are no less important for that.

To start with Arnoldian culture, music and literature and drama, middle-class Parsis identify with the British. In general Parsis are fond of western music, and if you go to a concert of classical western music in Bombay, many in the audience will be Parsi. The most famous musician of the community, Zubin Mehta, is a conductor of western music; an American-educated Parsi remarked cynically that when Zubin Mehta and Ravi Shankar performed together in New York, "though they both came from the 'East,' the gulf between their respective music systems is so wide that the concert assumed 'East-meets-West' proportions."[29] Parsis also flock to the evenings of classical western music offered by the Bombay Madrigal Singers Organization and the British Women's Council. "The audience was always at least 99 per cent Parsi and foreign," an admirer explained over tea at the CCI Club (Cricket Club of India); "Parsis like western music." She was of course exaggerating, claiming for Parsis a greater musical sophistication than that of by middle-class Hindus. But a taste for western music is not uncommon in the community. And the community has contributed many excellent musicians of western classical music.

Another unchanging Parsi (and elite Indian) staple is the club. Following the imperial tradition—"in any town in India the European Club is the spiritual citadel, the real seat of British power, the Nirvana for which native officials and millionaires pine in vain"[30]—many Parsis are members of some institution or another. Parsi membership will concentrate in certain clubs which are not themselves exclusively Parsi—the Princess Victoria Mary (the PVM), at the Willingdon, the Cricket Club of India (the CCI), the Bombay Gymkhana, all of these heavily supported by Hindu membership—and in the evenings Parsis will gather in small groups around the tables and eat cheese sandwiches with their tea. The Willingdon Club is a good example of such institutions. It is a gracious piece of Raj architecture, with sweeping staircases and grand rooms. Sometimes a brass band would play in the garden.

The club was founded to enable the British and Indians to meet on neutral turf—most nineteenth-century clubs were racially exclusive—and the great Parsi industrialist J. N. Tata was among its founders. The striking point, to an outsider, is the very western feel of the building, its rooms, and its dinner service; it seemed to me much more like the New York Yale Club than even the westernized dining rooms of the best Bombay hotels.

To my knowledge, the Ripon Club—named for the Marquis of Ripon, once Viceroy of India—is the only exclusively Parsi club. Founded in 1884 by Pherozeshah Mehta as a venue where both nationalist and conservative political factions could meet, it has become a favorite lunch spot in the heart of the city center. When it was first established, the prospective member had to be male, prominent, and British-returned (in other words, he had to have been to Britain). These days the entrance and monthly subscription fees are fairly low, which allows younger professionals to join. Still, membership hovers around four hundred people.[31] It is a pleasant place to gather for lunch, either at the long common table or at smaller private tables. Like most Parsi food, the menu is western—the lunch service includes spinach souffle, Irish stew, and apple pie—but on Wednesday they served *dhansak*. Tall, dark screens mark off the various portions of the room, and heavy dark cabinets line the walls. Oils of distinguished members hang on the walls. In the afternoons, older Parsis come to read their papers beneath the fans, and to sleep.

The "Parsiness" of Parsis, though, is not in its quasi-westernized middle-classness but in its style, in a kind of pragmatic jolliness. The community self-image, many Parsi will say, is "hail fellow well met"; "eat, drink, and be merry"—Parsis, one Parsi told me, are a lot like hobbits—and apart from western music the cultural activities that Parsis themselves sponsor tend towards the jovial. In the last few decades Pervez Doctor's Coffee Concerts, a kind of Pops, have played the bright recognizable tunes of the great composers. A Time and Talents Club and the Bottoms Up Review have offered either classical western music or burlesque and other amusing fare.[32] Like other communities, Parsis perform western plays, preferably musicals and off-color comedies. For years Adi Marzban's plays defined Parsi humor. They were performed in Parsi-Gujarati; you went to see them on New Year's day, and by all accounts they were raunchy, rude and (supposedly) very, very funny. There was little content to the plot itself, I was told by the couple who were his main actors. It was the gestures, the mannerisms, the Parsiness of the humour, that gave it life; Parsis, they said, and many Parsis confirmed it, are famous for laughing at themselves. The audience would also laugh at the double entendres, titles like *Mari Nichem Daulit*, "this is my downstairs neighbor Dolly," which could also mean, "the wealth of my downstairs anatomy, of my sexuality." Once (they said) a show was about to start at 6:30: at 6:15 Marzban handed the main actor a banana and a sheet of paper and asked him to sing these words to the tune of "My Bonnie Lies Over the Ocean" while peeling the banana:

> My one skin lies over my two skin
> My two skin lies over my three
> My three skin lies over my foreskin
> Oh pull down my foreskin for me . . .

This, the actor said, brought hysterical laughter from the audience. And these plays were immensely popular and seen as quintessentially Parsi. Parsis flocked to see them, and while there were some who cringed at their crudity, far more Parsis told me that "Adi Marzban—now there is Parsi humor, we loved him."[33]

Even Parsis with a sharply subtle wit will talk about the average Parsi bellylaugh and obscene puns in Gujarati.[34] The Gujarati-English community paper, the *JameJamshed,* carries a weekly column in Gujarati, Jamas and Jilloo ("Jamasni Jilloo") . Much of its humor sparks off the sexual and scatological—and also off the Parsi self-image. For example, the August 26, 1989, column includes a story about a Chinaman who was dismissed from his job after the birth of his tenth child; it focused on the way the Chinaman could exploit the mild, trusting Parsi temperament to gain support.

> *Jilloo:* But Jamasji, without a job, the poor man and his wife and ten children, how will they eat, from where will they buy their clothes, shoes and socks? . . .
> *Jamas:* Don't you worry. Our Parsis are very generous-hearted and now it is the auspicious days of Pateti Khordad Sal [the New Year] and so children are making appeal after appeal, in like manner the Chinaman will do and if some Children's Fund begins, the kind-hearted Parsis in it will definitely contribute and increase their spiritual merit . . .

The column also plays on the idiosyncratic—and often, poor—Parsi control of Gujarati, using a character's incorrect Gujarati to turn a joke on India. For instance, the February 25, 1992, "Jamasni Jilloo" contains this exchange:

> *Jilloo:* For our country's "shrikhandata" [this is an incorrect Gujarati word; she means *akhandata,* unity or integrity] animals should also play their part along with humans.
>
> *Jamas:* Your Gujarati is becoming as poor as your English. It is neither *shrikhand* nor *sheero* [both of which are sweet dishes]—the correct word is *akhandata.*
>
> *Jilloo:* Whatever that is. You are not Gujarati scholar either.[35]

Bapsi Sidhwa's light-hearted account of the community, for a time the best known Parsi novel, has a distinctly scatological strain:

> Now Billy's thunderbox [his toilet], being part of the dower received from Sir Noshirwan Jeevanjee Easymoney, had to be special. It was! It was large, it was carved, and it was inlaid with brass. When the lid, which was also the backrest, was shut, it looked like a chest.
>
> Enthroned, Billy sipped his tea and read the newspaper. As soon as the cup of tea was emptied, it was replaced by another. Often Billy sent for ledgers and scrutinised them on his princely perch. This was the hour of his business audience. Those who wished to see him at his house, and at his leisure, visited in the morning. One by one the contractors, land-agents, purchasers and dealers would cough outside the reed curtain . . . of an occasional evening when it was dark outside, they saw Sethji in all his glory, lean shanks gleaming between pyjama-top and pyjama botton—brass inlay and carved thunderbox! (Sidhwa 1978:276–77)

There is a jolly English-matron feel to this humor: direct, naughty, innocent of violence, and essentially untroubled.

And yet at the same time, despite the cheer and placidity and pragmatism, there is a strain of discontent, of embarrassment and alienation from modern India that runs through Parsi discourse. The flip side to Parsi confidence is the fear that Hindus will laugh at them, think them eccentric, belittle them as weak. "To me," an adult Parsi admitted, "a Parsi is an old man in a *dugli* [a white Parsi coat] trying to get off the bus in a crowd." The image evokes a struggling, aging community in harsh and overcrowded modern India, a lurching bus where the old are pushed and teased and may have their wallets stolen; but they cannot afford to take taxis. The

Parsi character in the *masala* films is an old, eccentric man, the kind of elderly man who needs to get off the bus, battling his way to the door, at exactly the wrong moment for everyone. Why this should be the recurring image I am not sure; Parsis are widely respected for their benevolence in Bombay, and the image may have more to do with Marzban-inspired self-deprecating humor than with any more complex antagonism. Still, the existence of this stereotype of the crazy *bavaji* [Parsi] is a little unsettling.

Perhaps some of this uneasy anxiety spills into the increasingly shrill tension within the community, which is the most argumentative society I know.[36] "Everybody talks: no one does anything," the late Lady Hirabai Jehangir remarked dryly when asked, as the then President of the Parsi Panchayat of Bombay, for a diagnosis of what ailed the community. "Their vaunted unity is not the unity of agreement," she added "but that of quarrelsomeness."[37] Some Parsis suggested that their quarrelsomeness arose because Parsis still thought of evil as something in the world they were responsible for rooting out. Others told me that Parsis were all individualists, proud of their own and different viewpoints. Some said that Parsis were extroverts, and loved the sound of their own voices. Some explained that the quarrelling was a sign of their dried-up powers, of panicked impotence. Some suggested that it sprang from desperation, from the attempt to maintain an identity in a shifting world. All of them joked about their strife: if there are three Parsis in a room, runs a common joke, there will be four arguments. "If there is no one to argue with, a Parsi will look into the mirror and argue with himself." Yet the arguments do more to bind the community together, make it stand out from others, than do they tear it apart.

To an outsider, the most remarkable characteristic of this remarkable community is its intense ambivalence about its place in India. Parsis in general are proud and even boastful about the community's role in modern Indian history. Bombay is full of statues of important Parsis as well as hospitals, schools, and libraries built with Parsi funds. More than one Parsi, when I asked what it was to be Parsi, said that it was these monuments which moved them and gave them pride and made them feel Parsi. Many more than one Parsi said that they were Indian first and Parsi second. Articles on Parsi history start with proud, ringing declarative sentences about Parsi importance in India, their benevolence, their charity, their intelligence, and their love of the country that sheltered them so generously. And yet a stream of little remarks continuously underwrite Parsi alienation from modern India—and also attack that alienation. "If you look into the core of a Zoroastrian heart, most Zoroastrians really feel like strangers in India." The woman was explaining to me why I was not allowed into a fire temple, and went on to describe how my bodily vibrations would be damaged by the great purity and power of the temple fire. "I never felt like an Indian," an upper-middle-class woman explained. Like most Parsis (and elite Indians), she went on to say, she went to the best school her parents could afford. It was an English school, probably a convent school—many Indians attend schools runs by Catholic nuns and Jesuit priests—and she grew up on Jack and Jill, western comic books, and eventually Wordsworth, Byron, and Shelley. She never listened to Indian music—she couldn't understand it, she said—but she developed a taste for Tchaikovsky; she learned to ride and was known for her seat on a horse. She had felt nostalgic for the Lake District before she ever left India. But when she finally went to the Lake District, she said, it didn't touch her. It wasn't her country, and she found this confusing. In India, she said, Parsis are very pale. They feel superior to other Indians, and they do not feel Indian. "When I went to Britain," she said, "suddenly I had a dark skin and I was foreign. We are like the Jews," she said. "They have Israel, we have Persia and the Shahnameh. Our loyalties are directed towards our ancient homeland." "Never believe a Parsi who tells you that he is Indian first and Parsi second," another young woman told me over tea.[38]

Compared to my Hindu friends, Parsis seemed to me more comfortable with criticizing India, more at ease in deriding the poverty, the dirt, the noise, and the corruption that is so much of urban India. Many Parsis told me that the dynamic, successful Parsis had all emigrated. An eminent senior journalist told me that his vision of the community was of young men and women growing up in America. Many of them *have* grown up in America and elsewhere; 22 percent of Parsi families surveyed in a 1982 study reported that they had family members who lived abroad (Karkal 1984). Despite the fact that many middle-class Indians boil their water, several people spontaneously described the Parsi refusal to drink unpurified Indian water as an index of their stance towards India—and roundly declared that India and Bombay were falling apart. When

I told my Brahmin friend that my father was coming to visit, she exclaimed, "how lovely, where will you take him"? while a Parsi remarked, "that's wonderful, but I hoped you've warned him. I always feel," she said, "that westerners should be prepared before they come to India."

One afternoon I met a women who called herself a Parsi, but not a Zoroastrian; she had renounced her Zoroastrian faith to join the Christian Science Church. She was one of the relatively few Parsis I met who wore Indian dress instead of the standard Parsi western dress. When I commented upon this she said, "Parsis should be more integrated into India. I remember coming home around Independence, so excited, feeling that we were now a free India, and my mother said, we're not Indians, we're Persians. My sisters and I would never let her live that down. After 1300 years we're still Persians?" And then this woman added, "But most Parsis live like that. They still have their pictures of King George and Queen Mary—*apra raja, apri rani,* they will say. They think that they're better than the Hindus." (There *are* Parsis who have pictures of English royalty on their walls. There are many more Parsis who complain about Parsis who have pictures of English royalty on their walls.) A senior Parsi man explained: "when Hindus go to America or England, they often remain very much within an Asian world. We Parsis do not," he said; "we are more open-minded, we absorb more western ideas, they come more naturally to us."

And yet the exclusivity is sharply criticized. Marrukh Contractor would complain bitterly that Parsis hung out only with Parsis, that when you went to a Parsi party only Parsis were there, and so she herself spent most of her time with non-Parsis and her mother despaired of her ever meeting a Parsi man to marry. The same was true of another, older friend who was fiercely critical of the community and would write scathing essays about their colonialist mentality for the Bombay press. "As part of the post-Independence generation I have often been embarrassed by my compatriots' colonial hangovers and their insensitive jeering of Indian culture and customs."[39] And from my modest perspective, I rarely met a non-Parsi through a Parsi, and I often heard Parsis comment on their own exclusiveness. A young woman who had been educated abroad since age twelve explained: "I should say right from the start, going to school in Bombay with other Parsi children, we felt a secluded group. Right through childhood we stayed together, in classes, even in ballet and other activities. Parsi kids tend to group together." Again, this is hardly uncommon in communal India. But Parsis comment extensively on their exclusivity as something wrong. That is what makes it interesting. Debates over conversion, intermarriage, and theological orientation are consistently confused with larger issues of community positioning within India and the west. Parsis are Indian and that is bad (they don't care enough about the community to maintain its purity and assets); they are not Indian and that is bad (they keep to themselves, they don't allow conversion); they are too western (their westernness has destroyed them); the problem is that they aren't western enough (if they were more westernized, like their grandparents, they'd work harder). The feelings expressed are contradictory, incompatible, and fervent.[40]

The western-identified Indian—the Brown Sahib, as the phrase has it—is hardly a uniquely Parsi phenomenon, no more than the sticky, quarrelsome enmeshment of the community as a whole. When Nirad Chaudhuri dedicated his autobiography to the British Raj and described England, a land he had never seen, as one of the settings of his childhood, he outraged his countrymen but he was describing with superbly subtle irony the dilemma of the Anglicized middle classes that colonialism had created. The Anglicized middle classes are often taught more about Wordsworth or Shakespeare than Americans are; they send their children abroad for college if they possibly can; their men wear suits and their women a range of Indian and western dress; they drink scotch and play Trivial Pursuit and listen to reggae; they serve cocktails in the living room with Indian temple carvings on the walls and they have "discovered" rural India in handblocked Gujarati prints the way the American middle class has "discovered" a southwest style. In none of these activities are Parsis unique, except in what seems to me a greater degree of ambivalence about their Indianness. In the nineteenth century they reached farther and deeper, as a community, for the traits of westernization, and—as a later chapter describes— they reinforced their cultural move with a new enthusiasm for their non-Indian Persian past. Now many Parsis will stress their sense of difference from the rest of India, and however skeptical the observer might be that Parsis are "less Indian" than other Indians, it is crucial to understand how deeply engaged many Parsis have been with this sense of difference, of being fundamentally more like the west, and how deeply self-critical they are not only of their own Indianness, but of their failure to be more Indian.

On a train from Oxford to London, Yasmin—whom I had met through friends—talked to me about her sense of shame at being Parsi. "It is the feeling you might have if you went to an elite school, and then you attended a polytechnic. You feel proud of your elite school, but you're embarrassed if other people know. You're embarrassed because you think they think you feel superior to them, and you do and know it's wrong. You're also embarrassed because they might think you're no better than they are, and yet you've had these privileges, and that's also wrong. And you are horrified when your community seems to boast at your Hindu friends' expense." This conflicted attitude was not uncommon, she said; young Parsis who were liberal and sophisticated would be sharply conscious of what non-Parsis might think of them, and would almost insistently attempt to marry out of the community, to dress like Hindus and not like Parsis, to do anything to be different from the Parsi world in which they'd grown up. "They don't want to take on the *burden* of being a Parsi," she said. "On the one hand, you are immediately thought to be intelligent, far more intelligent than you think you are. On the other, people think of the inbreeding and the Hindi film image of the crazy *bavaji*, and they think you are a fool. You're pigeonholed anytime someone in Bombay hears that you're a Parsi. But you also feel pride. It's a mixture of pride and shame that you feel."

"Sure," Yasmin went on, "there were the Zoroastrian Study types" (a revitalizing youth movement). They were not ashamed at all of being Parsi, she said; they were so energetically against being ashamed that Yasmin thought they were a little weird. "They are dead certain that they'll marry a Parsi, and that's unnatural," she said.

> Most of that changes when you go abroad. Parsis in India ape the western standards. Everyone in Bombay wants to do *everything* that someone in the west does. But the strange thing is that a Parsi in Bombay who has not been abroad will get embarrassed about speaking Gujarati in public with her grandmother, whereas the Parsi who's just returned from abroad will think nothing of it, because they've got nothing to prove. I used to answer my grandfather in English when he spoke to me in Gujarati, but now that I've been away I try to use Gujarati.

These of course are the natural feelings of a person who participates in a diaspora and then returns home. Nonetheless the experience is shaped by her sense of the community's aloofness.

"I never wanted not to be Parsi," Yasmin said; "that was never an option." But she said she'd mumble the word "Parsi" in a mixed group. She'd make people guess what she was. "My skin is dark enough so that people don't think of me being Parsi, and that's great." "My uncle seriously thinks," she said, "that black people are closer to monkeys." She felt horribly embarrassed by her uncle's views. She herself dressed almost always in Indian bangles and Punjabi suits, not like the Parsis from the colonies. So no one really knows she's Parsi, she said, unless she tells them. She told me that her father's family had been doctors for generations, and she lived on the elegant Cuffe Parade, but "when you say that you're Parsi to Hindus they put you in a category. No one would ever criticize; they respect Parsis. They think of the hardworking industrialist when they think of Parsis. But maybe they also think of the crazy *bavaji*. If you do anything eccentric, a Hindu will make fun of you. My Hindu boyfriend used to make fun of the Parsi accent."

"You're ashamed," she said, "but you'd never want to belong to another community. Every Parsi would admit that. You might even not be ashamed but you'd feel in Bombay that you should act ashamed in front of Hindus. But it's great that there's all this interest in reviving the community." And the current generation, she said, really is achieving, not like the generation just after Independence. "That's something to be proud of."

A thousand years is a long time in a foreign land, and no matter how deeply identified they were with the British, Parsis live within a Hindu culture and within a predominantly Hindu land. The inevitable story about the elderly Parsis with photographs of British royalty is usually told as a self-deprecating joke about other people. And yet many Parsis tell you that they are Indian but they are not of India, they are not comfortable with things Indian, and then they disparage the Indian world in which they live; they speak of and often decry their own westernization, and laugh at their fellow Parsis—most of the community, they chuckle—who are more British than the British; they hang photographs of Iran on their walls and hold competitions in the recitation of the Shahnameh and yet dismiss their Iranian cousins as backward. "The Parsi community is one of the most imitative communities on the surface of the globe," a Parsi writer remarked around the time of Independence

(Dastoor 1944:6). This comment is strong, but it indicates a pro found discontent with community identity that fifty years have not chased away.[41] These are crude generalizations, and like all generalizations, dangerous. Nevertheless these themes seemed to come up and up again in my conversations.

The ambivalence, the sense of being out of place, is well represented in the literature and poetry Parsis have written: in some sense, the anomaly and, ultimately, the decay from the perceived fixity, authority, and rightness of the past *is* the theme of that literature. Keki Daruwalla's "Parsi Hell" (1982) includes these lines:

> Standing at the dark house of my dreams . . .
> Like a fire temple I hoard my inner fires
> Hoard my semen, brown with inbreeding. Genetic rust?
>
> Death hums over the wires: what affects the spawn
> Is rickets, polio, a drug gone rogue. Daughters
> Walk out on the tribe . . .
>
> A Parsi carries his hell.

The poem memorializes community and individual decay. Daruwalla asserts both that his semen has decayed (the symbolic importance of semen is widespread in South, if somewhat idiosyncratic here) and that lust has destroyed his faith.[42] There is no real hell after death, he says, but the Parsi hell is here on earth as the community falls apart at its seams. Parsi literature seems to circle ceaselessly around this sense of a decaying, sexually devitalized community. There are more positive portraits of the community— Boman Desai's *Memory of Elephants* (1988) is a notable one—and modern Indian literature is not an optimistic counterpart to these tales of rotting gloom. But Indian writing in English, such of it as I have read, tends to find its despair and motivation in the seemingly intractable problems of poverty and politics. Rural India is romanticized, modernity condemned or celebrated, the metaphysics of self-consciousness explored and politicized.[43] I, at least, do not see a thread as coherent as that which runs through Parsi poetry, a thread of a deracinated, anomalous, decaying culture within the confusion of a bustling postcolonial world. Consider, for instance, one of the most famous poems of one of India's best known English-language poets: "The Ambiguous Fate of Gieve Patel, He Being Neither Hindu Nor Muslim in India" (1966).

To be no part of this hate is deprivation.
Never could I claim a circumcised butcher
Mangled a child out of my arms, never rave
At the milk-bibing, grass-guzzling hypocrite
Who pulled off my mother's voluminous
Robes and sliced away at her dugs [breasts].
Planets focus their fires
Into a worm of destruction
Edging along the continent. Bodies
Turn ashen and shrivel. I
Only burn my tail.

In the land of recent horrors Parsis are not responsible for the horror, nor have they suffered by it—not in comparison to those who saw their mothers mutilated—nor are they particularly relevant to the horror's existence. And yet Patel told me in the late 1980s that he no longer felt this way about India, that he felt that India was now more his own. Adil Jussawalla, one of the major Parsi poets (again, like all Parsi writers, an English-language poet), entitled his first book *Missing Person*. The two title poems, long and segmented, describe what he perceives to be the fragments of his identity: post-Independence, post-British, neither Indian nor western, an intellectual in a country crying out for concrete aid, a middle-class citizen in a nation of paupers. In this poem Jussawalla sees himself almost as an insult, he sees himself as eliciting rage and laughter from those around him, and he feels that he has no identity but that of the "missing person." What is missing is the person in him. And he himself is confused, angry, and tormented by his own being.

A mill of tubercular children
Is what he wears
The wretched of history storm into
They smash
His house of ideas

Who puffed up an Empire's sails?
Still fuel the big-power ships
Still make him fly
High to jet-setter fashion
Blood tumbles down his sleeves

> Hung upside down
> To dry
> In his flat
>
> He'll wreck himself yet
> Docked in a bar with a criminal friend
> His shirt wrapping him like a wet
> Sail, his wood carcass breaking and
>   burning in mutinous sweat. (1975:19)

The poems are bleak and difficult, filled with anger: his own, at himself and other people, and their anger at him. "God of our fathers, of the broken tribe and the petrified spirit, why did you send us this horror?" (1975:20). And much of this anger he at least perceives to be connected to colonialism and his people's colonial involvement—the wet sail, as it were, that he has wrapped around himself.

> In the fist of a rotting people
> His rotting head
> A mirror fires at him point blank
> And yells, "Drop dead
> Colonial ape,
> Back under an idealist spell
> Yes, you've made it to some kind of hell,
> Backslide, get liquidated"
>
> "Wait! You know whose side
> I'm on" he shouts
> "But the people, their teeth bright as axes
> Came after my bride.
> I've said all my prayers.
> O pure in
> Thought word and deed have I been
> Delivering sun,
> Yet you gild street urine—
> Theirs!" (1975:22)

I am part of India, he says, but they revile me as a traitor. And yet I have been good—and he uses the standard Zoroastrian phrase: good in thoughts, words, and deeds. In spite of being a good Zoroastrian, they hate him: the poem suggests that it is because he

is a good Zoroastrian and thus a compliant colonial—that they—
India—see him as the enemy. Now he fits in nowhere, and must
only rot.

It makes no sense. Wadia's thumping talks
On working for the happiness of those
Unborn generations and my kids;
Bund Garden picnics, tempers, squabbles, slaps,
All boil down to grease-stains in a pan,
Four rooms in London—broken taps, no rugs—
Meters gulfing shillings by the shoal,
Mothers sinking in a Willesden home,
The children sulking with the telly gone,
And me among a suitcase full of notes,
Three thousand years of notes—one manuscript
Containing words as dead as all my dead
Ancestors unpacked in silent towers.

I thought it was my life's one task, you see,
To disabuse the West of fantasies
About the ways of prophets, what they taught;
To prove a gentler vision to my own
Than Nietzsche seemed to see. Those sordid years,
When Hitler lashed his name's electric whip
Across the backs of caterwauling Jews,
The concentration of my hopes began.
Nietzsche did not know that Superman
Zarathustra was the Jews' first brother.

Such folly, such thick wit. I still worked on.
Then suddenly the Mahatma and his crowd
Got what they wanted. Uncertainties
About the growth of "parasites"
(so a Hindu called us then), an excitable Wadia
                    advising us to pack,
I came to London—my scholarship a tail
I'd learn to wag in public fairly soon.
Hilda says I'm sitting on it still.

I have a lovely family, of course.
Silloo's tongue a pipe of poisoned darts,
Nozer off his rocker for his June,

Ordering a gross of condoms by the post . . .
They've learnt too much too soon
Smacked Niloufer
For calling Eric "nigger"
And she so dark herself.
I see the boys are fighting shy of her,
An ugly child but one with a brilliant voice
That falls around my mornings like those coins
Grandfather let me throw at peasants once.
I'd send her to a singing school, of course,
But what can a girl do
With a trained voice and looks so wrong and black?
I wish the pop she picks up would not stick.

The little one will probably succeed
If he sticks to what he wants to be:
A fireman.
I must see Abe or Clive about that will.

Three shirts to wash. And Silloo's nosh-ups
Always stew.
What does she find in that Miss Eruchshaw
to talk a Sabbath through? Me, I supposee . . .
"Bread loser," "running dog" . . . I've heard it all.

Dressing Nozer's nose last night, I shook.
They beat him 'cause they thought he was a Jew.
Facial similarities—further notes—must work—
Forget my fears—must start work again—
Must work. (1975:40–1)

He leaves India because as a colonial parasite he is no longer
welcome there; but he also has no place in England. So he works,
tormented by the idea that it cannot be his culture, it cannot be
England, it cannot be his history which condemns him. If only he
works harder, somehow his true goodness will find identity and
peace for him.

Rohinton's Mistry's well-reviewed *Tales from Firozsha Baag*
(1987) describe life in one of the Parsi *baags*.[44] This urban community is actually a little village. "Soon after moving in, Dr. Burjor
Mody became the pride of the Parsis in C block. C Block, like the

rest of Firozsha Baag, had a surfeit of low-paid bank clerks and bookkeepers, and the arrival of Dr. Mody permitted them to feel a little better about themselves. More importantly, in A block lived a prominent priest, and B Block boasted a chartered accountant. Now C Block had a voice in Baag matters as important as the others did" (1987:79–80). The dominant tone in these short stories is a peculiar, deep ambivalence about Parsi life in India, which is presented as warm, endearing, communal, but also as aging into dilapidated eccentricity. One of the most poignant stories, "Lend Me Your Light," describes the wreckage of a friendship amidst the strains of emerging adulthood. Jamshed was the best friend of the narrator's older brother. He was wealthier than the narrator's own family: where the two brothers crowded into the grungy school dining room for lunch with all the other boys, Jamshed reclined in the back seat of the chauffeur-driven, air-conditioned car which arrived with his lunch inside a cooler. But apart from that, Jamshed and Percy, the narrator's brother, spent their time together.

The narrator and Jamshed left India the same year, the narrator for Canada and Jamshed for the United States. Jamshed couldn't wait to go. "Absolutely no future in this stupid place . . . Bloody corruption everywhere. And you can't buy any of the things you want, don't even get to see a decent English movie. First chance I get, I'm going abroad." But Percy stayed, and began to organize a charitable agency to help destitute farmers in a small Maharashtrian village. Jamshed writes to the narrator from New York: "Glad to hear you left India. But what about Percy? Can't understand what keeps him in that dismal place. He refuses to accept reality. All his efforts to help the farmers will be in vain. Nothing ever improves . . . Bombay is horrible [Jamshed has just returned from a visit]. Seems dirtier than ever, and the whole trip just made me sick. I had my fill of it in two weeks and was happy to leave" (1987:181). Percy writes that his work is going well: for the first time in years the farmers did not have to borrow from the money-lenders. He was in turn appalled by Jamshed's visit to India. "We were supposed to be impressed by his performance, for we were in an expensive restaurant where only foreign tourists eat on the strength of their US dollars . . . Here was one of our own showing us how to handle it all without a trace of inferiority, and now we were ashamed of him" (1987:185).

The narrator then describes his response to Jamshed's letter.

I started a most punctilious reply to his letter. Very properly, I thanked him for visiting my parents and his concern for Percy. Equally properly, I reciprocated his invitation to New York with one to Toronto. But I didn't want to leave it at that. It sounded as if I were agreeing with him about Percy and his work, and about India.

So instead, I described the segment of Toronto's Gerrard Street known as Little India. I promised that when he visited, we would go to all the little restaurants there and gorge ourselves with *bhelpuri, panipuri, batata-wada, kulfi,* as authentic as any in Bombay; then we could browse through the shops selling imported spices and Hindi records, and maybe even see a Hindi movie at the Naaz Cinema. I often went to Little India, I wrote; he would be certain to have a great time.

The truth is, I have been there just once. And on that occasion I fled the place in a very short time, feeling extremely ill at ease and ashamed, wondering why all this did not make me homesick or at least a little nostalgic. But Jamshed did not have to know any of it. My letter must have told him that whatever he suffered from, I did not share it. For a long time afterwards I did not hear from him. (1987:181–2)

Then the narrator returns from Canada to visit. "Bombay seemed dirtier than ever. I remembered what Jamshed had written in his letter, and how it annoyed me, but now I couldn't help thinking he was right. Hostility and tension seemed to be perpetually present in buses, shops, trains. It was disconcerting to discover I'd become unused to it" (1987:187). Percy had not planned to return from the village to see him, because Jamshed was due back at the same time and Percy could not bear to see him. But he returns unexpectedly. The moneylenders have killed his co-worker. And the narrator feels helpless because there is nothing he can do to help.

Jamshed inadvertently *does* help. The next day, Jamshed appears, and listens to Percy's tale of struggle. "I told you from the beginning, all this was a waste of time . . . I still think that the best thing for you is to move to the States . . . There, if you are good at something, you move ahead" (1987:192). Percy turns to his mother. "Could we have dinner right away? I have to meet my friends at eight o'clock. To decide our next move in the village" (1987:192). The narrator flies back to Toronto and unpacks.

Gradually, I discovered that I'd brought back with me my entire burden of riddles and puzzles, unsolved . . . I mused, I gave way to whimsy: I, Tiresias, throbbing between two lives, humbled by the ambiguities and dichotomies confronting me . . . I thought of Jamshed and his adamant refusal to enjoy his trip to India, of his way of seeing the worst in everything. Was he, too, waiting for some epiphany and growing impatient because, without it, life in America was bewildering? Perhaps the contempt and disdain which he shed was only his way of lightening his own load. (1987:192–3)

The narrator sides with Percy. But he has chosen Jamshed's life. "There you were, my brother, waging battles against corruption and evil, while I was watching sitcoms on my rented Granada TV" (1987:184). All three of them, after all, agree that in India there is much evil and corruption—one of them risks his life to fight it, the other two leave for better opportunities abroad. All of them are uncomfortable in India, and respond drastically to their discomfort.

Most of the other stories are about an aging, aimless people: the fifty-year-old in dentures, with constipation, spat upon by a Hindu so that his pure, gleaming white *dugli* [a Parsi man's coat, worn on auspicious occasions] was stained scarlet by lower-class *paan;* the young boy who every Sunday plucks out his father's white hair, first resenting it and then overcome by his sorrow at his father's age and approaching death; the young couple who take in an older couple as paying guests, and try to get them to leave after a while, and then the older woman spreads excrement and trash at their door and eventually steals the baby and puts it in a parrot cage. The last story is about the narrator's letters home, and about the manuscript—this manuscript of stories—that they receive in the mail. His parents like the stories: they are, after all the letters that never arrived. And in the end:

In the stories that he'd read so far Father said that all the Parsi families were poor or middle class, but that was okay; nor did he mind that the seeds for the stories were picked from the sufferings of their own lives; but there should also have been something positive about the Parsis, there was so much to be proud of: the great Tatas and their contribution to the steel industry, or Sir Dinshaw Petit in the textile industry who made Bombay the Manchester of the East, or Dadabhai Naoroji in the freedom movement, where he was the first to use the word *swaraj*, and the first to be elected in the British Parliament where he carried on his campaign; he should have found some way to bring some of the these wonderful facts into his stories, what would people reading these stories think, those who did not know about Parsis—that the whole community was full of cranky, bigoted people; and in reality it was the richest, most advanced and philanthropic community in India, and he did not need to tell his own son that Parsis had a reputation for being generous and family oriented. And he could have written something about the historic background, how Parsis came to India from Persia because of Islamic persecution in the seventh century, and were the descendents of Cyrus the Great and the magnificent Persian Empire. He could have made a story of all this, couldn't he?

Mother said that what she liked best was his remembering everything so well, how beautifully he wrote about it all, even the sad things, and though he had changed some of it, and used his imagination, there was truth in it. (1987:245)

This is quintessentially Parsi: the sense of the glories of the community's recent and distant past, the embarrassment about a lesser present. Shortly before I left from my first visit I lent the book to a Parsi friend. It offended her: why couldn't people write about Parsis as they really were? Today's Parsis weren't like that, so crabbed and crazy, she said. People would laugh at the community if they read the book; it wasn't right.

Another, final, example is the play by Mistry's brother, who stayed in India (Rohinton Mistry did emigrate to Canada) and married a non-Parsi; his work is different from his brother's in many ways and its emotional tone is quite distinct. Nevertheless, community ambivalence about India remains a core theme. *Doongaji House*—the playwright told me that the house is a metaphor for the community as a whole—is about a once elegant building, now old and dilapidated, in the heart of Bombay.[45] It was once the tallest building around for miles, and one of the first buildings in Bombay to have electricity. It used to be a matter of pride to live in Doongaji house, we are told. But now the electricity has stopped working and the inhabitants fear that the roof will collapse on their heads.

The play is about a Parsi family living in Doongagi house. The father is an old man, a drunkard, who no longer holds a job because—he says—his brother cheated him out of his business. He copes by living in the past and the play opens on his reminiscences.

> Do you remember those days? When Rusi was only five or six, and Farli was still learning to walk? Things were so cheap then, we had plenty of money. Every evening, coming home from work, I'd pick up something—pineapple cake, chocolate liqueurs [note that this is not Indian food]. [The Hindus] think it is their Raj now. Was a time when they would bow and scrape to us. If a Parsi got on a bus, they would rise to offer him a seat. Today, walking down the street, they make fun of you. . . . Those days are gone. This is a generation of sissies. . . . The blood has been polluted.

The mother cannot bear the father's helplessness, and nags him constantly. The son is shiftless and irresponsible; the daughter, still unmarried, brings home the only paycheck in the family.

The play describes the dissolution of the family as one illusion is dispelled after another. They learn that the father was not cheated in his business, but that the business fell apart of its own accord. The daughter accepts a job from the man who brings this news, and decides to move out of Bombay, leaving the jobless father sharply aware of his inability to support his family. To make money he steals his daughter's last paycheck, places a bet, and loses. In his drunken daze following this adventure, when the city goes crazy in the premonsoon heat, he taunts Hindus in the street. They beat him up. The play ends when the roof caves in under the weight of monsoon rains. It kills the upstairs neighbors, the building is condemned as unfit for human habitation, and the parental couple is taken to charitable housing for the destitute. Before the play ends, the wife has a dream:

> I was going back to my father's estate, outside Lahore. I was happy to be going back home. But when I reached it, I saw that everything was ruined. The garden was overrun with brambles and wild grass. The bungalow was decayed and crumbled . . . Then I saw Avan [the daughter]. She was standing in the middle of the ruin, carrying an infant in her arms. It was a monster . . . Swollen head, two holes for a nose . . . eight fingers on each hand . . . "Who is its father?" I screamed at her. She just pointed: some distance away, in the tall grass, was a body . . . covered with a white sheet. I went up to it and pulled back the sheet . . . It was my father, Kaikhushro. I touched

his cheek. It was icy cold. Then he opened his eyes and smiled at me.
I felt happy.

The dream's weirdness reinforces the play's refrain: the Parsis are dying, their past has disfigured them, but it is the illusory belief in their past superiority that keeps them happy.

Among contemporary Parsis, and especially younger Parsis, the sense of being non-Indian seems to be weakening.[46] The woman who had once been nostalgic for the Lake District told me that she was raising her children to be more Indian so that they would not feel these tensions. Middle-class Hindus told me that Parsis were more Indian in this generation than they have ever been before. One Hindu man explained, for instance, that he lived near Dadar, where a large Parsi community is located. It used to be that when the Hindi films came on—there is a popular one on television every weekend—the Parsi neighborhood was silent, he said. You never even heard Indian music, only western classical music. Now, if you take a weekend walk down those streets, he said, the collective sound of many televisions is of Hindi films and Hindi music. In the building where I stayed with the Contractors—it was a Parsi building, with Parsis on most of the five floors of flats—I heard western music and the sound of western films. But I also heard Hindi films. In recent years, Parsis have begun to take more interest in their religion, with the youth in particular demanding to know more about their rituals and traditions. A group called Zoroastrian Studies formed around fifteen years ago under the leadership of a charismatic scholar, Khojeste Mistree, has become a vital community presence, offering lectures, classes, and retreats. Yet while the community may be changing, to an outsider there still seems to be a sense of uncertainty, anomaly, and ambiguity about what Parsi identity should be. Parsis are inordinately proud of their past and deeply critical of their present. And anomaly brings with it something more profound than simply not belonging: a sense of decay, dissolution, and emasculation.

IN THE
BEGINNING

2

Parsi Comment: Shirin

In a conversation with me, a young Parsi woman reflected on her community as follows:

What does the community think of itself? Speaking for myself, when I look back in time, about ten years ago I think that my generation was experiencing a religious identity crisis.[1] There was little sense of Zoroastrian identity. No one understood the religion or the rituals and practices. I felt ashamed when people called us *bavajis*.[2] I felt ashamed to wear the *sudreh kusti*.[3] I didn't understand its symbolism and couldn't explain the religion to non-Zoroastrian friends. . . . Many in our generation experienced this. Nor could we go to our parents for help, for even they knew more about Christianity than their own religion, because of the Christian missionary schools they attended.

So we felt inferior because of our religion. And yet at the same time the community was proud of its past achievements in almost every field: science, technology, literature, arts, business, philanthropy, and so forth. Practically the whole of Bombay was developed by Parsis— hospitals, theatres, you name it. Because the parents couldn't explain the religion to their children they tried to make them proud of their community by telling them about its achievements. So on the one hand we had an inferiority complex and an identity crisis and on the other hand we boosted up our egos with constant bragging about our past glories, and we felt superior to the rest.[4]

◆ ◆ ◆

All societies have a historical consciousness; even the once timeless primitive has acquired the right to a complex memory of the past.[5] But the past can be used in different ways to different ends. Parsis use their past to define their primary sense of the present, and—particularly important in their current insecurity—what they remember are their achievements: their power and ambition during the British Raj, their greatness in the Persian past. These achievements, both ancient and modern, were memorialized in the period of Parsi flowering under colonial rule, and they express what the Parsis came to see as the community's essential nature. Large chunks of undistinguished yesterdays—for instance, the first eight hundred years the Parsis spent in India—are ignored. Much cultural heritage—religious ritual and theology—has been determinedly forgotten by those who identified the community, through Anglicized eyes, as progressive, modern, and rational. The reconstructed past now provides an important and valuable sense of capability. But it contains a destructive edge, for the construction of memory during the Raj served a purpose which is no longer relevant for the Parsis in modern India, and what has been forgotten could perhaps more effectively serve their current needs.

The next few chapters describe the substance of modern Parsi historical awareness. This is not—I repeat, not—a historical analysis of the Parsi past. The anthropologist in the archives is always suspect, for the foray among the papers is guided by concerns directly centered in the present. Nevertheless, this is also not quite the way a Parsi would tell the tale. Most Parsis know the general outline of what I describe. Many Parsis will know little beyond the framework of these community-salient facts, and many of them would question the details which I provide out of contemporary scholarship—Zarathustra's birthdate, his birthplace, the correct interpretation of his teachings, the reason for the fall of the Sassanian empire and so forth. So the following is the skeleton that the community recognizes, fleshed out by respected scholarship and some foraging in the archives.

◆ ◆ ◆

Zarathustra probably lived in the middle of the second millennium
B.C., a rough contemporary of Abraham and of the creation of the
Rig Veda.[6] His were a nomadic people, herding cattle, sheep, and
goats, and he may have lived in the heroic age of his culture, for
the holy book which describes his doings makes reference to warriors and charioteers: "even as a mighty chariot-warrior should
fight, having girt on his sword-belt, for his well-gotten treasure."[7]
These nomads descended from the Indo-Iranian peoples who had
wandered on the southern Russian steppes in the fourth millennium B.C. By the third millennium these people had separated into
two cultures, but even a thousand years later, they shared similarities. The early Iranian religion echoes much of the Rig Veda, and
the Veda can be used to interpret early Zoroastrian texts.[8]

Zarathustra is thought to have been a priest of the early Indo-
Iranian religion.[9] Central to that religion was the concept of *asha*
(Sanskrit *rta*, later *dharma*), righteousness or—as scholars and
some followers describe it—natural law.[10] The term is thought to
imply order and right working, and it remained central to
Zarathustra's understanding of religion as he reformed it. In connection with human action *asha* is translated as truth. The leading
western scholar describes its original meaning thus:

> This term, it is now generally accepted, represents a concept which
> cannot be precisely rendered by any single word in another tongue.
> It stands, it seems, for "order" in the widest sense: cosmic order, by
> which night gives place to day and the seasons change; the order of
> sacrifice, by which this natural order is strengthened and maintained;
> social order, by which men can live together in harmony and pros-
> perity, and moral order or "truth."[11]

This remains salient for the contemporary Zoroastrian. Most
Zoroastrians would probably give a roughly similar account if
asked. The central foci of the early Iranian cult were fire and water;
again, these elements, particularly fire, remain at the heart of
Zoroastrianism. It is thought that milk and the sap and leaves of
a sacred plant—it may have been hallucinogenic[12]—were offered
to the water, and fat and incense, along with fuel, to the fire.[13] And
as fire and water were conceptualized as divine beings, so too were
other natural presences: the sun and moon, the wind, the rains, the
trees.

Parsi comment: Shirin

The conversation continues, with personal expressions of religious sentiments that are yet communally representative.

> I believe very strongly that if you take one step in the right direction, God takes 10,000 steps towards you.[14] I would just come into contact with people who wanted to help. I am certain that if you are absolutely sincere and honest about something, God provides. You shouldn't worry about resources or even doubt your abilities—HE PROVIDES. All along I've had this personal relationship with God, and I can see him guiding and moving me along. My sense of God has never changed. He's always been kind, giving and loving me unconditionally. He is always just. He has performed many miracles for me. I've also been aware that anything good in life must be worked for. I'm aware of an evil force, obstacles, hurdles, pain and unhappiness that we must face. I'm also aware that not all human beings are TOTALLY GOOD, like God is. I know that life is not a bed of roses. There are many stumbling blocks. But as long as you TRY and live and work for the sake of truth and righteousness, I believe that you are doing well. If you allow a little evil in, it grows and grows disproportionately until it wipes itself out. There are a lot of things I still can't quite understand. I see injustice, I see truth being suppressed, I see evil temporarily triumphing over good. I say temporarily because I have total faith in HIM and HIS plan and I know that in the end truth will prevail.

◆ ◆ ◆

Tradition says that Zarathustra was born laughing, that he rejoiced in God's love and beneficence and felt no need to fear. For "those who are made to cry have seen mortality as their end, and those who have laughed have seen their own righteousness."[15] Men tried to destroy him at his birth, but failed. They tried to burn him over a fire, but the wood refused to burn; they put him in the midst of oxen, and then of wild horses, in the hopes that he would be trampled, but in each case a member of the herd stood over him to protect him. They left him in the care of a she-wolf, but a divine power protected him.[16] In his youth he was brilliant and wise, as a young adult he withstood privation, as an aging man he was calm and pious and then, curiously, he was killed at prayer.[17] In short, he was a hero, the subject of the traditional stories of the birth of a hero and perhaps even of his death.

Selection from a Modern Parsi Children's Book

Zarathustra grew up to be a big fine boy. Everyone loved Zarathustra. They asked him "Why are you always smiling and happy?" Zarathustra would explain: you can be happy too if you try to think and do all that is good, share what you have with others and be kind to everyone. There was a time when there was a shortage of food in Iran. Zarathustra and his parents gave away all the good they had to the hungry people. They became poor but were glad that so many people were made happy by their action. Zarathustra now wanted to speak to the world about God. He left his house in search of TRUTH. . . . Zarathustra taught all people to be good and have kind thoughts about everyone, to do good to all and to help others to be happy. People loved Zarathustra and began to follow his teachings. He became a great prophet of Iran. (*Zarathustra*, by Piloo Lalkaka[18])

♦ ♦ ♦

Tradition says that Zarathustra was thirty years old when revelation came to him. He had left his parents' home at twenty, against their wishes, to seek for truth.[19] He went to a river to fetch water for a seasonal ceremony, wading into its depths. Upon emerging on the bank of the river (and having bathed, thus being ritually pure) he saw on the bank a shining figure—"a man, handsome, brilliant, and elegant, who wore his hair curved-tailed, because the curved tail is an indication of duality"[20]—who led him into the presence of God (Ahura Mazda) and five other radiant beings, before whom "he did not see his own shadow on the earth, owing to their great light."[21]

Exactly what Zarathustra taught about these beings is not clear, for his teachings, preserved in seventeen hymns known as the Gathas, are elliptical and obscure.[22] At the heart of the uncertainty is the question of dualism and the degree of God's power in the universe. Perhaps the most famous passage in the Gathas is this:

Truly there are two primal spirits, twins, renowned to be in conflict.
In thought and word and act they are two, the good and the bad. . . .

And when these two spirits first encountered, they created life and not-life, and that at the end the worst existence shall be for the followers of falsehood *(drug),* but the best dwelling for those who possess righteousness *(asha).* Of the two Spirits, the one who follows falsehood chose doing the worst things; the Holiest Spirit, who is clad in the hardest stone [i.e. the sky] chose righteousness, and (so shall they all) who will satisfy Ahura Mazda continually with just actions.[23]

The leading western scholar from whose work the translation is taken argues that these words indicate that early Zoroastrianism is dualistic.[24] There are two beings, each of whom has made a choice between good and evil, which is like the choice each individual must make in his or her life. Ahura Mazda could not destroy the evil spirit (Angra Mainyu) directly (spirit cannot destroy spirit), but by creating a material world, he created a trap for the evil. In the beginning, explains a later text, there were both God and evil, both uncreated, both infinite, with a void between them.[25] God knew that he must destroy the evil but that he could not do so in its spiritual form, so he created the material world as a trap for the evil, in the same manner, say the texts, that a gardener sets a trap for the vermin in his garden. Human beings, God's creations, can, by choosing good action over bad, force the trapped creature to expend its power in a futile struggle to escape. Death, pain, and suffering have an independent and external cause; God is responsible for none of the sorrow which grips this planet.

Most contemporary Parsis disagree with what is called the "continuity thesis"—the argument that their religious theology has been consistent over its history, and that the later texts, which are clearly dualistic, can be safely used to interpret the Gathas. Most western scholars of Zoroastrianism—at least, the leading scholar and her students—argue for the continuity thesis, and explain that the religion is a dualism in which God and evil are independent and opposed. Without taking sides, it is important to indicate that the question of dualism is heated and emotionally laden for Parsis, and that most Parsis know of and reject the views of recent western scholarship. A recent book entitled *What a Parsee Should Know* asserts: "There is no Dualism in our religion in the proper sense . . . in the course of time, it was forgotten that the Evil Spirit was the creation of Ahura Mazda himself and it was raised almost to the level of a rival of Ahura Mazda . . . the so-called Dualism . . . merely denotes the tendency in the human soul to deviate from the path of righteousness."[26] This is not an atypical modern text. Again and again, I met modern Parsis who had heard the term "dualism," had at least a vague sense that in dualism evil was not fully controlled by God, and straightforwardly denounced dualism as having nothing to do with Zoroastrianism.

Dualistic or not, Zoroastrianism is a doctrine in which moral issues are very clear and very important. God is good, rational, and knowable; he is truth—and truth, or truth-telling, is a Zoroastrian tenet which even a Zoroastrian untutored in the faith will tell you is the heart of the religion. God is also purity. Evil is the lie: all acts which are irrational and hurtful are due to evil. A human being is essentially good, but he or she can choose to be influenced by Ahriman, the Satan-equivalent. The central story of the religion is that the human individual participates in a battle between good and evil in which his or her own freely chosen actions determine the battle's outcome. It is usually accepted that God will ultimately win the war, but only through human initiative.[27]

Zarathustra also seems to have taught that each human being is judged at the end of life. Upon death the soul comes to a bridge over a chasm, the Chinvat Pul, and a woman representing the person's life deeds beckons the soul to cross over. She is either old and ugly, or young and beautiful, in accordance with the soul's deeds, and as the soul steps upon the bridge the path either widens to enable the soul to cross to a blissful, natural heaven, or narrows so that the soul falls off it into the hellish depths. And yet regardless, at the end of time all souls will be redeemed, and the earth returned to an Edenic godly paradise. It is said that Zarathustra was the first to teach the doctrines of an individual judgment, Heaven and Hell, the future resurrection of the body, the general last judgment, and life everlasting for the reunited soul and body; it is sometimes said that Zoroastrianism is the source from which similar Christian and Judaic teachings derive.[28]

Then as now, God was represented by fire. He is not fire personified, and contemporary Zoroastrians hasten to point out that they do not worship fire. They use fire to represent God, more or less as the cross represents Jesus. It is not quite clear when the first fire-temples were built; Herodotus refers to Persian fire-worship, and it may have been that there were very early temples. Scholars seem satisfied that fire-temples were entrenched in Zoroastrian worship by the end of the Achaemenian period (4th century B.C.).[29] In contemporary Bombay there are 44 fire temples, each with an ever-burning fire fed on sandalwood by white-frocked priests.[30] Some of them are highly sacred, in temples designated Atash Behrams: these fires have been consecrated by fires takes from 16 sources (lightning being one) and purified 91 times.[31]

Literary Vignette: *More of an Indian*

Crossing the garden quickly, she sniffed once, and again, harder, but the *mogra* nestling in leafy nooks hadn't blossomed, and in any case their fragrance would be too delicate to withstand the suffocating sweet of the frankincense and sandalwood burning in the temple. The triangular white blur against the verandah's yellow was no doubt the priest sitting cross-legged, and from the pause in his heated discussion with the sandalwood seller at the gate about the future of the city, she sensed his curiosity as she sprinkled water on to her fingers from the brass vessel in the porch and untied her *kusti* before entering the temple. Her hands went nervously through the movements, lips mumbled the accompanying prayers she had known by rote since the age of seven when she was initiated into the faith. The prayers were in Avesta which she couldn't understand, although she knew vaguely what they meant, because dad had told her. But her voice kept mingling with the priest's and the sandalwood man's, making sense in a confused intercalation of the spiritual and the temporal, about guarding her and her dear ones, as only Ahura Mazda could do, and about the police reinforcements expected to arrive in the city, about driving the evil spirits to the north and governing Bombay directly from Delhi, expressing her repentance for evil thoughts, words and deeds and their doubt whether the figures of wounded, arrested or killed given in the newspapers were correct.

Lest the click-clack of her high heeled sandals disturb the worshippers inside, she tiptoed past the photographs, the portraits in oil in pompous array of the departed worthies and founders of the temple, with mention underneath of their names, lineage and the thousands and lakhs [a lakh is 100,000 rupees] contributed to its building. The photographs were heavily stained by the smoke which, without an outlet, swirled around the pillars and gathered darkly under the satin-covered ceiling. The smoke had not spared even the portrait of the Prophet Zarathustra Spitama, he of the golden light, his forefinger raised, and in her hurry to face the Fire she passed the portrait without realizing that she had done so, then took a step back to salute it twice with both hands to make up for the lapse. The Prophet's kindly brown face against the sun hardly gave evidence of the fiery spirit she had come to associate with him.

By force of habit she pushed back the sliding glass front of the wooden cupboard and picked out a cloth-bound Avesta less frayed than the others, although she had no intention to pray from it. The sandalwood's sizzling and crackling across the walls of the inner altar punctuated the muffled singsong of the priests who recited prayers for the dead. They sat swaying in front of vases in which small fires burned and vessels containing sacred bread, grains of pomegranate and eggs, ghee or clarified butter, symbolizing the vegetable and animal kingdoms. She started, turning a pillar on which the golden shadows played, to find herself confronted by the officiating priest, white robed and capped, who held out a metal ladle with ash from the Fire. "Dust to dust" his impassive eyes yet spoke to her. She applied the ash to her forehead, fumbling in her purse for a coin to place in the ladle, and handed over her offering of sandalwood without looking up at him.

Now she found herself facing the inner altar, shocked and momentarily blinded by the bleeding gash of sun in a cloud-contused sky. She turned round to the other worshippers of whom there were only a few at this hour—a middle-aged couple, three or four old ladies crouching over their prayer books and a young man who stood swaying from one leg to another like an animated toy. The susurrous of their prayers, the priests' singsong, were orchestrated weirdly by the hissing and crackling of the little fires responding to the big one, echoing and re-echoing under the cavernous roof sloping away from the central dome. There was a child, too, solemn in its embroidered cap, which stared without blinking at the Fire. She took wisdom from the child and turned to the altar once again. From the enormous silver censer high on a marble pedestal, the flames freshly fed with sandalwood leapt up like tongues to lick the dome—no, like arms multiplying, bending and stretching in quick casting-off movements, casting off the defiling smoke which rose in draught after swishing draught to the ceiling. As she looked around at the metallic tray suspended over the Fire and the swords and maces hung against the inner wall, the flaming plumes smouldered down, without fury or hunger, to embers that blazed day and night since the temple was consecrated and would continue to blaze long after she herself was dust. . . .

She saw the priest change his *sapats* [slippers] for a pair especially reserved for the inner sanctum, pull white gloves over his hands and tie a piece of cloth over his mouth so that his breath might not defile the sacred Fire. The ceremony of feeding the Fire, performed five times every day at the commencement of each of the *gahs*[32] was about to begin, and she stepped sideways slowly to have a better look as the priest bent to wash the marble slab on which the censer stood with well water that had itself been purified. Reciting a short prayer, he sprinkled some frankincense and arranged six pieces of sandalwood on the fire carefully in pairs, one pair on top of the other and at right angles to it in the form of a throne. At his majestic, measured periods, reciting the prayer of all prayers, his resonant orotund voice soaring and subsiding with the flames, goosepimples crept up from below her ears to her cheekbones. "Oh God, the one and only! We praise Thee through Thy fire. We praise Thee by the offering of good thoughts. We praise Thee through the Fire. We praise thee by the offering of good deeds. We do all this for the illumination of our thoughts, for the illumination of our words and for the illumination of our deeds." He moved around the censer, ladle held aloft, invoking Ahura Mazda eight times from the four sides and the four corners, reverting finally to his original position facing east. Thrice he rang the bell, shattering the temple's silence, expressing the determination of the true worshipper to shun evil thoughts, words and deeds. (Karanjia 1970:1–4)

♦ ♦ ♦

Tradition says that for ten years Zarathustra was unable to find any converts among his own people, save his own cousin Maidhyoimanha.[33] So he left his people and, after some wandering, arrived in a community in which the king and queen, Vishtaspa and Hutaosa, acceded to his teachings. A story—again the focus of a dispute—ascribes this decision to Zarathustra's ability to cure the king's favorite horse. When he came to King Vishtaspa's court, evil courtiers insinuated that he was a sorcerer, for fear that his teachings would make him important and displace them. Zarathustra was imprisoned. But then the king's favorite horse grew ill.

From the modern *Pictorial Gatha:* "King Gushtasp had a beautiful horse, which was dark in colour and hence was called Asp-i-Siah [the black horse]. Once this horse had great pains in all its legs and could not move an inch and fell down. Nobody could cure him, but Zarathustra made certain conditions before curing the horse, which Gushtasp accepted, and the animal was fully cured."[34] Zarathustra said that he could cure it, and did so, extracting a promise from the king for each of the four legs that he restored to health: that the king, then his son, and then his wife, must embrace the faith, and finally, that his traducers be put to death.[35]

Ethnographic Vignette

In 1986 a film entitled *On Wings of Fire* was screened before the Parsi community in Bombay. Up until two hours before the scheduled showing, it was not clear that the film would be permitted to run. The Bombay High Court had been approached twice by orthodox Parsis—in particular, by an organization which called itself the Council of Vigilant Parsis—to prevent the film from being shown.[36] The order failed, the film was shown but picketed; by this time reams of paper had been devoted to the topic.

The film-makers of this feature-length film had set out to describe Zoroastrianism, but their interpretation of Zoroastrianism and the reaction to it became mired in the messy emotional quicksand of the Parsi romance with the west. The director was an ambitious American Parsi and his charismatic adviser had studied Pahlavi in Oxford, and their Zarathustra was an enlightened but quite clearly human philosopher. The orthodox Council of Vigilant Parsis saw their Zarathustra as a near-divinity, with all the magical, thaumaturgical respect that South Asians show for their human avatars. The treatment of the horse scene, then, was like a spark to a packed fuse. In the film, Zarathustra blesses the horse, but does not appear to effect a supernatural cure. To give some of the feel of this controversy, I will quote some of the letters to the editor published in *Parsiana,* a widely read community magazine. This one is from three community high priests (March 1983:49):

> This mind-boggling interpretation is a downright insult to the memory of a great prophet . . . The prophet is not only relegated to the level of a philosopher and thinker, but by this scene in the film, he

has been dragged down to the ridiculous role of a horse-doctor, a man of special veterinary knowledge! This is one such scene in the film, but there may be many others with various such implications, denuding the prophet of his supernatural status and showing him as a mere mortal.

From the director (April 1983:11):

> The curing of King Vishtasp's horse is a legend which nearly all Zoroastrians grow up with. It appears allusively in the Denkart (DK VII 4.70) but is fully developed in the Zardusht Nama.[37] In the film we are using the story to dramatize a point. In no way are we suggesting that this single act (curing the king's horse) is the only reason why Vishtasp accepted Zoroaster's religion . . . In no way would we like to portray Zarathustra as a veterinary doctor.

From a reader (A. B. Bhiwandiwal) (May 1983:4):

> Bharucha [the director] intends to portray Zarathustra as healing a sick horse and this is definitely improper and blasphemous. In actual fact Zarathustra was capable of and could perform any miracle or create supernatural phenomena.

From another reader (P. D. Sunavala)(August 1983:11):

> So-called miracle cures by mystics or faith healers of which there are quite a few these days, will not convince any educated person in this scientific age. It is evident that Bharucha is averse to casting Zarathustra in the role of a mystic healer effecting cures by chanting mantras; the man was a profound scholar of many parts, the one under context being veterinary medicine.

From another reader (Phiroz D. Dotiwala) (September 1987:40):

> When Zarathustra is shown curing a lame horse, it reveals ignorance. Our pristine prophet had vehemently decried any such hocus pocus miracles. How then could he himself perform such magic? All these were fabrications to impress the ignorant laity. There never was a lame horse and no such incident actually happened. Zarathustra told King Vishtaspa, "Behold oh King! You are riding a lame horse, you are going away from the right path ordained by Ahura Mazda—the path of righteousness. As a King, liberate your people from igno-rance, superstitions, deity worship and sacrifice of blood, and uplift

them for the cause of humanity." This was the lame horse that prophet Zarathustra cured and not a lame animal.

Fury was further fueled because the film presented Zarathustra's doctrines as they are understood by western scholarship. Thus not only was the prophet depicted as a mortal, but as advocating a dualism of the sort already described. This conception of dualism is accepted neither by the liberal majority of the community nor by the ritualistically orthodox followers of Ilm-e-kshnoom, an esoteric interpretation of Zoroastrianism. The members of the Council of Vigilant Parsis were for the most part kshnoomists. Their distraught leader articulated these almost hysterical objections in *The Parsee Voice:*

1. The Divine status of Holy Prophet Zarathustra has been denuded to an extent where he is projected merely as a philosopher and a thinker, a rational mortal, who is more like "The Prophet" of Tagore, than the Divine, Yazatic [angelic] Being of the Gathas and the Avesta.

2. The poisonous philological dogma of "Freedom of Choice" is wrongly supposed to have been propounded by Prophet Zoroaster, and has been woven into the fabric of the film. In fact, the very theme—a maddening and suicidal one—of the film is, "One must first learn to think and then to believe." Thus the very bottom of the belief and faith, whether blind or intellectual, brought by the first and the most exalted Messenger of God is being knocked out by the film.

3. The new-fangled heresy that Lord Ahura Mazda is not yet omnipotent, because there is evil in the world, and all that poppycock, is being bandied about in this celluloid catastrophe.

4. As a corollary of the bizarre concept of evil expounded in the film, death is supposed to be evil, as it is (wrongly) believed to mean destruction, which is the handiwork of Ahriman!

5. That highly objectionable scene of a "mock" funeral, shot at Doongerwadi last May, is very much there in the film.[38]

In the end, the film was not an artistic success in the eyes of many Parsis. But the controversy drew the attention of the members of the community to it, and a number of them were proud of it. Many of them also liked the way the religion was portrayed. "Yes, yes," one family explained to me over tea. "That is how it is, the light and the darkness, we do good to fight the evil. That is what our religion tells us to do."

♦ ♦ ♦

Vishtaspa seems to have prospered under Zarathustra's theological guidance. His territory grew, and although these are the "unrecorded centuries," and there are arguments about when he lived and where, it seems probable that he lived somewhere in the east or northeast of contemporary Iran. Historical records first mention Iranians centuries later (in the ninth century B.C.).[39] As described by Herodotus, these were the Medes, who were established in western Iran. They overthrew the Assyrian empire in 614–612 B.C. and extended their sway over the Iranian peoples in the east and southwest. Zoroastrianism seems to have spread quickly during the sixty years of their rule.[40]

In 549 B.C., the Persians—the term here is used properly to describe people from the southwest area of Iran—led by Cyrus, scion of the Achaemenians and son-in-law of the reigning Median king, rebelled against the king, defeated him, and founded the first Persian empire. Cyrus went on to conquer Asia Minor and Babylonia (with all her subject territories) and brought all the eastern Iranians under his control. In all likelihood Cyrus and his Persians were Zoroastrians.[41] Certainly Herodotus assumed that he was, and ascribed to Zarathustra a venerable antiquity.[42] In any event, it has been argued that postexilic Judaism owes much to Zoroastrians through the Jews' appreciation for Cyrus, who freed them, and that Judaic concepts of heaven, hell, and even of a messiah arise from their enthusiasm for Cyrus' ideas (Boyce 1979). Herodotus describes the customs of these Persians thus:

> Their wont . . . is to ascend to the summits of the loftiest mountains, and there to offer sacrifice to Jupiter, which is the name they give to the whole circuit of the firmament. They likewise offer to the sun and moon, to the earth, to fire, to water and to the winds. . . .
>
> There is no nation which so readily adopts foreign customs as the Persians. Thus, they have taken the dress of the Medes, considering it superior to their own; and in war they wear the Egyptian breastplate. As soon as they hear of any luxury, they instantly make it their own; and hence, among other novelties, they have learnt unnatural lust from the Greeks. . . .

Their sons are carefully instructed from their fifth to their twentieth year in three things alone,—to ride, to draw the bow, and to speak the truth. . . . The most disgraceful thing in the world, they think, is to tell a lie . . .[43]

Parsis sometimes know about Herodotus and his account of the adaptable ancient Persians, but more often they do not.

The Persian empire was expanded under Cambyses, who added lower Egypt to it, and continued expanding under Darius. In 331 B.C. it fell to Alexander, the Macedonian, who invaded Persia and in five years conquered almost all the territories of the Achaemenian empire. Alexander had no religious mission, but the death of priests and the sack of temples was a wound to the Zoroastrian faith, and in a Sogdian fragment he is described as among the worst sinners in history. But he ruled for only seven years; then one of his generals, Seleucus, took command over a large part of the Achaemenian empire. A generation later a tribe of Iranian nomads invaded Parthia, in the Iranian northeast, adopting their language and Zoroastrian religion. They then revolted in mid-third century B.C., as did Greek-governed Zoroastrian Bactria, and one of these converted nomads, Arshak (known to the Greeks as Arsaces), took control. Within decades his lineage had established rule from the border of India to the western borders of Mesopotamia. Zoroastrianism was once more declared the official faith of an empire.[44]

In 224 A.D. (or thereabouts) the Arsacid emperor was overthrown by an Iranian from Pars, who established the Sassanian dynasty in Iran. This was a powerful and less tolerant Zoroastrian dynasty, greatly influenced by a priest, Tosar, who enforced a number of doctrinal and ritual reforms. The relevant feature of this rule for the Parsis and their contemporary students is that in this period the Avesta—the canonical body of religious texts which include the Gathas—was written down. These texts seem to have been transmitted orally until an alphabet was invented specific to Avestan. Also in this period—and indeed past the Islamic conquest, through the ninth century A.D.—additional religious texts were written, in another language, Pahlavi or Middle Persian, which were commentaries on and translations of the original texts. These, unlike the Gathas, clearly incorporate the doctrine of dualism. Those who want to defend Zoroastrianism as a dualism point to these late texts as proof of the argument; those who seek to rescue

Zoroastrianism from the dualistic label claim that the late texts are
paranoid, superstitious fantasies.

In 636 A.D. the Muslim Arabs overran Syria, crossed into Mesopotamia, and met the Iranian imperial army at Qadisiya. Within
fifteen years they controlled most of Iran. Zoroastrians were probably not properly considered "people of the book" at this period,
but they were tolerated as such, and were forced into the payment
of tribute. Parsis usually assume that the Zoroastrians were tormented for their beliefs.

Parsi history begins when some Zoroastrians left their homeland,
probably for reasons of religious freedom, and landed on an island
off the coast of Gujarat in the early tenth century.[45] As the standard
nineteenth-century Parsi history proclaims: "The Persian or Parsi
fugitives, after undergoing numerous hardships and nearly incur-
ring destruction in a manner which recalls the adventures of Aeneas
and the surviving Trojans, succeeded in gaining the shores of India,
where the rights of shelter and settlement were conceded by a
Hindu ruler" (Karaka 1884:I:xv).

Tradition says that the pioneer Parsis learned to speak Gujarati
on this island of Diu and sailed over to the mainland in 936 A.D.,
whereupon they presented the case for their settlement. This intro-
duces the most famous story of Parsi history. A recent novel retells
it below.

Literary Vignette: *The Memory of Elephants*

Jadav Rana, the rajah of Sanjan, the fishing village near which the
ships had been beached, met officially with the Persians less than a
month after their arrival. A *darbar* [meeting] was conducted on a
wide flat *maidan*. Jadhav Rana wore a long violet satin robe, red
satin slippers, and a diadem of gold with a ruby centerpiece. He sat
on a covered throne with embroidered drapes surrounded by noble-
men in satin and velvet robes and turbans and guards in white with
spears glittering in the sun. He raised his hand and the Persians were
brought into the center of the assembly and invited to tell their story.
The most senior of the *dasturs* [priests], each of whom wore a red
sash around the waist, had been elected spokesman. Jadhav Rana felt
sorry for the Persians but was uncomfortable with their stern warlike
appearance. "This is a sad story," he said when the *dastur* was
finished. "What you wish—a place to stay where you may worship

freely, where you may cultivate the soil so that you are not burden-
some to others—is fine and honourable, but it is not that simple. Let
me show you how it is."

He clapped his hands twice and a jug of milk, filled to the brim,
was brought out. "Sanjan is like this jug of milk," he said. "There is
no room for more."

The old *dastur* reached into his robe for a coin. "Your Highness,"
he said, slipping the coin carefully into the jug without spilling a
drop, "we Persians will be as the coin is in the milk. You will not
even know we are there."

The crowd applauded the *dastur;* Jadhav Rana was impressed but
did not smile. "This is well," he said, "but a coin is tribute, and the
hospitality which can be bought with a coin is not the hospitality of
Sanjan. How will you repay our hospitality?"

The *dastur* dropped a pinch of sugar into the milk, taking care once
more not to spill even a drop. "Your Highness," he said, "as the
sugar sweetens the milk so shall we endeavor to sweeten your lives
with our industry."

Members of the crowd jumped as they cheered. Jadhav Rana
smiled and gave his consent but also named five conditions: the
Persians were to give him a full explanation of their religion, they
were to adopt Gujarati (the language of Sanjan) as their own, they
were to adopt the local forms of dress, to surrender their weapons,
and conduct their ceremonies after nightfall to avoid influencing the
Hindus.[46]

◆   ◆   ◆

This meeting, even these conditions, may be apocryphal; however,
strict Zoroastrian endogamy, coupled with the refusal to convert
non-Zoroastrians or even to allow them within the fire-temple,
may date from this era, as none of these customs of exclusion are
now found in Iran.[47]

For the next seven centuries Parsis lived peaceful, unremarkable
lives. Some Parsis left Sanjan and settled in other, nearby areas:
Navsari, Surat, Broach. For the most part they were agriculturalists
and weavers.[48] They also engaged in a little trade and probably
began their involvement with the alcohol trade, tapping the date
palm to produce a weakly fermented milky drink called toddy.[49]
During some of this period Islam again governed them, and they

paid the *jizya* (tax on nonbelievers), but were comparatively untroubled. In 1322 a traveling Dominican monk remarked upon their existence: "there be also other pagan folk in this India who worship fire; they bury not their dead, neither do they burn them, but cast them into the midst of a certain roofless tower, and there expose them utterly uncovered to the fowls of heaven. These believe in two First Principles, to wit, of Evil and Good, of Darkness and Light, matters which at present I do not purpose to discuss."[50] And while there is uncertainty about when the custom of exposing the dead to be devoured by vultures emerged, it was certainly in evidence by this period.[51]

Ethnographic Vignette

In 1979 Time/Life books published, in their series of Great Cities books, a portrait of Bombay. Parsis appear throughout the text but are most famously illustrated by a photograph of the *dokhmas*, taken from above. The *dokhma*, or Tower of Silence, as an Englishman supposedly dubbed it, is a high-walled, circular platform where the Parsis leave their dead, to be eaten by vultures and kites. After the vultures have disposed of the flesh, the *nassasalars*—a special, impure, caste-like subsection of the Parsi community who handle the dead—push the bones down into to a central pit. So powerful do the Parsis remain in Bombay that the photograph of four pallbearing *nassasalars* and their corpse, along with some text, were inked out after publication to avoid offending the community.[52]

"Other communities never get embarrassed about their practices," a Parsi friend said in passing. "It indicates something about the level of community insecurity." I myself thought that Parsis were markedly irrational about their vultures. Many Parsis adamantly told me that the vultures consumed the entire human corpse in half an hour, and then the skeleton, whitened by the sun, slowly disintegrated into dust. The custom, they said, was hygienic, ecologically pleasing, and philosophically appropriate. One evening I attended a lecture entitled "The Zoroastrian Custom of the Disposal of the Dead: Scientific or Barbaric?" A fellow listener rose afterwards to support the lecturer's contention that the practice was wholly scientific. Vultures, he said, had a "rational" and "scientific" mentality, for they plucked systematically at only cer-

tain portions of the body.[53] In a 1906 prize essay the writer remarked, "My object in publishing this essay is to show my educated co-religionists how well the laws of the Vendidad [to a great
extent these cover the disposal of the dead] enacted for the preservation of health and for the observance of the purity of things are
in harmony with the laws of hygiene and the principles of the
science of medicine."[54] I repeatedly heard arguments for the eco-
logical soundness of the method, and many people pointed out that
this final act continued the famous Parsi spirit of charity even after
death.

Yet other Parsis told me that near the site the stench of rotting
flesh was pungent, that there weren't enough vultures, that the
practice was wildly unhygienic, that the Panchayat secretly sends
in butchers to finish the job the vultures could not handle; that the
method was appropriate for ancient Iran but not contemporary
Bombay.[55] In 1973 a tough-minded Panchayat trustee surrepti-
tiously entered and photographed the precinct where bodies are
laid out. He found unconsumed bodies rotting in the open air. "We
saw only one vulture, one kite and two crows devouring a body
. . . Is this the most ancient, civilized and scientific system?"[56] There
were enough vultures for most of the year, he said, but in the dank
monsoon heat and rain they stayed away. His report catalyzed an
agonizing controversy. The ghoulish British fascination with
dokhmenashini had precipitated both embarrassment and dogged
pride in the nineteenth century—but the claim that bodies were
rotting winched both responses to excruciating tension.[57]

It is apparently true that vultures are shy of busy, smoggy cities
and that they dislike rain, and I have seen photographic evidence
that at times the bodies are not quickly eaten. Yet I have also seen
the sky thick with birds. Funeral prayers are held in long halls in
the *doongerwadi* precincts. Many people come in white; it is the
color of religious Parsi dress (and of Hindu mourners). At the end
of the prayers those Parsis who choose may file past the body to
pay it final respects. Then it is taken by the pall-bearers up into the
garden in which the Towers stand, the men following, often linked
in pairs by a white scarf held between them. By this time, thirty or
more birds have begun to dive and circle in anticipation.

The point, of course, is the flushed distress that concentrates
around a distinctly non-western and emblematic custom. The passion bleeds the community's emotional core and its confusion over

how western a Parsi truly is. The vultures, dwindling, still circle over Bombay's most exclusive suburb.[58]

"Parsi Poem" by Keki Daruwalla

With vulture ended
The black vigil of the eyes

The silence of lost distances
Is on eyes as they slow down
To a blank opacity
One eye jellyfish, the other stone
As he probes, the violence
Of metal in his beak

Time is a vulture-wing on the glide
Under a blue sky

Between me and the vultures
—the scrawny neck, the bald head,
Splayed wingtips edged with black,
The wing-span 9 feet from tip to tip—
Is something personal

As they gather like a brewing storm
—a wilderness on wings—
An abstraction is skewered
A perversity is bitten to the bone
A secret urge, pickled in the loins
Is cleansed, purified
The scorpion severed from the tense arch of his tail
The poison in all its purity, its passion
Displayed as if in a glass phial

Bones in talons
Ah the buoyancy of it!
An upward incision in the clouds
And then the release
Eyes scanning the flight
Wings swooping in pursuit
The bone, red with friction
Merging in the clay and dream

Of another star
A meteor in its own right
Til it hits the rock-ledge
And the marrow spills
Like vision from a shattered mirror.[59]

To return to our chronological narrative, it is not clear what kinds of lives these early Parsi farmers and merchants led, but it is possible that they were a community of note.[60] A pre-British text— *Qissah-i-Sanjan* (History of Sanjan), written c. 1600 A.D.—presents Parsi life in India as a blessing. Moreover, the sixteenth-century Moghul Emperor Akbar discoursed upon Zoroastrianism with the priest Meherji Rana. It is true that Akbar showed a keen interest in a diversity of religious approaches, but also true that an impoverished, low-status community would be unlikely to send a representative to the imperial court. And when the British first arrived in Surat and were having difficulty with local merchants wary of the competition, it was a Parsi who interceded for them with another Moghul emperor, Aurangzeb, and obtained valuable help for them. It seems reasonable to assume that at least some of the community had done well after its transplant.

In any event it is known that Parsis spread out in the areas around Sanjan, where they first landed, and began to build fire temples and *dokhmas*. Most accounts assume that the community was primarily agricultural. In the fourteenth century Parsis played an important part in the Hindu resistance to Islam, but as the resistance failed, they were forced to flee the immediate area.[61] Very little is known of this period, but Parsi historians have given vivid legend-like accounts of the days before the Raj, when Parsis were brave, clever, and warlike.[62]

Then the British arrived.

In 1905 J. M. Framjee Patel—a Parsi—published a book on Indian cricket, which the Parsis dominated for many years. In passing, Framjee drops a casual, explanatory aside: "A Parsi in England feels quite at home. He knows well the history and traditions of its people, and is no stranger to their manners and games. He esteems their sports, liberties and literature. Many a wealthy and educated Parsi now-a-days takes an annual holiday to England, just as a Mahommedan or a Hindu goes to Mecca or Benares" (1905:47). This is a remarkable comment, and Patel shows no consciousness of the oddity in comparing Mecca for the Muslims, Benares for the Hindus, England for the Parsis. Between roughly 1600 and 1900, this tiny group of respected farmers— probably no more than 100,000 of them[63]—became the most English-identified, westernized community on the subcontinent, albeit in an Indianized, Persian manner. England had become Mecca indeed.

By the sixteenth century Europe had begun to sniff out foreign markets, and adventurous merchants learned to trade the risk of tropical fever for the promise of great wealth. During this time Surat became the most important seaport on the west coast of India, and the center of trade for Moghul and European merchants. By the seventeenth and eighteenth centuries Surat had become the largest Parsi settlement, and Parsis became intimately involved in that trade and in banking, brokering, and moneylending, and although there are scholarly debates about the degree of their power, there is general agreement that it was considerable.[64] The reasons for their success are less clear. The fair Parsi skin may have been reassuring to Europeans;[65] they may have been less constrained than other communities by longstanding trading networks;[66] they may simply have been savvy, smart, and lucky.

For whatever reasons, Parsis were able to engage the commercial trust and interest of the European community, and it was in international trade that money was made. The century from 1650 to 1750 has been called the "prebourgeois phase" of Parsi economic bloom (A. Guha 1982). The community became deeply involved with trade, but had not moved *en masse* from Gujarat to Bombay, and was not as widely urbanized as it would become later.[67] The principal nineteenth-century Parsi historian records that in this period "the Portuguese, French, Dutch and English factories all employed Parsis as their chief brokers" (Karaka 1884:II:9). And in the last quarter of the seventeenth century, a Parsi, Rustom Maneck, became the broker for the East India Company—a position of considerable importance. Parsis were not, in general, involved in major trading in the second half of the seventeenth century, although several of them were shipowning traders and ships owned jointly by Parsis and Portuguese are mentioned in Dutch shipping lists.[68] But by 1746, according to Dutch reports, Parsis accounted for 10 percent of Surat's estimated trading capital—a figure far above the percentage of the population. The striking figure, however, is that while only 6 percent of the Muslim trade and 38 percent of the Hindu-Jain trade was dependent upon Europeans, 100 percent of Parsi trade depended on them.[69] "With the eclipse of the Dutch and the rise of the English as a major territorial power in India in the 1750s, it became obvious to [the Parsis] that they had much to gain as traders from individual loyalty to the English" (A. Guha 1982:10).

And the British appeared to like them. Most of the European accounts from this period speak highly of the Parsis. From John Ogilby's *Asia* (1672):

> In most places of Surat dwell a sort of Persians . . . clothed like Indians, except for a girdle or sash of camel's hair or sheep's wool [the *kusti*, still worn today] . . . They live here like natives, free and undisturbed, and drive what trade they please. They are very ingenious, and for the most part maintain themselves with tilling, and buying and selling all sorts of fruits, tapping of wine out of palm trees, which wine they sell in houses of entertainment . . . Some also traffic, and are exchangers of money, keep shops, and exercise all manner of handicrafts, for they are not allowed to quench fire with water. (in Boyce 1984:129)

From J. Ovington, *A Voyage to Surat in the Year 1689:*

> The "Persies" are a sect very considerable in India . . . They own and adore one supreme being, to whom, as he is the origin of all things, they dedicate the first day of every month, in solemn observation of his worship . . . They show a firm affection to all of their own sentiment in religion, and are very ready to provide for the sustenance and comfort of such as want it . . . In their callings they are very industrious and diligent, and careful to train up their children to arts and labour. They are the principal men at the loom in all the country, and most of the silks and stuff at Surat are made by their hands. (in Boyce 1984:129)

In 1670 the Governor of Bombay, Aungier, a man with a vision of Bombay as a great trade center, wrote back to England thus: "[Parsis] are an industrious people and ingenious in trade, therein they totally employ themselves. There are at present few of them [in Bombay] but we expect a greater number of them, having gratified them in their desire to build a burying place for their dead on the island."[70]

There are several striking elements in these accounts: that even 600 years after landing the Parsis were readily described as Persians; that they were hard-working and ingenious and took care of their own kind (Parsi charity later becomes famous); that they were involved in a variety of economic pursuits and had a possibly undeserved reputation for honesty, and that their theology is recognizably monotheistic, although (as many accounts mention) they recognize two principles or types of being, good and evil.

When the British first acquired Bombay in 1662, as part of the dowry for the Portuguese Catherine of Braganza, Bombay was seven swampy islands inhabited by a Dravidian fishing people, the Kolis.[71] Despite the fetid atmosphere and stagnant heat, Bombay soon appeared to be a desirable alternative to Surat, where Marathas worried the countryside and the Mughals imposed heavy taxes. The British fought concertedly to keep the local Portuguese from reclaiming the seemingly worthless property their crown had given away, and rapidly settled the harbor. Parsis were encouraged to move there by the British, who gave them land, and their casteless status may have enabled them to do so more freely than other groups. And as the Governor of Bombay had hoped, the erection of a Tower of Silence around 1672–74 seems to have increased the flow (David 1973:435). An early twentieth-century British guidebook to Bombay remarked, "Among the many strange people who accepted the Company's offer of hospitality none was more welcome than the Parsi and none has become so completely identified with the fortunes of the city" (Newell c. 1914).

One of the first Parsi enterprises with many British customers was shipbuilding; indeed it was at least in part for this reason that the British were so eager to have them in Bombay. A Parsi (he came to be called Wadia, from the Gujarati *vadia*, shipbuilder) had been recognized for his shipbuilding skills, and the British invited him, with ten others, to help establish the shipyards in Bombay. Parsi workmanship—at least according to Parsi historians—was excellent. "History has established beyond doubt that vessels built at Bombay, by the Parsi Master Builders, whether for the Navy or for private owners, were vastly superior to anything built anywhere else in the world, and examples of vessels being fully tight and serviceable after a century over their construction is an indication of their magnificent construction" (Wadia 1983:182). The superiority owed at least something to the teak used to build the ships,

in contrast to the oak of the English shipbuilders.[72] Wadia seems
to have been a man of spirit, followed in this respect by his family:
reportedly, one of his grandson's ships was found bearing the
phrase, "this ship was built by a damned Black Fellow!"[73] A recent
history of the Bombay shipyards presents this delightful, sly account:

> The expression "Black Fellow" in reference to Indians was in com-
> mon use by some Europeans and was naturally resented by many
> men who were in no sense inferior and most certainly superior in
> point of intellectual and professional abilities in the arts and crafts
> to those who used the expression. It was, however, greatly resented
> by Jamsetjee, the Builder who felt it so much that, according to Lt.
> Col. John Briggsbook, he had carved on the Kelson of the "Corn-
> wallis" the words, "This ship was built by a d-d Black Fellow A.D.
> 1800." These words were carved in such a manner that they were
> not noticed till many years later, when the ship returned to the
> Bombay Docks and Jamsetjee himself pointed them out to his friends.
> (Wadia 1983:191)

The grandson's audacity seems to have been tempered by political
caution. In any event Wadia earned a fortune and founded a dynasty. From 1735 to 1885 the only large dockyard in India was
commissioned to the Wadia family. Parsis told me that in the battle
of Trafalgar most of Nelson's ships were Parsi-built. But shipbuilding does not, by itself, produce the capital of grand wealth and
great investment. The wealth that made Parsis famous was the
opium trade with China.

By 1813 there were 29 large Bombay ships in trade with China.[74]
Of these 12 were Parsi owned; 17, British owned. They were
phenomenally successful: addiction makes good customers. The
most famous of these merchants was Sir Jamsetjee Jeejeebhoy
(1783–1859). Born to a humble family, he later spent his prodi-
gious earned wealth on charity, for which he was knighted and then
given a baronetcy, the first Indian to receive one. Over time his
financial feat was touted as a moral victory. A 1939 biography
asserts: "On one of these voyages [to China] his ship was captured
by the French, who were then at war with England, and he was
taken prisoner. . . . The unfortunate result of this voyage did not
damp the ardour of Jamsetjee; on the contrary, [it strengthened]

his enterprise, industry, tact and perseverance" (Darukhanawala 1939:81).

But other trade also contributed to wealth. As non-British colonials, Parsis were not allowed to trade directly with Britain. They remained a primary mediating link between Europeans and the Indian hinterland, and they managed much of the trading world in Bombay; it is said—admittedly, by a Parsi chronicler—that all trade through Bombay of any nature in some way passed through Parsi hands.[75] Parsis also entered into symbiotic patron-client relationships with the British, in which they would advance the capital and the British would advance their name, apparently a profitable relationship for both (David 1973). Around 1830, Sir John Malcolm, Governor of Bombay, remarked that: "there is no body of natives in India so remarkable for their intelligence and enterprise as the Parsis. Bombay has owed its advancement in a great degree to this class" (Karaka 1884:II:116). By 1840, Parsis owned 24 percent of the shares in the Bank of Bombay, next only to Europeans (A. Guha 1982:13). By 1864, Parsis accounted for only 6 percent of the Bombay population, but 17 percent of those involved in wholesale trade, banking, and other financial pursuits. More than half the community was urbanized, and many of them could speak English. In 1869 the Suez Canal was opened and Bombay became India's chief port. By this time, the Parsis were already deeply involved in India's industrialization. And by this time, at least some of them were rich.

Literary Vignette: "The Crow Eaters"

Bapsy Sidhwa's light-hearted satire—so named to celebrate Parsi talkativeness, not the manner of the disposal of their dead—is the story of a nineteenth-century family which starts life very poor and in the second generation produces one of the richest men in India. Freddy marries and moves, in his bullock cart, to Lahore, taking with them his mother-in-law, whose dominating ways threaten to destroy him utterly. Back in the days when insurance companies were making their first inroads into the Indian population, Freddy took out a policy on his store—and promptly burned it down, to his regret not taking his mother-in-law with it. He collects on the insurance and building on this initial deceit gradually becomes a wealthy man, in part due to his ability to flatter the English and milk them for business. But his son is perhaps the best caricature of the stereotypically successful late-nineteenth-century Parsi businessman.

> You knew right away where you stood with him [Billy], and his values, once you grasped the one-track bent of his mind, were straightforward. He was suspicious, and this aspect of his personality showed at once in any transaction. He was avaricious. His dealers knew exactly where they stood with him. Their faith in his cunning was seldom misplaced.
>
> Billy had a simple vocation in life. MONEY! (Sidhwa 1878:188–189)

By the mid-nineteenth century, Parsis were well established as the leading community in Bombay—at least the leading Indian community, and Bombay, city of commerce, was less dominated by imperial hierarchy than the other great cities of the country. As a handsome British album of old Bombay remarks, "Foremost among Indian communities we must place the Parsi, for to him the city owes more of its enterprise and stateliness than to any other."[76] The community not only owned half the island but by Independence had built much of its imposing architecture, often for benevolent ends. They were known to the British through their business, from shopowners to great industrialists—an 1862 *Visitor's Guide to Bombay* lists a shopping guide which features almost exclusively European and Parsi names—and were widely perceived to be rich. An 1831 London account of Bombay remarks that

> The Parsis, descendents of the ancient Persians, and disciples of Zoroaster, are the principal and most wealthy men in Bombay . . . Active, intelligent, persevering and industrious, they applied themselves to the domestic arts and foreign commerce, and have everywhere been protected and esteemed, and are now the richest individuals on the western side of India; they possess most of the best houses in Bombay, acquired either through purchase or building, and enjoy every privilege, civil or military, in common with Europeans, whose manners and customs, as well as those of the Hindus, they have in many particulars acquired. They are a handsome race, much fairer than the natives of Hindoostan.[77]

A 1900 *Tourist's Handbook to Bombay and India* describes Bombay as the "Paris of the East" and defines Parsis as "Persian, sect of fireworshippers: a very rich, commercial and influential part of Indian cosmopolitan population."[78]

By 1864 there were nearly 50,000 Parsis in Bombay, occupied in primarily middle-class activities.[79] At that time 90 percent of the Bombay Parsis worked in five occupational areas: trade, money transactions and real estate (40 percent); secretarial and book-keeping jobs (14.5 percent); wood processing (12.5 percent) and clergy (7 percent).[80] These figures indicate a community more engaged in clerical work and banking than in business—even today, although widely known as businessmen, more Parsis are involved in the service professions: medicine, law, journalism. In 1974 fewer than 10 percent of the male heads of household had their own businesses, and 80 percent were involved in some kind of service profession (Axelrod 1974:63).

Nevertheless, it was the entrepreneurs, and in particular the industrialists, who set the standard for the community and became its symbol for the outside world.[81] A native non-Parsi chronicler remarks of them in 1863: "Name any business and the Parsis would go into it."[82] In 1885 the Governor of Bombay introduced a speech by a Parsi priest by remarking that through their wealth and charity, "long before I came to Bombay, I knew that the name was a household word in England."[83] The 1908 *Imperial Gazetteer* of India summarizes these impressions formally:

> The Parsis exercise an influence much greater than is implied by their numbers. They commenced to settle in Bombay soon after the cession of the island to the English, and now by the force of their inherited wealth, their natural genius for trade, their intelligence and their munificent charities, they hold high rank among the native community. Their position was recognized by the Crown when Sir Jamsetji Jeejeebhoy received a baronetcy in 1857; and a member of his family was chosen to represent the city of Bombay at the coronation of the King-Emperor in 1902. Next in importance to the Parsis are the Hindu traders or Banias . . .[84]

And these remarks reverberate in modern Parsi life. In the collective myth of the past, nineteenth-century Parsis were businessmen. They were politically eminent and economically successful, and all the English knew it.

The fortunes that Parsis made in trade in the eighteenth and early nineteenth centuries were later invested in the emerging Indian industry. Between 1854 and 1870, 13 cotton mills were established in Bombay. Nine of them were founded by Parsi entrepreneurs.[85] Cotton became in essence India's first industry, profiting enormously from the American Civil War. Parsis dominated this emerging modern entrepreneurial class at first, and Indian industry was initially concentrated in Bombay. Khojas, Bombay Jews, Gujaratis, and Marwaris then followed their lead, and soon surpassed them (Kulke 1974:123). But the Parsis deserve much of the early credit. The Bombay Spinning Mill was the first mill in India to run by steam energy. It was founded in 1854 by a Parsi and can be said to have founded the textile industry in India. In 1895, as in 1925, Parsis were found in almost half the managerial and supervisory positions in the Bombay mills (Kulke 1974:126). A Parsi started the first iron foundry in India, as well as its first flour mill. And by the late nineteenth century Parsi industry had branched out to many fields.[86]

In addition to these activities Parsis became deeply involved in finance. They played an important role in the founding of all Bombay's important banks: the Central Bank of India, the Government Bank of India, Asiatic Bank, and so forth, and for many years served as their chairmen and managers. In a photograph published in 1904 of the Native Share and Stockbrokers Association, Parsis clearly predominate in the gathering.[87] They became prominent as bankers for Indian princes in financial difficulties.[88] As trade with China opened in 1833, and with the rise in price of the American cotton, the number of independent European mercantile firms in Bombay increased dramatically. Nearly all of the broker-guarantors, who advanced the capital for trade, were Parsis, and the first Indians to establish a mercantile firm in London were Parsis.[89] The Stock Exchange was founded, primarily by Parsis, in 1860, and for years its presidents were Parsi.[90]

The dominating Parsi figure of this period became the symbol of the modern Indian entrepreneurial class as a whole. Jamsetji Nusserwanji Tata (1839–1904) became by far the most prominent of Indian industrialists and the most famous Parsi. The Tata group of companies, one of India's most famous business names, includes truck makers, hotel owners, insurance brokers; they run a town in eastern India—Jamshedpur—which formed around the steel industry that Tata created in India, and they operate major businesses in energy, textiles, jute, tea, and trade, among other things.

Tata seems to have been a remarkably shrewd and able entrepreneur. In 1867 the ruler of Abyssinia provoked the British government into attack by imprisoning some British subjects, and J. N. Tata, then a young man, obtained the commissariat for 16,000 troops.[91] He turned a profit of four million rupees, and began the enterprises that would make him famous. In any event he was responsible not only for the major impetus to the cotton industry, but for the founding of the Indian steel industry, the introduction of the hydroelectric system, and the first major institute for technical education and research (the Indian Institute at Bangalore). Tata is also known for his progressive treatment of his employees. In Jamshedpur, the town created for the steelmills, the employees have their own schools, hospitals and parks, and the factory has seen little in the way of employee disputes, a most unusual history in India. Tata also built the best hotel in India—at least, in Bombay—the Taj. Bombay's biographer reports the story that as a youth, Tata was asked to leave the exclusive Watson's Club on the grounds that he was a native, and swore to build a hotel to outdo it. The story is probably apocryphal, but Watson's has long since vanished while the Taj remains a focal point for *le tout* Bombay.[92] Not apocryphal is the story of Tata's legendary stature in his own time and in our own: when he died, Lord Curzon—the Viceroy— remarked that "no Indian of the present generation had done more for the commerce and industry of India" (Harris 1958:275).

However, the English were not entirely pleased with Tata, and their displeasure leads us to one of the most important and contrary strains in the Parsi legacy of identifying with the British. Tata was a nationalist. He believed that India would achieve her real freedom only through widespread industrialization and the capacity to educate her own scientists and generate technological innovation. This was his motivation for founding the Indian Institute at Bangalore, and the idea behind the steel and iron industries and other industrial developments. He canvassed for capital investment in these enterprises for avowedly nationalistic ends, and he acquired the investments. In fact, he was probably denied a title on account of his nationalism. In the climate of the time, that was a sizable price to pay.[93]

Tata was not the only Parsi with nationalist sympathies. Dadabhai Naoroji, the Grand Old Man of India, helped to found the Indian National Congress and wrote a famous tract accusing Britain of draining India of her wealth. He stressed the importance of education for modernity and the debilitating effect of traditional custom; it was generally assumed that the adoption of a western political structure demanded a transformation of traditional Indian social structure. Indeed, when Parsis protested Naoroji's pro-Indian, pro-Congress political stance, they objected to it on the grounds of Hindu backwardness.[94] Pherozeshah Mehta was another powerful, liberal, progressive Parsi, as was the violent revolutionary Bhikhaiji Rustom Cama (Madame Cama), the first to unfurl the future Indian flag in public, at the Second International Socialist Congress at Stuttgart in 1902.[95] She not only advocated violence as the means to shake off British shackles, but was considered seditious enough (and sufficiently well born) to be exiled to Paris, from whence she carried on with her agitations. Most Parsis seem to have been embarrassed by her activities at the time; indeed, only recently has the community taken steps to commemorate her life.[96] Still, in the early twentieth century there were many Parsis who shared nationalist orientations, many who wore the Gandhian *khadi* and argued for their country's independence. This is an important piece of community history which Parsis regard with justifiable pride.

But it would be a mistake to infer a shared Parsi political vision from these reformists; the rejection of Hindu "superstition" was common, but the political criticism of the Raj seems to have been rare. All the evidence—Parsi, British, the oral history of the present—suggests that the majority of Parsis remained loyal to the crown throughout the political agitation of the early twentieth century.[97]

There remains the question of exactly how wealthy the famously successful Parsis were. Communitywide data for the nineteenth century are spare. However, what data there are—particularly from the turn of the century, out of the sunniest Parsi and British accounts—provoke thought. In 1901, Parsis were 43 percent of the population in the North Fort area, which could be a fairly well-to-do area; on the other hand, they were 32 percent of the population of Dhobi Talao, a much poorer area, though by no means the poorest in Bombay. In 1911, a smaller percentage of Parsi families lived in one room than of any other community; nevertheless, 42 percent are reported to live in one room.[98] In 1911 Parsis are primarily distributed between Fort North, Dhobi Talao, and Khetwadi.[99]

The *Gazetteer* does show a disproportionate number of rich Parsis in 1901. Parsis constituted only 6 percent of the population. Nevertheless, they constituted a third of those natives whose annual incomes exceeded 100,000 rupees (there were four Muslims, six Parsis, seven Hindus and about thirty-five Europeans in this category), a third of the natives whose income was between 50,000 and 100,000 (fifteen Hindus, thirteen Parsis, nine Muslims and about twelve Europeans fall into this category), and about a fifth of those natives whose incomes were between 20,000 and 30,000 (72 Hindus, 29 Khojas, Bohras, etc, 23 Parsis and 20 Europeans are in this category). These were very rich people: income tax was required of all whose income exceeded 1,000 rupees. However, only 62 Parsis of the roughly 18,000 Parsi workers earned so much. The *Gazetteer* mentions a notorious band of poor Parsi thugs in the 1850s.[100] And certainly British missionaries noticed the existence of poverty-stricken and slum-dwelling Parsis.[101] Wealth was not ubiquitous among Parsis. And as I have suggested before, the Parsi standard of living may have risen—not fallen—in the last one hundred years.

Still, let me leave this historical chapter with an unabashedly optimistic vision of "the past glory of this enterprising community" (Darukhanawalla 1939:253). In 1939 Hormusji Dhunjishaw Motabhoy Darukhanawala published what became the first volume of a collection of short biographies entitled *Parsi Lustre on Indian Soil*. (It would be followed by a second volume in 1963.) It is a remarkable document, and somewhat nostalgic: this was a period when a note of discontent appears in community literature, but no doubts disgrace this text. There are perhaps 500 short biographies of eminent Parsis, most of them born in the nineteenth century. The entrepreneurs abound, but also painters, politicians, doctors, lawyers, journalists, philanthropists, and many who made significant contributions in varied fields: a founder of the Indian National Congress and the most important nineteenth-century Indian politician (Dadabhai Naoroji); all three Indian Members of British Parliament (Naoroji, Mancherjee Bhownaggree, Shapurjee Dorabjee Saklatvala); the first Indian baronet (Sir Jamsetjee Jeejeebhoy); the only Indian appointed to the committee to establish the Bank of Bombay (Dadabhoy Pestonjee Wadia); the first Prime Minister of the Bombay Presidency (Sir Dhanjishah Boomanji Cooper), the "Uncrowned King of Bombay" (Sir Pherozeshah Mehta, another baronet); "Parsi Rustomjee," Gandhi's right hand man in South Africa (Rustomjee Jivanjee Gharkhodu); the first Indian Grandmaster of All Scottish Freemasonry in India (Sir Tehmulji Bhicaji

Nariman; many Parsis were involved in Freemasonry); the first
Indian M.D. from London (Dr. Kaikhasru Nusserwanjee Bahadur-
jee); the first Indian to serve on the Council of the Royal Institute
of British Architects (Burjor Sorabshaw Jamshedji); a coach builder
who introduced rubber-tired carriages to Bombay (Pestonjee Press);
a tradeswoman (Aimai Jehangir Commissariat); the "Potato King
of Bombay" (Burjor Framroze Joshi); the pioneer of coffee production in the East (P. E. Polson); the first Indian to fly from Europe
to India (Dara N. Masters), scholars, writers, photographers,
builders of religious buildings, hospitals, and scholarly institutions,
owners of princely fortunes and the benevolent managers of their
wealth.

Yet the Introduction by J. R. B. Jeejeebhoy, a scion of the house,
is the most notable section of the book. The ringing prose reaffirms
the late-nineteenth-century ideology of a noble Parsi character,
unsullied by Hinduism, which needed only the opportunity of
western contact to emerge at the top of civilization.

> [The reader] will be left to wonder how this exiled band of ancient
> Persians could ever have, with such a short period of civilization and
> education, achieved in all walks of life, what the nations, even of the
> West, had taken centuries to accomplish. The explanation is clear.
> They lived in the purity of heart conscious of their strength, they lived
> humbly, soberly and happily, they forgot pride of self, they had their
> hand on the plough and realized the dignity of labour, they were
> honest and frugal, hard-working and persevering, they identified
> themselves with all the beneficial reforms, and far-reaching influences
> of Western culture, they kept their purse strings loose and lightened
> the burden of their neighbors, they swerved not, even in the midst of
> slaughter and fury, from their ancient creed which has survived for
> thirteen centuries all the vicissitudes of time and fortune, in short,
> they have attuned their heart strings to their God and their religion,
> and they have so far succeeded not only in saving Parseeism from
> utter extinction but, by adding to its laurels, have restored it to the
> high pinnacle of its pristine glory.[102]

Jeejeebhoy's Parsi is pure, humble, sober, happy, hardworking,
honest, determined, westernized, charitable, religious and manly.
And very successful. Virtue has been rewarded.

THE POWER
AND THE GLORY

$$3$$

In the late nineteenth century and early twentieth century, at the zenith of Parsi success, a cluster of self-attributes becomes established in the Parsi literature. These attributes—symbolic markers of identity—transform and extend the fundamental ethical attributes which the Zoroastrian religion ascribes to the good person: truthfulness, purity, charity. They also include other attributes which can be supported by the religious texts and by Zoroastrian history, but which would have been less obviously central to the precolonial Parsi self-conception: progressiveness, rationality, and a particular kind of civilized masculinity. They are part of a general package which consistently represents the Parsis as the most westernized—and most worthily successful—community in India. In other words, what appears to happen in this period is that a set of essentially universal moral ideas, many of them shared closely with Hinduism, are transformed into a powerful political argument for community superiority and difference from other Indians. Parsis thus represent themselves as having by religious fiat the character thought to be acquired only on the playing fields of Eton, the character which dominates the chivalrous idiom of the imperial imagination, the character which in imperial discourse not only justified colonial rule but demanded it as a moral necessity. Inevitably, this politically motivated positioning reiterates a somewhat unfair colonialist characterization of other Indians.

Historical memory is shaped by need and desire. In 1884 one Dosabhai Framjee Karaka published a two-volume *History of the*

Parsis that captured and celebrated the cheery confidence of a colonial elite at the height of its achievement. The volumes are dedicated to the Prince of Wales, from the "most loyal" of the Asian subjects beneath the "beneficent sway of the British crown."[1] Karaka's Parsis are rational, progressive, worthily prosperous and intensely loyal. And they are all these things because they are not Hindu or Muslim—not *really* Indian—but Persian. "The Parsis pride themselves on being the progeny of a mighty race of people . . . Their grandeur, magnificence and glory were unsurpassed by any other nation of ancient times . . . [Their Persian past] is claimed by the modern Parsi as animating his spirit and firing his blood" (Karaka 1884:I:2,5). Persian ancestry, in Karaka's eyes, spurred Parsis to rise above and beyond a land Karaka almost called barbaric. This fiery blood enabled Parsis to prosper like no Hindus could have done.

> Descended originally from an enterprising, courageous, industrious and self-sacrificing people, who at one time were masters of a great empire, they did not absolutely lose those characteristic qualities of their race, although adverse circumstances forced upon them a life of inactivity for more than 1000 years. The old fire of their ancestors continued to burn, however faintly, in their breasts, and it only required the least encouragement to revive. . . .
>
> It will thus be seen that the Parsis were the first to bring prosperity to Bombay, which prosperity, as times went on, supported and fostered by British power and the enterprise of British merchants, has raised Bombay at this day to the proud position of second city of the British Empire.[2]

Other Parsis seem also to have believed that the British presence had enabled the basic qualities of Persian nobility to emerge from under the accretion of Hindu custom. For instance, the entry on Parsis in the *Maharashtra Gazette* remarks: "Thus we see that after the advent of the British in India, the dormant qualities that lay concealed in the Parsi bosom for several generations obtained free scope."[3]

Karaka describes at some length Parsi truthfulness—(it makes them better businessmen)—and charitableness; he implies that Hindu charity wastes money on irrational, idolatrous religion, whereas Parsis use their money for progressive ends, to improve educational opportunities and health care.[4] He explains that

Zoroastrians are religious, but in a rational, secular, western way. They have left behind their rituals and have turned towards Science. Even the women, he muses, who have lagged behind the men and still follow foolish, superstitious, traditional customs like covering their heads, have begun to change under the influence of western tradition: thus, following the colonialist symbolic logic, even the tradition of the society was becoming progressive.

> A great change, however, at last began to take place. The young men who had been educated in Government schools and colleges viewed the question of female education in its proper light. They felt the mental inferiority of their better halves. They plainly saw that their own domestic life could not be rendered happy if their wives remained uneducated, nor could the Parsi community be said to have made any great advance from a moral or social point of view if their women continued in a state only worthy of a semi-barbarous age and society. (1884:I:304–05)

But the most remarkable feature of the text is its breezy assurance of Parsi and British near-equivalence.

Parsis, Karaka explains, had learned Hindu habits to live among the Hindus, but that was merely a surface accretion which enabled them to survive. "As [Parsis] advance every year in civilization and enlightenment, they copy more closely English manners and modes of living" (1884:I:123). Under the British their natural nobility, and more to the point, natural "mastery," products of a civilization even greater than the British, sprang forth. Soon, Karaka speculated, they would be indistinguishable from the English. "Some of those [Parsis] who adopt European dress might even be mistaken for Europeans, for the population possesses a vitality and an energy inherited from their ancient ancestors the Persians that is equal to those of European populations living in more bracing climates than India" (1884:I:95)—that is, Parsis are more vital than either Indians or Englishmen in India. "The highest proportion of children in any class in Bombay under one year of age is found in the Parsi population."[5] His last paragraph is obsequious, and with no hint of a play of contestation:

> With regard to the present position of the Parsis, it may be said that they are well launched on the path of progress. With the advent of British power in India better and brighter days dawned for them.

With the rise of that power they have risen from poverty and oppression to security and wealth. Upon that power they depend and implicitly rely. It has developed again in their race those high qualities which history attributes to their early ancestors. With its aid they have been able to help and relieve their oppressed brethren in a distant land.[6] To it they owe everything and from it they hope to gain still more.[7]

One hundred years later a young Parsi Harvard student described Karaka's text as a self-conscious attempt to lay claim to the "civilizing process," as she put it, "a historical concept of self-differentiation by which urban, educated Parsis have sought to differentiate themselves and their community at once from the Indian population and from their rural heritage."[8] Their ideology, she argued, led them to perceive their history in irregular progression: a period of greatness and civilization in the Persian past followed by greatness and civilization during the British rule—ignoring a thousand years of agricultural labor in India, let alone Iran. The problem with this vision, as she saw it, was that undying loyalty and commitment to colonial ideals were not particularly adaptive in postcolonial India. Whatever the community's fate, her point is vivid: the community's sensibility was profoundly altered by the experience of British rule. Parsis had power and success at the height of the Raj, and both as a means to achieve that power and as the consequence of it, they identified themselves as like the British and unlike their Hindu countrymen. That identification probably altered them forever.

The Attributes of the Good Parsi

The salient virtues clustered around the concept of good Parsi in the late nineteenth century are described in the English-language, British-focused, Parsi-authored literature of the late nineteenth and early twentieth centuries. At least some of the Parsi-Gujarati literature of the period also reinforces these accounts—there is a particularly rich literature explaining that the religion is rational and monotheistic, and that Ahriman, the spirit of evil, is only a metaphor for bad thought—but I do not know that literature in any depth. It is also not clear how many Parsis adopted these self-descriptions—if it is difficult for an anthropologist to be certain of her claims for a live community, it is far more difficult to wrest the secrets of lived reality from the archives—and only quarter of the community spoke English in 1901 (although that is a remarkable percentage; less than one percent of the Hindus or Jains spoke English).[9] Yet from the representation of Parsi life in photographs and from British descriptions, it does seem that the community was remarkably westernized and was widely regarded as charitable, truthful, racially pure, and as like the British as a native community could be. I read the comments in the English-language literature as a kind of political rhetoric, supposedly directed at the Parsis but in fact aimed at the British, which argued that the moral qualities of the Parsis must be classified as more European than Indian, and, like the British, as superior to the moral qualities of the native Indian. The concept of the good Parsi must be read as a community ideal as well as a strategic economic gamble. And whatever role these self-descriptions played in the cognitive life of the community members in the late nineteenth century, they seem to play a powerful role in the lives of late-twentieth-century Parsis.

The attributes perhaps most strongly associated with Zoroastrianism in the religious texts are truthfulness and purity. *Asha*, cognate with and similar in meaning to *dharma*, is perhaps the most important word in the religion. It evokes a seamless fabric of truth, purity, and goodness.[10] To reiterate its centrality: Taraporewala, a much-admired priest and translator of the Gathas, says: "And what then is *Asha?* Scholars translate it variously as 'Purity' or 'Righteousness' or 'Truth,' but it is far more than any of these words in their *ordinary* sense. It is the Eternal Truth, the One Reality."[11] *Asha* is the centerpiece of the two standard Zoroastrian Avestan prayers which accompany all the daily prayers and are recited before and after most religious lectures and community functions; even if a Parsi has no idea of what the Avestan words mean, he will recognize the word *asha*. And the general resonance of the word "truth" in the contemporary community would be hard to overestimate; it carries the penumbra of meanings that *asha* does. What is good is true, and what is true is good. Parsis pride themselves on their truthfulness and not infrequently contrast their honesty with the dishonesty of non-Parsis.

At the same time, a reputation for keeping your word has obvious business advantages. In a study of colonial *sheths* (great merchants) in Surat, Haynes points out that *abru*, reputation, carried the connotations of both religious appropriateness and economic credit. "The ability of local merchants to generate reputations as wealthy and trustworthy persons made possible their participation in a vast commercial economy that functioned without legally enforceable contracts or modern financial institutions" (1987:342). At least by the late nineteenth and early twentieth century, and presumably much earlier, truth seems to have taken on this aspect of business reliability for the Parsis. The business heroes of the eighteenth and nineteenth centuries are presented as gaining commercial credit through their uprightness and truthfulness; contemporary Parsis certainly adulate their past truthfulness as a past commercial asset.[12] Parsis repeatedly told me—I must have heard the story fifty times—that all the banks in Bombay employed Parsis as their clerks, because "in earlier days" Parsis always spoke the truth. I was told—I remember in particular by a priest at Udwada (in Gujarat, home to the most sacred fire)—that business under the British had been honest, which is why Parsis had succeeded. An older friend, born at the first decade of the twentieth century, told me many times a story about a building that her father decided to sell. Someone approached him, they agreed upon a price, and then the buyer wanted a written contract of the bargain. Her father was furious, she said. "I am a Parsi-Zoroastrian," he announced; "my word is my oath." And he refused to sign a contract. He also stood by his word, she said, although a man later approached him with an even higher bid. A reputation for truthfulness would have been important in the trade of precolonial Surat; but in the rapid economic expansion of colonial west India, in which the Europeans could pick and choose amongst potential partners, Parsi honesty seems to have become entrenched as a status marker to affirm the validity of past profits and to promise them to future clients.

A similar transformation also took place with the concept of purity (also very much a Hindu sacred idea), which was refigured from holiness into racial superiority. "Purity really is the key to the religion" a Parsi friend told me. "Purity enters the way people talk about their prayers, their minds, their lives." In some sense Zoroastrianism is no more than a ritualistic commentary upon purity and pollution. Its theology, doctrine, and ritual practice all focus on purity. The central cosmological struggle of good against evil is described as an effort to achieve purity—that which is evil is impure; that which is impure is evil. Zoroastrians often have a concrete conception of evil, with rituals and garments literally designed to keep the evil from the self.[13] Parsis wear—at least, are supposed to wear—a special shirt, the *sudreh*, beneath their other garments, which carries this protective intent.[14] Traditional constraints on menstruating women are elaborate and among the most severe in India, a country particularly hard on menstruating women.[15] Those Parsis rediscovering their religion refer, with delight, to their discovery of the religious injunctions behind their urge for cleanliness. "I've always been a very *clean* person, fanatic about keeping the house tidy, taking baths and so forth," someone would say. "Now I know why." The major ceremonies—the *yasna* ceremony, the ceremonies of birth and death, the *navjote*, and marriage—do this job of carefully creating an enclosed, purified space within which certain actions are done, or statuses transformed, purifying a body to enable it to function effectively in the world. As another, Western, scholar says, "it is not an exaggeration to say that Zoroastrian piety and spirituality begins and end with the body."[16]

So dramatic grew the Parsi sense of difference from Hindu and Muslim Indians that as the century turned, Iran became the central symbol of Parsi ethnic—that is, non-British—identity, and the emphasis on the difference clearly included and extended the religious rhetoric of Parsi purity. "The Parsis are the one race settled in India (not excepting the Kashmiris or any other) that could for a moment be called white," proclaims a Parsi journal in 1906.[17] The considerable European philological interest in the ancient religion, united to the energetic Parsi attempt to detach things Parsi from things Hindu, was probably sufficient to ignite practical Parsi efforts to create the sense of a clearly Iranian Zoroastrianism. In 1858 K. R. Cama, scion of a leading Bombay family, travelled to Europe to learn Avesta and Pahlavi from the great European scholars. He subsequently founded the Zarthosti Dinni Khol Mandli (the Society for Furthering Research on Zoroastrianism), home for Parsi scholars of the texts,[18] and in league with others argued that non-Zoroastrian elements should be purged from the faith.[19] In 1911 two leading religious reformers founded what they called the Iranian Association. For a society of this name its goals are remarkable.

    1. To maintain the purity of the Zoroastrian religion and remove the excrescences that have gathered around it.

2. To expose and counteract the effects of such teachings of theosophists and others as tend:
    a. to corrupt the religion of Zarathustra by adding elements foreign to it;
    b. to bring about the degeneration of a progressive and virile community like the Parsis, and make them a body of superstitious and impractical visionaries.
3. To promote measures for the welfare and advancement of the community.

To call the association the Iranian Association was in fact a polemical claim about who a Parsi "really" was, and a political assertion about the undesirability of anything Hindu.

Awareness of Iranian ancestry was further exemplified and heightened by the philanthropic urges towards the poorer, less educated reformists in Iran. In 1854 the community sent Maneckjee Hataria to Persia to inquire of their coreligionists' state, and in the same year it founded the Persian Zoroastrian Amelioration Fund, with the ultimately successful aim to persuade the Iranian government to release the Iranian Zoroastrians from the *jizya*.[20] By the early twentieth century, the modern Iranian nationalist movement had improved the status of Zoroastrianism in Iran, and in 1923 the community was semi-officially invited to return— and clearly, this notion had been present in the Parsi community for some time. By 1922, the Iran League had been founded in Bombay. Its goals included: to better the conditions of Iranian Zoroastrians, to encourage the study of Zoroastrianism and Iranian history, to encourage Parsis to make commercial connections with Iran, to travel to Iran, to invite Iranian Zoroastrians to visit Bombay, but most strikingly: that Parsis "should continue to regard Iran with patriotic fervour as in the past."[21]

It has been argued that this new Iranian identity and the fantasies of community repatriation emerged because the reality of an India without British rule approached.[22] Whatever the reasons, today many Parsis will have pictures of Iran on their walls. Parsi tour groups regularly revisit the ancient sites of Persian greatness. There is still an Iran League, although more anemic than in earlier years. There are contests in recitation of the Shanameh. In the esoteric philosophy of the religion, Ilm-e-kshnoom, Persian words are considered to be more pure, of greater potency, than words in Gujarati or English. And most palpably, Parsis will speak of their Iranian ancestry, their unique, untainted Iranian blood, and why that blood and body distinguishes them from their Hindu brethren. In the debate over intermarriage, as we shall see, this biological superiority is hotly contested—but passionately defended.

The British unconsciously (perhaps) colluded in the use of Parsi religiosity to establish racial superiority, because Zoroastrianism proved strategically useful in the bid to retain the importance of Christianity against the late-nineteenth-century attack by science on religion. The discovery of a contemporary monotheistic religion which was demonstrably ancient indicated to some Englishmen that religion could not have followed the evolutionary development postulated by anthropologists, and thus could not be explained as a psychological phenomenon.[23] Only God, as it were, could have created so noble and ethical a religion as ancient Zoroastrianism. The abstract emphasis on truth in the Gathas is admittedly quite different from the nineteenth century anthropological description of an early animistic world. *Ipso facto,* the religion must have been inspired directly by God, and not by gullible humans. As an Englishman argues,

> [The Gathas] present truths of the highest moral and spiritual significance, in a form which constantly reminds us of the teaching of the Pentateuch and the Prophets . . . They are absolutely irreconcilable with the theory which regards all spiritual and soul-elevating religions as developed by a natural process from a primitive and naturalistic polytheism; they support the view, which alone supplies a true, rational and adequate account of the movements of human thought, according to which religious beliefs were first set in motion by communications from God.[24]

In part because of the Christianity of the German scholarly translators of the texts, in part because an early form of Christianity added weight—proof—to the argument against evolutionary atheism, Zoroastrianism was described by western scholars as the earliest monotheism and as source for both Judaism and Christianity.[25] Ultimately, these writings fed back into the Parsi desire to purify their religion and the community, to strip it of all accretions of Hindu tradition, and to see that religion as more evidence that Parsis were like Europeans—they were even the *source* of European religion—and very different from the other communities in India.[26]

The concept of charity also moved from the religious realm to the political and economic arenas; in fact its role as a virtue may have been promoted as a consequence of its persuasive power in the politico-economic field. A young Parsi woman said in 1988: "The word 'good' for many many Parsis has to do with charity, maybe because we moved from Iran to India and India's a poor country and the Parsis became a prosperous community. For some reason being good and being charitable are often linked. And now you often hear someone say, so-and-so's a very good person, and you look into what they've done and 99 percent of the time it's something charitable." Charity had always been a religious virtue commended in the ancient holy books. But during the Raj, charitable activity became the primary indicator not only of religious goodness, but of political and economic power, the means through which a secularized, progressive, westernized Parsi achieved recognition. Much of Bombay was built with charitable Parsi funds, the more so as the British government began to confer knighthood on those who were outstandingly benevolent. Between 1820 and 1940 the Parsis built over 160 fire temples; in the same period they erected over forty *dharmsalas* (resthouses, often used to house the poor) and *baags* (colonies); and they donated funds to 350 schools, libraries, educational centers, hospitals, clinics, and wards.[27] Parsis in general provided funds in such amounts that the total recorded Parsi charities reported annual incomes of well over one million rupees—and at one point, up to seven and a half million rupees— during the first forty years of the twentieth century.[28]

The emphasis on charity continues today. Throughout their writings Parsis refer to their community as charitable; they talk about their achievements in community and cosmopolitan giving, they show you, the visitor to Bombay, the hospitals, schools, and other institutions built with charitable funds. Jamshetjee Jeejeebhoy still remains the goal and stereotype of the Parsi success story: you struggle, you rise through hard work to wealth, and then you give that wealth to others who are in need. The following is an excerpt from an interview with a very wealthy, powerful Bombay businessman, known for his charitable activities.

I was the only son of my mother who had six daughters. So the logical inclination would be for the mother to spoil the only son she had. That would be the natural inclination. But she didn't. On the contrary she brought me up more strictly than any of my sisters. For example, my family had three cars. Yet quite often I was told by my mother after I had matriculated middle school, "you come home by bus." And I questioned why I should come home by bus when my sisters get to come home in the car. So she said, "but I would like you to appreciate how others live. And that everybody doesn't possess a car. Travelling by bus or train inculcates in you a sense of appreciation for what God had given you and of the best use you must make of it." And that was when I was something like 14, between 12 and 15 years. And I began to appreciate that.

You've got the money. You're sitting on it. But my first reaction would be, since I've made so much money, I must give part of it to people who are in need of that money or in need of that help.

This is the standard stereotype—the script, as it were. The speaker was said to give a notable portion of his wealth and time to the less well-to-do, and indeed, as I sat in his office, some of the poor waited outside for their appointments with him, and he took a string of phone calls about housing and medical care for members of the community. As Karaka did, so do contemporary Parsis explain that Parsi charity is worthier than Hindu charity: that the Hindu will build a temple for his people or even just himself, while the Parsi will build socially useful buildings and fund scholarships.

The tough-minded historical analysis of philanthropy suggests that it is intimately involved with the establishment of *abru*, reputation, credit-worthiness, and commercial authority. Rudner, for instance, writes of the circulation of religious-cum-economic goods in South India. "Nakarattars 'invested' profits from the salt trade in religious gifts. Religious gifts were transformed and redistributed as honours. Honours were the currency of trust. And trustworthiness gained Nakarattars access to the market for salt" (1987:377). Haynes points out that the philanthropy of Surat merchants in the colonial period functioned to maintain their reputations, gain political influence, and ease relations with political authorities; he remarks that what appeared to the British Civil Service as the diffusion of a new Victorian ethic of humanitarian service was less evidence of the merchants' progressive modernization than of their conservative business acumen (1987:340). Berry suggests that philanthropy enabled the native businessman to transform his subversive and dangerous wealth into a sign of his integrity (1987:306).

White (1991) points out more generously that Parsi philanthropy in Bombay helped to establish a material infrastructure for the community and create a sense of community unity and boundedness. It must be said, however, that the motivation for Parsi philanthropic gifting was sometimes simple and direct. The India Office library contains the correspondence of an outraged Parsi donor who refurbished a large room in the Imperial Institute with the apparently explicit agreement that he should be knighted in exchange; alas, the government changed after the redecoration but before the title had been rewarded.[29] Nevertheless, it is important to recognize that charity figures powerfully in the romance of the successful Parsi.

"Progress" is another virtue whose religious significance may have been promoted after its social virtues became clear. Certainly the ethical notion that the world progresses was transmuted, over the nineteenth century, into the argument that Parsis are rational and socially progressive. By the late nineteenth century, being tolerant, liberal, open to the kinds of change the British had encouraged, and a member of the most modern and advanced community in India, was what being a Parsi was about. Parsis were prominent in the nineteenth-century Indian reform movement, which emerged with the aim of removing the supposedly irrational, archaic customs which impeded modernization. In the late nineteenth century Behramji Malabari, for instance, became a noted reformer of Hindus, focusing on child marriages and the prohibition on the remarriage of widows.[30] He saw in these customs the cause of the inferiority of the Hindu people. "What could you expect from a nation whose mothers have a life in perpetual infancy? Can these be mothers of heroes and patriots and statesmen?"[31] Naoroji, Madame Cama, and Pherozeshah Mehta of course stood identified as reformers, and there were others, more or less famous, who worked to educate the poor, to improve health care, or to make legal rights practically attainable.

As Parsis came more and more to see themselves as a progressive community, they downplayed the ritual of their religion and sought to describe Zoroastrianism as a rational ethics entirely compatible with science. "The special claims of the Zoroastrian system are most obvious in its relations to science . . . There are several features of the religion of Zarathustra which have appealed particularly to the scientist as such."[32] In the late nineteenth and early twentieth centuries Parsi secularism grew rapidly. Publications addressing the Parsi religion stressed that it was primarily a rational ethical system under the benevolent guidance of God rather than a religion which—like Hinduism—was abundantly endowed with supernatural entities. Zoroastrianism was described as scientific, and its obsessive concern with purity attributed to the need for hygiene (for example, Dubash 1906). Even the most beloved Karachi priest of the period presents his reformist orientation almost as a conversion experience, and certainly as a necessary change. Upon returning from Columbia, where he studied with A. V. W. Jackson (the most noted Iranist of his time), he declared: "I was now eager to become the thinker of new thoughts, the student of new ideas, and the propagator of new concepts. In 1905 I had set foot on American soil as an orthodox. Now in 1909 I was leaving the shores of the New World as a reformist" (Dhalla 1975:158).

Much quoted during this period was *The Modern Zoroaster,* by the English writer Samuel Laing.[33] Laing argued that recent scientific work had demonstrated that behind all aspects of life there lay dualism, as between the poles of a magnet and as between positive and negative electricity. Zoroastrianism reflected these scientific truths more fully than any other religion: "In its fundamental ideas and essential spirit, [Zoroastrianism] approximates wonderfully to those of the most advanced modern thought, and gives the outline of a creed which goes further than any other to meet the practical wants of the present day and to reconcile the conflict between faith and science."[34] And Laing quoted Andrew Carnegie—as Parsis would do for the next hundred years:

> This evening we were surprised to see, as we strolled along the beach, more Parsees than ever before, and more Parsee ladies richly dressed, all wending their way towards the sea. It was the first of the new moon, a period sacred to these worshippers of the elements . . . There was no music except the solemn moan of the waves as they broke into foam on the beach. But where shall we find so mighty an organ, or so grand an anthem? How inexpressibly sublime the scene appeared to me, and how insignificant and unworthy of the unknown seemed even our cathedrals "made with human hands" when compared with this looking up through nature unto nature's God! . . . Nor do I ever expect in all my life to witness a religious ceremony which will so powerfully affect me as that of the Parsees on the beach at Bombay.[35]

It is a romantic, attractive description; Laing quoted it, however, because he approved of a religion without ritualistic trappings, without apparent dogma, in which God is understood as essentially another term for nature. This is recognizably the western intellectual's romantic agnosticism of the period, but it is a far cry from an orthodox Parsi's ritual-laden life. Yet in the late nineteenth century Parsis began to endorse this vision of a scientifically accurate, spiritually aesthetic, reform-oriented and ritual- and dogma-free endeavor, and it remains relevant today. I remember dropping in, fairly early in my stay, on a course of lectures on the Zoroastrian religion at Kharegat colony. Sitting next to me were two women in their seventies, both very proud of their religion. They had always worn the *sudreh-kusti,* they said, but when they were very young no one had explained the religion to them. Now they had begun to read about it and to come to these lectures. "It's a very scientific religion. We worship the sun and the moon and all the elements. That's why it's scientific. Everything is nature."

Biographical Vignette: Professor Dubash

Late in my stay, as the afternoon faded into evening, I met Professor Dubash, a frail, elderly man. The street outside his wooden shutter seemed very Indian. He lived in a world that seemed more Hindu than Parsi, with more clutter, less Edwardian furniture, more distinctly Indian food; when I remarked upon this he said, you must see the Indian Bombay, north of the Victoria Terminus. The Parsis do not understand India, he said.

I must understand three things about the religion, he said. First, I must separate the ritual from the liturgy. The professor is anti-ritual; ritual is a late, superstitious accretion spurred by power-hungry priests. Second, Zoroastrianism is very scientific. Zoroastrianism holds that the scientific view of the world is the correct one. Third, Zoroastrianism is simple: one single creator, and that is that. The Amesha Spentas—the seven spirits mentioned in many important prayers—merely represent different human qualities of the creator. This is the spare, scientistic Zoroastrianism of the late nineteenth century, and Dubash approves of it. And yet, tellingly, he also reads the devotional, mystical love poetry of Sufism. Religion, he explained, was ultimately about love, the love that a mother bears for her child, and Zoroastrianism doesn't talk about love, so he was Zoroastrian and more, because religion to him was more than scientific.

He then commented upon the superstitious nature of the community. They all turned to a variety of gods and other faiths, he said, but it was like practicing magic, always to get something, because your back is bad or the job difficult. Sai Baba—a contemporary divine miracle-worker—appeared particularly powerful to them. This may be because some of the things Sai Baba spoke sounded Zoroastrian, like his talk of living a good life. Part of the problem, he said, is the fault of the priests. They may care about the texts, perhaps, but they do nothing for the people. They are either scholars or ritualists. They do not reach out.

When I write about the community, he said, I must read the Victorian historians to see their self-satisfaction with the community as it was then. But above all I must be aware of the community's charitable nature—such facts as that Tata founded the first hospital in Bombay in 1845, before India knew anything of modern medicine. The young people today don't give a damn about the poor. Nothing is what it was. The community is committing suicide with all this intermarriage. You cannot allow outsiders into the fold. The sense of history is not deeply ingrained in the Parsis, he remarked; perhaps this is what makes it possible to die. Even the Theosophical Society, to which most of the cultured people belonged, is not as it was. We are dying out, he said.

The candle was burning before his ancestors on the table, and he wore the *sudreh-kusti,* and Zarathustra's picture hung upon the wall.

◆ ◆ ◆

Perhaps even more dramatically than the religion, the Parsi lifestyle became westernized. Turn-of-the-century photographs show the men in suits, albeit wearing the traditional *pughree,* a conical Parsi hat. The women usually wear saris, but sometimes European dress, and they wear stockings, English shoes, and pearls. In publications like *Men and Women of India* (1906) the Parsis are consistently more western in appearance than members of other communities. The furniture, similarly, is European in design. Many modern Parsi homes are full of the heavy, boxy furniture (and pianos) of their Edwardian ancestors, and the community seems to have adopted, earlier than other communities, the dictum that the colonial domestication of space indicates a colonial orientation of mind.[36] Both in the early twentieth century and today, Parsis placed a premium on privacy and lived with fewer people per room than other communities—for example, the Jains—of similar socioeconomic standing. (Even today, one of the most commonly cited reasons for remaining single is the unavailability of a room or apartment for the young couple). The mimicry went at times to absurd but unironic lengths. In 1890 a Parsi—at odds with the community because they had dismissed him for converting to Christianity; apparently, conversion was the only unacceptable imitation of the British—observed drily that "this ambition to appear exactly like the British is so great that some of them put on solar hats [*topees*]."[37]

And the admiration was mutual. In 1870 the Hon. C. D. Postan remarked that "since the conquest of India by the British government, [Parsis] have been esteemed the most faithful, the most intelligent and the most enterprising subjects of the Indian Empire."[38] Again and again the British sing praises to the Parsis and applaud their westernization. In English records of the period, the "stately Parsi" pushes through the milling crowd of Indian humanity in an English buggy; his brilliant-hued, beautiful women wear quantities of gold lace and handsome ornaments, and they laugh merrily, as Hindus never do; Parsi women openly travel the roads, like western women and unlike well-to-do Hindu and Muslim women who are, according to tradition, secluded from public gaze.[39] Parsis have shops and houses in the English part of town.[40]

Books printed for the European market return the compliment and give thanks for the worthy virtues of colonial rule. A late-nineteenth-century *Portrait Gallery in Western India* is illustrated by pictures of stiffly posed Parsis with biographical captions that speak of their reform and advancement, and usually, their moral weight. One biography explained that "Mr. Cama has been a thorough-going social reformer, and has waged a continuous and strenuous war against all kinds of superstitions, which have crept in among the Parsis through contact with other communities; and in this field more than any other he has been most successful" (Jalbhoy 1886:68). In the *Portrait*, even the women are reformist, progressive, not really like the rest of Indian women, who are mired in tradition. The caption for a female educator (Franscina Sorabji) reads: "the ideal wife and mother, educationist, philanthropist, imperialist, and citizen of the world of true progress, of the true emancipation of Indian womanhood" (Jalbhoy 1886:101).

Indeed, the Parsis displayed their progressiveness in their Anglicized women and civilized men, a display all the more convincing in a context of colonial discourse in which Hindu women stood for the traditional backwardness of their people, regardless of the sophistication of their men.[41] In 1838 an anonymous British author commented in the *Asiatic Journal* as follows:

> Work-tables fitted up after the European mode, are not infrequently found in [Parsi women's] possession; they know how to use English implements in their embroidery, and they have English dressing-cases for the toilet. Considerable pains, in some instances, are bestowed upon the education of the daughters, who learn to draw and to play upon the piano; and one Parsi gentleman, of great wealth, contemplated the introduction of an English governess, for the purpose of affording instruction to the young ladies of his family. (Chaudhuri 1986:240–41)

In 1852 the English author of *The Parsis* remarked on further changes:

> Of late the Parsi Ladies of Bombay have betaken themselves to wood-work, and a variety of European amusements and tasks. English hosiery has been in use among the better classes of both sexes for some years, and the men have a weakness in displaying fine English shoes ... The spirit of improvement leads the better educated youth to make English the chief medium of communication. Many of the Parsis speak English with a facility scarcely credible for foreigners.[42]

The author exclaimed that "Of all the tribes now indigenous to the soil of British Hindustan, the Parsis must command our warmest and most lively sympathy." Another Englishman, writing in 1922 (the book was called *Our Parsi Friends*) reported in a similar vein:

> The last half century has seen a complete change, especially in Bombay. Parsis of both sexes now eat together after the manner and from the crockery of Europe. The Parsi lady has exchanged the Hindu bodice and petticoat for the English bodice and the English coat. Instead of slippers she wears high-heeled shoes. She has adopted stockings, stays and combinations ... Over her combinations the

Parsi girl wears her sacred shirt and her sacred coat and the Parsi youth wears them under his Bond Street linen. (Kincaid 1922)

Parsis began to treat their women like western, progressive women in the nineteenth century. A turn-of-the-century Parsi woman proudly explained that Parsi women "live a natural life, enjoy their games, can admit of a girlhood as well as a womanhood, and are fast becoming splendid companions for their husbands; it is not longer a rule but an oddity when a Parsee husband spends his evenings away from his home" (Cavalier 1899). Parsis were among the first communities in India to educate their women, doing so in English from 1860 (Hinnells n.d.). By 1870 over a thousand Parsi women had received a secondary education (Kulke 1974:104). One article pointed out how the community realized by 1849 that "for the social and intellectual advancement of their respective communities, no means could be more hopeful and fruitful than the education of girls."[43] Private homes were used for some years until, in 1858, the Parsi Girls School Association was formally inaugurated. There are pictures of students of the Tata Girls School at Navsari taking first-aid classes, and accompanying essays on a convalescent home for women and children and "Parsi Ladies as Educationists."

Most dramatically, Parsis spoke English. In the mid-nineteenth century Parsis built more schools and attended school more regularly than other communities, proportional to their numbers (Hinnells n.d.:1). By 1881 74 percent of the community was literate (Hinnells 1978:52). By 1901 more than a quarter of the community spoke English, as compared to less than one percent of the Jains and half a percent of the Hindus (Axelrod 1974:31); 63 percent of Parsi women were literate and nearly all the men (Hinnells n.d.:2). In 1899 an English newsletter remarks, "The Parsis are most loyal to England, and nearly all the younger generation speak English well."[44] In 1906 a journal article comments: "the love of English literature has spread among the womankind of Parsis more widely and more rapidly than among any other nationality in India. Of this there can never be two opinions."[45]

Early twentieth-century accounts reiterate these themes. The recorded memories of a Bombay-based British businessman describe the Parsis as "completely westernized in their habits" and acting as a kind of bridge between Indians and Europeans. "Mind you," he remarked, "we had nice Indians in Bombay": for him, the Parsis were different from the Indians.[46] In 1911 the English author of an illustrated exhibition book of Old Bombay remarked: "It is Bombay's peculiar pride that there is no city to compare with her in the number, intelligence and public spirit of its leading Indian citizens. In this matter Bombay would be pre-eminent even without reckoning the Parsis, but this small community alone has produced a number of men of such eminence as would lend distinction to any city in the country."[47]

Men and Women of India—self-advertised as the only society magazine in India—devoted a special issue to the Parsis in 1906. Among other pieces it featured the Parsis' share in the industrial development of India—"it is men of the type of Mr. Shapurji Sorabji who draw the tie between England and India much closer together—to the material benefit and honour of both countries"[48] and displayed shops like Kapadia and Sons, the milliners, mercers, and drapers whose store was stocked by buyers who went frequently to Europe for the latest styles. Bombay Parsis, the magazine suggests, are delightfully English, and (it implies) the English must have been relieved to find this civilized island in the raging, backward chaos of greater India. After I had written the first draft of this book I ran into a man in the library who had been stationed in the British military in Bombay during the war. I asked him what he thought of the Parsis. Oh, he said, we thought that they were the very *nicest* of the Indians, and they were so well educated.

The very sense of superiority and set-apartness of the community, coupled with their steadfast adherence to Zoroastrianism—however much the religion seemed to be re-envisioned by Parsis as a kind of secularized moral philosophy—made Parsis a catch for missionaries, and at the century's end a small group of Cambridge University women formed an organization specifically intended to convert them. The pamphlet written to advertise the Missionary Settlement for University Women asserts that "there are few communities so intensely interesting as the Parsi community. . . . They profess to believe in one God, a belief which grows hopelessly confused in the endeavour to account for the origin of evil . . . It is national feeling, rather than religious conviction, that makes the Parsis thankfully receive all he can of Western culture and scornfully reject Christianity."[49]

The Parsis, the pamphlet continues, present special difficulties to the enterprise of conversion. They are strongly bound together by national pride, they can become Theosophists without ceasing to be Zoroastrians, and because they have their own schools and hospitals, they are more self-sufficient and difficult to reach in the conventional ways. But one could, after all, meet the Parsis—"there is much in the social life of Hindus and Mohammedans, even in the upper class, which precludes meeting them on an equal level. This is much less the case among the Parsees"[50]—and they were thought to be susceptible. "The Parsis, as a rule, do not care to mingle much with other races in India, but they are willing and ready to associate with Europeans . . . [they] are becoming more and more civilized and tolerant; they regard missions with friendly feelings."[51] Little came of the mission—in fact, one of the study questions for the mission course was why so few conversions resulted from the work—but hundreds of pages of diaries record encounters with Parsis of all economic levels. Running throughout the diaries is the zealot's frustration of dealing with a community eager to Anglicize but sweetly refusing to convert.

So the British admired the Parsis, and the Parsis strove for their attention. Until the emergence of mass nationalist politics under Gandhi, the tone of English-language Parsi discourse was of upward mobility and almost-to-the-summit success. Nowhere is this strain in Parsi thought, and the thrust of British identification, more starkly revealed than in a publication called *The Parsi: The English Journal of the Parsis and a High Class Illustrated Monthly,* published monthly in 1905. The first issue assesses the year:

> Turning from the year that has just passed it is but natural to ask what can be the hopes and aspirations of the Parsis standing on the threshold of the year . . . What but that the career of enlightenment and progress in which they have embarked since the advent of the British in India may be advanced, and that the task of social amelioration, domestic reform, intellectual and moral improvement and material prosperity to which they have set their hands may be further accomplished? . . . The peoples of the West whom they decided to copy are yet to be closely studied and the good that is found in them is yet to be engrafted on their social constitution.[52]

Throughout the year the enmeshment with the British is stated in brilliantly clear assertions. "The [Parsi] destiny is bound up with the British in India; when the latter leave India the Parsis follow them. There will be no standing room left for them once the British have left his soil—a day, let us hope, which is hundreds of years distant."[53] "The Parsis, on contact with the English, have thrown off their slight Orientalism and stand revealed, by thoughts, mode of speech and ideals, as 'a western nation living in the heart of Asia.'"[54] "The complete Europeanization of the Parsis is now a mere matter of time."[55] "The Parsis are so differently constituted from the rest of the Indians that any close union of the two is well nigh impossible."[56] Not surprisingly, the community is not reported as identified with India in this magazine; indeed, when the Alexandra Girls' School for young Parsis is named the Alexandra Native Girls' School, there is a storm of protest.[57] Still, one of the striking features of the magazine is the comparison of the community to the Japanese. In the news at the time, the Japanese had just taken three Pacific islands from the Russians. *The Parsi* treated the event in a manner that sounds simultaneously miffed and jealous. "Among Asiatics, the Parsis have undoubtedly stood in the forefront, until recently, when the Japanese, hitherto considered little short of barbarism, pushed themselves forward in the most marvelous manner."[58] The writing has the tone of an attention-seeking, eager-to-please, somewhat insecure adolescent who has momentarily been eclipsed by a less obedient sibling.

Biographical Vignette

I met Rusi Davar, an elderly man, through a Parsi relief organization. He lived in charity housing in Tardeo, north central Bombay, in a dilapidated neighborhood. His colony had little of the manicured grandeur of the more southern Parsi colonies, and stray dogs panted in the shade of the dusty buildings. Rusi lived in the back of the colony, in a two-room flat with his sister. Rosewood cabinets lined the walls. Some of them had been confiscated by those to whom he and his sister owed money, and their parents' clothes, which had been kept in the confiscated furniture, were piled in the empty spaces between the cabinets that remained. There were large cracks running up the walls and damp patches on the ceilings; still, the building must have seemed quite sturdy when new. Parsis sometimes see these now crumbling buildings as a symbol for the community as a whole. The Davars had lived there for many years. There were pictures of Zarathustra everywhere, and one of Kookadaru, an unofficial Zoroastrian saint;[59] there was a Sai Baba near the kitchen fire. There were pictures of all of Rusi's relatives, some of them in frames embroidered by his mother. Next to the cluster of Zarathustra pictures, with the family portraits and Kookadaru, were the prayer books, now dusty. Rusi could no longer read because his eyesight had deteriorated, but he did what he could from memory. In the bedroom there was a picture of the Duke of Windsor. His uncle, he said proudly, was on the first Indian team to go to England to play cricket. They were all Parsis on that team.

♦ ♦ ♦

At the heart of these semiotics, at the dead center of the Parsi construction of self in the economic and cultural arena of the colonial Raj, figured the gentlemanly manliness of the Parsi man, a schema which translated the muscular Christianity, the main argument for British supremacy and their white man's burden, into Parsi terms.[60] Characteristic to Parsi descriptions, however, is a stag-like contestation: Parsis not only sought to be *as* manly as the British, but more so; their virility was not only equivalent but, they seemed at times to argue, ultimately superior. This is the real thrust, I suspect, behind Karaka's enthusiasm for the Parsis' Persian past— that Parsis have "a vitality and an energy" equal to that of Europeans in Europe. It is the point behind the famous story of J. N. Tata standing his ground to brash, ungentlemanly Englishmen (although it is perhaps not surprising that there is psychological but not physical confrontation in the story). This is a fictionalized account:

The rows of rickety wooden chairs had long been filled, but hundreds of Indians were content merely to squat at the perimeter of the official seating arrangements. Within the select enclosure of chairs an altercation was taking place: a tall, gangly uniformed English official was trying to remove a chair "for one of the English ladies who just arrived" he explained, while a young Parsi in a *dagla* [coat], white pants, and *paghri* [hat] was trying to restrain him. "I'm sorry" the Parsi said, "but this chair is reserved. My friend will be back in a moment." The Parsi was smaller, but with the thick density, the quick strength of a dwarf in his body. He spoke politely, but his face was stern. "In fact, here he is now," he said without turning away, as his friend came up beside him.

"Let me go," the Englishman said, trying to get free.

"Put the chair down," said the Parsi.

The Englishman looked nervously from the Parsi to his friend and back. "Who are you to speak to me like this?"

"We know our rights," said the Parsi with the same politeness, the same unswerving gaze.

The Englishman might have backed off then if he could have saved face doing so, but it was too late. "I could have you confined for the night," he said.

"That is a risk I will have to take."

Fortunately for everyone, a second uniformed Englishmen called from a distance, "It's all right, Roger. We've got all the chairs we need."

The first Englishman thumped the chair down without looking at the Parsi, and walked away immediately. The Parsi put the chair calmly back where it had been and said something to his friend with a confidential smile as the first rockets flashed into the darkening sky and fountains of flame erupted in the heart of the enclosure. (Desai 1988:118–19)

The Parsi is stern, tough, built like a fighter, and moreover in the right. He is also unshakably polite. He is more of an English gentleman than the English gentlemen themselves. This superior manliness is also probably the spirit behind a remarkable book which is an encyclopedic paean to Parsi athleticism.

In 1935 H. D. Darukhanawala published a book entitled *Parsis and Sport*. Four years later he went on to publish a myth-making book entitled *Parsi Lustre on Indian Soil*, with about five hundred short biographies of eminent Parsis. But *Parsis and Sport* seems to have been his first attempt at community glorification, and its entirely unsubtle message is that the Parsis are the most physically vigorous men in India. "The sporting instinct is inborn in members of the Zoroastrian community . . . The Parsi's achievements in sport touch a high level of excellence; he has led the way to other communities in manly games and athletics" (Jeejeebhoy in Darukhanawala 1935:15,19). The text reads like a believe-it-or-not encyclopedia of unsurpassed feats; one of them is a record for swimming in place in a small pool. The book contains picture after picture of burly young men in scanty clothes: wrestlers, swimmers, weight-lifters, cyclists, cricketers, men balancing on skates, posed with rapier and helmet, calmly surveying the dead tiger stretched at their feet. The sports chosen are English-inspired; the dress is English-inspired; the manliness itself has an English public school-boy feel; the book is extraordinary testimony to the impact of colonialism on colonial elites.

Of all gentlemanly athletic pastimes, cricket was the most esteemed. It was fitting to the ethos and aspirations of the community that Parsis played cricket sooner and better than any other community. Parsis dominated cricket—now, the national pastime of India—until the early twentieth century. The first great players were Parsis, the first all-India team to travel to Britain was an exclusively Parsi team, and the yearly match between the Europeans and the Parsis—the Presidency vs. Parsee match—was apparently the highlight of the Bombay cricket season. "A Presidency-Parsee match is the Indian Duty. People go to see it, just as the Greeks went to their Olympic games or the Spaniards go to witness bullfights in Madrid." Of the first cricket team to go to England, an Englishman said: "As pilgrims go to Jerusalem to worship at a shrine, so now the Parsees are going to England to do homage to the English cricketers."[61] The chronicler shares the basic insight of the Englishman—"just as 'the history of the shirt is the history of civilization,' so the history of Parsi cricket is partly the history of physical, social, and moral progress of the go-ahead and imitative Parsi youth"[62]—and there is no doubt in his mind of the nature or importance of the cricket-playing enterprise. "Who is the father of Indian cricket? It is the child of progress, of the friendly embrace of the East and the West" (Patel 1905:174). English commentators seem also to consider Parsi participation as a sign of the achievement of the colonial enterprise. A Governor of Bombay remarks in 1899 that "I may be a little partial, but I really do not know a sight more creditable to the British capacity for administration than that of a cricket match on the parade ground between the Presidency European Eleven and the Parsis" (Lord Harris 1899:70). And a British commentator of the time exclaims, praising the Parsi enthusiasm for cricket: "the Parsi fraternity is the most intelligent as well as the most loyal of the races scattered over our Indian possessions."[63] Nandy's perspective is somewhat more acid: "the Parsis, of course, did not have to produce a new westernized class for cricket; they opted as a community for the model of English gentility and cricket came in as part of the same baggage" (Nandy 1988:53).

In 1905 Patel described the Parsis as "a fine product of Persian pluck and English culture" (1905:2) and Parsi commentators in general seemed to conceptualize this breeding as ideal. An 1896 Parsi commentator remarks, "in physical matters, too, Parsis are rapidly developing robuster qualities of body, which will in the long run make them the equals of many Western nations, and on which Western supremacy rests. In social matters they easily take the lead of their Hindu countrymen" (Karkaria 1896:50). Again and again, the themes are set out: Parsi men are easily more masculine than Hindu and Muslim men, and perhaps at least as masculine as the British, who after all are newcomers to the tropical heat—and masculinity is the basis of western supremacy.

Indeed, all of the virtues reconfigured and acquired during the Raj—the honesty of commercial trustworthiness, the purity associated with European-like racial superiority to the native Hindus, the philanthropy of successful business, the English-style rationality and progressiveness of Parsi religion, lifestyle, educational aims, and even the status of their women—all of these construct a semiotic package of the Parsi as an English gentleman. Why go to so much effort?

The symbolic role of gender identification in the colonial period is so well established that it would be inappropriate to reargue it closely here. Students of colonialism in India and elsewhere describe a cluster of desired characteristics associated with the colonial men in authority and opposed to the characteristics of those over whom they ruled. The colonial authorities were interpreted by the colonizers as rational, progressive, controlled, and masculine, in contrast to the supposedly irrational, traditional (primitive), untamed, effeminate people over whom they ruled. Some scholars understand these semiotics as a psychodynamic scramble on the part of the colonizers to master the terrible sense of isolation and worthlessness created in the foreign overlord through the colonial encounter. Wurgaft suggests that this (interpreted) dread produces "the psychic need to bring India out of the shadows of pure fantasy into a more reassuring sphere, where it could be controlled and tailored to the requirements of the imperial imagination."[64] It has been suggested that in Victorian society generally there was considerable anxiety about the nature of masculinity, and that some of these anxieties were projected into the colonial situation (see Das 1986:68). Other scholars focus more upon the emergent notions of chivalry and muscular Christianity in the code of an English gentleman: the man as protector, the woman in need of protection. "Chivalry represents an idealized doctrine for the dominant side of an unequal relationship, a model of altruistic relations between the powerful and the weak, the rulers and the ruled, the autonomous actor and his dependents, and what was considered to be the strong male and the physically fragile female."[65] The colonized not only were conceptually feminized as a group in a manner that legitimized colonial rule, but native women in particular became the ground on which many of these legitimizing strategies were played out. Woman became a concrete metaphor for tradition, and the helpless victim who truly needed protection from maltreatment by her native men (this is why, some have suggested, *sati* was a source of such horrified British fascination).[66] The intense regulation of sexual interaction can be seen as a prominent attempt to regulate the boundaries between colonizer and colonized—to help create, in legislative fact, the colonized and the colonizer—and by these regulations to articulate a hierarchical relationship between them.[67] In actuality the enactment of these symbolic identifications served to legitimate the moral authority of colonial rule: the colonizers ruled from a sense of chivalrous duty, out of the moral obligation to care for those weaker than themselves.[68]

As did many of the Hindu elites—one thinks of the followers of the Brahmo Samaj, or Vivekananda's exhortation that "what we want is muscles of iron and nerves of steel. No more weeping but stand on your feet and be men" (Das 1986:72)—nineteenth-century Parsis strove to persuade the British of their British-style masculinity in a complex cultural climate in which legitimate authority could be claimed only for those with certain characteristics. Callaway points out that "for colonial society, the concept of the 'gentleman' served as a category for mapping the social world" (1987:42). As a community, the Parsis were more enthusiastic than most, not only in claiming gentlemanly masculinity for themselves but also in acquiring English characteristics. They could claim, moreover, a historically distinct origin from the Hindus, one which was allied with classical antiquity, the reputed cultural source of Victorian civilization. But like all assertive strategies, these moves could be counterproductive if they failed, and in the early twentieth century the winds had begun to blow from another direction.

Biographical Vignette: Sorabji Shapoorjee Bengalee

Parsi biographies—hagiographies—often have a common tone. The man is born impoverished, but struggles hard, goes into business, becomes very successful, devotes his money to public welfare and liberal causes, and dies beloved, usually with a statue to commemorate his civic virtue. The thick volume on Sorabji Shapoorjee Bengalee exemplifies this process of memory.

Sorabji was born in 1831 to poverty. The family business had failed and his father had died, leaving his widow and infant son with no more than the house. Bhikhaiji, his mother, mortgaged the house to support them and then rented it to meet the payments. She was able to send her son to school, but he left it early at his uncle's wish: even so, "his education began when it apparently ended" (n.d.:6), when he began to read systematically. He began to send commentaries to Bombay newspapers at age fourteen, and became a professional journalist at nineteen, a job that found an "outlet for his bouncing enthusiasm for public service" (n.d.:7). His salary, however, he earned in banking; by 1855 he became Deputy Accountant at the Mercantile Bank, a post never before given to an Indian. But it was still a clerk's job, and he left it in 1858 to enter an English business concern. He did brilliantly. He was sent to England and then to the Middle East; he was asked to open a branch of the firm at Calcutta; he became the firm's chief broker and his commercial acumen was regarded as the firm's greatest asset (n.d.:13).

Sorabji was a progressive thinker. He became part of a group which included Dadabhai Naoroji and K. R. Cama and which attempted to reform certain Indian customs like child marriage (Sorabji himself was married at nine) and also to increase knowledge of the Zoroastrian religion as it was originally, untainted by a thousand years of Hindu contact.[69] Together they started the *Rast Goftar*, the primary vehicle for reformist, liberal sentiment in the community and indeed in all of Bombay. Sorabji helped to establish schools for girls and to develop sports in boys' schools. He intervened in municipal mismanagement and public health issues. He became famous as a reformist and a public servant; he was, his biographer tells us, "one of the moral forces of his time" (n.d.:79). But he stood aloof from the Indian National Congress because he felt that the country was not ready to govern itself. Like many Parsis, he was devoted to British rule.

In 1892, shortly before his death, he published some articles reviewing the condition of the Parsis. They had made striking progress in the last fifty years, he said, primarily in social and educational development. Because of their advances they had claimed the leading positions in the professions and other walks of life. Wealth had become more widespread—but so too, he warned, had the expensive habits of the wealthy. Women had more status in the household, thanks to more extensive education and the decline of child marriage and polygamy.

> I notice only one unfortunate feature. I have only one misgiving regarding the future, that our educated Parsis wish to be regarded as being separate from the other communities of India. If this feeling persists in the future, it will cause them a lot of harm. The Parsis were [sic] a very small but important part of the Indian population. As natives of the land, they had intimate relations with other communities and receive as such all benefits. If they break off these ties, they will remain like Eurasians and Indian Christians, apart from the body of the people, begin to hate the vernacular languages, be reduced to the position of an intelligent but uninfluential community and forgo the honourable place they hold in Indian circles. I pray that Parsis may never regard themselves as separate from, their Hindu and Mahomedan brethren . . . Barring this one fear, I count the future of the Parsi race as being promising in all respects. (n.d.:75–76)

◆   ◆   ◆

Parsis led the initial attempts to acquire greater self-rule by Indians—Dadabhai Naoroji was among those who founded the Indian National Congress; he coined the word *swaraj,* home-rule. But Naoroji did not actually encourage the British to leave; he wanted to improve the process of British rule until some time in the distant future, when its goal would have been accomplished.[70] When mass politics took over and the message became "Quit India," the Parsi community refused to participate. In 1921 the Prince of Wales paid an official visit to India. The nationalists boycotted the occasion, but the Parsis came to greet him. The subsequent riots lasted four days and left 53 people dead. At a meeting with some 150 representatives of the Hindu, Muslim, and Parsi communities, Homi Mody—a prominent Parsi politician—was invited by Gandhi to speak. He asserted that the riots were not random but aimed at the Parsis, because as a community they had failed to join the non-cooperation movement and had been unable to adopt Gandhi's nationalist program, so other communities had become incensed at them. Mody's biographer asserts that Mody particularly impressed upon the audience that the Parsis were not to be bullied. They were second to none in independence of character and would not join a movement just because many Hindus insisted that they do so.[71]

In conversation after conversation, Parsis told me that the majority of Parsis had been unhappy with Independence. Older Parsis in particular remembered that the community was uncomfortable with Gandhi and with his insults to the British. The upper class, they said, may have been nationalist, but not the majority, which generally consisted of deeply committed Anglophiles. A middle-aged Parsi woman told this story: a friend of hers was taken by her father to watch the flag-crossing ceremony on August 15, 1947. As the Union Jack descended and the Indian tricolor rose, the father said to his adolescent daughter, "With that flag going down, law and order in this country have disappeared." And yet—certainly now—most Parsis remember their nationalist leaders with pride and honor. It is part of the attempt to readjust to the whims of history.

Parsi consciousness of the past should prepare us for some uneasiness in the present. In order to succeed under the conditions of colonial rule, Parsis attempted to behave and believe in a manner akin to the westernized, secularized, civilized English—at least, many Parsis presented themselves as doing so. To maximize their opportunities in the colonial context, they treated themselves as unlike their fellow countrymen; so successful was this strategy that they created a standard of entrepreneurial success hard to match in independent India. They were indeed Herodotus' adaptive Persians and it had served them well, but their adaptations proved less effective in the different postcolonial circumstances.

"Father-in-Law"

After a bath
Having cleansed his body
Of the plague of matter
And after his prayers,
Having cleansed his spirit
Of the plague of desire
He entered the fire temple

Bowing before the flame he touched the ground
And applied on his forehead camphor and wood ash
Which the Dastur had ladled out of the fire-bowl
Then he lit a butter-lamp—
Ahura Mazda had to be told that the flame of devotion
Had been kindled in his heart

Sitting down to his prayers
He meditated on *Asha,* the divine law
And *Vohu Mana, the Good Mind*
And having crushed Angra Mainyu the evil principle
And Ahriman, the devil,
He asked Ormuzd for favours,
The same favours which a warrior or peasant
Or a trader in skins and spices
Would have asked in the days of
Zohak or Zarathustra
Long life for his son
Long life for his daughter
And peace for his ancestors,
A ghost-wall of fungus faces
Receding into time
Like the avenue of sphinxes.

And he stepped out of the fire-temple
To discover
That his shoes had been stolen.[72]

WE ARE NOT
WHAT WE WERE

... 4 ...

In the 1920s and 1930s, when Gandhian mass politics took center stage, when many Indians had labeled the British as morally bankrupt, and when Hindu-Muslim politics made it clear that small minorities had no place at the center of power, a self-denigrating tone emerged in Parsi literature. It is a remarkable tone. Parsis had perhaps always argued about their identity. Turn-of-the-century complainers whined that Parsis had not gone as far as they should have, or had lost religion or tradition in the frenzy for success.[1] But thirty years later, when independence becomes an inevitability, both content and ethos change: why have we fallen from the top? Why are we not as we were? And as the complaints mount in intensity and continue on into the present, they circle around the decay of the almost-English attributes of the late nineteenth century. The modern Parsi is not truthful, his purity has made him genetically rotten, his charities have drowned his ambition, he is stuck in his traditional, nonprogressive ways, and—most intriguing—his sons are effeminate and incapable. He is the reverse of the almost-English gentleman.

Modern Parsi Distress

Many Indians are deeply critical of modern India. The problems of mass poverty and political corruption seem intractable and overwhelming. Popular distrust of elected officials now runs through all levels of society and across all group boundaries. The newspapers cry out ceaselessly about political deceit and manipulation; the rape of the poor by the rich; the lot of peasants enticed to leave the land for manual labor in the city and then tossed out like refuse when the construction job is done; the heroin addicts encouraged to sell their kidneys for cash to maintain their habit; the government officials who invent fictitious relatives in order to claim compensation in the settlement of the largest factory-based accident in history. There is much to fear, much to attack, much to argue over.

Parsi self-criticism is not like the general criticism of India by Indians. It speaks of the moral failure of the criticizer's own kin, the failure of sons and fathers as well as the failure of distant political leaders. It is personal and apologetic. We are not what we were, people will say. There is a sense in this discourse that the community has lost direction, lost steam, that the young men can no longer function effectively and in any event no longer care, that the community is dying and decrepit and has long since passed its zenith. Parsis say that the community no longer has moral integrity, that Parsis will lie and steal. In this discourse priests are accused of smoking—smoking, as a casual defilement of fire, is in theory absolutely unacceptable to Parsis—and young men are suspected of homosexuality and impotence. And most of these criticisms seem linked to talk of the community's downfall and of a past utopia from which the present has declined.

"We have fallen from the top," "the prestige and the vitality of the community have gone"—these themes of decline and deterioration, of something being wrong with the Parsis and certainly with their supposed pre-eminence came up again and again in my conversations with Parsis. Most Parsis with whom I spoke—young, old, male, female, rich, poor—remarked on community decline. It was also clear to me that this was a shameful topic, at least when displayed in public to non-Parsis: a Parsi friend who wrote a letter of complaint about the community to the *Times of India* was sharply chastised for her choice of publication venue. Another example: the BBC had produced a documentary about the community which I knew to be widely condemned by Parsis as inaccurate, misleading, and disrespectful. When I finally viewed it I was taken aback, because the filmmaker had simply recorded the kind of remarks—we are not what we were, our young women do not want to marry our young men, our community is dying—that I took to be routine in conversation with Parsis. The community was distressed, several Parsis remarked to me, because the film was shown internationally. Yet the letters-to-the-editors columns published far worse condemnations regularly in *Parsiana* and in the weekly Parsi column of the *Bombay Samachar*. The corollary to the shame seemed to be a vehement denial that anything is wrong at all, and if it was, it should not be mentioned in public.

The discourse of critique came from vociferous busybodies and alienated cynics—but also from happy-go-lucky adults. Parsis spoke to me about the sense of "something wrong" in many different ways and with many different intensities, as the metaphors of decay and displacement appear in different ways in Parsi literature. There were those who trashed the community brutally and those who casually dropped comments like, "oh, he's one of the Parsis who thinks the British forgot to take him with them." Individuals are as idiosyncratic in their accounts of the community as they are in their choice of profession, partners, and daily activities.

Not every Parsi voiced criticism, and not all the time, and there still remained a vibrant, cheerful pride in the community and particularly in its past. Nevertheless, these critical opinions were entrenched enough and similar enough to persuade me that they were symbolic markers, symbolic self-descriptors that were widely shared at least within the Bombay community, and were often articulated by Parsis when they spoke privately with me about the community (this was not the discourse of after-dinner speeches).[2] I did spend most of my time with the upper half of the community—the same socioeconomic group that would have been most responsible for the nineteenth-century quotations—but I heard these critical comments from Parsis in every tier of community life. One of the more poignant moments for me came in watching a family argument between a mother in her sixties and a daughter half her age. The daughter had been irritatedly dismissing the community's relevance, saying that it was in decline from the past. The mother stood by the table, clutching the back of the chair, saying "we *have* got, we *have* got" (meaning, we *do* have men in our current community of equal status to those in the past)—but with obvious distress on her face and unable to give convincing details. This is not to say that the young are more critical than their seniors; if anything, the reverse is true. Yet the mother's pain did accurately represent the community's emotional sensitivity to criticism.

While there are very real problems facing the Bombay Parsis

community, many of these criticisms are not realistic. To be sure, I cannot demonstrate that most young Parsi men are neither gay, nor pathetic, nor impotent. I cannot prove historically that most Parsis are more or less as truthful as they were a hundred years ago. In fact I cannot even imagine how one might be reasonably expected to carry out the proof for such an assertion or its opposite. All that I can suggest is that it violates my commonsensical interpretation of the Parsi social world to describe the majority of young Parsi men as homosexual, impotent, or pathetic (terms that are used as synonyms) and to dismiss the community as no longer truthful. None of these claims is—in my eyes—in any obvious way connected with the Parsis I met. I can (and later, do) point to assertions which are contradicted by available statistical evidence, and I can also claim, following statistics presented in an earlier chapter, that economically the average Parsi is probably at least as well off today as his forefather was a hundred years ago. Furthermore, while the relative social status of the community as a whole may have fallen, there is still a remarkable number of politically, economically, artistically, and socially visible Parsis.

It seems to me that the anthropological task is to wonder whether there is not some possible cultural explanation for this self-criticism. And while most of the critical remarks invoke claims which are not clearly realistic, they are clearly related to the nineteenth-century construction of the Parsi as an almost-English gentleman. In fact, to an outsider's eyes—at least to this one's—the criticism constructs the modern Parsi—particularly the young Parsi man—as the inverted image of that glorious figure. What seems to have happened is that by the end of the nineteenth century the Parsi mapping of what it was to be a good Parsi—the cultural model, complex prototype, or schema—had shifted in ways exemplified by Karaka's *History*. Few Parsis would have matched this ideal, as few Americans in the Depression have ever exemplified the characteristics of Horatio Alger, but the Parsi experience was such that the ideal could evoke the possibility of realism. The ideal Parsi was a very successful man whose truthfulness backed his commercial authority, whose pure Iranian blood guaranteed his superiority to native Indians, whose rational progressiveness demonstrated his achievement in civilization relative to other communities, and whose general characteristics made him as much of an English gentleman as it was possible to be. Then, as the external political and economic hierarchy shifted—the British left and other communities achieved political and economic dominance—it became difficult for Parsis to match themselves to their cultural model. Their response seems to have been to criticize their contemporaries and turn for validation to the memory of the now utopian days when the model seemed at least rhetorically persuasive. Thus departing from the observation that Parsis are no longer commercially and politically powerful, they conclude that therefore they must not be truthful; their purity must be suspect; their progressive rationality questioned; they must not, indeed, be manly gentlemen.

Underlying this inversion is what I will call the trope of decay. Throughout the myriad of specific, particular complaints about the community there is a potent association of purity, blood, and moral goodness which is very Indian, but with a Parsi slant. (In this context the shared parentage of both Vedic and Zoroastrian religious idioms should be recalled.) And all of this malaise conveys a sense that this vital core has begun to rot. Some of the complaints are that corruption comes from without, that it is the corrupt surroundings of Hindu-Muslim India that are causing the amalgam to decay; more of them suggest that the dying core itself spreads the rot. But all of the niggling worries and angry attacks agree that there is corruption; that Parsi purity is being polluted; that Parsi blood is going bad; that the moral fibre of the community is putrefying. And while the complaints sometimes mention these themes directly, it seemed to me that it was more that the criticism circled around and around this tangibly existential fear.[3]

Ethnographic Vignette

"If you write one thing in your book," my Californian Parsi friend told me, "you must write that the community is destroying itself by all this quarrelling, by not helping one another. You must write that the fruit rots from within." Rustom was born in India and his children were born in India, but like many Zoroastrians he has resettled in the America. Parsis call him Irani.[4] His grandparents came in a wave of Iranian Zoroastrians who emigrated to India around the turn of the century.[5] Many of them became restauranteurs, purchasing the small, lucrative tea-shops that line southern Bombay's main artery. The tea-shop fare is rarely expensive so the shops are always crowded, and above the people, over the door or in the corner, will hang a picture of Zarathustra gazing Christ-like at the heavens, a wilting garland around the frame.[6]

Parsis tend to look down on Iranis: the Iranis tend not to value education and so-called culture—western music, literature, the arts—as highly as the Parsis, and they lack the distinguished history of the Indian community. To Parsis Iranis seem rather crude: to Iranis Parsis seem aloof and self-conscious, stiff and not so fun-loving. There are distinct cultural differences between the two communities. One week, for example, I went to both an Irani wedding and a Parsi *navjote,* both parties of several hundred attended primarily by their own communities. At the Irani wedding there was less gold jewelry than at the Parsi *navjote,* and none of the Chinese-embroidered saris, now worth a small fortune, that Parsis acquired in eighteenth- and nineteenth-century trade with China. More liquor was consumed and much more Gujarati spoken at the Irani wedding; English tends to predominate at elite Parsi functions. I was most impressed by the differences in the dancing. At the Irani wedding there was a good deal of dancing: but it was the men who danced, a great clump of them, to *lambada* music—I was told that they were drunk—while the women watched. At the Parsi *navjote* few people danced, but those that did danced in couples.[7]

Both Parsis and Iranis will tell you that they are one community, that Parsi marries Irani, that their shared religion is the most powerful of bonds. But the overtones of mutual hesitation remain.[8] And one of the real differences between the two is their attitude to their own communities. From the Irani side, many perceive their community as flourishing. These small restaurants are extremely profitable, and many Iranis own farms and businesses outside Bombay as well.[9] Parsis, they say, do not work with their hands as Iranis do, and they no longer have the determination of their forefathers. Look at their marriages. Iranis marry and usually marry young (in their early twenties), and then they have children. Parsis, a Bombay Irani told me, have no more sex drive, no more business sense. "They are too effete to dirty their hands with real work. They have lost the adventurous spirit and enterprise that made them potent. They have lost their virility. They have been weakened by their long time on Indian soil, by their intermarriage with Hindus. They can't even have children any more." We Iranis, he said, are the ones who thrive.

The Particulars of the Criticism

To my mind, the most interesting complaint among the Bombay Parsis is that the young men are inadequate. Today's Parsi boys—the terms "boy" and "girl" are used of young adults until their mid-thirties—have lost the manliness of their forbears, at least in what I will call the trope of decay. They are presented as spineless, unambitious, and—in some descriptions—impotent. The standard colony-raised boy, in the stereotype, wants enough money for movies and a motorbike. He wants an easy life and a secure life, enough money not to worry but not so much responsibility that he has to think. Yes, an important lawyer sadly nodded in his air-conditioned office, the community is demoralized, the spirit has gone out of the boys. They want security; maybe they always wanted security, but in the Raj there were fewer risks. Now the power the Parsis had in the Raj has passed them by, he said, and the entrepreneurial zest has gone out of the community.

I spent some of my second visit to India casually asking Parsis if this criticism of the young men had any truth. I was disconcerted by the frequency with which Parsis confidently affirmed it. This vision of spineless young men is by no means confined to letter-to-the-editor writers and frustrated single women. It is as widespread and ingrained as the account of community failure; indeed it is part of that account, used to explain why the community will no longer reach great heights. Most Parsis, particularly if they were middle-aged or older, said yes, that it was true; there were of course the dynamic boys, but such boys always emigrated to America. Several young men affirmed the validity of the stereotype (for other young men) and young women went to some lengths to explain its appropriateness. Yes, a friend said, she thought that generally the stereotype held—and yet, she said, somewhat surprised at herself, when she thought of the individuals she knew, the stereotype did not seem to fit them. Sometimes other women made similar remarks: there was so-and-so, he was a real mama's boy, but *their* friends were not like that. Others were quite certain that the stereotype held more often than not. "I never date Parsi boys" one Parsi teenager told me. "They're so effeminate. Didn't you know that lots of Parsi boys are gay?"

Few men referred to young Parsi men as impotent, and relatively few women. When I heard that said I assumed it was a metaphor, a screen memory, as it were, for something else. Sometimes the metaphorical status of the remark was clear. For instance, I spent an afternoon with one of the community poets in his beautiful apartment in one of the once most elegant residential areas in Bombay, now still crowded with Parsis. "Time," he said, "stopped for the Parsis around 1950. Even a few years after Independence the community had confidence. Then everything broke down. Parsis are deskbound, while the rest of India is very physical. The Parsis have lost their physical sense of well being, their enthusiasm in all senses. They've become more and more schizoid," he said, "some of them throwing themselves into activity, others withering away." And then he used the term "impotent": "Parsis," he grimaced, "are emasculated by their women and by their society. Parsis have lost their nerve, they have [he quoted Auden] an ingrown virginity. They want to shut themselves away to protect themselves from a world that has emasculated them."[10]

One of my Parsi female friends—middle-aged and divorced—was convinced that Parsi men often suffered from a genuine problem. She knew many Parsi men who married and lost their interest in sex after the first or second child. It led one friend to divorce, another to have affairs, and so on. Why, she said, she knew a couple who were in trouble because the man wouldn't make love in Bombay, and then his parents sent them to Paris, and still nothing happened. (There is a characteristic assumption in the story that what is wrong in Bombay is more likely to be right in Europe.) This, she said, you do not hear about in the Hindu community. "That is why our population is declining." A geneticist (Undevia 1984) has suggested that the close inbreeding within the community has led to a lower standard of fertility for Parsi women, but no evidence is available concerning male fertility. In any event, real frustration with male sexuality—which is widely reported in India (Kakar 1989)—does not, to my knowledge, as readily contribute to a public discourse of inadequacy in other communities. My reason for treating Parsi discourse as a displacement of anxiety from some nonobvious source is that among the Parsis the idea of impotence is associated not only with Parsi men, but with the end of empire.

Rightly or wrongly, the criticism of the young boys is relentless, and universally affirmed in the area of education, particularly in contrast with the young women. Parsi boys, I was told many more than several times, are not as clever as Parsi girls. Parsi girls are hard-working, ambitious, and well-educated. Parsi boys are spineless and undriven. Parsi girls are independent, strong-minded, and determined. Parsi boys are dominated by their mothers until they reach adolescence, when all they want is a motorcycle and an easy life. Who blames the girls for not marrying them? A recent Bombay leaflet proclaims:

> This is what is happening with our boys and girls today.
>
> *Paradoxical as it may sound,* it may be stated again that, *the very higher standard of education* we are seeking to have for our youngsters, seems to have gone *by itself to militate* against our numerical strength.
>
> This happens to be particularly so with respect to our girls who having once obtained higher education are often found to *outstrip* our boys in many fields by securing posts oft times more lucrative than the boys by virtue of their somehow displaying *better Personality, Academic background, and better Application to work.* This happens to make the incompatibility between them and the boys noticeably pronounced.
>
> *They get quick jobs . . . But despondent*
>
> It is not just because of any disregard of their Parents or of their Religion that they unconcernedly choose to stray away [marry out], but it is because of desperation born of frustration for not finding enough number of Zoroastrian boys around the corner *and of a standard* despite being in quest of them, that they, if they do, do so. It is not without passing through a tormenting period of distressing thinking that they, if they do, do so.[11]

"Yes, it is very true" a bank clerk confided, "the girls work hard. The boys are pampered. Then they reach adolescence, and all they care for is movies and a motorbike. So they fail in school, it does not bother them." I attended a Youth Congress at which yet another eminent lawyer, in this community of eminent lawyers, addressed the audience of young adults. He urged them to marry inside the community, and then announced that some people said that the boys were not as achieving as the girls. And he said—it was remarkable that he felt the need to say this—"but I have personally inspected each application to work in my office, and I tell you, the boys are every bit as well-qualified as the girls."

The interesting aspect of all this is that the account of superior female education and earning power is false. Parsi women do not earn more, work more, and acquire more education than Parsi men, although it is certainly true that young Parsi women work more and are more highly educated than the average urban Indian woman. The figures obtained from a careful 1982 survey of the community (Karkal 1982) reveal that 44 percent of the Parsi men had gone to college or better, and 45 percent of the women, but fewer of the women had higher degrees than the men. The average income of all Parsi men was 1,455 rupees a month, of women 1,117 rupees; 33 percent of the men earned more than 2,000 rupees a month, but only 14 percent of the women.[12] The stereotype of the undriven, apathetic Parsi male and the high-earning, better-educated Parsi woman does not gain substance from these figures. This makes the stereotype all the more intriguing.

And what is striking is the sweep of the stereotype. I heard it very often. And the explanation offered for it is itself stereotyped: Parsis adopted English education very early and took full advantage of British patronage, but then other communities began to educate their young and drive ahead, and what can one do in the competition for so very few jobs? "We are now outnumbered in India," someone told me, a remarkable comment because the person spoke as if this were a new phenomenon. We are being swallowed, Parsis would lament. A remark made in 1941 is still characteristic:

> Today . . . [Parsis] are facing another crisis, and it is largely of their own making. This comes from the almost wholesale imitation of the manners of the West . . . The relatively much higher standard of life which the Parsis have adopted for themselves . . . has brought many social and moral evils in its train and has proved disastrous for the well being of the community . . . (Dadachanji 1941:xxiii–xxiv)

Most of the published accounts are versions of the conviction that westernization is the source of the community's woes. Bulsara's 1935 summary captures this aspect well:

> From the first quarter of the nineteenth century [Parsis] came out on top as a marked community among their sister communities in India,

and like the European Sahib the Parsis came to be generally looked upon as addressed by the proud and apparently gratifying appellation of Sheth.

The Parsi mentality underwent a change and with that change and greater contact with the expensively living Europeans, their standard of living also rose considerably in comparison with their sister communities. They gradually developed a sense of pride regarding their status and vocations of life and by and by shunned certain occupations as beneath their dignity, also developing a certain amount of scorn for manual or so-called menial labour, unworthy of those called Sheths.

The above virtues and a higher standard of life did considerably help them for a time and were largely instrumental in the phenomenal rise of the Parsis in the latter half of the nineteenth century, both in economic prosperity and general education and culture. When the other communities began to awake and come marching on along lines similar to those the Parsis had traversed, the Parsis gradually failed to keep pace with the others in their relative cultural advancement, social solidarity, closer organization and individual efficiency. The sudden spurt of advance and prosperity seems to have lulled them into a false security and superiority, which cannot be maintained without active and intelligent efforts and constant individual and communal betterment.

Besides, during the time of their general prosperity the poor and middle classes, by a natural law of infiltration, adopted without discrimination between the lasting and the ephemeral, the ways and modes of life of their richer brethren, which they would not be able to maintain under adverse circumstances. Times began to change, but neither our poorly devised education system, good for its days, nor our mode of life were modified in response. Our spirit of adventure and pioneering habits of commercial and industrial enterprise largely left us as we became more smug and comfortable in easy going services. Familial and social cohesion began to loosen and various other communities with their vastly outnumbering hordes began competing with the Parsis shoulder to shoulder until their almost monopolized positions were taken from them. Our position of advantage in the governmental machinery and the commercial world was lost, our standard of life, however, still remained as it was, and most of our false values cling to us like barnacles, until today the Parsis are increasingly finding themselves in awkward holes in various spheres of life-activities. (Bulsara 1935:376–77)

Again and again I heard variations on this theme: we got rich, we were for a time the richest community in India; because of our wealth our men became complacent and lazy and felt no need to adjust to changing times, and now we are burdened with our expensive lifestyle without the means to maintain it. It happened in Persia, it happened in Rome, and now it is happening to us: when men get rich they lose their drive and the culture crumbles.

Literary Vignette: *Jamasni Jilloo*

"Jamasni Jilloo" is one of the oldest and best loved Parsi columns, appearing regularly in *JameJamshed*. Jilloo is a silly, bossy woman; Jamas is a more knowledgeable but lazy man. The following is excerpted from the column of January 20, 1991:

> *Bomanji:* "In those days our young Parsi men were so well built. Unlike the thin, sickly looking young men of today, they did not flit aimlessly wearing t-shirts with meaningless slogans like 'I love you' and 'Kiss me quick.' They used to go to Pestonji Marker and to the Physical Culture Home at Gowalia Tank and did exercises to make their body fit and healthy. Our Parsi musclemen used to perform physical culture shows as well."
>
> *Jilloo:* "Well, talking of these old times tales reminds me of what I had read in the papers a few days ago. It seems that at the Alalampur airport, a muscled body builder pulled a 28-ton Boeing with his hair, much to the amazement of the audience."
>
> *Baimai:* "An entire plane, merely with hair on his head? Did you hear that Bamanu dear? Would you be able to do that?"
>
> *Jamas:* "But how could he pull anything with his hair, when he has none on his head?"
>
> *Bomanji:* "You are talking of these men of modern times. But our Parsi musclemen were no less. In the olden days, our Parsi 'pahelwan' Tehmurasp Sarkari would tear a thick telephone directory to pieces merely with his bare hands."
>
> *Jilloo and Bamai:* "Truly those were the days and those were the men!"[13]

Even more intriguing is that the contemporary complaints (the ones I heard in 1987–1988 and 1990) concern the failure of the Parsi youth to be as aggressive and competitive as the Hindus. In the literature and in the discourse community failure is not ascribed to the inadequacy of the westernized model so much as to the failure of the community-and particularly the young men—to live up to the drive of the men in the model, to emulate their manliness. The boys, I heard many Parsis say, are used to comfort, which the Hindus are not. The Parsi boys, being used to comfort, will not venture into unknown territory and they will not take risks the way Hindu boys will. They want boring white collar jobs which will be secure but will never make them wealthy or powerful. They won't even leave Bombay for better opportunities outside, as the Hindu boys do (although many are clearly leaving India, this criticism is launched against those who want to remain in Bombay if they do remain in India). They have no *danda*, none of the entrepreneurial drive the Hindu boys have.

One of the most common criticisms by Parsis about Parsis is that Parsis live in the past and so are ineffectual in the present. This was the point of *Doongaji House*—as a middle-aged female journalist explained, the novel is a good representation of this community, which enforces old values, lives in the past, and perceives the men as ineffectual and the women as gutsy and smart—and also of many of the stories by Rohinton Mistry. Another friend explained the young men's supposed impotence directly by the Parsis' refusal to engage with the present. "The Parsi man came up the hard way. But what is he today? Today he is—out of place. Out of pace with the times around him. He is stuck. They still talk about the British. They're stuck in the past, they haven't come to terms with the present. And they want to believe that the values of those days are superior to the values of today and so they cannot get anything done." A housewife told a *Parsiana* reporter in 1974: "in British times, Parsis were the number one community. Now the English have lost their position as a world power, as we have lost ours as a community. During these times Parsis had initiative, integrity, grit and go. They were more educated, and enterprising—went out of Bombay and did things. Today they live on past glory, on their grandfather's money. Parsi youths want too much entertainment, and an easy life. They want soft jobs . . . Parsis have lost their business sense."[14] The cream of the community men, one young woman said, always goes overseas. That is why the women don't marry. In short, the British have declined, we have declined, and somehow the world has changed for people like us.

So the Parsi men do not compete, and the aggressive Hindu male is taking their business away, and it is more or less the Parsis' own fault—so goes the cultural configuration. At different points in recent decades Parsis have argued that places be reserved for them in medical schools, technological institutes, and so forth—as is the case for the so-called "backward castes." There has been a great deal of community conflict about this demand: when it is made, the explicit argument is that Parsi men cannot succeed in an open competition against Hindu men, and it is not right that India should allow this remarkable minority to perish. For all the enthusiasm for the ambitious women, not a single Parsi suggested to me that those women would restore the community's honor. This seems to be a man's obligation: "It is the boys who can lift up the community; neither the girls nor their elders. It is the boys who have the energy, the potentialities, intellectual and physical, to move mountains if only knowledge is poured into their brain cells today" (quoted from the Suntook pamphlet cited above).

In 1990 a young Parsi filmmaker released a film about a Parsi household (*Percy,* based on a story by Cyrus Mistry). Almost the entire community—I met two exceptions—hated the film. It portrayed a young, dependent boy, dominated by his mother, too shy to ask women out and too weak to defend himself from the Hindu bully whose dishonesty he reports to his boss. Why film such a story, the Parsis asked? Why not film the Tatas, the Godrejs, Dadabhai Naoroji, the Parsis who helped to give India her greatness? "There are so few films on the Parsis," a middle-class Parsi mother remarked. "Yes, there are some mama's boys in the community, but not all the boys are like that. So if you portray the community, why show that? We have had so many great people in the community, it has done such good. They should make a film about them." "They will laugh at us," another, more elderly Parsi remarked. There was, inevitably, a letter in *Parsiana* that reflects accurately the tone and content of the criticism I heard: "Does the Parsi community comprise only of individuals like Percy and his mother? Don't we have a better class of people? . . . Why not show that music changed Percy's life and he threw off his shackles, stopped being a mama's boy and became a new man? He could have inspired the youth."[15] Few Parsis seemed to view the film without conceptualizing the theme as a judgment on the community for all the world to see. "Parsis," another friend said when I was talking about the film's reception, "have lost the ability to laugh at themselves. All those years of Adi Marzban's humor, when they split their sides laughing at the Parsi idiocies he ridiculed, and now they can't see these films as artistic products in their own right. The community is very insecure." But the film had depicted the entrenched stereotype. The filmmaker told me that Parsis hated his film because it cut too close to the bone. A reviewer exclaimed: "Pervez Meherwanji had managed to create the perfect Parsi ambience—the house with the four-poster bed and round marble table, the good-for-nothing colony *chokras* [boys] hanging out all day, the morning and night *kusti* prayers, the *sukhad-loban* [sandalwood and incense], the character—everything was just right."[16]

Cinematic Vignette: *Percy*

This is a representative section of the story which became the basis of the filmscript, as printed in the magazine *Bombay:*

"You'll splash hot oil on yourself, you ninny. Don't even try!" she had brushed him aside, once when he had put the pan on to try and make his own breakfast. "And how much oil! *Matere mua,* you've finished half my tin! Do you know how much this one tin costs now?" She bullied him too much, she sat on his head. He knew it. Sometimes in his heart, he rebelled against her tyranny, her strict routines. But he never spoke his resentment. It was better to be obedient, if you were a duffer. And Percy had had a long training in servility. Maybe he could manage on his own, better than she thought he could. But he wasn't sure. He had never been without her, and the thought had never occurred to him that he might some day.

Half an hour later, Percy was getting dressed to leave for office, when he discovered that there was not a single button left on the fly of his trousers. His other two pairs were with the dhobi.

"Mumma!" he called out to Banubai in his fluty, quavering voice. "Mumma, *all* my buttons are gone. Not one left. Stitch me some now, will you? How can I go like this?"

"My eyes don't work so good anymore. Haven't I told you, start doing things with your own hands now. How much can one person do? I have but two hands," Banubai harangued her son. "If something happens tomorrow and I become supine, God forbid, what will become of you? . . . Give, give . . . Bring the needle and thread. And my specs."

The short, wiry Banubai was 68, and very active still. Holding the needle within an inch of her nose, she threaded it skillfully, at first try. Then, bending over the trousers, she muttered under her breath, softly but audibly, "Where will I find you a wife? Who will marry you, a chap like you? . . ."

And Percy, who was standing beside her in his shirt and his shoes, with a towel wrapped around his midriff, declared, "I don't *want* anyone, Mumma, I don't want! I'll stay here with you. You can look after me better than any wife."

"*Ja, ja gadhera!* Show some sign of brains when you open your mouth," Banubai shouted at him; but it was playful ire, and a half-smile diffused her grouch of concentration.[17]

◆　◆　◆

Let me turn for a moment to the first wave of community criticism, because it captures the image of the corruption out of which the effeminacy supposedly grows. "There seems to be a feeling, however, in certain quarters that the community has reached or passed its zenith" (Markham 1932:xi). One 1933 report explains that the Parsi birthrate had declined, that insanity was on the increase, that unemployment had risen, and that even literacy seemed on the decline.[18] The author quotes one Dr. Moos on "the steady fall of the prestige of the community" (1932:45). In 1935, Bulsara speaks of "the alarming problem of growing economic misery and the physical, intellectual and spiritual impoverishment of an increasing section of the community" (1935:330). In 1940, Desai asks, "where have the great men of the last two centuries gone? Are the Parsis deteriorating? How often that question is dinned into our ears and how often it is as vehemently affirmed as denied!" (1940:4,49). And in 1945: "the Parsi was a product of culture, tradition, civilization, religion, temperance, tolerance and other gainful virtues. Today this coherent life appears to be disintegrating" (1945:2). Or a 1937 comment: "I say, in Education the Parsis were the first and foremost in India. How then came the decay, when and where from, it is necessary to know . . . Ye sons of Rustom, where are those charms of yours ancestors that are to this day being boasted of by lovers of Firdoosi?"[19]

The two most devastating critiques were published just around Independence. One is a book by P. A. Wadia entitled *Parsis Ere the Shadows Thicken,* published in 1949. It remarks that "a small community like ours can escape the process of decadence and degeneration, if it has the art of rejuvenating itself from within . . . Our community, however, seems to have exhausted by this time the chances of bringing to birth leaders who with courage and understanding can break the ever tightening grip of its dead past" (1949:138–139). This book presents the community as sinking into poverty and death. Its diagnosis is that Parsis glorify their past and cling to western values which are maladaptive for modern India. They are maladaptive because the western lifestyle is very expensive—and yet Parsis refuse to work to maintain that lifestyle; they feel that they can rely on community charity, which is easier than hard work. They have lost their entrepreneurial spark.

The other jeremiad is *A Community at the Cross Roads,* by S. F. Desai, published in 1948. The foreword asserts:

> The broad facts that emerge from any consideration of the problem are that a deterioration in the moral fibre of the community has set in. We have an idle rich class, contributing little to the general well-being of the community beyond indiscriminate charity, and our poor are getting poorer and losing their self-respect. There are many individuals and agencies at work amongst the poorer sections, but their efforts are disjointed and we can see no signs of a definite recovery.[20]

The work is primarily a treatise on population and the means to increase the number of Parsis since the Parsi reproductive rate is slowing down. The book sets out, however, a fairly comprehensive list of flaws:

> Socially, the Parsi of yesterday formed a small unit and lived a more rural than an urban life. Biologically, the Parsi was a healthy, happy being who believed in a settled, married life with an expanding family. Socio-biologically, the Parsi was a product of culture, tradition, civilization, religion, temperance, tolerance and other gainful virtues. Today this coherent life is disintegrating. The Parsi has left his usual expansive rural habitat in favour of an ever circumscribing urban life. The tendency is definitely disruptive and uncongenial to a well-knit social fabric. In such an atmosphere the human mind undergoes a severe strain. The spirit of give-and-take becomes displaced by dissension and discord; that of mutual accommodation . . . by the intolerance of a section; that of religious fervour by ridicule;

that of cultural preservation by an oblivious disposition; that of inventive ability by an unwitting superimposition of a misfit; that of pleasant relationship by a dislocation of amity; that of virtuous intent by a profanation; that of replacement of the dying genius by a wilful murder of the superior germplasm. A small community can ill afford to indulge in such unprofitable ways of living. Poverty is growing from year to year. A larger number is getting submerged from year to year. A section is growing up in parasitic existence and like every parasite is strangling the host it feeds on. A larger effort than hitherto is now warranted to cement the hiatus and build a superstructure that will endure. (1948:15)

For this author, the core problem is biological. "In its biological career the Parsi community has arrived at a cross road" (1948:73). He argues, essentially, that the breeding of like with like produces infertility (too much racial purity, in other words, is bad). In bold type he declares "that the decline in numbers is bound to be linked up with a decline in quality also" (1948:74). Desai's solution is, explicitly, eugenics: the deliberate improvement of the race by the breeding of the desirables and the sterilization of the undesirables. The notable point is the perception of community decay, the decline not only of numbers but of quality.

This distressing shift to despair in community self-perception is well recognized within the community. As a letter to the *Times of India* remarks in 1944, "Any sane member of the community who observes the present movements and doings of the Parsis will, in spite of all his inborn enthusiasm, affirm that they, as a community, are deteriorating not only physically but also morally, economically, as well as socially and politically . . . *For the last few years this communal depression of the Parsis is being openly admitted.*"[21] And in 1977 Dr Lovji Cama, second-prize winner in a competition entitled "The Lost Generation" (the reason for this intriguing name is not clear), remarked in his essay that "Anyone who reads *The History of the Parsis* [Karaka's 1884 text] cannot but be impressed by the confidence and the sense of identity and direction the community possessed. Yet, only seventy years later, we appear to have ground to a halt, our confidence lost, our numbers diminishing, our commitment to our religion weakened."[22] Self-confidence has given way to insecurity.

◆ ◆ ◆

Alongside this self-criticism of Parsis India itself is criticized on the grounds that it has changed without the British, and that Parsis cannot compete within the new India because they are people of integrity. Hindus, the argument runs, live in a less dichotomous world than the "people of the book," those of monotheistic faiths, and particularly Zoroastrians. "There are gods for everything, and the poles of right and wrong are just less far apart." As one Parsi writes, criticizing Hindu society and urging it to change: "The Hindu has a much greater capacity than most to live with ambivalence, and with the gaps between aspiration and achievement, between promise and performance, and between high moral aspiration and plain human selfishness" (Moddie 1968:77). Parsis, the argument went on, need integrity, honesty, directness, and Indian society does not have this character. Now the Hindus have taken over, the argument continued, bribery and fraud are rampant, and India is in decay. Parsis cannot succeed in a corrupted world.

Certainly it is true that to do business in Bombay one must walk around the very edges of the law. Governmental regulations tend to encourage people to take a flexible attitude towards compliance with the law. Income tax, for example, is severe, and income is regularly underreported.[23] Members of the Parsi community gave me the impression that Parsis actually did pay their taxes, although they tried legally to avoid heavy penalties for their wealth. The Contractors, for example, worried about how to pass their money to their children without great taxation, but the routes they chose were within the limits of the law.[24] The common feeling was that Parsis were more honest than most, and hence in this contemporary society, they suffered for that honesty. "I pay my taxes," a member of the CCI club told me as we had tea on its lawn, "and because I do they question me more. People laugh at you if you try to be honest here." Parsis often complained that they could not function in such a world, that they were incapable of living on the shadowy slopes of deception and dissimulation. This, they would say, is why they were not able to match our earlier business success. Parsis, they reiterate, are honest; they cannot live with the lies and bribery the businessman needs to survive. And so the new postcolonial Bombay bears in part the causal burden of Parsi decline.[25]

Yet the more important (and contradictory) thread of this self-criticism is that Parsis are no longer as truthful as they were, that the moral strength of the community has weakened. This is in part an account of truth-telling itself. An elderly women told me that the community had lost its moral integrity. Now, she said, people will lie and steal. "Up til now, truthfulness, honesty, have been predominant. But it is not as it used to be before." Their word, she said, now means nothing; the moral fibre of the community has decayed. Along with the famous story about all the banktellers in Bombay being Parsi in earlier years goes the disclaimer that "these days, of course, it is not like that, why there was a Parsi bankteller who just the other day . . ." And Parsis will recount Parsi misdeeds with a kind of prurient interest. It used to be—and still is—that used cars were sometimes advertised for sale in the *Times of India* with the phrase, "Parsi-owned." It used to mean that the car was in excellent condition; you would never be swindled. "But now, what does it mean to be Parsi these days?"[26]

Parsis also used the concept of truth to argue that the moral integrity of the community had lessened. A young woman explained: "These days, because there have been so many years of blind religion, Parsis see truth as what built up [as ritual], not as understanding the right way. For example, if I tell a Parsi that my grandma is sitting in the funeral prayer halls, after her bath, they will tell me that I can't touch her, that it's impure to give her sandalwood. I say that that's not truth. It's just a set of built up beliefs. These customs are only symbolic of what is really the truth, and that is to remain always clean and pure." The community, some Parsis would explain, had confused rituals with ethics, had as it were mistaken surface for depth. The concept of truth had changed, so that now the community assumed that truth and goodness lay in the superficial traits of the proper ritual action, rather than in ethical behavior. My elderly Parsi friend went on: "If you take a hundred Parsis and a hundred Hindus you will find more truthful and honest Parsis than the Hindus. That I am proud of—my community. But it is not as it used to be before. . . . That is because of changing times, and they have lost that; you see, they have become so mixed up with rituals and tradition that they have lost religion. As long as I wear a *sudreh-kusti,* as long as I do *jashan,* I'm a good person. Doesn't matter what I do afterwards. That recognition has gone."[27] The implicit argument is that Parsi money is made by honest hard work: whether because of contemporary Parsi character or the modern Bombay environment, less of that work is possible now.

Untruthfulness and effeminacy are construed as symptoms of the deeper rot, consequences but not causes of decay. The biological treatise quoted earlier cast its argument in the language of early-twentieth-century eugenics, but its emotional reverberation was far more profound. The well-established worry is that "racial purity" has produced an inbreeding which is destroying the community from within. Concern about this is so great that it is a piece of common knowledge about Parsis: more than one non-Parsi has asked me, upon hearing that I have spent time with the community, whether it is true that there is too much inbreeding. In 1932 one Parsi observer commented:

> The Parsis of India, the legitimate heirs of the Iranians and inheritors of the light of Iran and Iranian character, continued the noble traditions of their forefathers for over a millennium, earning their income by the sweat of their brow, obeying the moral and physical laws, and always giving away a good portion of their worldly wealth to the relief of the sick, the unhappy and the destitute. But today the balance appears to shift the other way. The Parsis themselves are getting poorer day by day. They do not seem to stand the strain of racial competition, physical exertion, and moral bankruptcy. One can but wholeheartedly wish that the Parsis possessed the Iranian glory even in a foreign land. Nothing but degeneration and demoralization appears to have set in among them.[28]

Literally, the race has been corrupted, its stock has gone bad, the strain has degenerated. In the late twentieth century the rhetoric of genetic decline continues, and has become a weapon in both sides of an intense debate about intermarriage. A comment about the Fourth World Zoroastrian Congress remarks:

> Mercifully, the fourth Congress, unlike the third, was spared home-spun theories on genetics. The constant reference to the virtues of thoroughbreds, both animals and humans, at the third congress, had led Aspi Modi, a business consultant, to the remark that he was not sure whether he was at a world congress or a stud farm.
>
> At the fourth Congress only one speaker from the floor began to wax eloquently on the merits of thoroughbred dogs. He was immediately contradicted by . . . Homi Sethna who remarked that genetically pariahs are the strongest dogs.[29]

I heard inbreeding debated on public podiums as a battle raged about whether non-Parsis married to Parsis should be allowed into the community, one side using thoroughbreds to press its advantage and the other bringing up the case of Egyptian royalty.

The orthodox position, rabidly against intermarriage, fervently asserts the religious (and economic) power of racial purity. Alien blood has already and will further corrupt the blood and the body; impurity (through the mixing of bodily substance) must be prevented lest more corruption occurs. One attack on conversion, for instance, includes a chapter entitled "The Supreme Importance of Genes and Lineage in the Religion" (R. A. Irani 1985:43–44). The argument is that unless purity is preserved, the genes will alter and the race will weaken or be debilitated out of existence. This point is reiterated in the following excerpts from letters to the editor:

> Is it not a fact that the period of peak glory in the history of the Parsis in India was attained in the last century after over a thousand years of not only in-breeding, but more precisely, cousin marriages? And then is it not obvious that the present downfall of the community is apparently due to an increasing tendency of bringing non-Parsi blood into the community?[30]
>
> Why are our Zoroastrians afraid to die out and not afraid to defile the very essence of Zoroastrianism? If need be let us die out—but let us die as true Zoroastrians.[31]

Genetic purity has made the community strong, they assert; it has given Parsis their particular characteristics. If the genes are distributed the characteristics will disappear. An official Parsi report submitted to a governmental body explains that adopted children cannot naively adopt their parents' religion.[32] The reason is that "each human has a certain wave-length of devotion towards his own Prophet and Religion: and that wave-length is embedded in his gene. This wave-length should not be disturbed either by conversion or a marriage mix-up. That is why Parsis are anxious to preserve their racial gene, which has the religious germ of Zarathustra embedded in it."[33] In this context, the oft-cited comparison of Parsis and Jews is pressed into service, mostly to defend the orthodox.[34]

The other side—usually elite, sophisticated Parsis—cries that inbreeding has reduced Parsi drive, sapped their fertility, and driven them mad.[35] "We need fresh blood" is a common refrain.[36] Once I spoke with the teenage son of a well-established professional about

his cousin's child, born "spastic." The cousin had married within
the family, and her father before her also within the family; now
that cousin was firmly convinced of the need for intermarriage, and
the teenager spoke with bitterness about his commitment never to
marry a Parsi. The genes were too close, there was too much risk,
he said.

It is a weird and telling argument—in India, where in-group
marriage is taken for granted—that in Parsi endogamy the blood
of the community should be said to fold in upon itself, implode,
and self-destruct. The blood is bad, there are strange diseases, the
blood has been corrupted—this worry is striking, shared even by
some of the orthodox in private. It was with great fanfare that a
geneticist discovered that there *is* something "wrong" with Parsi
blood, that Parsis carry an odd enzyme which renders some of them
violently allergic to aspirin. With similar fanfare, some years ago,
another geneticist announced that the community was genetically
more similar to Indians than to Iranians, a source of glee and
outrage, and yet perhaps another emblem of the ambivalence about
Parsiness and Indianness and their connection.

Along similar lines is the belief that inbreeding has spawned a
high incidence of mental illness among Parsis. The mad *bavaji* is a
common community stereotype, so common, indeed, that it enters
as the primary Parsi stereotype in Ruth Prawer Jhabvala's stories.[37]
A Parsi psychiatrist casually remarks in an article on the community: "I have often been asked by both Parsi and non-Parsi friends
whether there is a high incidence of mental illness in the Parsi
community" (Marfatia 1972:62). In the mid-1980s Shiavax Vakil,
once a trustee of the Parsi Panchayat and an active participant in
community debates, published a small booklet entitled *Parsis and
Conversion: An Objective Study,* in which he argues forcefully for
the need for conversion. He quotes from a study which suggests
that the incidence of mental illness in the Parsi community is the
highest as compared with other communities, and also from a
study which suggests that the community suffers more from cancer
than any other community in the world. He concludes: "we are,
compared to other communities, mentally and physically ill"—and
thus Parsis need to marry out to fortify their stock.[38]

The pro-intermarriage Parsis also launch against the community
the complaint that it is made up of stick-in-the-mud traditionalists.
"If a man refuses to change his thoughts and habits in the context

of his times, he stagnates and stagnation is death, biologically speaking."[39] The liberal wife of a liberal priest—she was also one of my greatest friends—wrote to the *Bombay Samachar:* "Custom, and some customs which have become traditions, are all man-made, suitable and important for the time and age. When the very time, age and the whole world changes, MAN himself changes, and the customs man made also change."[40] This woman was in her seventies, so evidently liberal distress was found within the whole community, from the younger to the eldest members. But it was particularly young adult Parsi women whose friends had married out, or who contemplated outmarriage themselves, who would—in the perennial fashion of the young—accuse the community of being traditionalists. One woman fumed to me about "close-minded priests" and exclaimed that if they didn't let her sister's children (from an intermarriage) enter the *agiary* (fire temple) she would build them one herself. What brings this conflict out of the eternal struggle of youth and old age is not only that young and old are to be found on both sides, but that both engage in a specific exchange about tradition itself. And, as I shall go on to argue in the next chapter, the construction of the argument is that those who argue that racial purity is good are vehemently against pro-gressive development and for traditional customs; those who argue for a progressive, liberal reform of the old traditions claim that racial purity is inherently suicidal. To my knowledge, the argument pitting one Parsi virtue against another and demanding that one choose between them is new in Parsi discourse in the twentieth century.

One could argue, I suppose, that this discussion of blood is simply a ploy in the more purely economic issues of intermarriage and access to community funds. But the controversy about charity, which by that logic would also be a purely economic issue, lands squarely on the issue of corruption-from-within, and while the debate over intermarriage (which the next chapter describes in more detail) is clearly figured in class terms, the debate over charity is not. Charity is also now, like racial purity, regarded as something which may have destroyed the community from within. It is harder to be a charitable Parsi donor now than it was in the past—there is simply less wealth around—and people fear that the rich cannot or will no longer give. Accompanying this worry is the pernicious and powerful notion that charity itself has undermined the community and sapped its strength. The not-so-implicit message is that what is best in the Parsis has contributed directly to their fall. When I visited a Parsi Panchayat (the central administrative unit) in Gujarat, for example, I was told in no uncertain terms that the problem with the community was that the young were lazy.[41] All they wanted to do was to sponge off the charities. Charity, I was told, has ruined them. There is no enterprise in the community, because everything was given free. You can see a Gujarati and a Parsi set up garages next to each other, the trustee told me. The Parsi will be given concessional rent and a grant yet his business will fail, while the Gujarati's prospers. Parsis, he told me, were pampered, and did not like to work with their hands. As a Parsi woman explained, the fear is that the Parsis have no *danda,* no money-making, deal-driving ambition to succeed in business. The literature is replete with these comments:

> [1948] Decades ago the Parsi community boasted of not having a single beggar in its ranks. Today that proud boast lies low. Apart from actual and professional beggary, we have before us a sorry spectacle of armies of economically hard-hit families asking for help from funds and philanthropic individuals. Whether these armies arise because of the prevalence of the dole system or whether the dole is there because of the armies is a moot point. But . . . the dole system is bad. (Desai 1948:8)

> [1955] A point always to be borne in mind is, the dole given to able-bodied unemployed persons, without making an effort to provide them with any suitable employment, is charity in the wrong direction and it has done more harm than good to this class of unemployed . . . The psychological factor . . . creates a vicious circle. (Sidhwa 1955:12)

> [1978] Prosperity of bygone days made Parsis soft and lacking in initiative, enterprise and hard work. With families largely dependent on charities, this has definitely contributed to increased pauperisation. Self-respecting families, who would otherwise have refrained from asking for help have become accustomed to systematic begging.[42]

It is probably an exaggeration to say that charity relief is responsible for financial hardship in the community, and there is no hard evidence that Parsis are lazy, relative to other communities. It does seem to be true that the charities are organized poorly and that they do not operate to provide incentives for those in need. A detailed thesis on the charities concludes:

> With an increasing amount of charity and relief, the number of those in real or apparent need has gone on steadily increasing. The multiplication of Trusts and profuse private benevolence without any attempts for years to coordinate their efforts has lead not only to wastage and overlapping of funds but to beneficiaries seeking unethical ways of retaining relief. The complete isolation and non-cooperation among charitable trusts is responsible for this. The most striking phenomenon is that almost all relief is mechanized mass treatment of distress today, and there is a shortage of constructive developmental or preventive welfare work of any kind, substituting or supplementing the disbursement of relief and doles. (Mobedji 1987:103)

The author of the report condemned those who ran the trusts for what she perceived to be their negligence. They are so dole-oriented, she said, that they do not realize how doles might rob the community of its initiative and will to work. Now even youngsters go to trusts and cry their hearts out, she said; and because there is no central coordination between the trusts, although there is supposed to be, these people sometimes get funded from more than one trust. So they see no reason to strike out on their own. A 1935 report asserts that "Charity relief in such cases *acts as a dope* . . . The possibility of an all too easy access to charity relief not so well organized as it ought to be, and *the temptation of easy money* have also led to the encouragement, creation or perpetuation of *a beggar mentality* and *a beggar class* in a certain section of the community."[43] The charity which embodied the business prominence of the nineteenth-century Parsis is now perceived to have beggared them in the twentieth century.

It is important to bear in mind how wide and capacious this charitable net is. The Bombay Parsi Panchayat, founded in the 1670s, is the central administrative unit regulating community behavior. Other community centers have died out, but the Parsi Panchayat became a powerful body and, by the end of the nineteenth-century, the warden of considerable community wealth.[44] The Panchayat controls assets of 10 crores rupees, or 100,000,000 rupees, which produce a disposable annual income of 15,000,000 rupees (about $1,000,000) for a community of 60,000.[45] There are

Parsi hospitals, Parsi clinics, Parsi schools, Parsi housing coopera-
tives all founded on a charitable basis. As one speaker remarked
at the 1990 Youth Congress in Hyderabad:

> At the outset, I would like each of you to look back and ponder upon
> how much of our lives have been benefitted by the generous vision
> and philanthropic legacy left to us by our forefathers. Speaking for
> myself, I was born in a Parsi hospital, lived for several years in a
> beautifully maintained Parsi *baag,* went to a Parsi school and lastly,
> my M.S.W. [Master of Social Work] thesis was sponsored by a couple
> of Parsi trusts. At this juncture, I ask myself as we all should, what
> will my contribution be, in thought, word and deed—especially
> deed—to carry forth this legacy for the well-being of our future
> generations.[46]

Parsi charity is truly remarkable and a great testimony to nineteenth-century Parsi achievement, which makes it all the more
striking that some Parsis point to it as one of the causes of their
decline.

Ethnographic Vignette

I met Cyrus and Banu as I wandered through one of the poorer
Tardeo colonies, camera in hand, trying to find an elusive but
reportedly beautiful *agiary.* An old couple watched me from behind
a barred window, and I stopped to ask directions. He wore a
skullcap and a thinning *sudreh,* she was in a Parsi dress. We fell to
chatting, and they invited me inside. They seemed overjoyed to
have met me, particularly the second time I returned. They hugged
me, and exclaimed and gave me presents and sat me down to tea
with home-baked goodies.

They lived in the typical two-room charity flat, the outer room
with four dark wood wardrobes, with a fourposter bed, two tables,
and several chairs; there is little room to move. A battery-operated
clock hangs on the wall, a present from their son. Banu sometimes
sat in the front entrance, by the window, with her foot-operated
Singer sewing machine; from that window she could see the whole
length of the street. The kitchen, adjacent to the outer room, has
two high-standing bunsen burners, and behind it is a small, light-
filled bedroom in pink. Photographs of the relatives hang everywhere: in the outer room, in the inner room, inside the wardrobe

doors. The second son still lives with them, a short thin man in his twenties. He came in once at the end of one of our teas. Cyrus introduced him and then said accusingly, "he has failed to take my advice. He studied up to the thirteenth standard, for B.Comm. [Bachelor of Commerce], and then he failed, and I told him to try again. But he will not, and now he has a bad job." The son had turned away by this time. It was not the only time Cyrus shamed his son in front of me.

Banu was born in the late thirties in Bombay, at the Parsi Lying In Hospital, the daughter of Banubai and Aspandiar (her father was a priest). Banu, like her mother, stayed in the hospital for 41 days after giving birth, during this time she could not be touched. Her mother died when she was only five, and she was sent to Surat to live with her aunt and uncle, also a priest. Her father died seven years later. She returned to Bombay when she was fifteen, and married Cyrus seven years later. Cyrus had lived as a child on the floor above their present apartment. His father was a clerk in a textile company. Cyrus studied up to the sixth standard—changing schools so that, as his father's insistence, he could study Persian as a second language—and left school in 1945. I asked him what he had thought of the approaching Independence. "Even now I prefer the British Rule. It was a Golden Rule, now we have less than an iron rule. I pray to the almighty that we might live to see another rule. All these politicians are *chors* [thieves], they are bad." He was given a job in a kind of accountancy because he said, they wanted Parsis for the job because Parsis were supposed to be honest. "Not any more," Cyrus fumed.

Cyrus and Banu had two sons. Cyrus said: "Once someone told me that if I prayed the *Atash Niyash* properly and sincerely, then God will grant that any wish of yours will be fulfilled."[47] He remembers praying that prayer and asking for sons. They had sons, he said. "But look at them now, they are useless to me." Both sons went to excellent Parsi-founded schools, and the eldest was particularly clever and a very good sportsman. Now he is employed at the same firm that his father worked in for thirty-one years, but as a computer operator, a better job; and he gets more than the salary Cyrus got after his thirty-one years with the company.

But in 1984 this son married a South Indian—not only a non-Parsi, but a dark-skinned woman. His parents did not attend the wedding and have nothing more to do with him. "My boss said, you must go to the wedding and give you son your blessing. My foot, I said. Once my son even brought her to the office for my blessing. And I said, my foot." He found out about his son's interest in this outsider when his office mates started "making mischief" with him, saying that his son will marry a non-Parsi.

> I thought they were teasing. Then I came to know the story. I called my son, and he came that night. I explained so much, how the marriage would be wrong, and then Mr. Dubash, you met Mr. Dubash, came and talked to him, and then I took him to my boss, my boss's wife, and they all explained, so many people. I said, give me six months, I will find you a wife, any kind of wife you want. And he said no, and then he said, if you break my marriage I will murder you. And so I took this knife [Cyrus reached for the kitchen knife] and I said, take this knife and murder me now, you are no son of mine.

Now, they do not speak. "It [the marriage] cannot last, how can it last? There will be differences in food, in faith, in everything." Apparently the wife's uncle and father also work in the same firm as Cyrus and his son.

"My second son is also useless," he went on to say. "He is going to RTI (the Ratan Tata Institute). I know he leaves work at 5:30 but he only comes here by 9:00, and when I ask him why so late, he gets mad and leaves. And he earns only 750 rupees a month, with breakfast, tea, and lunch. It is nothing. He failed his B.Comm. and he will not retake." At this point in the conversation Cyrus pulled out a poem tacked to his wardrobe. In translation, it reads in part:

> You may forget everything else
>   never forget your parents
> Innumerable are the things they have done for you
>   don't forget that
> The stones of the earth were worshipped by them
>   only then were you born
> The hearts of these good people
>   never crush them

Both his sons, to Cyrus, are destroying their ancestry and insulting their parents. One humiliates him by marrying out—not only a non-Parsi, but a dark-skinned woman, which throughout India is a stain upon the family. The other humiliates him in a more Parsi, less Indian, manner: he fails to achieve, and Cyrus suspects him of being immoral. This Gujarati poem, with its many resonances for the tensions in the Parsi family, brought tears to the eyes of the woman who read over my translation with me.

Cyrus, at 62, has been retired for two years. Banu still works, the kind of jobs that many of the poorer women in the *baags* take on. She does some packing for a firm, spins wool for *kusti*-weaving (the Panchayat supplies this wool at reduced cost) and bakes Parsi dishes like *karkaria* (a sweet fried wheaten cake), *bhagia* (a fried salty gram-flour-banana mixture), and then also *pillaus, biryanis, dhal, dhansak,* kabobs, *patrana macchli* (a Parsi fish dish), chutney balls, and much else. She also volunteers in several hospitals at least one day a week.

They are a very religious couple. Banu usually wears a scarf around her head and Cyrus wears the Parsi skullcap; religious Parsis are meant always to keep their head covered, but while turn-of-the-century photos show whole groups scarved and skull-capped, few modern Parsis follow this injunction. Cyrus explained to me that very religious Parsis also drink *nirang,* bull's urine, in the morning, but that this they did not do. Banu prays for fifteen minutes in the morning, fifteen minutes at night, the *kusti* prayers and perhaps some others. It is Cyrus who is the most devoted. He will pray for one, one-and-one-half hours on ordinary days, and up to three hours on an auspicious day. And now, in retirement, he attends almost every lecture on the religion that is offered: lectures by Khojeste Mistry, a western-trained dualist; by Adi Doctor and K. N. Dastoor, both esoteric kshnoomists; and by the orthodox Peshotan Peer. All of these gentlemen disapprove deeply and publicly of each other, but Cyrus enjoys all their talks.

When Cyrus retired, his pension funds yielded 250,000 rupees, a substantial sum, although not much if you estimate that he and his partner would each live another twenty years. But he spent about 75,000 rupees to realize a dream: for three weeks he and his wife visited Europe. The first time I met Cyrus and Banu, they pulled down the photo album to show me pictures of Banu against the Alps and Cyrus in Amsterdam. Cyrus loves to travel, and has seen the length and breadth of India. Another substantial sum (about 25,000 rupees) went to renovate the flat.

In retirement his days are simple. Cyrus drinks pure water when he rises and then stands on his head for several minutes, doing yoga like Nehru, he said. Then he drinks his tea and has breakfast. After breakfast he goes to the library to read the papers and then bathes and prays. Sometimes he goes to the fire temple. Then he has tea and returns to the library. At the end of the workday he meets several Parsis at the bus stop and they talk for an hour. He returns home by eight, says his prayers and eats his dinner, and reads the papers until bed. Sometimes he will visit his brother in the State Bank.

Cyrus does not think of himself as engaging in cultural critique when he discusses his second son. Yet when he describes the community, he focuses on the problem of the young men in a way that is very similar to the complaints he has of his own son. He thinks that intermarriage is a bad thing, a big problem, spurred in part by the need for housing and in part because Parsi boys aren't learning enough and the girls are learning too much. What aren't the boys learning? They roam here and there, they watch TV, they go to the movies, they don't have any drive, he says. Why do they act this way? Cyrus didn't know. But the community, he said, is in trouble. What to do? Still, as he says, "I am thankful to God that I took birth in the Parsi community." Parsi birth, he thinks, is the last birth in the karmic wheel, the highest birth, before one is released from the painful demands of reincarnation. Parsis are moderate, he says, and very neat and clean. They are honest, hardworking and charitable. "And we are jolly," he said. "We are good people."

◆ ◆ ◆

The temptation to blame others for our troubles, real or imagined, is profoundly human. Even when the criticism amounts to self-condemnation, self-blame at least gives to events the illusion of predictability and control. If only we had acted otherwise, we would not have had these consequences, and if only we had been wiser, we would have known. The belief that we can govern the events in which we live our lives, that we can be masters of our destinies, is one of the most valued human ideals. The rude factuality that we are tidepool dwellers subject to the moods of a vastly large and powerful ocean of historical particularities—these are uncomfortable truths which all our religions and psychologies teach us to deny. Parsis, as a community, made cultural choices which propelled them to the top of the political and economic world of late nineteenth-century Bombay. The tide flow of history has left them in a vastly different place from where they once were.

In vehemently deriding themselves, in tearing apart the fragile foundations of their self-congratulation, they are using a very ancient, very powerful, means to cope with suffering: to name despair by representing it. Parsis speak and behave not only as if something but someone were responsible for the pain, the humiliation, the embarrassment, as if the pain would go away if only their young men would get their act together, act more effectively, and persuade the women to marry them. These self-critical Parsis do not accept the accidents of history with clear-eyed resignation and humility. They act as if their suffering arose from identifiable faults which can, with time and wisdom, be righted. In attempting to identify those faults, however illusory and rooted in nineteenth-century culture these attempts may seem to us, they are doing what all people do in their struggle to come to terms with the vagaries of life: to assert that events can be mastered, that decisions can be implemented, and that we live lives that we have freely chosen.

UNCOMFORTABLE
REALITIES

$$\cdots \;\; 5 \;\; \cdots$$

There is a hard edge of reality to Parsi complaints. Parsis have been arguing for years, with trauma and ambivalence, about how to fix the boundary around their religious community. Whatever they decide and however long they argue, the disputes have made one thing brilliantly clear: something fundamental to the community's sense of itself has changed dramatically in the last fifty years, and the community has no shared moral vision about how to come to terms with it.

◆ ◆ ◆

In 1990 the most dramatic, emotionally laden event in the community was the death in a car accident of a young Parsi woman, Roxan Darshan Shah, and the question of whether she was or was not a true Parsi. She had married out of the community, as perhaps one in six Parsis do these days. But she was the daughter of a prominent family, she practiced the religion, and she had even married by a special marriage ceremony which legally asserted that she remained of the religion of her birth. Nevertheless, when her grieving father brought her body to the Towers of Silence, the caretakers—who called the Parsi Panchayat—told him to take it away. The abrupt finality of this decision, seemingly sanctioned from the top, and the compelling image of her father abandoned by his religion in the hour of his greatest need, shook the community badly.

Intense journalistic coverage continued for months. The *Bombay*

Samachar published, in an unusual move, a booklet of its articles and to-the-editor letters; *Parsiana* ran a front-page editorial, which I had never seen them do. There were committees and affidavits and meetings with hundreds of people. "Stop the *dokhmas* from being defiled" one orthodox meeting flyer read, printed in English on one side and Gujarati on the other. "How many of us are aware that it is only because of these consecrated, sacred institutions that a relatively [small] handful of Parsee Zoroastrians have survived and kept their separate identity for nearly twelve centuries?" I heard about this case constantly, over tea, over lunch, in scholarly gatherings, as people discussed strategy and urged me to see the issues as they saw them.

Unfortunately, one of the high-priests—on his way abroad—hurriedly sent off a letter of support to the Panchayat without realizing how public it might become: "I was very happy to learn that the Trustees refused to offer the Bungli facilities at Doongerwadi to the relatives of late Mrs. Roxan Darshan Shah."[1] The letter went on to explain that "to marry outside the fold is next to adultery . . . a child born in such a situation is considered to be illegitimate."[2] The letter was published, despite the priest's subsequently obvious embarrassment.[3] And a predictable letter to the editor articulated a popular response: "Now what manner of man is Dasturji? 'Very happy' about anything connected with the death of a vibrant youngster snatched away in a tragic accident? Not a word of sympathy; not an expression of regret. Is this Zoroastrianism? Does such a man deserve his title?"[4]

The invective grew increasingly shrill. The Panchayat began to consider taking legal statements from Parsi women in similar positions, who had married by this special civil marriage and were now agitating for what they took to be their rights. The orthodox were outraged by this sign of the Panchayat's liberal weakness. One of the spokesmen produced a pamphlet with these stinging words: "Dither and pusillanimity—the Bane of the B.P.P. [Bombay Parsi Panchayat] Trustees. In the last three of four decades, one weakness of the B.P.P. Trustees that has stood out is the gutlessness and a tendency to panic at the slightest turning of the worm, particularly if the worm happens to be a mere threat of a legal notice!"[5] And the tirade continued from other Parsis: "it was a crying shame that a Parsi should write such blasphemy"[6]; "I have always been nauseated by the oft-repeated comment heard when sanctimonious Parsis get together . . . How pure is our religion!"[7]

Why was this so heated? The Roxan case took to the extreme the question of whether a Parsi fundamentally changed through intermarriage. This was not the question of whether an outsider or even a child would be admitted within the fold; the issue was whether someone who was clearly a member of the community, and moreover continued to practice her religion as a member of the community, had somehow changed her very substance in marrying a non-Parsi, as if her birth had somehow become invalidated. And the question was sharply dramatized by the family it involved. Roxan's father was a well known doctor, very well respected in the community, known as a kindly and religious man. He was in many ways the paradigm of the good Parsi: highly educated, western-identified, sophisticated, charitable. One of his daughter's friends told me that if it had been anyone else, the community would have reacted differently. Roxan, she suggested, was too much of an ideal for the community to tolerate her intermarriage.

Here the tension arose between those who identified the community through its ethnicity, and those who identified it through its sophistication, upward mobility, and tolerance for change. It is tempting to argue that the liberals are the most privileged and the best educated; they are the ones most likely to have descended from the well-to-do nineteenth-century Parsis (class status is often reproduced) and the ones with the least to lose if the doors of the community are thrown open. They are also possibly the most likely to have outmarrying daughters, although there are no figures to confirm this.[8] Similarly, it is tempting to describe the orthodox as penny-pinching nonintellectuals who care more about access to Parsi charities and housing than about intangible ideas. There is some truth to these stereotypes. Generally, the more privileged a Parsi feels, the more liberal he or she is likely to be, just as the reformists of the Parsi past came from the elite. But there are some very wealthy, educated, committed Parsis who fervently oppose outmarriage, and some poor priestly families who support it. Nevertheless, the dilemma remains: are Parsis progressively Parsi-like, or biologically Parsi-pure? Sadly, they cannot now be both.

The conservative argument emphasized custom, and as they argued from history, they spoke in Gujarati, covered their heads, treated the priests like privileged authorities, and drew on the symbols of traditional religious authority. Much was made of a letter from seven high priests of Bombay and Gujarat:

> That question [of outmarriage] has come up in the past, and the leading *dasturs, mobeds* and common people of the community emphatically rejected it. Based on books on the religion, edicts, customs, tradition, strong reasons were presented to support them, all of which are in the records of you gentlemen.
>
> We once again inform you that sacred rules in the books, the customs and ceremonies of the religion accordingly state that after marriage the lady who had such a marriage [an outmarriage] cannot be a Parsi Zoroastrian and so cannot use any religious institutions or *dokhmas* . . .⁹

Many of the letters to the editor, in Gujarati or English, from priest or layperson, make similar assertions.¹⁰ Mixed in with this is the argument, from history, that biological impurity leads to weakness. "History testifies that mixed marriage was one of the main causes for the fall of the once mighty Sassanian empire. Do we want history to repeat itself?"¹¹ And religious purity cannot be maintained by the offending outsiders. As a high priest explained, "A woman marrying outside the community cannot observe the rules of purity as laid down by the Zoroastrian religion. She cannot perform ritual ablutions [*padyab kusti*] and do prayers [*farziyat* and *bandaj*] in a non-Zoroastrian environment. When she bears children of a non-Zoroastrian seed [*tokham*] and participates in Zoroastrian ceremonies, this woman does great damage to the Zoroastrian religion."¹² Such women, he implies, physically defile the Parsi community.¹³ The argument—elaborated particularly by those drawn to an esoteric interpretation of Zoroastrianism, *kshnoom*—is that religious prayers have to do with "vibrations," almost physical emanations. *Dokhmas* can purify bodies only if they have been prepared by certain ritual prayers which can only be performed on Zoroastrians. Thus the non-Parsi defiles the Parsi, and the most powerful of tools in the fight against evil is rendered useless. Zoroastrian prayers, whose aim is to purify, are rendered invalid by the non-Zoroastrian environment in which they are uttered.

On the other side, the liberals—and they were quite visible in the press—uniformly pressed for the need to change with the times. Customs are made for the times and do not define the people.

Dokhmenashini is just a method of disposal of the dead. In the past as well as our own times, it has changed and will keep on changing according to climate, circumstances and the laws of the land.[14]

As charity begins at home, it is now time to reexamine our customs and jettison them if they clash violently with the demands and aspirations of a changing world.[15]

When customs and traditions become the prime focus towards which the whole religion of the community is directed, when these are allowed to supersede the true religious precepts of the religion, then they become a serious threat to the true religious and spiritual development of the community.[16]

Rituals are customs. They have no power in themselves; they are chosen by the dictates of need and circumstance. When need and circumstance change they can also change, it is argued. It is horrifying, a wealthy woman remarked to me, that the community can be so backward.

It is true that at least some of the voiced concerns are rather more pragmatic—if our children intermarry will the Hindus take our flats?—although in my experience liberals tend to accuse conservatives of this fear more than conservatives seem to express it, and conservatives manipulate this fear amongst their followers. "The vocal majority is most concerned with the erosion of valuable assets," a liberal lawyer bitterly complained to me; "all this talk of racial purity is sugar-coating for the real thing." "There are three questions" a conservative speaker announced at a major community meeting.[17] "Do you want the community to die? Do you want the religion to disintegrate? Do you want your flats taken by non-Parsis?" But it is hard to believe that resources dominate the debate. Most of those who had married out by the Special Marriage Act (and all of those who had written to the Panchayat to request the future use of the *doongerwadi*) were well-to-do.[18] And the discourse about the mixing of the unmixable is angry. A lower-middle-class man asks pointedly: "Does a horse go with a camel? Does a dog go with a mouse? No." A remark from the floor at a lecture: "if you sow potatoes, you don't get cabbages. If we crossbreed, the intelligence may be there, but the morality always goes down." More than resources are relevant to the debate.

"One Parsi is an individual," a lawyer told me, "two create a controversy, three create chaos." Conflict is part of the community self-image, but this conflict seemed quite severe. Where does the debate now stand? Two community leaders told me that they thought that sixty percent of the community supported the Panchayat and thought it right that Roxan's body had been turned from the *doongerwadi*. Forty percent, they said, would have allowed it. Another man—the lawyer just quoted—remarked that seventy percent didn't care. Of those that did, he said, two thirds supported the Panchayat. But I very rarely met anyone who was actually indifferent to the issue of conversion and to the Panchayat's decision about the case of Roxan. I have documented most of the debate with published sources, but that is because the community cares enough to make me careful to cite all of my sources. In my experience, the lawyer was unduly cynical when he remarked that 70 percent of the community just didn't care.

• • •

The roots of the current conflict go back to the Raj, when the first attempts to violate ethnic purity in the name of reform took place. But they were few, and elite, and basically nonthreatening. The community remembers only one case, and the reformists won that one.

In 1903 Ranaji Dhadabhoy Tata, scion of the most respected, most adulated, most Parsi of Parsis, brought home a French bride, had her *navjote*[19] done, and then married her according to Zoroastrian rites.[20] Tata claimed that his wife had become a Parsi and professed the Zoroastrian faith, and that this entitled her to enter the fire temples and upon death to be taken to the Towers of Silence. The community became distraught. The more progressive (presumably also members of the elite, although there were elite detractors as well) supported him, the more conservative did not. In July 1903 a petition signed by 2,300 Parsis reached the Panchayat. Some weeks later there was another, signed by 769 Parsis (Desai 1977:13–14). A committee was appointed but it reached no resolution. In 1905 solicitors representing Tata along with a number of the community elite began a discussion about the convert's rights in the community.[21] Could she indeed enter Parsi Panchayat property? Could she draw on the community's charitable funds? This led to one of the most famous cases in Parsi history.[22]

The suit arose because the Panchayat, after some dithering, for-
bade the use of all their funds and properties—including the *agiaries* and *dokhmas*—by people who had not been born Parsi. The
cream of the elite then sued them.[23] They first contended that the
Panchayat Trustees were not properly appointed and had no rights
to make such decisions. Secondly, they argued that Zoroastrianism
positively enjoined conversion. The Trustees, then, were not only
illegal but incorrect. The Trustees, in return, argued that they were
carrying out the intentions of those who had founded the trusts
and established the properties, and that their intentions had been
that only Parsis should use them. And while the religion as
Zarathustra described it might seek converts, the community in
India had never done so, and so those who had given money could
not have included such converts in their concept of a Parsi.

In 1908 the High Court's judgment produced a conservative
compromise. The religion of Zoroastrianism does indeed enjoin
conversion, Judge Davar concluded—but then he distinguished a
Parsi from a Zoroastrian. A Parsi, he explained, was a direct
descendent of those who had come originally from Persia, and only
a Parsi was eligible to use Parsi funds and institutions.[24] And yet
he made what appears to be a new and significant concession which
was accepted by the Panchayat: that while Tata's wife could not
have access to Parsi institutions, her children could.[25]

In general, as Davar stated, "during the progress of this case, it
was abundantly clear that the Parsi community of Bombay, as a
whole, most strenuously objected to the admission of *juddins* [ali-
ens, non-Parsis]."[26] The community feeling seems to have arisen
from two fundamental fears: defilement and resources. Davar remarked that the community worried that the lower elements of
Indian society—Bhangis, Mahars, Kahars, Dubras—would convert
in order to gain access to the charitable funds reserved for Parsi
Zoroastrians.[27] Davar agreed that this was important, but then
went on to argue as if defilement was the real concern.

Centuries of association with Hindu brethren have made the Parsis
entertain the same feelings towards a Hindu of the lower castes as
Hindus themselves entertain. The Zoroastrian religion inculcates
doctrines of purity and teaches cleanliness at every turn. Parsis,
however poor, have never taken to occupations which may bring
them in contact with unclean things. There is no Parsi—and there

never has been a Parsi—that has followed the occupation of a Sweeper, a Barber, a Butcher or a Shoemaker.[28]

The statement is undoubtedly false historically; certainly Parsis performed these functions in ancient Iran. But in any case the problem is not of castes; Davar extends the fear of contamination to all non-Zoroastrians.

> Though in all other matters they have lived on terms of great friend-ship with their Hindu and Mahomedan fellow-subjects, in religious matters they have been most singularly nervous of any association of any kind with Durvands [non-Parsis]. This word again is not used in any offensive sense. To a Zoroastrian, his best friends among Euro-peans, Hindus or Mahomedans are as much Durvands from a relig-ious point of view as the humble Hamal or Massal who serves in his household. No Durvand is ever admitted inside a Zoroastrian's Atash Behram, Agiary, or Dare Meher. No Durvand is allowed to remain in the edifice where Muktad ceremonies are being performed. No Durvand is allowed to go beyond a certain limit in the grounds of the Towers of Silence. No Durvand is allowed to look in when any of their religious ceremonies are being performed; and this feel-ing is carried to such an extent that the most honoured guests who are sometimes invited to witness a marriage ceremony are not al-lowed to have their chairs on the carpet over which the chairs of the bride and bridegroom are placed. Even at the present day, as Dastur Darab told us, "an old-fashioned Parsi will not drink water touched by a Juddin, and he will not eat food cooked or prepared by him."[29]

In general the worry over defilement occupies more space and more argument than the concern over competition for resources. Whether this reflected the common Parsi view is unclear. It is a more respectable theme for a people who define themselves as charitable; it is also a very understandable theme in purity-con-scious India. Purity appears to be, in any event, the dominant theme expressed in all major Parsi controversies over conversion.

As a result of the High Court's compromise judgment, men are allowed to marry out of the community and to call their children Parsi. Most Parsis say that it is because Tata married a European that this precedent became established. Had he married a Hindu, the cynics remark, it never would have happened. And despite the near-century of legal support, when a son chooses to marry a non-Parsi his father may well throw him out. As Cyrus said on that occasion: take this knife and murder me, you are no son of mine.

The agony over intermarriage is very real. One of the few arguments I ever overheard in the Contractor household was when they disagreed about whether the eldest daughter's children—she had married out of the community, to a well-to-do man—should have their *navjotes* done. The standard community line is that this is unacceptable, and the priests have been threatened by the orthodox that if they ever do such rituals they will be hounded from their jobs. Still, a few priests—either desperately poor or bravely compassionate—will carry out these rites of religious passage for the offspring of mixed marriages. "No," Mr. Contractor shouted. "Whatever your community says, that is what you will do. *Bas* [stop]." "But times are changing, Pervez," Mrs. Contractor said, almost tearfully. "In America, elsewhere, it is done. They do it without thinking. All members of the [mixed] family see all the rites." But she would not, she said, take her grandchildren with her when they went to the *agiary* if the *navjotes* had not been done. "Yes," Mr. Contractor agreed. "People would talk about us. That would be bad."

"Pervez very much believes that Marukh should marry a Parsi," Mrs. Contractor told me.

> I have accepted my eldest daughter's marriage. It has changed my views. These days children do what they want. And I wanted first that my daughters should have a college education and their freedom. They must have their salaries. There are so many Parsis who are so miserable in bad marriages, and stick with them because they don't see any way out. Now Parsi girls seem to work harder, to qualify better. The boys don't seem to bother. And yet I still think that Marukh should marry. She says, marry for the sake of marriage? I agree, it's silly, but still, I think it's good.[30]

Again and again I saw mothers and daughters, fathers and sons, torn over tradition and change. "When it happens to your child, you accept it," Mrs. Contractor said. "You cannot lose your child." Except that people could and did, depending on the strength of their feelings. At least one of the orthodox watchdogs of the Committee of Vigilant Parsis had seen two sons marry out. I was told that he never forgave them, although they spoke.

Literary Vignette: *The Fire Worshippers*

The middle-class Parsi boy in this novel wants to marry an upper-class Brahmin girl. He breaks the news to his father:

> "Over my dead body!" Pestonji roared. "You'll bring this girl into my house over my dead body, understand! I never never thought I'd live to see the day when I'd be ashamed of my own flesh and blood. Ashamed, do you hear? The day you wed this girl, you cease to be my son. . . ."
>
> [The sister now tries to soothe her father]:
> "Look, Papa, I've always admired you as one of the most reasonable and practical of men . . . All this heartbreak and unhappiness for the sake of a promise made by our forefathers eleven hundred years ago? Do you think it's worth it? . . . We are living in a different age . . . Zoroastrianism is no longer a faith to be lived, it's just a unique cultural heritage."
>
> [This opposition is as strong as the orthodox would like to draw it: disown your son, or accept that Zoroastrianism is culturally dead. Later, the mother—again the mother, responsible for the emotional life of the family—relents.]
>
> "I refuse to go on with this. Nari can do whatever he wants to. I am an old woman and I want to die without any regrets . . . I'm not saying [Papa] will ever approve but I don't think he'll make a fuss now." (Bharucha 1968:189–90; 191–94; 211)

From *More of an Indian*

> "I love him, Dad . . . I love him so much I can't think of life without him."
> "All I've ever taught you, Shirin, this is the test for it. How our sacred texts were burnt, how our religion was torn from the soil that had nurtured it for centuries. Yet how it survived in a different soil . . . This fire that has burned for a thousand years, the light of our lives, may soon be quenched, these temples closed for lack of both priests and worshippers. Because people are turning their hearts away from the light. People who should know better. Like you, Shirin." (Karanjia 1970:91)

◆ ◆ ◆

This is, of course, not a uniquely Parsi problem but a problem throughout India. As different ethnic groups move to the city, parents no longer control their offsprings' social life at college and at parties; children move to different cities and send back word of a *fait accompli*. Intermarriage is particularly a problem for those who have emigrated to America and England and must adjust to standards for young adults quite unlike the accepted behavior in India. Knowing that a phenomenon is part and parcel of the modern world, however, does not always ease the pain. But the Parsis put an unusual spin on a common problem in two ways: first, the arguments harken back to the community self-image under the British—why can't you today be progressive like they were—and second, the resolution really matters, because if the Parsis do not do something about the way they marry, their community will disappear in generations.

The Parsi population is decreasing rapidly in Bombay. Until 1941 the Parsi population was slowly but steadily on the rise in India. But in 1961 they were down to over 100,000; in 1971, over 90,000; in 1991, there were 76,000 Parsis in India, with around 54,000 in Greater Bombay.[31] Some of this drop is due to emigration and outmarriage, but probably no more than half of the decline.[32]

After the 1981 Census, the Bombay Parsi Panchayat initiated a population survey of Greater Bombay. On their behalf the International Institute for Population Studies in Bombay interviewed a random sample of 2,000 households from the seven constituencies in Bombay where most of the Parsis live. Among the many interesting facts the survey confirmed was that one in five Parsis is over 65, making the community among the most aged in the world.[33] And the marriage statistics were striking. The mean age of marriage may now have reached 27 years, one of the world's highest marriage ages.[34] Not only does the community marry late, but the number of never married women is quite high. By 1982, more than one in five Parsi women—21 percent—never married in their lifetime; for the general population of India in 1971, that figure was 0.58 percent.[35] When they did marry, they did not reproduce. Twenty percent of the married women had no children; another 26.5 percent had one child. The average number of children per female for all interviewed was 1.62, and for women of completed fertility, 1.85. This figure is well below replacement rate and below the rate for college-educated American women.[36] In comparison,

Irani women marry at around 20 and only 8 percent of Irani women over 25 had never married (Axelrod 1974). It is important to bear in mind when considering these statistics that the community standards for sexual interaction are fairly strict; while I was aware of some married couples who tolerated infidelity, I encountered little premarital sexual activity. Other anthropologists have also been persuaded that Parsis are not sexually adventurous before marriage.[37] These statistics for delayed or rejected marriage indicate a trend towards celibacy and abstinence.

Why on earth would this happen? Parsis often explain that their marital foot-dragging is caused by the difficulty of finding appropriate housing for newlyweds. The society highly values a western lifestyle; it sees neolocal relocation on marriage as intrinsic to that lifestyle; because Parsis refuse to marry until they can live neolocally—so goes the argument—they often refuse to marry at all. It is, realistically, extremely difficult to find housing in Bombay, particularly in the once-colonial areas where the Parsis are concentrated. Stringent rent-controls result in a dearth of rental housing, and flats are often passed down within the family or left vacant for decades rather than sold and lost forever to the family. The city bursts with ever more migrants each month, all competing for space. Nevertheless, it seems bold to pin the reproductive failure of an entire community on the paucity of land, when Hindus in the same dilemma reproduce with ease.

The best explanation, to summarize the studies, is that Parsis hold a western ideal of marriage, prefer to marry up, are hesitant to marry non-Parsis, and the women have neither an economic incentive to marry nor a social compulsion to be partnered. The combination of these factors seems to be sufficient to impede marriage. The problem of maintaining marriage rates in highly educated communities that value a woman's economic freedom and do not demand marriage is, again, not unique to Parsis. But the added pressure of the westernized ideal, endogamy, and an obviously shrinking population size make the problem unusually present for Bombay Parsis.

Paul Axelrod carried out a painstaking study of the community's marriage patterns, comparing them to the Jains and the Saraswat Brahmins. Single-family housing was his first-choice variable.[38] "It has often been called to my attention that 'those Gujaratis and Maharastrians don't mind sleeping on the floor in one room; but we Parsis like to have a bed, and we are used to privacy. We have a higher standard than the other communities'" (1974:86). He pointed out that it is not even the housing itself, but the location of the housing, that is important. Saraswats are as a community less wealthy than the Parsis and face the same housing shortage; and still they settle in independent households at a rate comparable to the Parsis, marry at an earlier age—and nearly all the women marry.[39] They manage this by settling farther out from the main center of Bombay. This means traveling an hour or longer on horribly crowded trains. But the cost of living is substantially lower in the suburbs, and many of the professional middle class commute. Parsis do not. "Parsis have very specific ideas about the quality and location of their residences, and they are reluctant to make a sacrifice for the sake of a more expeditious marriage" (1974:113). They like living in the old, colonial, traditionally Parsi-British areas of Bombay.

Education was Axelrod's second variable. He found again that it is not education as such, but something about the ideals and self-image of the educated Parsi that encourage the preference for neolocal, western-style marriage. Statistically, educated Parsis are more likely to settle in their own flats than less-educated members of the community. "Parsis often assert that it is the educated members of the community who have the more 'modern' ideas about family life and want to settle neolocally" (1974:99). College graduates from Jain and Saraswat families—even graduates from English-language, British-style universities—still move in with the groom's family as often as the less educated.[40] And Axelrod summarizes: "Education and neolocal residence are both associated with the rejection of 'traditional' ways which are not compatible with the progressive outlook of the Parsi community. . . . On the other hand, in the Jain and Saraswat communities education has for many years been a means through which they could carry on their tradition" (1974:101).

Love marriages are part of a similar pattern. Sixty-two percent of the Parsis who had not graduated from high school described their marriage as arranged; only 30 percent of those with college degrees did.[41] Yet again Axelrod emphasized that education itself is not the obstacle, but something about education in the Parsi milieu. In the Saraswat and Jain samples, there was no association between higher education and love marriages (1974:127). "This pattern is seen again and again. In the Parsi community love marriages are associated with many criteria that can be categorized as non-traditional" (1974:127)—those who are born in Bombay, are wealthy, are less orthodox, and so forth.

In short, Parsis associate being progressive with being highly educated, living in their own flats, wearing western clothes—with being westernized altogether. The preferred marriage embodies this ideal. Parsis marry for love—55 percent of Axelrod's sample described their marriages as love marriages, as compared to 6 percent of the Jains and 7 percent of the Saraswats (1974:123). They want to live on their own when they marry. And the women—most of them highly educated—seek men who are educated, nontraditional, and—as becomes clear—at least their social equal.

At the same time, there are powerful disincentives against marrying out, such as being disowned by parents, friends, and culture. Nor is there much pressure to settle, if the ideal is not available. In Hindu society, unmarried women shame their parents and are even perceived as violating *dharma,* religion and duty. This is not true in the Parsi community. Marriage is perceived as a good, and as the true Zoroastrian way (and young women may be eager to keep pace with their peers and marry when they do), but no stigma attaches to those who do not marry. Indeed, for many years Parsi women have been able to inherit money that would have been theirs as a marriage portion, and use it for themselves (1974:138). Certainly many women work, and do not need a marriage for their support. Many Parsis explained this to me as a sign of the advanced standing of the community, though bemoaning the consequences it has had for reproduction. And while the Bombay Parsi community is tightly interwoven, in a community of 50,000, a fifth of whom are over 65, scattered throughout a city of about 12 million, it can be difficult for a man and woman to meet and fall in love. Of the 200 unmarried adults Axelrod surveyed, most of them women, 35 percent said that they did not marry because they could not find a suitable match. Simply stated, the costs of marriage with a non-Parsi are very high, the costs of remaining single low, and the likelihood of finding in the small Parsi population a love match that comes up to ideal community standards is relatively low. The Parsi Panchayat has established a marriage bureau to facilitate marriages within the community; when I spoke to the secretary in 1988, the bureau had arranged 25 marriages in two years. There are plans to make available flats for couples on the condition that they marry, though few of these plans have seen fruition. A recent paper suggested that there were over five hundred couples looking for a place to live in before they married or had children.[42]

Two subsequent studies support Axelrod's findings that expectations of a westernized, sophisticated lifestyle, coupled with the disincentive to marry out and no social incentive to marry, impede marriage within the community. Gould's demographic analysis incorporates the old Gujarati records of community life along with contemporary interviews. She argues that Parsi birthrates have been declining since at least 1881, when the age of marriage was 19 and less than 1 percent of the population remained single. This was prior to the spread of female education and had something to do with internalized conceptions of ideal family size. In fact, she remarks, highly educated women now consider themselves more likely to marry than uneducated ones. Potential lifestyle and class level influences the decision to have children more than the young couple's response to social pressure. Moreover, her informants did not consider the housing crisis a significant factor.

> People say that Parsis do not get married because they do not have houses, so let's provide them with houses so that they will get married. I consider that a simple solution. Housing might get people to marry a little earlier—only the ones that are postponing marriage for that reason. But I am not convinced that if you do something like providing houses tomorrow for everyone, somehow our number of single people will go down.[43]

Parsis will not move out of the center of Bombay to find room for marriage or more children, but at the same time, housing alone will not explain the problem. Another study, by Billimoria, reports that housing may be a significant constraint in the desire to have more than one child (22 percent of those surveyed gave limited accommodation as their explanation; 32 percent mentioned economic limitations). But her primary explanation for the low marriage rates is the low achievement of the Parsi male relative to the female's expectations. "The Parsi woman has high expectations regarding the man she marries. Perhaps the expectations are too high . . . either the girls will have to be educated to lower their expectations or the men will have to work harder, earn more, be more educated. [Otherwise] the Parsi women will remain single or marry out of the community."[44] And she summarizes the issues thus:

> [The women] wanted their spouses to be educated, talented and qualified. Hence, failing to meet the expectations, some of them chose to remain unmarried even up to a late age, though they were not averse to marriage as such. In fact they were not dedicated career women and were quite willing to give up working if required to do so. Married women were more keen on working than unmarried women since, if there was a clash between their home and hours of work or job transfers, they wanted to retain their job. Hence they [the unmarried women] were not against marriage as such, but were choosy and had high expectations about the spouse they wished to marry.[45]

Whatever the factual basis of this complaint against the men, as an emotional reality it is very powerful.[46] Certainly the women's discomfort with traditional marriage seems to be real for many, and it seems that this factor—again, hardly Parsi, but exacerbated in this career- and education-oriented community—has a powerful influence over the Parsi woman's decision to get married.

Literary Vignette: *The Memory of Elephants*

Bapaiji settled herself in her favorite armchair in the verandah of Hill Bungalow, resting her feet up on one of the slats, to read the daily *Jam-e-Jamshed*, the six-page Gujarati newspaper she had co-founded with Tehmina Cama almost thirty years ago. I remember it best for its only English features: Ripley's Believe It or Not, and comic strips of Dagwood and Blondie, the Phantom, and Mandrake the Magician. She was proud of the newspaper as she was of so many of the projects sponsored by the Woman's Committee. They had classes in sewing, dance, music, embroidery, Hindi—whatever someone could teach someone else wanted to learn. The Maharajah of Baroda had come to one of the annual presentations of their work which they had supplemented with music and a skit written by Bapaiji, and had been impressed enough to initiate an annual donation of five hundred rupees, making it fashionable to donate to the cause of the Women's Committee, which enabled them to build a library and a club for the women. Bapaiji was the club's first president and remained so until she died. She wished Hormusji [her late husband] could have been with her for the next day's event, when the Maharajah of Baroda conferred upon her the title, Rajya Ratna, the Jewel of the State, and awarded her the solid gold medal embossed with her name and new title; he had been so proud of all her honours and medals. She wished that Adi [her son] would come with Pheroza [his wife]; the ceremony was to be held in the school compound where Hormusji had been the headmaster and Adi the pupil, but her relations with Adi were not like they had been with Hormusji; Adi resented everything about her that Hormusji had encouraged; he had even chosen a docile, pleasing, pretty wife, everything she was not—but if Pheroza had been more like herself they might have had arguments about everything; there wasn't room for more than one Bapaiji in the family and Pheroza was wise enough to know it; but Bapaiji wished she understood Adi's discontent better. (Desai 1988:71–72)

◆ ◆ ◆

Parsi women are generally perceived by Parsi men as very powerful. "I had a [so-called] Jewish mother. Sera had more that twenty centuries of Persian blood is her veins, but any little Jewish boy from Brooklyn would have recognized her as his very own."[47] Parsi women are not infrequently held to be the strong partners in the household. A biography of a leading Parsi politician describes his mother as "a frail and gentle creature"; nevertheless, "he would literally not do a thing without obtaining her consent" (Mankekar 1968:14). A Zoroastrian woman in Gujarat—an Irani—was famous as a hotblooded political fighter who kept a nuclear power plant out of the area: "*there*'s your real Parsi," I was told.

Shirin is a handsome woman, in her late twenties when I first encountered her, and a good example of a strong Parsi woman. She lived with her parents in a largish flat in Colaba, the fashionable central district of south Bombay, a flat which her parents could not afford to buy again at current prices. The rooms are distinctively Parsi: heavy dark furniture, English knickknacks, a portrait of Zarathustra. Shirin has been intensely involved with the community, for example working to ameliorate the priests' appalling living conditions. She was also involved with other sorts of social projects. She loved the work and was noticeably effective in it. When I met her, she was working for a local mission and also for the Parsi Panchayat. She described her own upbringing as follows.

My grandmother and mother played a major role in my life as far as religion was concerned. My grandmother tried to give us knowledge by telling us stories, teaching us about good and evil, right and wrong, and how to conduct ourselves. She was orthodox and very strict about following various rituals and customs and enforcing high laws of ritual purity. For example she was very strict about laws of purity being maintained with regard to menstrual periods. We couldn't touch her or her belongings during this period, and if we asked her why she just said this is the way it happens, the way it is. She said, my parents did it and I know that it is the right thing.

My grandmother didn't stay with us—she was very independent, but she would visit us every day and at times when she was ill she stayed with us. We saw a lot of her as my parents had an active social life and we were always left in her care. She insisted on living within a certain income left from her husband's savings. She was very righteous and straight about everything. Occasionally we were frightened of her. If you didn't say your prayers or said them too fast or didn't get up early there would be a cane. Later on in life when she was sick and old she had mellowed; and I became very close to her.

My mother was the backbone where my spiritual growth was concerned. From childhood I have always admired her for her quality of giving. She was always giving, not thinking of the costs or rewards. As a child I noticed that if there was a beggar on the road, or a destitute or poor person, she always helped, and she instilled these principles within us. She created this impression in my mind that we should always give. There were many rough periods for us as a family, emotionally and financially, but she was a pillar of strength, giving us love and care. She is honest, sincere, hardworking and good. She worked hard to send us to the best of schools to give us the best in education. She didn't have to put us in the top school in Bombay. But she did. My achievement drive comes from her, to work hard and to study. I remember one incident very clearly. I was in the second year of college and had measles. I was very sick with high fever, I couldn't even keep my eyes open, but my mother insisted I give [take] my exams. She sat next to me, reading to me. I had a high fever the morning of the exam. She came with me and said if you feel real bad come home, but you have to TRY and make an attempt. I got a first class that year.

Dad is very much an extrovert. He loves being outside. He had little influence over us, especially with regard to children. He is not that religious minded.[48]

I would hesitate to say that most Parsis would give such an account of a strong, inspiring mother. Nevertheless, Shirin's account is hardly idiosyncratic. Gould describes Parsi women as "tiger women," and many in the community openly praise the success of the young Parsi women in professional life. Indeed, their perceived success figures in Parsi explanations for Parsi male spinelessness in the face of the women's westernization and education and eventually their earning power, all of which make their expectations of marriage too high. And intriguingly, some Parsis will suggest that the marriages are difficult because couples are caught between two sets of values: westernized, educated women who as Indians expect their husbands to be far more educated that themselves; westernized, educated men who as Indians expect a docile, homebound, dutiful wife. Certainly this kind of tension between the woman's work and the husband's expectations create problems in the western world—but in the Parsi context they are often articulated as the result of friction between a westernized Parsi culture and a supposedly more traditional Hindu society.

"In my generation," a fifty-year-old Parsi told me, "there is a lot of tension. The men all expected Indian wives, but we no longer wanted to kowtow." Several Parsi women, like this writer, told me that marriages from this period—and perhaps before then—had been stormy. Parsi women had been more educated than their Hindu counterparts for many years. But it was women born shortly before Independence who went to work in significant numbers, and they explained to me that they felt trapped by marriage, torn by conflicting demands, that their daughters looked at the tension, knew their earning power, and decided not to marry.

> The Parsi father, the husband of my generation, saw his father, and thought that he had the right to be as autocratic as his father had been. But the women were well-educated; they were earning. And they didn't feel that their husbands' demands were justified. So there was friction. And they didn't want their daughters caught in the same trap. So here I am, I am so conscious of the community declining, and yet I cannot advise my own daughter to marry. Let them establish themselves in a career, let them feel independent—and then, if they want, let them marry.

The writer went on to explain that Parsi women of her age pushed their daughters to be independent, to fight, and she thought that perhaps less pressure was placed on their sons, because when there was trouble with the husbands the wives met their emotional needs through their involvement with their sons. The mama's boy, in this account, is created by the mother's westernization, her consequent difficulty with her husband, and then her overinvolvement with a son she encourages to be dependent. There is, in India, a well-described pattern of powerful mothers, distant husbands, and dependent sons, always closer to their mothers than to their wives (Kakar 1981). What is significant in the Parsi account is the belief that this pattern is created not by the influence of Hindu culture, but by the tension generated by holding western values in an eastern world.

Another variation on this east/west problem is as follows: Parsi women are highly educated—a western trait—and still they and their husbands expect the male to be superior to the woman—an eastern trait. So the women do not marry because they cannot find a suitably superior husband—or when they do marry, they dominate their household. A Parsi psychologist asserts:

> Parsi mothers are well known for over-protectiveness. The child may be pampered, given the best of food and clothing, but no liberty to do anything, no freedom to choose a career, no freedom to take any decision . . . They keep badgering the child, rousing anger, hatred, guilt, anxiety. What is more, the children become dependent on the mother for everything. . . . Maybe it is in the nature of the woman to be a little dominating, because she has been suppressed so long.[49]

Again, the mother is overwhelming, powerful, dominant, more involved with her children than they need—and probably less involved with their husbands than they could be. "Often, the girls are more educated, hold better jobs than the boys, and earn more and thus wear the pants and have a lot to say about everything."[50] Another Parsi psychologist explained to me that the strong mother created the dependent, passive son of out her own expectations that he would fail to live up to the achievements of her ancestors. This psychologist describes the Parsi mother-son relationship as a "double-bind." The explicit verbal statement to the son, he said, is "succeed." But, he said, the underlying message is, "don't succeed, you can't." These days, he said, mothers discount the natural ability of the boys to succeed. "Mummy, I've got a lot of homework," the boy will say. "Don't worry," she says, "I will do it for you." There is now, he said, an ingrained belief in the community that it is the woman who has the ability, not the man. This is probably true throughout India, he said: women do very well in the competitive examinations. But in the Parsi community this success goes along with a very negative image of the man. Don't think and don't succeed, the mother manages to convey. This is all different from the Jews, he said. The Jewish woman does not take over completely. The man remains the thinker. In the Parsi family, the woman takes over completely in the household. By now this has become a situation in which the Parsi woman becomes disinclined to marry a Parsi man. The average Parsi man, he said, is a hail-fellow-well-met kind of guy. So, he said, the standard male is perceived as inadequate by the mother and then discarded except as an emotional comfort; as young adults the men, responding to this expectation of inadequacy, move into jobs which do not require much thinking, like the job of a bank clerk for instance; and yet the Parsis still identify with the British, so they hang around the coffeeshops in the five-star hotels. Community mythology tells them that they are successful and driving, but the actual expectations around them tell them that they are incapable of success. The Cusrow Baag boy—the colony boy—he suggested, is a typical example of this impasse.

Intermarriage, delayed marriage, marriage rejected if it does not allow the woman freedom, marriage where the woman marries down: such utilitarian issues grip many sophisticated communities these days. This sort of community has broken free of traditional models of male-female relations. There is no cultural command to marry unless one wants to, no cultural command to have children—and further crowd the crowded flat—unless one wants those children. From a global, even an Indian, perspective, this is no bad thing. From a community perspective, be that community Parsi, Jewish, American, or Swedish, the perception may be different. And from an individual's perspective—and the individual is the decision-maker—the problem is still differently arraigned. Parsis are now trying to instill the concept of reproduction as a civic virtue. But in crowded, expensive Bombay, western-identified Parsis are not buying. And so the worries remain. One cover of *Parsiana*, for instance, pictured an Indian tiger and a Parsi on its cover. "Endangered species?" the caption read.[51] Articles on declining numbers constantly appear in the English and Gujarati press; as my Gujarati teacher sighed when we were going through the paper, "here is another essay on the topic with which the Parsis are so obsessed, why their numbers are declining, and whether they will die out."

The interesting anthropological question is, however, how is this figured from a Parsi perspective? And the answer, surprisingly, takes us back to conversion, and to arguments surrounding conversion, which have nothing directly to do with marriage at all.

Joseph Peterson's Conversion

On March 5, 1983, an American with no marital connection to the religion but with an intense desire to become a Zoroastrian underwent the *navjote* ceremony in New York. It seems that he was completely sincere in his devotion, and that he had for many years read nearly everything about the religion upon which he could lay his hands. Certainly he memorized the long Avestan chants necessary for the *navjote* ceremony, and performed them well. At least two Zoroastrian priests officiated in the ceremony, and around a hundred American-based Zoroastrians were present. Judging from the contemporary press coverage and recent casual conversation, this was the controversial community event of the decade. "The Managing Committee of the M. F. Cama Athornan Institute and the M. M. Cama Education Fund strongly condemns the alleged 'navjote.'"[52] "Peterson has rendered a great service to us all, and more so to our religion."[53] "The welcome that [Peterson] received from some four hundred true Zoroastrians was tremendous."[54] "The best remedy is to socially boycott Mr. Kersi Antia [the chief priest officiating at the *navjote*] and his associates from all communal and religious associations."[55] "I for one would like to see the community bestow a gold medal on mobeds Kersi Antia and Hormazdiyar and their associates."[56] "For ill-gotten fame or reasons of expediency, they are attempting to bulldoze in reform."[57]

The community went into an uproar. Probably the most important immediate response was that of three of four high priests in Bombay who collaborated on a statement which appeared in *Parsiana* in August 1983:

> We have read with grave concern reports appearing in a certain section of the press regarding some irresponsible members of our

priestly class residing in North American having performed the so-called *navjote* of a 27-year old American of Christian faith . . .

This so-called *navjote* in an insult, mockery and a cruel joke perpetrated against both the Zoroastrian and Christian religions . . .

The very idea of conversion is contrary and repugnant to the principle of Divine Justice.[58]

They contend that conversion is profoundly inappropriate on two counts, both of them essentially historical. First, the very notion of conversion is antithetical to the religion. The argument runs as follows:

People professing religions may be divided into two groups: those who preach that man will be judged by God according to the actions performed in this life; and those who preach that man will be judged by God according to the religion professed in this world. . . . Naturally and logically, the religions of the first group cannot and do not practice conversion . . . The propagandists of the religions of the second group preach that one can go to heaven simply by adopting a certain religion.[59]

In other words, Christianity values conversion because only if you are a Christian can you be saved. According to Zoroastrianism, it is not your beliefs but your actions which determine whether you are saved or damned, and thus no conversion is necessary.

The second argument, upon which the authors spend more time, is that Zarathustra never converted anyone (why break tradition, is the implicit corollary). Conversion is not a concept present in the Rig Veda, nor in Brahmanical tradition (they rely here on Zoroastrianism's historical relationship to the early Hindu texts, and the knowledge that the Vedic texts are often used to interpret the Avesta). They cite the Bhagvad Gita's *sloka*, "better one's own duty [*dharma*] to perform / Though void of merit / Than do another's well / Better to die within [the sphere of] one's own duty / Perilous is the duty of other men," and they interpret this to mean that one should never accept a religion other than the one into which one was born. Although some passages in the Persian Rivayats are thought to support conversion, they in fact refer to the treatment of Zoroastrians who have left the religion of their birth.[60] Zarathustra, the authors say, merely clarified the religion of the pre-Zoroastrian Iranians and enabled them to understand its ethical core.

The priestly authors then remind the readers that there are Zoroastrians living in Iran, marginally tolerated because they do not attempt to convert others, and that conversion has brought "strife, destruction, devastation and misery" on humankind.[61] (Actually, conversion is tolerated and at least occasionally practiced by Iranian Zoroastrians.) And they conclude with the plea that "We therefore earnestly hope that this puerile attempt and anti-Zoroastrian action on the part of a very small band of dissidents will not be tolerated, recognized and accepted by our co-religionists."[62] Conversion creates chaos when it is allowed—and anyway we do not allow it—and it defiles us, the priests suggest in other contexts.

Against this rejection, liberals argued that unless conversion is tolerated the community will die. Pragmatism and adaptation demand social change. Appended to the account in *Parsiana* was a letter from the president of the Zoroastrian Association of Metropolitan Chicago, reportedly signed spontaneously by over 90 percent of the members present at the monthly general meeting.[63] "Many of us from the Chicago area were very disturbed" to read a letter written by a member condemning the priests involved in the conversion.[64] Their major counterargument centered on survival in a world in which intermarriage is becoming increasingly more frequent.

> Of over 15 marriages in Chicago in recent years, in only two cases were both partners Zoroastrian. Our brethren in India cannot conceive of the calamity that would face us here in North American if we did not adopt a more tolerant approach and accept these marriages . . .
>
> Did not our forefathers, when they came to India, make some concessions to their new homeland? Does not everything in nature adapt and mould to its environs in order to survive, improve and grow in stature? The basic teachings of Zarathustra are universal and will remain relevant to all peoples for all time; they are immutable and unchanging and transcend all bounds. But in matters of social import let us bend a little with the times. To take an absolute and unbending position may be dangerous.[65]

Wê are, they argue, a progressive people who are not tied to customs. We interpret the religion in its universal meaning.

The priest most centrally responsible for the convert's *navjote,* Kersey Antia, wrote a single-spaced, forty-seven-page reply to his collective critics; it was entitled "The Argument for Acceptance." It is an impressive document, drawing widely on western and Indian scholarship. Most of it is devoted to a detailed consideration of the ancient texts, from which Antia concludes that in the early days of the religion people were, in fact, converted to the faith, and that Zoroaster felt that his religion was one which would be appropriate for all people to accept.[66]

The nonexegetical argument is here integral to a progressive, nontraditional liberalism, based in this particular case on the sophisticated claim that Zoroastrianism is the ultimately adaptive religion that finds its greatest expression in work and lifestyle, not in religious strictures.

> It is worth noting how the Parsis themselves . . . see the realization of their traditional religious values in their efforts at industrializing India and providing jobs to its poor. Thus, replying to a staunch critic of Mr. J. R. D. Tata's Parseeism and standing in the Zoroastrian faith [Tata is often criticized because of his secularism], Mr. S. Vakil retorted that such critics "forget that *the greatest cosmopolitan Fire Temple in the private sector has been kept burning at Jamshedpur by the Tatas day and night, which is feeding half a million mouths."*[67]

This approach is part of a debate over whether religious restriction and requirements are trappings over an ethical core to which they are irrelevant, or whether Zoroastrianism depends upon the specific prayers and rituals which make reference to the divine and which are not shared by other religious communities.[68] Again, it is a reformist, progressive, perspective. Antia is clear that ethos, not etiquette, is the essence of religion, that the modern world demands change, and that adaptation to that change in no way devalues the religion but rather demonstrates the sophisticated tolerance of an elite community.

Other arguments from this period are intense. Each side, of course, accuses the other of suicide and assumes the worst case of the opponent's strategy.[69] But the most fascinating feature of these other arguments is that the discourse about purity has been biologized and, as the previous chapter recounts, the discourse has established a liberal critique of the backwardness of tradition and the genetic corruption of racial purity. And the arguments have made it clear that the debate over conversion has become a negotiation over what parts of the traditional identity are least hard to lose. On the side of purity there is history, tradition, orthodoxy, and what makes Parsis different; on the other side are the ideals of westernized sophistication, of liberalism, reform, and progress. From early on, as the elite adapted to and identified with the British, these aspects of the community have been in tension with each other. The archives are full of debate over the importance of religious ritual and the backwardness of custom. And yet in the earlier period such controversy really did not matter. The community was flourishing and important, and the internal debates perhaps even made it feel vital and alive. Now it becomes necessary to choose, and the fact of having to choose probably makes the inappropriateness of old aspirations embarrassingly evident.

As more Parsis resettle in North America and elsewhere, it seems likely that the balance of opinion will shift towards intermarriage. At the Seventh North American Zoroastrian Congress, held in 1990 in Houston, there was relatively little controversy. A session designed for those under twenty-five [older people could attend but not speak] came to a widespread agreement that it would be best to marry a Zoroastrian—but that it would be very hard to find one person who was also financially stable and emotionally well-suited. Another session presented five dialogues between parents and children. The parents had mostly been raised abroad; the children had been born and raised in North America. And the dialogues demonstrated that despite tension and fear, the generations had gracefully agreed to the inevitability of change.

In North America, it seemed clear, the children are likely to marry out, and the parents are adapting to that prospect. Certainly parents attempt to marry their child within the fold. Boys are sent to Bombay over Christmas vacation, ads are placed in *Parsiana* ("London-settled, Dubai-based Parsi boy, 30 years, seeks alliance with slim, pretty Parsi girl";[70] "Parsi parents of 23-year-old, attractive, educated daughter from a very decent family and good background seek alliance with a tall, mature, educated Parsi boy from similar background. Girl willing to settle abroad")[71]—but ultimately, young Parsi adults, raised as North Americans and in a religion which explicitly asserts the freedom of choice, make their own choice, and the parents are forced to live with it. As I was told by mothers in Bombay whose daughters had married out, "You cannot lose your child, you just have to accept it. In Delhi, in London, in Hong Kong—in all the far-flung communities—there is more tolerance for intermarriage than in Bombay."

The problem in Bombay is that the community is large enough so that intermarriage need not seem inevitable, yet small enough so that it often occurs. There is justification for outrage on both sides of the debate: outrage that the woman married out because there *are* available Parsi men in the community, and outrage at her ostracism because given the small number of such men, finding a soul-mate in the community is hard. Inevitably there is denial. There are those who assert that dwindling numbers are not a problem; in any event, the messiah has already been born, the world as we know it will vanish, and a new world will emerge which will be entirely Zoroastrian. Others claim that in the depths of the Armenian mountains are the lost tribes of Zoroastrians, numbering in the millions, who will shortly be discovered and they will resuscitate the community. The people who cling to these notions are those who refuse to accept any change to the traditional concept of the pure, progressing, populous Parsi. For most Parsis, however, the choice is between purity and progressiveness, and many articulate a preference for purity over survival.

Bombay exacerbates the problem. In London, Chicago, or Hong Kong, a new community self-definition may seem more reasonable. Bombay—a world of widespread caste prejudice and concern for purity—carries all the semiotic signification of the community's past, and it may be too painful for its Parsi residents to acknowledge the reality of new circumstances against those embedded memories. To move to Los Angeles is to acquire a changed identity, by nature of the changed surroundings. To debate a new identity in a city where the Parsi buildings decay and the statues of Dadabhai Naoroji and Jamsetji Jeejeebhoy corrode in sulphuric rain is to call attention both to the monuments and to their slow destruction, to the tangibility of the loss of once real power.

Denial goes only so far. When a good Parsi's daughter marries a Jain but claims to remain a Zoroastrian, and over thirty other young women of respected families present the Panchayat with affidavits affirming that they are in similar situations, the community is confronted with change. In this situation, the process of making the calculation dramatically forces the recognition that, literally, "we are not what we were," the world has changed beyond comprehension, our life—with its preferences and interpretations—cannot go on as it did before.

To an anthropologist the most remarkable feature of this struggle is that it is not merely another face of Indian communalism, of the caste or religion-based loyalty that has thrown the contemporary Indian world into turmoil. This is about the failure of the community to maintain the Raj ideal of western-identified progress and at the same time to preserve its racial purity. The very existence of the debate forces the community to become aware of the inadequacy of its options in the contemporary context. And the hysterical tone of the debates may reflect not only passion about possible outcomes, but also the fear that the community cannot agree on a solution, cannot resolve this central problem, because no resolution is possible using the established Parsi concept of the good self. Under these circumstances, with the feel of shotgun urgency, the debate has become extremely painful. "Conversion is to Parsis like a red rag to a bull. Zarathustra's preachings are forgotten, rational thinking leaves them, and the Parsis rush to fight an enemy that does not exist."[72]

ON POSTCOLONIAL
IDENTITY

··· 6 ···

When I met Roshan again after many years, in the imitation-baroque marble entry to Harvard's Widener Reading Room, she recognized me at once; but I couldn't place her.[1] She was thin, almost gaunt, and looked very South Asian as she stood with her coat bunched above a knee-length *kurta* and pants, with a long ponytail down her back. She had been ill, which accounted for the gauntness, but I realized later that I hadn't recognized her because in Bombay she had seemed so confidently part of the well-bred westernized Parsi world of old money, good lineage, and impeccable behavior. She had seemed to me, that is, profoundly Anglicized. Her father, a senior executive with a multinational company, was a fair-skinned, elegantly suited man whose style reflected years of upper-level management and international business. Roshan had grown up with the status symbols of his foreign travel: hard, high-bouncing superballs from America, dolls from Switzerland, little blue dresses from Yugoslavia. She and her sister would clamor to wear their foreign outfits at company parties, but their father made them dress in Indian clothes. Their mother spoke with the imperturbable clarity of elite English and she seemed indistinguishable, at first, from an upper-middle-class London mother, with the same brisk efficiency in arranging dinner parties and charity events and children's after-school lessons. Roshan had short dark hair and she wore shorts, in a world of saris and chaperones. She took ballet lessons and piano lessons, even at twenty, and she met friends at the Willingdon Club, where all their parents were members. Both Roshan and her sister had been sent at ten to an exclusive boarding

school in England, the way English children in the Raj would be
sent back home, for schooling, and they spent their final two years
at a select school for their exams. Roshan's sister went on to
Oxford, but Roshan, who had announced that she hated England,
chose almost at random a small college in Massachusetts. In Bombay, where they came to join their parents for the holidays, they
lived in the tree-lined heights of Bombay's exclusive Malabar Hills,
and went to their country house at Poona on weekends.

By my first trip to India I had been in England myself for six
years and had glimpsed the British template for this elite colonial
world: the long dinner parties with their bewildering, rigid but
unspoken etiquette; the elegant balls at which the well-placed un-
dergraduate women wore their satin nonchalantly and danced
among the wineglasses left on the grass at dawn; the recognition,
one afternoon, that the Stilton in the Fellows' Parlour was part of
an attempt to mimic a culture in which few intellectuals would ever
be natural members. It both repelled and fascinated me, this Evelyn
Waugh casualness of horses and country houses and Lord Mountbatten's relatives. In England, as a foreign scholar, it was a world
into which I had never been invited, and I resented Roshan for
growing up so comfortably in its Indian simulacrum. The irony of
this resentment was that she too had felt awkward and disinvited
from the world of the old-monied upper class, and she would assert
herself at Harvard as someone whose critical stance rested on her
identification of herself as non-American, nonwestern, and more
or less nonprivileged. And this of course is the larger irony: that
many of the postcolonial critics who write with outraged moral
distance about western privilege (although Roshan had not yet
entered the literary-political arena in this way) have in some way
or another been privileged themselves.

When I first met her, Roshan was twenty years old, and she was
back from her first year at an American university. I had heard
about her for months as a "good Parsi"; a "brilliant girl" who
cared about the community, was determined and energetic, and
made things happen. She had returned to India from England for
a year before college and been bored by the tennis and riding at
the Willingdon, and then she went into the Parsi General Hospital
to get her tonsils out. "Being wheeled out after surgery I saw the
wards and looked—and I suddenly got the idea." When she recov-
ered, she took her guitar and a friend down to the hospital and
they sang for the patients and the patients loved it. So she brought

back more friends, and then a group of friends, and then she organized school parties. The projects diversified. Under her direction, students planted trees in the *doongerwadi*. They sang at another hospital. They found television sets so that chronic patients could do something with their time. And Roshan become famous (to Parsis) and the source of affectionate, teasing stories. When I was told that Roshan had returned to Bombay I dutifully scheduled an appointment and, tape recorder in hand, met her and for several hours sat and listened to her tell me about concepts of truth and purity and goodness and how she wanted to become a priest.[2] She trusted me, and she talked to me about boyfriends and careers and her views about the community. She was the age of my youngest sister, and evoked in me an elder sister's protectiveness, but I didn't feel that I had any real sense of her. It was not until I saw her in America that I felt I could begin to understand her.

At this time Roshan was twenty-six, and she was struggling with conflicts over who she was and where she belonged. She had lived outside India, (other than visits on holidays), for sixteen years, first in England and then in America. When she returned home, all her friends were married, and they no longer had what she thought of as the tree-climbing abandon of the unmarried woman. She hated feeling out of place and envied their confident membership in Indian collective life. But she wasn't sure whether she wanted to live in India, and she was horrified by the thought of compliantly accepting an Indian husband's authority over her life. Roshan saw herself as a writer and as someone who, like Anita Desai, might spend part of her time abroad, and she desperately wanted to avoid the stifling trap of a traditional South Asian marriage. This was a worry I had heard before: the woman's hostel I had stayed in during my first trip to Bombay was full of highly capable, career-oriented single women nervous about the constraints of traditional marriage, despite the accepted wisdom that in India a woman's job outside the home did not challenge her role as a mother and only brought more honor to her family.[3] But they at least were clearly elite Indians. As an India-born Parsi who had lived most of her life abroad, Roshan's hesitation was wrapped up in even more complex issues of belonging.

> I went off to school in England at ten, or eleven, and the biggest emotional crisis you face is being torn between where do you belong. A little bit happens subconsciously. You turn British. And depending

on your personality that little bit may be more than others or less than others. But a large part of it is also very conscious, and you find yourself saying, well this is an English thing and this is an Indian thing and shall I dress like an English person, shall I talk like an English person? Or shall I be Indian at this dinner party tonight? And it's a very big crisis because you're one or two kids among hundreds and you have no adult to reinforce your behavior. And my younger sister took a conscious decision: "I go to India for summer and Christmas vacation, nine months of the year I'm in Britain. It's easier to cope with being a little out of synch in India, than being out of synch ten months a year while I'm in England." I tried, I did play with my own psyche, I tried. But I was much more rooted in India, I had a much fiercer loyalty to upbringing and family and the people I truly loved and I knew I didn't love or really care for anybody in Britain. So I decided to take the hell I thought I'd get in Britain for ten months, and stick with the identity that I thought would be approved of by my parents, because I needed them more than any- one. The approval of schools and teachers didn't matter to me as much as it did to my sister. But if you do this, you have to take a lot of flak from the other students, particularly in your teens, because you are foreign.

As Parsis, neither Roshan nor her sister looked particularly foreign; the assertion of foreignness is something she perceives herself to have chosen.

> In Britain, you are looked down upon. The question is how much you can tolerate in your teens being different from the rest, and to me it mattered more to cling to the intense love of my parents than to seek the love of my peers and to have a comfortable life and such. My sister adapted the opposite way. In games, in lessons, she could do just what the British did. And at dinner parties and balls she could wear dresses just as the British did and she had no problem with that because she prefers to be one of them. There was always something strangely Indian about me which I was defensive about.

It was never clear to me how much of this anxiety I should take seriously as anxiety. Roshan was expressive, and she flourished with an audience. But the drama was also a way to deal with the anguish of not fitting in, and not counting. That pain and powerful emotions were involved was obvious. At the school where the two sisters studied for their advanced exams, Roshan was invited to neither of the two dances which marked the end of the two years. (Her Anglo-identified sister was asked, of course). Roshan was, however, a responsible student, and she became a school prefect—one of the cadre of students that essentially run and discipline an English school. Her post was to patrol the grounds after dark and catch the students out after hours. Most prefects see their job not only as following the rules but as interpreting them, so that they turn in only those whose crimes are particularly egregious. But Roshan was a Parsi, with a by-the-book understanding of truthfulness; and by that time, she was also very angry. Each morning she reported offenders to the authorities with the particular nature of the crime: usually, kissing.

When I came to America it was the biggest psychological break. For the first time I was seeing Indians and Parsis out of their own land. It was a novelty in San Francisco, seeing the Chinese, seeing them coming to school and being American and going home and eating noodles and speaking Chinese. It was the same with Indians. I started to see Sardarjis [Sikh men] who'd wear turbans and girls in *salvar kameez* and slowly, slowly, that broke down the defenses and I started to see that we're different but it's a great honor to be different, we're revered for being different. Teachers would say to these boys and girls, stand up and tell the class where you're from. Americans ask these questions. Other cultures don't ask much. So I realized pretty soon that it was to my advantage to be what I wanted to be and I played it up to the hilt. I changed my wardrobe completely. I could draw upon my culture and not be ashamed to present it in any way. And that's what made me draw on Hindu culture and not just being Parsi. In boarding school I did draw on being Parsi, because that was nice, neutral ground, neither too western nor too Indian. It was a sort of middle way. But here I've found that's not enough, because Parsi culture is something that is not so difficult to understand from the western point of view, our lifestyles at home, etc. Going to the Willingdon, British India, legacy of the Raj. That was not such a novelty to the Americans, being Parsi. So therefore I drew on more Indianness, the other things of India, eating more Indian food, not just Parsi food, wearing more Indian clothes, polishing my Hindi, going as far now as to learn Urdu, and going as far now as shunning everything western. And it's quite frightening, because my American roommate points out that you haven't worn American clothes in four weeks, and you haven't cooked western food for weeks, you haven't eaten western food for weeks, and when I first started to cook it would be a roast chicken, mashed potatoes, peas, and now I don't touch the stuff.

Roshan's dilemma—who shall I be tonight, how shall I choose out of my heritage—would now be described as postcolonial. The term often refers to highly westernized third-world intellectuals who traffic in the discourse of colonialism and its aftermaths, and who rewrite themselves for the multiple others in their audiences. (In fact, the heterogeneous category includes all whose identities have been marked by the colonial experience.) "In the west they are known through the 'Africa' they offer; their compatriots know them both through the west they present to Africa and through an Africa they have invented for the world, for each other, and for Africa" (Appiah 1992:149). These are elites. They are not the poor Parsis in Tardeo, recklessly spending severance pay to visit Europe for three weeks, but the ones who live out the middle-class dream of enlightened transnational freedom. Postcolonials in this sense alter identities for others through transacting identities for themselves, through displaying the insistent complexity of their own group affiliations—at times, refusing to be categorized at all—as a means to destabilize simple stereotypes. One thinks here not only of Anthony Appiah, but also of Sara Suleri, Homi Bhabha, Chinua Achebe, Gayatri Spivak, Lata Mani, Jamaica Kincaid, Arjun Appadurai, and other postcolonial critics who have reshaped the imaginative landscape of cultural criticism. As with Roshan, it is easy to be cynically suspicious that they capitalize upon white liberal guilt and the current vogue for multiculturalism, and they do: but to say this is to ignore the way their stance may help to resolve the pain of a marginality that has been imposed upon them.

In a broad sense, of course, Roshan's dilemma is merely an exaggerated caricature of the impact of modernity, of the profound and unalterable way the geopolitical boundaries of the mid-twentieth-century world—before frequent flier miles and fax machines—have shifted and grown grey. In Clifford's diagnosis of contemporary identities, "intervening in an interconnected world, one is always, to varying degrees, 'inauthentic': caught between cultures, implicated in others. Because discourse in a global system is elaborated vis-à-vis, a sense of difference or destructiveness can never be located solely in the continuity of a culture or tradition" (1988:11). This is the experience of someone like the writer Bharati Mukherjee, who (like Nirad Chaudhuri) had many "homes," not all of which she had seen when they were hers: "I was born into a class that did not live in its native language . . . My 'country'— called in Bengali *desh,* and suggesting more a homeland than a nation of which one is a citizen—I have never seen" (in Mariani 1991:24). She moved to Canada; to Iowa; to Atlanta; to New York. "There is a sense of the interpenetration of all things" (in Mariani 1991:27). Mukherjee is a postcolonial critic also in the narrow sense, but her interpenetration is a condition of modern London, Boston, Los Angeles, Bombay. I myself grew up on the east coast of the United States, spent my twenties in Europe, and now live on the west coast, but I write this in Boston. There are African masks on the walls and Indian clothes in my closet, and around the corner, at Union Square, there are Brazilian, South Asian, and East Asian markets and a restaurant famous for its French-Cambodian cuisine. Like most American cities, Boston is in this larger sense postcolonial, full of immigrants and emigrants, carrying their culture with them and reweaving it with the rags and patches of others. And perhaps as Sartre said of himself (and Paris) in relation to Fanon, urban America is losing some of the "settler" quality, some of the complacency of assumed domination. It is an extraordinary time.

Yet despite its broad latitude the politics of this cultural concatenation are most obvious and most exigent to those, like Roshan, who speak from what are called the margins: people who are not white heterosexual middle-class western men. And the challenge for a Roshan is to know how to play marginality to advantage, to know how to deal with exclusion so that its pain is mitigated and its power enhanced. The more traditional approach to these politics have been the torn dreams of all disempowered groups: confronted with the inferiority of your gender, skin, or accent, do you adopt the mainstream style and hope to be accepted, or reject the mainstream in order to build a world in which its values will not matter? These politics of assimilation or rejection have been attacked (in large measure by black women) as simplistic; Cornel West, in a thoughtful discussion of the dilemma, points out that the attack has been the creative push towards a new "politics of difference."[4] These new politics, he argues, represent blackness through its complex diversity and through the deconstruction of simple racial categories. For him this is the attempt to manage simultaneously the "double consciousness" of the rejection of the mainstream (and its association of blackness with inferiority) while assimilating into it; to be what he calls a "critical organic catalyst." These are "cultural workers who simultaneously position themselves within (or alongside) the mainstream while clearly aligned with groups who vow to keep alive potent traditions of critique and resistance" (in Ferguson et al. 1990:33). The effort to straddle both assimilation and rejection has become the inherent problem of the marginalized postcolonial subject, and the creativity forced by its tensions the hope of its resolution.

Roshan sits uncertainly on the edge of this mined political arena, and her ambivalence about which stage presence to choose—complete assimilation, radical rejection, daytime conformity and ethnic noodles at night—has become the trope, the representation, the politics, and the experience of the postcolonial culture of which the Parsis are so remarkable an example. The postcolonial discovers again, after Fanon's generation has passed, that he is a man of color, as Appadurai (1993) movingly details, yet he lives in a white world in which his color is liberated as a commodity. In the politics of difference, ambivalence is not a symptom of the problem but the modus operandi of the cure. Cultural studies as a discipline could be described as a struggle to accept the proposition that, in Kobena Mercer's words, "it is no longer possible to map the terrain in terms of simple binary oppositions" (in Grossberg et al. 1992:425). (This was undoubtedly always true; the claim has, however, become an insistent challenge around the concept of self and other, colonizer and colonized.) One of the telling indications of this transformation is a dazzling set of arguments over the writing of Indian history, in which ambivalence emerged as the durable good for both sides of an important, high-profile dispute. In 1990 Prakash's manifesto for a "postfoundationalist" history unveiled a history without rigid categories of individual, institution, and class, without rigidifying "Orientalist" foundations.[5] O'Hanlon's and Washbrook's reply is a tour-de-force that argues that the call to avoid fixity assumes a mistaken notion of the certainties of the historian's enterprise; it is inevitable that the historian impose meaning on the material, make it "good to think."[6] They quote Searle on Derrida, pointing out that the attack on foundations itself implies a belief in foundations and is intellectually unsophisticated as an account of human reasoning. They argue that Prakash does not take his own poststructuralism seriously, that he is in fact committed to a political agenda which his writing should persuade him to reject. And they say that although Edward Said, too, tries to ride the two horses of deconstruction and Marxism, he at least knows which side he is ultimately on. As a cogent argument, this essay is brilliant. But Prakash's rejoinder is more moving: if O'Hanlon and Washbrook seek mastery, he finds comfort in ambivalence.[7] "Let us hang on to two horses, inconstantly" (1991:184).

The hope of this confidently theorized rejection of a single subject position, a clear political agenda, a lone mastered steed, comes out of the urge to transcend the inevitable degradations of the colonizer-colonized dichotomy. "There are, in the end, only the colonizer and the colonized" (Dirks 1992:1): all these formulations of marginality and colonialization depend upon the accepted existence of a dominant group and a subordinate group, an us and a them, upon the acceptance of what is called alterity. The world remains full of profound power asymmetries. Nevertheless many contemporary projects see the route to the political resolution of their problems through the deconstruction of the basic colonial opposition and the transcendence of what Greenblatt calls the "sentimental pessimism" of a world globally defined through hegemony and subordination.

Thus, for instance, two of the most recent postcolonial texts are a frontal attack on this entrenched colonial dichotomy and a plea for productive ambiguity. Sara Suleri asserts that the study of colonial rhetoric deconstructs its simplifying rigidity. "To study the rhetoric of the British Raj in both its colonial and postcolonial manifestations is therefore to attempt to break down the incipient schizophrenia of a critical discourse that seeks to represent domination and subordination as though the two were mutually exclusive terms" (1992:4). The danger of the contemporary discourse on colonialism, she argues, is that alterity becomes an easy trope, too easy a trope, to reach for: that whatever the cold realities of the political system which gave rise to the trope, our understanding of it will not advance us if we reify it. And so Suleri proceeds to analyze the binary trope as a defensive strategy against merging and against the homoerotic bonds of sameness. In a different book about a different place Anthony Appiah also uproots and abandons these ungainly dyads of Africa and the west, black and white, colonized and colonizer. The Africa that Africans invented was in part a response to the configuration of Africa in the European discourse, and must, he suggests, be refashioned without this bent mirror. We are already "contaminated" with each other, he says: the vision of a unitary Africa as against a monolithic west is an easy sophistication we must learn to live without. And he says with compelling wisdom, eyeing the strewn carcasses on our intellectual battlefields, that the abandonment of these charged political categories is not an embrace of moral anarchy. "We can surely maintain a powerful engagement with the concern to avoid cruelty and pain while nevertheless recognizing the contingency of that concern" (1992:155). In doing so, he reaches out to soothe the debate over how to retain our critical, moral vision while acknowledging the limits of our cultural certitude.

But in these thicketed discourses there is also a negative yearning for ambiguity which arises from the fear that definition leads to the loss of freedom and possibility: it is not the desire to embrace multiple positions, but the fear of embracing any, lest the impossibility of holding it should lead to self-destruction. This unwelcome uncertainty is the heart of the ambivalence that Homi Bhabha diagnoses for the colonized subject, for (to restate) the colonial subject identifies with the colonizer and yet cannot be the colonizer. If he identifies with his nativeness, he confronts his own condemnation; if he identifies with the westernization he has adopted, he confronts his own alienation. "The taking up of any one position, within a specific discursive form in a particular historical conjecture, is then always problematic" (in Ferguson et al. 1990:81). This is most famously elaborated in Bhabha's (1990) account of the ambivalence of nationalism: the postcolonial cannot find peace in nationalist identity because of the unhappy dualism of colonial identifications.[8] Through this politics of difference, which Bhabha says is the condition of modernity, the concept of nation becomes a fantasy of certainty (powerfully depicted by Benedict Anderson) disrupted by the panicked denial of fixity.

Bhabha, who is a Parsi, is among the most anguished of contemporary postcolonial voices because he mercilessly refuses to transcend the psychological vise of the colonial position, although it is clear that the recognition of this split-subject position causes him anger and embarrassment. Indeed, his famed obscurity may arise from the willful resistance to see what he finds so clearly before him: that he cannot control his subjecthood; that he is constructed to react against the dominant culture—whether English or Hindu; that he maneuvers betwixt and between an array of subject positions whose rigidity he finds appalling but which he cannot transcend. This is the problem of hybridity, the multiply defined self which both reiterates colonial categories and ultimately subverts them, but through echoes and not direct opposition. And it is to him both terrifying and liberating. Bhabha shows us that the postcolonial subject, the marginal subject, is someone who feels that her capacity for self-declaration has been taken from her again and again, through a long history in which she has been forced to conform to the dominant culture's prejudices and biases. Her demanding refusal to be identified with others, which mainstream observers of postcolonial discourse view with frustration and perplexity, must be seen as a fear of suffocation. Lata Mani's introduction to her essay in a fat foundational text for cultural studies exemplifies this anxiety:

> [Cultural studies] sets up problematic chains of equivalences between, say, people of color in the United States, people from the third world, lesbians, gays. . . . It is not as though difference is not acknowledged, for an inventory of difference is crucial to this narrative; rather it is that difference is insufficiently engaged . . . This makes a mockery of the escalating racial, class and social tensions which characterize the United States today . . . (in Grossberg et al. 1991:393)

Affiliation becomes possible only through acknowledging difference, because these politics are as much about selfhood as about political economy.

And so the hope of transcendental ambiguity arises through the pain of illegitimacy, the subject caught within multiple subject-positions, and through the fear that grasping one identity will deprive the subject of any at all. A literary critic calls the modern fascination with ambiguity and fragmentation a "late imperial romance," and claims that the literary vision of this romance is not one of cultural despair but of transformation: of a curiously isolated, asocial, transforming merger with the infinite and not with a fellow human. *Heart of Darkness* and *A Passage to India*, McClure argues, denote a new type of imperial romance, in which "the discovery that imperial power is limited, and the prospect of an endless struggle with Otherness, become paradoxically redemptive" (1991:118). Marlow's disintegrated world and his disintegrated telling of that world is disruptive but not destructive. In contrast to the early voyages to marvelous possessions and the wonder and excitement that the first colonizers evoked, the late imperial romance finds the wondrous by breaking apart the mundane, controllable possessions of an exhausted empire, and gaining from these remorseless deconstructions a kind of transcendental peace. But again it is a joy of strange solitude, a kind of dissociated and apolitical ease in which the real difference of other people is reconfirmed as hell.

Perhaps what we are seeing in Bhabha's ambivalence, West's political gambit to be both mainstream and marginal, Suleri's rejection of colonial binarism and Appiah's of racial opposition, in the abundant complexities of a postcolonial politics of difference, and finally in Roshan, wondering "shall I be Indian tonight?" is a kind of intellectual's counterpoint to the literary critic's late imperial romance. There is a hope, certainly, that the ambiguities will lead us out of rigid conceptual corridors, and out of the intolerable bind that confronts the marginalized critic with a choice to assimilate or rebel. And surely one answer to those who are angry at the evocation of fragmentation and contingency is that through these explorations, a culture which has caught itself on the barbs of outmoded concepts can lead itself around the thorn bush. My father once said to me, when I was carping about what I took to be exclusionary feminist claims, that although arguments look foolish from an external vantage point, if the country can work through them they will change the way the genders relate in American culture more profoundly than if we had argued rationally to that end. This, perhaps, is the work of culture, to heal our suffering through means we cannot recognize directly as a healing.[9] In the postcolonial idiom this healing seems to take the form of consciously chosen multiple identities which the subject ironically plays with and sets up against the dominant construction of his marginal identity as a means to transcend the pain of inherent difference.

The romance, if that is what it is, grounds itself in the daily contradictions of a noninnocent abroad, and in the playful, cynical, deliberate attempt to manage in a world in which the one who

manages is unambiguously different. In her efforts to be comfortable in American society, Roshan repeatedly assumes varied selves
in pursuit of her authenticity. She is (consciously) more Indian in
America than she would be in Bombay, and considerably *less* Parsi,
with her *gaghra* and *choli* as flimsy protection in Boston weather
that saw me in sweaters and boots; with her visits to the Hindu
temple; with the *puja* devotions in her Cambridge apartment; with
the Hindi and Gujarati that she would speak insistently to other
Indians at Harvard. She self-consciously and deliberately behaves
in ways which present contradictory and historically inappropriate
signs of identity. And yet she is horrified by the South Asian
Americans who are similarly "inauthentic" and "contradictory" in
their styles. When we went to *diwali* [Hindu New Year] together,
she told me that it was odd to see South Asian Americans, people
with Indian skins and Indian clothes, who when they opened their
mouths produced pure American sounds. And as we sat there with
a hundred South Asians at the Massachusetts Institute of Technology, eating the bland American Indian restaurant food provided by
a local eatery, a woman in a beautiful *kurta,* with a gentle, rounded
Hindu face, came up to us, smiled apologetically, and asked for
some soda; the food was so hot, she said; she was used to the mild
Bengali food. (Bengali spices are not so mild in Bengal.)[10] Roshan
was speechless (momentarily) when she left. "That's it," she said,
"that's what I mean."

> I'm seeing before me a whole culture with people who don't have a
> sense of belonging and are now grappling the wrong way, the only
> way they can. They are born and brought up in America, they're
> naturally American—gestures, talking, attitudes. Their whole sensi-
> bility is American. And yet there's some Indianness, which they see
> in their parents, and they all feel a certain sense of loyalty to that.
> And so what they're trying to do is something I could never do, which
> is to recreate, not real India in America, but what I call a mix and
> match, east meets west situation. For me, I'm not willing to compro-
> mise with mix and match. I don't like this world music phenomenon
> that's coming, of eastern and western music, I don't like this fiction,
> the Bharati Mukherjee people, mixing the cultures. I'm separating.
> I'm saying, this is my culture. Of course typically I live in America
> but I live a *true* Indian culture in America; not an east meets west
> culture. I'm seeing that as dangerous. They're not bringing the true

India, and they're afraid of being truly American, for fear of losing something. So they are creating a third avenue, which is an unknown avenue to me, and doesn't look terribly inviting and exciting either.

I see the west as the riches of America and the opportunities of America which have given me a lot, and I don't want to not have that opportunity, because it has resulted in a good person growing and perhaps I could do something good for the country and for India. So I don't want to lose the opportunity. But I'm not so sure that I'll stay here. I'm going through a phase right now that I'm shunning everything western; to the extent that not even Bombay's good enough, I want to go to Benares for Christmas.

What does it mean for an England-educated Parsi to live a true Indian culture in America? The concept of identity has a peculiar valence in American culture. We primarily see it in its loss. The phrase "sexual identity" acquired cachet only when it became clear that many people did not have a culturally tolerated one. Identity politics are politics of difference, in which the central desperate question is how to negotiate confident uniqueness in a hostile world that threatens to obliterate you. Indeed, if you search for identity in the classic psychoanalytic texts like Fenichel's you will find no listing for it in the index. You *can* find the term in the psychiatric diagnostician's manual, where it occurs in an illness called "identity disorder" and is marked by serious subjective distress regarding uncertainty about three or more of the following: long-term goals; career choice; friendship patterns; sexual orientation and behavior; religious orientation; moral value systems; group loyalties. Even Erik Erikson, the master bard of identity, is more comfortable with identity confusion and crisis than with identity itself.

We tend to think of identity as a clear and unambiguous assertion of selfhood, as a state of comfortable knowledge which directs our behavior and motivates our actions, and our attempts to describe this state have traditionally relied upon the matching of the social context to in-the-head knowledge. Erikson's account, for instance, emphasizes the mutuality of inner conceptualization and social recognition. "Identity formation . . . arises from the selective repudiation and mutual assimilation of childhood identifications and their absorption into a new configuration, which, in turn, is dependent on the process by which a society (often through subsocieties) identifies the young individual, recognizing him as somebody who had to become the way he is and who, being the way he is, is taken for granted" (1968:159). This definition is not dependent, perhaps, on the traditional concept of social role, but it relies upon the social placement of an individual within the modernist analogue of the role: the place, within the huge complex mechanism of the social whole, which the individual has chosen as his own.

Roshan, and others like her, have a much harder time achieving an acknowledged identity in this sense because (at the very least) the large social whole of their world is so chaotic: less a modernist mechanism than a postmodern kaleidoscope. But when Roshan struggles with the question of who she is—whether she should be western or eastern, and who it is that makes these executive decisions—she is not so much struggling to achieve social recognition as she is aiming to play with, challenge, and subvert the kind of recognition she consciously evokes. She manipulates what we think of as her selfhood: at least, she manipulates the appearance of herself to others. At the same time, her primary manipulation is the denial of the definitional power of her social contexts: she is *not* American, *not* English, *not* Hindu in Bombay. Roshan is passionate and desperate and sincere and she is terrified, I think, that if she does not define her uniqueness through differences she will dissolve into the amorphous common whole. The "terrible twos" style of stubborn defiance is a defiance in the service of survival; it is the last defense of the powerless against a power which is not only external but also partially internalized. This is why it is the salvation offered by Memmi and Fanon against the colonizer, and why it is the style adopted by those who lead the oppressed. Erikson suggested that Gandhi's childish "no" was one of the greatest and most effective of his character traits.

Because of Roshan's deliberate manipulation of her social role, it seems that her flailing is better captured as a search for what Lionel Trilling called authenticity than what Erikson described as identity. Being who you purport to be, being true to yourself, being genuine, seems—on the surface, at least—to be more difficult in a world in which one's nationality is not obvious, one's historical past cannot be assumed, and one's ambitions and hopes and achievable goals cannot be read from one's surroundings. The clear tags that might give easy identifications, the possessions and pasts that might, as Rousseau suggested, define selfhood in civil society, are not obvious guides here to the recognition of sameness and difference which comprise our crude Eriksonian intuitions.

Trilling argued that authenticity becomes the leading concept of selfhood in modernity because it captures the greater ambiguity and tension that we, as members of an increasingly kaleidoscopic world, experience in relation to our surrounding social demands. "Authenticity is a more strenuous moral experience than sincerity, a more exigent conception of the self and of what being true to it consists in, a wider reference to the universe and one's place in it, and a less accepted and genial view of the social circumstances of life. At the behest of the criterion of authenticity, much that was once thought to make up the very fabric of culture has come to seem of little account, more fantasy or ritual, or downright falsification" (1971:11). Authenticity is the account of selfhood that surpasses mere presentation, mere role-appropriateness, the selfhood of (in at least one of Trilling's senses) violent assertion that rips through the dull constraining fabric of the everyday, as Kurtz rips through the colonizing culture. Whereas sincerity is merely the commitment to a refusal to lie, authenticity implies a commitment which is deeper, more complex, somehow more true, like the difference between the fact of history and the truth of fiction, as Wallace Stegner might say. Authenticity as the "really real" of personal experience and selfhood becomes a particularly heightened problem in postcolonial culture because the anxiety over labelling is central for the selves whose history is steeped in cross-identification and rejection. In the postcolonial context, this authenticity is of the kind that Barbara Miller borrowed from A. K. Ramanujan to illustrate the terrifying complexities of Ayodhya, a new icon of Indian authenticity. A young prince falls in love with a beautiful daughter of a sage, and pretends to be a spiritual seeker in order to approach her father. The father intuits his real intentions, and sends the prince off to find Truth. After searching fruitless for a year, the prince prepares to go back empty-handed and confess his deception. But then he meets a shrivelled crone, and from her discourse, he realizes that she is Truth. He asks her to come with him; she refuses. He asks, "what message shall I take to the world?" "Tell them," Truth answered, "that I am young and beautiful" (Miller 1991:790). The lie can be more authentic than the apparent truth; mythic origins can seem more authentic than the facts; subverting labels can seem to feel more authentic than accepting them.

Roshan denies the identity ascribed to her either by history (her non-Hindu Parsiness) or by geographical context (her English schooling, her American education) and she chooses to annex the Indianness which others perceive to make her different and to emphasize it. Yet as she asserts her Indianness she does so in a way which calls attention to her westernness, and this is her authenticity, her "who"ness. At Harvard Roshan became the president of the South Asia Society and announced the Society's presence with a gala evening of music, poetry and dance from both South Asia and the West. Adams House students played Ravel, Rameau, and Mozart and recited their poems, and then other students from Harvard and M.I.T. read Urdu and Bengali poems, performed *kathak* (Indian classical dance), and sang popular, low-brow Hindi film tunes.[11] A trio on tabla, violin, and tambura, two of them from America (and one of them Roshan's roommate) performed a traditional *rag*, and a gifted mimic, playing all the parts, enacted a comic skit in which a B.B.C. commentator interviewed Maharishi Mahesh Yogi—the inventor of Transcendental Meditation—and Mr. Swami Rami, the American who sells two weeks of TM to American consumers for large sums. Roshan played a Mozart Fantasia and read a short story about her mother's attempt at matchmaking in Bombay.

In giving a public stage to her own ambivalence, in enacting confusion as creative tension, Roshan does what many great leaders have done. She transposes private crises into a vehicle sufficiently popular that others can identify with it. This was the source of Gandhi's brilliance, that he was able to use the conflict between his moral scrupulousness and his sensuality, between his identification with maternal caring and his ambition, between his intense desire to please and his stubborn individuality, and to craft from those difficulties a singular vehicle whose unique ambiguity enabled countless others to see in it the representation of their own struggles. Gandhi not only used the public arena but needed it, to assure himself, perhaps, of his mastery of these competing emotional intensities. Individuals who need the public arena in this way run terrible risks, but they are, when they succeed, the most remarkable members of a generation.

The point I want to make about all this is that ultimately,

Roshan's route to authenticity—and that described by West, Suleri, and Appiah—is to continually reinvent herself through sequentially identifying with contradictory narrative self-descriptions, while simultaneously learning to treat them as just that: narratives to be manipulated. Roshan, when I knew her at Harvard, was visibly casting around between alternate characterizations of the person she was perceived to be, and it seemed that the task she had set herself was to make these characterizations psychologically available, but not determinate. That is, she seemed to be teaching herself how not to be destroyed by the complexity and by the lack of a single prescribed social role, but rather to be enriched and to use the complexity to create a flexible space in which she could effectively act.

What I find remarkable in Roshan's development is that it is not unlike Roy Schafer's account of the freeing of the imprisoned analysand. The claim that Roshan's struggles are my own, or that Sara Suleri's emotional conflicts are merely a South Asian reflection of Diane Sawyer's, would confuse not only the postcolonial but the psychoanalyst, whose work is predicated (even more than the post-colonial critic's) on the insistent nuances of difference. But I think that Roshan's struggle for authenticity is emblematic—in a particularly extreme but everyday way—of the psychodynamic struggles that have emerged in the complex urban centers where psychoanalysis finds its natural home. Something about the experience of selfhood is changing in our urban centers, something that has to do with travel and uprootedness and cross-cultural identification and global awareness. Over the last ten to twenty years American cities like New York have become more ethnic, more culturally complicated, and their inhabitants have become perhaps even more mobile as a result of technological improvements in air travel and communication. This is of course (in part) a middle-class (middle-brow?) phenomenon—but then Roshan *is* middle class, along with the college professors and writers who become postcolonial critics and the analysands who enter psychoanalysis.[12] This is the world of Paul Gilroy's *Black Atlantic,* where the black English live between two great cultures and carve out structures of feeling that develop "through the special stress that grows with the effort involved in trying to face (at least) two ways at once" (1992:3). It is the world of Carol Gilligan's Harvard and Emma Willard School students, struggling to recognize and interpret womanhood in a world full of contradictory messages and multiple (but constrained and constraining) career choices. It is the world of Aihwa Ong's flexible citizenship among the Chinese businessmen in diaspora, happy to live anywhere so long as it is near a major airport. I don't suppose that in any fundamental way human nature has altered. But I do think that in response to this deracinated, transnational, neoprimordially chaotic village of a world, we have begun to conceptualize an individual's emotional adulthood in a different, more complicated manner. And while it would be naively arrogant to claim that the struggles of the white New Yorker reflect the anxieties of the postcolonial critic, it would be foolish to assert that they are utterly different. In many ways Roshan and I are more like each other than either of us like the small-town, rural farmers' wives in any of the countries in which we both have lived. But I do not want to argue for that strong claim here. All I want to do with this gesturing towards a middle-brow postcoloniality is to assert that Roshan is fascinating for reasons beyond herself, that her struggles mark out an anthropological arena which we are only now beginning to enter but which will become more and more important with time.

The "imprisoned analysand" is Schafer's name for a certain kind of analytic narrative, in which the analysand is jailed within a set of circumstances in the world of unconsciously developed meaning. "A job, a marriage, a vow of vengeance, a stain of dishonour, a dream of glory, a promise made or a promise broken, a tense body or a beautiful face, a small town or the whole wide world; every one of these and many more are potential prisons" (1983:257). The point is that many people in pain see their pain as the consequence of the unalterable circumstances of their lives. From Schafer's perspective, the analytic work is to enable analysands to see their responses to those circumstances as something they have chosen, something they can control, and something to which they have the flexibility to respond. "Briefly, the imprisonment story will no longer be used by the analysand to block more adaptable alternatives, and yet will not be altogether dismissed through the adoption of a manic position of untrammelled freedom" (1983:272). Identity, of course, is the most paradoxical form of imprisonment, for it limits the analysand by asserting his being, and the goal of the work is to reduce the fear of that assertion.

Emotional health—or however one describes the preferable state towards which the analysis supposedly aims—consists in seeing the narratives of one's life as multiple and selected, understanding the purposes they serve, sympathizing with the needs they filled; it means to understand that while one cannot rescript the stories of one's life, one has some choices in the way that one reads and even lives a life. It is a life one has chosen, with all its imperfections, inadequacies and unalterably circumstantial circumstances, and ultimately, it is a life aimed towards the good, in which one is able to love and to work, to find joy. "The new freedom, such as it is, will be that of a readiness to entertain multiple and less acutely conflictual possibilities of understanding and, along with these, multiple possibilities of feeling, revaluation and action in the world. But in another and equally important respect, the narrative redevelopment of the case leads to the analysands seeing the prison in a new and happier light, that is, seeing it also as one of the expectable, unconsciously developed narratives of committing oneself steadfastly to personal aims, values and human relationships" (1983:279–80). Closures are good because they imply choices; too much openness is as imprisoning as none.

I believe that Schafer uses the word "narrative" in order to convey this mixture of flexibility and commitment. He is usually called a constructivist, meaning that he understands the analysand's account of his experience to be constructed in the interaction between analyst and analysand, an interaction, moreover, in which the analyst and analysand are both fictive "second selves," with modes of feeling and behavior peculiar to the psychoanalytic context. The most therapeutic feature of analysis is not so much the understanding of the historical past, but changing our relationship to it. It is not that analysands come to remember a more complex past or even to understand more deeply; it is that they have experienced that past in a different way, and so have profoundly changed it. The analysand who breaks into torrential weeping upon remembering his father's actions in the past is not reliving the past; he is altering his understanding and memory of that past and relating it to his present in a different way. And he comes to claim it differently, as his own, as a piece of the world in which he made himself. In Schafer's "action language," the analysand learns to stop imagining himself as split apart by fragments of himself, feelings he cannot control, thoughts which force him to act against his will.[13] "Psychoanalysts may be described as people who listen to the narratives of analysands and help to transform these narratives into others that are more complete, coherent, convincing and adaptively useful than those they have been accustomed to constructing" (1983:240).

The primary contribution of this approach is the distinction between agency (the person who initiates action) and content (the person's idea of the "I"). The distinction accomplishes at least two ends for Schafer.[14] The first is to unsettle the notion that there is a single, describable entity which is the self. "Nothing here supports the common illusion that there is a single self-entity that each person has and experiences, a self-entity that is, so to speak, out there in nature where it can be objectively observed, clinically analyzed, and then summarized and bound in a technical definition" (1992:26). He sets a puzzle: how many selves and types of self occur in the following remark? A male analysand says to his analyst: "I told my friend that whenever I catch myself exaggerating, I bombard myself with reproaches that I never tell the truth about myself, so that I end up feeling rotten inside, and even though I tell myself to cut it out, that there is more to me than that, that it is important to me to be truthful, I keep dumping on myself" (1992:25). There are, Schafer suggests, eight selves of five types referred to in that remark.[15]

The second accomplishment of this distinction is to put more emphasis on intentional, self-conscious change by seeing the analysand as a *person* who gains increasing mastery over narratives of *selfhood.* Schafer points out that by using the word "self" to replace the word "person," we lose the explanatory power of the agent who uses concepts of selfhood for particular ends—destructive, inhibitory, creative and so forth. The analyst's job is to enable the person to retell important self-narratives in a way which is more adaptive, more complex, more productive; but the analyst can only conceive of that by distinguishing the teller from the tale. Indeed, the teller must come to share this distinction, because only he can change the tale and its motivational role. The distinction captures a theory of change not too distant from Habermas's (1972) distinction between communicative and reflective modes; it is the person's capacity to reflect upon her discourse that enables change to occur.

This redrafting of selfhood into a person with intentionally chosen self-narratives also emerges (more or less) independently from within psychological anthropology. Earlier theorizing emphasized culture as a constraint upon the individual. Cultures laid down more or less consistent patterns of thought and action to which people conformed, or against which they rebelled. Or culture created a "basic personality structure" from the formative experiences shared by members of a certain society, with primary institutions (like childhood discipline or kinship) doing most of the creating and secondary institutions (like religion and folklore) serving as the projective systems which reveal the conflict between institutional desire and cultural content. Later work stressed the difference between personality and culture, but still focused upon the way in which culture selectively pressured the affective and cognitive capacities of the human animal. These orientations were profoundly important as the means to encourage American awareness and toleration of the differences between cultures, to understand that the Japanese (for instance) had no option but to be different. Cultural needs are rather different now. In a world in which social communities are increasingly unsettled—in which people, particularly middle-class people, are increasingly likely to have friends and partners from a variety of backgrounds and to structure their music, their taste, and their desires out of a variety of ethnic traditions—the discourse in psychological anthropology has also shifted into a register in which people create themselves (their selves) rather than one in which they are constrained by culture.

The extraordinary feature of Vincent Crapanzano's modern psychological anthropology is its insistence that the individual chooses, consciously or unconsciously, her selfhood. Self-awareness, he argues, arises when the subject views herself from the vantage point of the other, and the self itself is dialectical and dialogic. Crapanzano describes a circular, continuous movement in which a person "casts the other"—decides, that is, how to characterize another person to himself—"in order to cast oneself" (1990:401). And conversely, one casts oneself in order to cast others. Crapanzano is acutely aware of the constraining forces of language and of the social norms, expectations, and desires which are embodied in the mother-tongue. But his approach is profoundly different from Ruth Benedict's (at times) cookie-cutter conception of culture's impact upon the individual. For Crapanzano, selfhood is a series of images, or narratives, created out of the dialectically evolving three-pointed star of ego, other, and ideal (which he describes in various ways). As I understand it, he distinguishes between the experience of self (which he uses to describe the agent, as Schafer would use the term "person"), the notion of the self (which he presents as contextually and pragmatically defined through dialogic interaction with a chosen other), and self-typification or characterization (which he articulates as the culturally available criteria or prototypes appropriate to the exchange at hand). The person constantly recreates and transforms concepts of his own behavior and being—certainly not freely, but within a highly complex description and behavioral environment that enables him to move in a variety of directions. We construct ourselves in relation to other people; to what we expect their expectations to be; to what they say; to the way we wish to see them and to control the way in which they see us, which is relevant to the way we see ourselves. Cultural limitations are highly important here, but as canals, paths, obstacles, opportunities, not as the high-walled one-way street through which traffic unthinkingly flows.

Contemporary cognitive anthropologists—in particular, Roy D'Andrade, Naomi Quinn, and Claudia Strauss—settle on a theoretical vision that is rather different in intellectual temperament but quite similar in content to the person-and-narrative account of selfhood. A recent volume (D'Andrade and Strauss 1992) underscores a distinction between content and agency by making a puzzle out of the relation of culture and action: how is it possible that people do what their culture tells them? The answer is that cultural models—shared, recognized, and transmitted internalized representations characterized as cognitive schemas—carry motivational force when they become internalized. For something to be a *cultural* model, it must have an observable correlate, which in its most powerful form is language. "Talk, we believe, is the external matrix of all deeply internalized cultural schemas" (D'Andrade 1992:230). Any individual will store, cognitively, thousands of these cultural models—the right way to be a wife, to be a factory worker, to react to witches, and so forth—and some of these will be more deeply internalized than others. The depth of internalization will have something to do with the personal schemas and needs of the individual.[16] The context in which the individual finds himself (on a date, talking to a cab driver, at a lecture) will have much to do with which schema is evoked and the manner in which it motivates him. What all this has to do with the self is that the array of highly salient schemas that motivate action ultimately account for the content of much of an individual's understanding of his "self." Quinn, for instance, argues effectively and at length that cultural models acquire motivational force in an individual's life through an individual's ongoing experience and interpretation of the world, and in the process become the primary self-understanding for the individual. Again, this very different theoretical framework presents a person and her multiple conceptions/narratives/ stories/ schemas about herself along with a theory that describes how it is that certain of these conceptions become salient and motivate behavior at certain times. There is no unitary, simple, coherent, entity which is selfhood; there are persons purposefully acting according to various notions of their selves.

And yet the "self" is terrifyingly overtheorized, and the tangle of contradictory goals which it evokes are both known and unavoidable. We yearn (good anthropologists) to argue against the concept of a bounded unitary self, to argue for multiple narratives, fragmented selves, I/eyes comprised by many roles and modes and cultural deceptions; we want to say that the western (American) self is limited, and inadequate to characterize the self in Bali, Japan, or for that matter, Asia, the iconical non-West. Still we are stuck with embodied persons displaying an undeniably human package of language and emotions. And so Geertz argues that the western concept of the person is "a rather peculiar idea within the context of world cultures"—this is undoubtedly true—but his ethnographies are full of recognizably person-like persons.[17] Kondo eloquently deconstructs the concept of the western, binary self, but uses personal pronouns in a quite familiar way. Lutz attacks universalist claims by pointing to a strikingly nonwestern linguistic anatomy of the person; McHugh attacks the attack by arguing that irrespective of linguistic referents, her Gurung informants feel and suffer in a way which is recognizably within the western idiom.[18] Spiro suggests that these awkwardnesses arise through the ease with which we conflate person, individual, personality and self-representation when speaking of the self.[19] Obeyesekere, in frustration, abandons the term altogether.[20]

I would rather explain this conception of a person gaining comfortable mastery over multiple narratives of selfhood as a theory of identity. The descriptive and analytic problem of Roshan (and others) is more precisely and less problematically stated as the problem of who she is: her authenticity or, more concretely, her identity. This perspective on identity is quite different from Erikson's naturalistic vision of an identity which can be intuited by an objective observer in a limited period of time. Roshan will probably be manipulating her interpretive contexts and flipping from one persona to another for years. Rather than locating her identity in the narratives themselves, or in the matching of the narratives to external approval, we capture more of her "who"ness in her experience of comfort and control in the slippage from one narrative to another. This comfort is what Schafer evokes in his account of the freeing of the imprisoned analysand: not that the analysand is unconstrained by narrative, but that the analysand comes to feel that her narratives of personhood, complex and even contradictory as they might be, are those that she has chosen, that rather than being controlled by the brute oppression of a narrative externally imposed, she is in mastery of the narratives which structure her presentations of personhood to the world.

In fact one could argue that the mastery of multiple narratives is the core project of the postmodern politics of identity. These ambitious texts, barnacled by theoretical jargon, enact Roshan's stubborn, tenacious, Gandhian "no." Their most insistent message is the refusal to be characterized by someone else's narrative, to assert their own authority in laying claim to a narrative of personhood that ultimately may be not so different than those they have rejected. When Lata Mani, for instance, rejects assimilation with heterosexual feminists, Chicana feminists, or black lesbian feminists she does so, I suspect, not because their narratives are so very different but because she seeks to choose them, not to have them chosen. When Gayatri Spivak denounces her characterization as a Marxist, a feminist, a deconstructionist, even as a disk jockey for contemporary culture, she does so, one suspects, not because she rejects those categories but because she resists having them imposed. When we, as members of an academic culture, are complicit in the dicta that only women can write on feminism, only men may write about the men's movement, only African-Americans may write on black politics, we acknowledge the importance of allowing those who have been disempowered to experience empowerment through the casting of their narratives of self-characterization.

From this perspective on the politics of identity, successful (healthy, appropriate) identity in a modern postcolonial context is less a self-characterizing narrative with a mirroring world than a sense of command over narrative complexity: narratives which one has to some extent chosen, whose mastery gives one a sense of direction, adequacy, and goodness. This sense of authoritative comfort is present in the Eriksonian reference: "the conscious feeling of having a personal identity is based on two simultaneous observations: the perception of the self-sameness and continuity in time and space and the perception of the fact that others recognize one's sameness and continuity" (1968:50). Erikson clearly means to imply more in this framework than the mere belief in stable embodiment; his studies of Luther and Gandhi suggest that the individual's quiet confidence in his capacity to act, feel, and be seen as the moral agent he chooses to be are important parts of identity achievement. Yet Erikson emphasizes, like our folk model of identity, the all-of-a-piece integration of intentional actor and social respondent. The cultural dimensions of late-twentieth-century America and its international interlocutors demand that we shift this emphasis.

Indeed, it is time to shift the emphasis in our social interpretation from cultural constraint to moral agent. I am scarcely the first to observe that Foucault badly undercut social theory's interest in the individual; nor should his blindness in that respect lead us to expel him textually and bodily from our thinking. But to conceive of ourselves as simply diagnosing the hegemony of the sociocultural is depressing. Far better, at least for our own sense of human possibility, to see individuals as struggling to achieve a manner of living in the world which is, for them, an exigent moral goal; and to see ourselves as anthropologists seeking to understand their historically and personally peculiar conceptions of the good. This is Charles Taylor's complex envisioning of selfhood and, in particular, of the tensions of modern identity. He argues that it is incoherent to conceptualize selfhood without an enmeshment with the moral, that selves must be understood as aiming at the good, and that our evaluative concepts enshrine this action of subjectively directing our lives towards moral affirmation.

The predicament of modernity, Taylor suggests, is the increasing power of this vision of individuals striving for deeply felt aspirations, while at the same time the frameworks which gave meaning to those aspirations have somehow gone awry, and multiplied. The most stubborn, awkward, recalcitrant problem in our attempts to theorize postmodernity is the effort to keep toleration for diversity

from collapsing into ethical licentiousness; to understand that multiplicity is not the same as complacent relativism, and that the
search for authenticity is not the same as self-indulgence but a
deliberate, intentional, and moral quest. In the face of this crisis of
meaning, modernity demands not that we despair, but that we
consciously, deliberately, with a heightened awareness of the twin
dangers of individual selfishness and communitarian oppresssion,
choose the contexts of meaning within which our lives can grasp
moral vividness.

These are large issues, but they are a compelling legacy for
anthropological orientation. When we take this theoretical frame
back to the field, and particularly if the field is a complex civilization, we are forced to see culture not so much as something
reified—there, as it were, for the observer to observe as a unitary,
constraining, personality-stamping whole—but as a series of pragmatic contexts to which individuals respond with narratives which
embody notions of the good life and judgments about right action.[21] Richard Shweder writes of an emergent view of culture that
would ground itself in the ends of everyday acts and interactions.
"A cultural psychology aims to develop a principle of intentional-
ity—action responsive to and directed at mental objects or representations—by which culturally constituted realities (intentional
worlds) and reality-constituting psyches (intentional persons) continually and continuously make each other up, perturbing and
disturbing each other, interpenetrating each other's identity, recip-
rocally conditioning each other's existence" (1991:102). Ultimately
the aim of Shweder's project is a moral one: to see meaning not as
something constraining what you can say but rather as enabling
what you intend, and to see it as morally saturated with notions
of the good. For all of its loyalty to older forms of anthropological
understanding, this people-centered approach to culture is quite
different from an earlier anthropological ethos.

It seems likely that the new leadership in Parsi cultural enactment
may come from the more than ten thousand Zoroastrians settled
in North America, because in these new circumstances, Parsi ethnicity moves from an ascription to a resource, a possibility, a
choice, an achievement, and the need to persuade young people to
choose wisely catalyzes a kind of cultural creativity. This collectivity—centered in Toronto, Houston, New York, Los Angeles, Chicago—has its intense battles, many of them between the Zoroas-

trians of more recent Iranian descent and those from India. And there are predictable Parsi tensions between the liberal and the ultra-orthodox. But nevertheless there seems to be an acute awareness that if Zoroastrians do not forge some new sense of commonality, they will literally disappear. The report from the 1993 Annual General Meeting remarked: "In his *President's Report,* Rohinton Rivetna stated that our greatest pride was our unity. Unity out of respect for each other's views, however diverse. He stressed that our top priority was to inculcate Zarthusti values in our children and make them proud to be Zarthustis."[22] Despite parent-organized skiing trips and congresses and marital ads placed in *Fezana* (the North American magazine) and *Parsiana,* it becomes brutally obvious that young Parsis, born and educated in America, are likely to marry out. The numbers are simply too small in any one area to create a viable pool of candidates. And so the enthusiasm of the congresses, youth gatherings, and newsletters is to forge a sense of Zoroastrian identity which is not dependent upon a habituated culture, which is literally not a *habitus.* Roshan remarks:

> Parsis are doing something which the other Indians are not doing, which I like. Second-generation Indians, as I told you, are trying to make this third avenue. You dress up in all Indian stuff on festival days, and go and blindly do a *puja,* you don't understand it, and basically your sensibility's American, you don't want to let go of that. I found that Parsis are not really trying to make a third avenue but to do what I'm doing. Bringing real Parsihood to America. For them it's easy to do because their lifestyles in India anyway are a real mixture of west and east. It's not so hard to keep that over here. Whereas the parents of these second-generation Indians were very Indian. For us it's quite normal. There's no artificial recreation that needs to be done. They can wear jeans and be just as Parsi, whereas Hindu families look at their children wearing jeans as now being an American thing.

But the evidence suggests that, in fact, it requires a great deal of intentional recrafting to make available a culture which is not based on unthinking imitation but upon some manner of teaching, particularly teaching the religion in a manner which can be consciously and easily learned. This is glaringly true with respect to Zoroastrianism, with its ancient, uncomprehended prayers and its solitary practice. And so the Gatha Studies Trust in Pittsburgh has produced a twelve-lesson home-study course on the religion, with essays by scholars geared towards making the abstract, piecemeal texts comprehensible as a contemporary ethical and spiritual vision. They are thoughtful, sophisticated essays, sprinkled with verses from the most scholarly translation of the Gathas, which argue for the salience of the religion to a middle-class, ethnically tapestried life. *Fezana* organizes congresses, symposia, tours of Iran; its fifty-page newsletter features news—with detailed accounts of the experience of unity at these various events, as well as the specifics of the lectures and celebratory prayers—accounts of Zoroastrian center openings, stories of the achievements and tragedies of particular North American Zoroastrians, historical profiles, upcoming events, traditional recipes, explanations of particular prayers, and more. A great deal of energy is spent on trying to teach *Parsi-panu*, Parsiness, in a form which is not embodied in food and gesture and everyday ordinariness, and is something that a student can deliberately learn.

This is not to say that deliberate teaching dominates Parsi encounters in America; on the contrary, there seems to be an immense number of purely sociable occasions. Roshan invited me to a Parsi event in December 1993 whose singular characteristic was a kind of multicultural insouciance in the service of reinforcing a sense of Parsi community. It was the Zoroastrian Association of Greater Boston annual Christmas party (there is also an Easter party). To this Roshan wore a demure Victorian dress. The venue was a Chinese restaurant and we ate Chinese American food. Santa came and distributed gifts to the children; the Walkman on our table helped the young men to follow the progress of the football game. Some Gujarati was spoken, and there was at least one person in Indian dress, and plans were eagerly made for future religious and social events. Nobody (not even Roshan) seemed to think that there was anything amiss with the cultural pastiche. In Boston, the week after the Christmas party there was a youth party; some young Zoroastrians were planning to come down from Montreal for a New Year's Eve party; and planning had long since begun for a symposium on the religion in February.

Nevertheless, it is the teaching, rather than the social gathering, that profoundly alters the manner of identifying oneself as a Parsi, not only for the children but for their parents. The newsletter with its recipes, historical sound bites, decoding of the prayers, the scholarly activities and the home study courses, even the very parties and gatherings, to which one must be invited and then decide to attend, figure Zoroastrianism in North America as an opportunity—and not as an ascribed identity. This is an inherent part of community-building abroad. Parsis in America must deliberately choose to subscribe to *Fezana* or *Parsiana,* neither of which is free; the congresses are expensive in time and money, even though efforts are made to lighten the financial burden; and social opportunities can be ignored. The concern constantly reiterated at the Seventh North American Zoroastrian Congress in Houston in 1990, a gathering of about 450, was how to pass on tradition to children growing up in the vastly different world of middle-class America, with its malls and discos and shocking mores. "When I hopefully have a family, what spiritual guidance will I choose to feed my child? . . . If we disagree on how to cook our food, we'll be eating hotdogs."[23] This is hardly a unique problem; it is one most immigrant communities must face, particularly if they are of the middle class and their members arrive in North America with jobs or schooling, usually with enough financial and social backing from the world that drew them that they can afford to ignore their fellow immigrants if they choose.

Often, the new immigrants do not ignore their fellow Parsis. At the youth session at the 1994 North American Zoroastrian Congress, a beautiful woman explained that she had confronted her ignorance about her identity when a Hare Krishna devotee stopped her in a Toronto street and offered to give her a booklet on the glorious Ram. She explained that she came from India and didn't need it, and he asked her with respect if she were Hindu. She said no, Zoroastrian, and he asked her what that was. Her calm superiority deserted her and she panicked. She told him that Zoroastrianism was the earliest monotheism and that it taught good thoughts, words, and deeds; then she announced that she had an appointment and fled. "When you come to this country," she explained, "there is a common pattern. First you shun all community events. You think of them as boring and unsophisticated. And then after you've been asked about Zoroastrianism by so many people, and you feel embarrassed but also curious, after you've come to terms with being different, you begin to attend the dinners and congresses and parties, and they don't seem silly but comfortable. And you begin to learn from the congresses how to verbalize what it is to be Zoroastrian." "It's true," Roshan said afterwards. "First you think they're stupid. Then after you've been here a while you find them comfortable. They remind you of home."

At the 1994 Philadelphia congress 500 Parsis spent three days attending sessions which constantly returned to what it was to be Zoroastrian and Parsi.[24] Most of the speakers disagreed with each other. One referred to the orthodox as benighted ostriches with their heads in the sand; the next said that orthodox ritual continuity was essential to maintain the faith. The youth sat in circles and discussed what it meant to be a Parsi, and all of them had different accounts of the threads that bound them to the community. It was obvious that individuals had radically different understandings of Zoroastrianism and their ethnic roots. This must be true for all communities, but as most never raise the question, their members go around in happy ignorance of the different shape of their neighbors' sense of identity. The North American Parsis seem to be developing an articulate tolerance of a community of disagreement, in which wildly divergent opinions—intermarriage must be accepted; intermarriage cannot ever be accepted; the *sudreh-kusti* is the only sign of true faith; the *sudreh-kusti* is an outmoded ritual irrelevant to spiritual commitment—mark out a shared arena, and in which asking the question, "what is it to be Parsi and Zoroastrian?" is more powerful than the answer any individual gives. In 1993 Farrokh Mistree, then located in Atlanta, pointed out in *Fezana* that it was no longer possible to expect passively that your children would be enculturated within your culture, and thus Parsi conceptions of Parsiness must deliberately embrace radical contradictions. "When I was growing up I knew that I was a Parsi Zoroastrian, and was part of an extended family. I knew where our fire temple was. I went to the fire temple and did what the others did. I ate lovely food, met the priests, and attended weddings and *navjotes*. I participated (at times with boredom) in the *jashans* that were held in my house . . . But what about my children?"[25] He argued that for parents to become active teachers of their children, they themselves must learn; they must acquire a self-conscious, intentional knowledge of their religion which they were never taught, and as they learn they will interpret, and their interpretation must be respected. Then without irony he quoted one of Kipling's patronizing remarks as a guide to sophisticated postcolonialism: "There are many issues associated with the religious education of Zoroastrian children in North America, and there are many different ways in which they can be resolved. I will end by taking refuge in Kipling's words: 'There are nine and sixty ways / to construct the tribal lays, / and—every—single—one—of—them—is—right!'"[26]

The repositioning of this postcolonial community away from its traditional home is remarkably interesting because it represents a kind of triumph of will over history. These are people marked by a complicity in a political order many of them would disavow. In India the community has been somewhat confused about its identity and affiliations and condemns itself beyond what the dull tread of history would merit. But Parsis do not seem to do this in North America. Judging from congresses and casual conversations in Boston, Philadelphia, Houston, Los Angeles, and San Diego, North American Parsis do not dwell on their failures and on the inadequacy of community members to the same extent as their Indian counterparts. They do not publicly chastise their youth but take pride in them and in their future. They are most concerned to keep hold of a past they see as precious and special; they do not live in a world in which the Parsi Lying-in Hospital is crumbling and the statues of J. N. Tata are surrounded by beggars and crows. Out of Bombay, as the young woman from Toronto said, it seems to have become easier for them to take joy in their bonding and to yearn for more. So at these congresses the youth get together in the pounding disco but wear little *fravashis* (a winged figure which is a Zoroastrian symbol for the spirit), and they talk about how much they want to maintain their Zoroastrian heritage and at the same time accept the statistical probability that they will marry out of the faith. The older generation takes pride in doing well enough to bring their families across the country for these gatherings, and they take pride in giving generously of time and money to maintain their ethnicity. Were they not so generous, their children would have none, and so some years ago Parsis began to create the networks and enthusiasm that has led to the congresses and youth gatherings and informal Sunday schools.

◆　◆　◆

From the perspective which presents Parsi self-characterization as a resource, Roshan's complexity becomes merely a dramatization of the problem confronting other Parsis abroad: how to manage

one's involvement with and commitment to the multiple contexts
of one's life—a human problem, to be sure, but one cast in particularly strong light by these exemplars of multicultural existence.
But not all styles of management have Roshan's multiplicity. Dina
is Roshan's closest friend in America, a woman she had grown up
with and also at that time a graduate student at Harvard. Dina was
unquestionably Parsi. She looked Parsi, she cooked Parsi food, she
spoke with a Parsi accent, she said her prayers every day and never
touched her prayer book during her period. She had been in America for about seven years. But while Roshan thrashed her way
through wildly different public personas, Dina had what her husband called an "identity bubble": she was the same, he said, in
Boston, Bombay, and Los Angeles, where he had met and married
her. And he was an American. Each of them had to manage, then,
the incoherence that surrounded the cultural commitments of their
lives. They did so peaceably, with a kind of deadpan, ironic humor
that seemed to give them command of the juggling-act quality of
some aspects of their experience together. The following conversation took place in December 1993.[27]

> *Richard:* We were an hour late for the reception. It wasn't actually
> a wedding. And when we got there nobody was there.
> *Me:* Nobody was there. It was a reception in Bombay?
> *R:* In Bombay. Everyone else was two hours late.
> *Dina:* We got married here.
> *R:* Under the "no fumar aqui" sign in the County Hall of Records
> in Los Angeles.
> *Me:* Did anyone know you were married?
> *D:* Oh yes. It's just that you need a month's notice for a plane
> ticket [in India] and we decided four to six days beforehand,
> that we would get married.
> *R:* Everyone in Dina's family had been married on December 12.
> *D:* It was a coincidence. My parents had gotten married then be-
> cause it was an auspicious day, you know, time and month and
> all of that. So my sister was the next to get married in my fam-
> ily, and December 12 turned out again to be a very good day.
> So then there were two, and then my brother said okay, we'll
> get married on December 12 as well.
> *R:* After a number of years of dating and having this crisis come
> up every December 12, I said, if we're not married on Decem-
> ber 12, and I said it very innocently—

D: I'm sure you did.

R: There's this tradition in America, that people are together forever, and usually what happens with a lot of my friends, they get drunk on the 4th of July and they get married. Or whatever. And I said innocently, you know if we're not married this December 12 we'll just go on in this pattern. About December 3rd or 4th. And Dina went into a panic, because she had read it differently than I had said it.

D: Ultimatum.

R: It was dinner conversation.

D: It was not.

R: So we were married. Four hundred dollars in phone calls later, because Naz had to get all this information.

D: Auspicious days. My mother said, we have to get married at 11:00 Bombay time, in the morning, and I said, that's midnight here, I don't think it can happen and she said oh all right, let me go to the nighttime part in Bombay. So by the time she had figured it out, and told me all the other rites to perform, it was $400 in phone bills.

R: I had to ask her father for her hand in marriage.

D: My father was so sweet. He said, "do it, do it."

R: They had met me in a variety of circumstances. There was the accidental three-month stay.

D: So we got married. And talk about auspicious. We go to City Hall and there was one line for marriage and one for divorce. I didn't tell my mother that. And here my mother was telling me about the time, and what to wear and how to do this or that. And at the divorce counter there were quite a few people and they were fighting.

R: I have a statement to make about Indian women. That the story becomes more embellished with time. There was one couple in the line, and they were stony-faced.

D: But my aunt and uncle happened to be visiting, just coincidentally, and she is my mother's sister, and I asked them to come on my behalf, and so my mother felt comfortable, and my dad was also very happy. And Ron's parents. And so we all trooped down to City Hall, and they signed as witnesses, and the marriage ceremony itself was quite short. Very short.

R: I imagine it's like getting married in a civil ceremony in Moscow. There are a lot of people who do that.

D: And then we went for a five-hour lunch. And it was a wonderful wedding, because we really enjoyed ourselves, instead of entertaining five hundred other guests.

R: And that night we had, oh, two thousand years of Zoroastrian history meets—

D: late twentieth century America.

R: Modern technology. So Dina has all these . . .

D: What my mother tells me, coconut, garlands, the *car* has a garland.

R: Sacred items, auspicious things. And there's a *dia* [small oil lamp] burning. And it's the middle of December, so the whole apartment's closed, and Dina put it in with the wick too tall, so it's very smoky.

D: Oil with a wax wick, Parsi style, and I didn't think.

R: It leaked into the other room and set off the fire alarm. It was an indication of the day that I just took the batteries out. . . .

D: So later on we went to India. Since my parents hadn't seen us.

R: We had a similar version of east meets west. Modern and ancient technology. They had this thing which they set up in the flat, Dina's mother, and you have to stand on the stand, and there are all of these chalk patterns, auspicious things, and they're waving coconuts and eggs and things and apparently these days you can't have a wedding without a video. And so there are these guys with lights running around. Sort of a blessing. We couldn't go to a fire temple.

D: We did have a Zoroastrian priest come to Pasadena and bless us, in our apartment. This was later. I thought, it would be nice to be blessed by a Zoroastrian priest.

R: We've been married three times.

D: My father is a priest, and the religion is very important to me, I do practice it, and I thought it would be nice to have a priest bless us, not to do any ceremony. And the priest we had was quite avant-garde in his thinking.

R: Sai Baba?

D [in a minatory tone]: No.

R: I've got a story for another time.

D: So we had this priest and he blessed us and my aunt and uncle were there, because it was just within a week. And he said a lot of blessings, prayer in our Avesta language, and then he translated in English so that everyone could understand. It was a very beautiful little prayer.

R: In the meantime everyone's children are running all over the apartment. It was quite a zoo.
D: It was very Parsi.
R: Typically Indian.

What makes humor humorous is contradictory juxtaposition: dignity and a slippery banana skin, a beagle and the character of a wily, war-toughened pilot. What makes irony ironic is simultaneous assertion and denial: "I can't imagine anything more interesting than watching grown men fight over a rubber ball." Common to both of them is tolerance of the conjunction. Humor isn't funny if it makes someone cry, and irony isn't subtle if it deceives.[28] These Batesonian acts and utterances, frames within frames, become an adaptively congenial way for this couple to handle the multiple framing expectations of their lives. Richard's culture teaches him that cars are never garlanded and that eggs have ritual significance only at Easter, and for children at that. Dina's culture teaches her that good weddings have five hundred guests and that eggs and auspicious times and father's permissions are part of the package. For them to laugh about their wedding(s) is both to acknowledge the incongruities of trained expectation and actual experiences and to assert that they are tolerable. Dina laughs with Richard about his egg-waving inlaws and the smoke-sodden apartment. Richard laughs with Dina about the small civil ceremony and the expensive phone calls. They laugh together, and with the laughter retain both the uniqueness of their own experience and the joy of their union. Unlike Roshan, Dina feels no need to master her frameworks by adopting them sequentially; but her laughter becomes a kind of skilled command over the tensions of multiple lives.

There has been a great deal of talk recently, both inside anthropology and out, that the discourse of multiculturalism has no moral guidelines, and that the cost of cultural democracy is moral anarchy. I see no grounding for this claim from my work among the Parsis. There are, to be sure, high costs to a multicultural life. It is very stressful to be a Roshan, or even a Dina. The daily conventions you absorbed when small no longer apply to your adopted culture, and you must learn to weave between many different cultural demands. The goals your parents had may be quite different from your own. Yet for all the complex semiotics in which Roshan and

Dina find themselves entangled, for all the representation of their first culture as a resource, and not an anchor, I never found myself in any doubt about the moral integrity of these two. The modern world contains an infinite variety of ways for a lax soul to manipulate others, to maximize his own advantage, to behave as a lax soul has always done. Roshan seeks for her authenticity in delineable ways: she attempts to develop her authority over complex narratives of personhood through dramatic enactment. She does so with seriousness, and in a manner which exhibits kindness and respect for others. It is easy to make mistakes in judgment. In many respects that is what this book has been about. But to say mistakes occur is very different from saying that agency is irrelevant, or that moral anarchy rules. And that, to paraphrase Evans-Pritchard, is where the humanist takes over from the anthropologist.

Coda

When I met Roshan at Harvard it was with hesitation that I brought up the topic of my book on the community, and did so only after she had enthusiastically announced that she planned to read the manuscript. I diffidently explained that I was writing about the criticism of the young men and hurriedly launched into an account about how this criticism might have more to do with the reversal of late-nineteenth-century identification with the British than with any actual behavior. Roshan listened patiently. At the end she said, "that's interesting, Tanya. Maybe it's true. But are you going to explain why all the young men are gay?"

ANTHROPOLOGICAL
REPOSITIONINGS

7

Can the Parsi move to self-critique in a time of change serve as a warning for the modern anthropologist? Modern Parsis are not unlike anthropologists. Both are middle-class, well-educated, often urban, and relatively urbane. Both are from communities which made great contributions to liberalism on the eve of their country's emergence as a modern polity. Yet both of them now fear that the steps their communities took at that time led them to a political position which they now see as morally untenable. Both of them fear that these steps have cursed them; that ultimately, because of them, they might die out; and both of them, in dealing with this fear, argue fiercely about change while change of necessity goes on. And both, unless they can adapt their vision of themselves to this necessity of change, will alter so dramatically over the next few decades that they will no longer recognize themselves.

What I fear is that in their anxieties to avoid the scourge of political correctness and their guilty suspicion that the attack is justified, anthropologists will critique themselves into irrelevance. Contemporary anthropological discourse sometimes carries a tone of moral condemnation—yet we attack each other often more because we are acting out anthropological anxieties about "other-ing" than because of substantive disagreement. Avant-garde anthropologists are sometimes held responsible for this disciplinary distress because they are the innovators. That is unfair. Few of them attack their own discipline. But somehow, their innovations are swept up in arguments they never generated and claims they never made. I do not want to target an attack of postmodernists against scientists, but a general malaise that runs through the denigration of anthropology by anthropologists of all intellectual stripes, in which postmodernism is seen as destructive rather than exciting and in which the classic ethnographies of the forties are seen as grand failures. As I see it, the problem lies not in the serious, thoughtful attempts to move the discipline forward but in what I think of as "hall talk," a carping, dissatisfied, troubled, sniping at one another behind each other's back. This is a malaise about what we are all thought to have said about each other, rather than anything we have said. I hear in the corridors and byways of the academy an anxiety about an anthropology in crisis, a condemnation of anthropology as a colonialist endeavor, a rationalization by graduate students who do not want to go abroad that anthropology is a reenactment of a colonialist enterprise. I hear anger that books like *Writing Culture* or *Tuhami* supposedly announced in a public place the worry that fieldwork is illegitimate; anger that putting in print things that we used to worry over amongst ourselves in smoky bars will discredit anthropology. I hear complaints that other fields do not take us seriously—at a time when anthropology has in fact had more impact in the humanities and social sciences than it has ever had before. Much of this anxiety flutters around the representation of anthropology as a colonialist enterprise, and much of it is a slightly hysterical displacement from more realistic worries about the discipline's rapid change.

In the eyes of many, anthropology stands condemned as the "handmaiden of colonialism," in Levi-Strauss' now famous phrase. "Now, whoever tried to deny that anthropology is the handmaiden of colonialism?" the Prices muse on an ethnographic collecting expedition. "In St. Laurent, even more than the Cayennes, we have been living pretty much the way visiting colonial white folks would have been expected to. . . . There's something about the definition of our role, and the way the town is set up, that leaves little choice" (1992:41). Their long discursus about their voyage is a distressed meditation on this problem.

> Much the same reasoning lies behind our initial non-negative (but still far from positive) decision about the museum—to participate in a project we don't fully believe in because if we don't someone else will, and the representation of Alukus, Saramkaa, and other Ma-

roons (and therefore those people themselves) would ultimately be the poorer for it. Who gets enriched (culturally, politically, spiritually, materially) by a project like this, and who is impoverished, is still very much on our minds. (1992:17)

In 1973 Talal Asad remarked, in one of the first substantial discussions of the problem, that "we are today becoming increasingly aware of the fact that information and understanding produced by bourgeois disciplines like anthropology are acquired and used most readily by those with the greatest capacity for exploitation" (1973:16). In 1992 Roger Keesing wrote that "whatever intellectual counterinterpretations we may entertain, we are products of an imperialist discourse that irresistibly shapes our language and our perspective" (1992:7). While it is clearly desirable to describe the world without asserting the supremacy of the west, and to know the nature of our enculturated biases, it seems to me that in some of these worries there is a defensiveness and an anxiety about anthropology as inherently dubious, an anxiety which responds to the nonanthropological literature which anthropologists often read.

The most trenchant critiques are launched at the discipline from outside. The sophisticated critique does not condemn the anthropologist directly (although this is not to deny that our imagination is shaped by the discourse of our times), but rather states that anthropology, as a discipline about the knowledge of others, re-enacts, by creating that knowledge, a relationship of domination over those others. By the asymmetrical acquisition of this knowledge, by the presence of scholarly tomes describing distant peoples and the absence of their books about us, by the objectification of people into knowledge, anthropology (from this perspective) displays the power differential which in fact made it possible for anthropologists to do their fieldwork. Evans-Pritchard could study the Nuer even though they didn't want him there because the Nuer had learned that to kill white men was dangerous. Gyan Prakash in his "postfoundationalist" manifesto presents anthropology as a "discipline that specializes in scrutinizing the Other" (in Dirks 1992:363), deconstructs the concept of cultural separateness, and suggests that the very fact that anthropology depends upon a concept of culture circumscribes the discipline within the Orientalist project. He suggests, in fact, that the claim to knowledge made by

the discipline is sufficient to destroy the involvement of the anthropologist in the society where she did her fieldwork. "Professional
training and expertise allowed the researchers to claim that partici-
pant-observation protected the observer's externality that had been
compromised in fieldwork" (in Dirks 1992:365). In this reading
knowledge is not only a domination over, but also a defense
against, other human beings.

Perhaps Said's work, more than any other, has popularized the
view that the attempt to know others cannot be isolated from the
desire to dominate them. And Said's view of anthropology is harsh
and unforgiving; his anthropology is an exclusively western enterprise closely tied to colonialism. "[Anthropology] [carries] as a
major constitutive element, an unequal relationship of force between the outside Western ethnographer-observer and the primitive, or at least different, but certainly weaker and less developed
non-European, non-Western person" (1993:56). He later goes on
to elaborate his point through a figure in Kipling's *Kim:* "The
native anthropologist, clearly a bright man whose reiterated ambitions to belong to the Royal Society are not unfounded, is almost
always funny, or gauche, or somehow caricatural, not because he
is incompetent or inept—on the contrary—but because he is not
white"(1993:153). This is anthropology as the discipline of pith-
helmeted explorers, presumptuous and possessive, traveling
through a land of collectible facts with the brave certainty that their
skin color brings them passage. This is an anthropology of voyeur-
istic curiosity, the anthropology of bare-breasted women in *National Geographic* and of the expert reconnoiterings of the Great
Game. Despite the caricature it is an inextinguishable image. James
Clifford reminds us that the "(inexpungable?) taint of colonialism
still makes anthropology untouchable in some progressive and
'third world' milieus" (in Grossberg et al. 1992:111).

The anger, of course, is not reserved for anthropology. Throughout the human and social sciences, in the writing of fiction and
history and music, there is anger about those who speak for others.
In the academy women are hired to teach about women, African-
Americans are hired to teach about African-Americans, Hispanics
about Hispanics. Names like Prakash, Suleri, Mani, Bhabha, not
to mention Appadurai, Narayan, Tambiah, Obeyesekere, now
dominate where names like Cohn, Singer, Bailey, and Dumont once
held sway.[1] Gayatri Spivak denounces the principle that only like

can speak on like; knowledge, she says, emerges through difference. But her answer to the question "can men theorize feminism, can whites theorize racism, can the bourgeois theorize revolution?" is "yes but": "it is crucial that members of these groups must be kept vigilant about their assigned subject positions" (1987:253). Her "must be kept vigilant" is ambiguous but has an ominous ring, as if to suggest that men can write about women so long as they are aware that they write from an apologetic position of patriarchal supremacy; that is, as long as they realize they are the power-holders and that, as such, are disempowered to understand the weak. This is not to say that I think that men should write with ignorance of women's history—on the contrary, dispensing with memory is one of the greatest of sins. I am in general an advocate of the anger that has restructured the academy's sensitivity to mainstream presumptions. But sometimes the anger is so great it seems to wash away all subtleties.

A heightened sensitivity about asymmetrical power relations now dominates the dialogue of humanistic knowledge. And it sharpens the anxiety that anthropologists not uncommonly feel about speaking for other people, a fear that speaking for the weak does not alleviate but emphasizes their weakness. "This book," Comaroff writes in the introduction to a well-known ethnography, "is the production of that privilege, and in conveying something of the logic and subtle creativity of those whose discourse remains stifled it can, at best, be inadequate" (1985:xi). Despite the suppleness of such disclaimers anthropology still carries its imperialistic burden for many of those whose ancestors suffered from imperialism. There, a "native" might think, goes another cocksure white person, swaggering in his ignorance but wealthy, wealthier than we are, because he has been paid to learn just a little of what we already know. It is not surprising that a history of anthropological informing has left a bitter trace. When the gifted Pueblo writer Leslie Marmon Silko wants to assert the depth of her storytelling knowledge she says: "Now this is a story anthropologists would call very old" (1991:89). She is being ironic, and a little cruel.

There is validity and invalidity in envisioning anthropology as the primary trope of othering. Certainly the guilt of speaking for others fits neatly onto a worry that anthropologists encounter as endemic in fieldwork: that they turn their friendships into data. Rabinow's (1977) night with a prostitute was perceived by some as offensive because although he accepted the prostitute to prove his affiliation with his male Moroccan friend, the prostitute seemed a powerful metaphor for the anthropological experience: you pay for friendship and write about it later. And we have a history of colonial complicity, conscious or otherwise, that we cannot ignore, and anxieties about the profound process of identification and return in fieldwork which become tangled with these more directly political concerns. But there is a danger that if we accept the implications of this trope as inevitable, we will become like Memmi's colonizer who sees the colonial exploitation, disapproves of it, but remains ineradicably in the category of the exploiter, and so becomes impotent. This is a simplification that can paralyze us and cause us to be overly harsh to our colleagues, and to distrust ourselves. I suggest that to condemn ourselves for the past is to use the semiotics of a past relationship to distort the realities of present ones. The postcolonial world is no longer configured in the stark opposition of self and other. Said—as Clifford suggests—is caught in the limitations of his own categories, and the way to move forward is to confront the power asymmetry directly and to see it as a tool in an effort to understand, and then to take that confidence into the new arenas for the anthropological exploration of modernity.

Power asymmetry is inherent in anthropological work. No matter what the political relations between the anthropologist's country and the country of the field (and they are often hierarchical), no matter what colonial history they share (and it is often considerable), no matter what the race of the anthropologist nor whether the anthropologist studies "up" or "down," the anthropologist ultimately controls the representation of the people she studies and as a writer she is more powerful—in that arena—than the people about whom she writes. Regardless of what they tell her, and even if they lie, the subjects of a book cannot control the pen the author sets to paper. The subjects trust her with their stories and she, sifting through her tapes and notebooks, represents them to the world. Usually, of course, her heavy-handed writing has poor circulation even if she is lucky enough to get it published. But if she is good at what she does—rhetorically persuasive and imaginatively bold—she will create a nearly indelible portrait of those she writes about, and she will change her readers' conceptions of them forever. Despite all the critique of *Coming of Age in Samoa*, for the millions of people who read the book Samoan lovers still whisper tenderly beneath the palm trees in the untroubled night. The Balinese will pit their cocks against each other in the minds of most anthropologists and historians no matter how many sturdy tomes attempt to unseat this central image. The Nuer will forever be obsessed with cattle and the Azande with their witchcraft. It takes not only sordid facts but artistry of great power and representational skill to disturb the impact of an effective anthropological writer.

This representational power of the author is the patent truth embodied in *Anthropology as Cultural Critique* and *Writing Culture,* both of them mild-mannered, thoughtful books that set off a hysterical storm of protest within the discipline—a storm far more emotionally heated than the reasoned insights of the books should have provoked. But they pointed to this unavoidably obvious truth of power asymmetry at a time when anthropologists were beginning to notice, in print, the complexities of the participant-observer relationship; it is no accident that the anthropological interest in colonialism emerged simultaneously and reinforced the point.

This power asymmetry makes anthropologists nervous and guilty, particularly in the current political climate of multicultural egalitarianism, and some of the recent vogue in experimental representation has been motivated in part by the desire to avoid the authoritative power of the author. Ewing, in a discussion of anthropological and psychoanalytic dilemmas about participant observation, points out that many of these attempts are naive. "It is precisely in this project of self-observation that anthropologists have had few guidelines for transcending their own self-criticism" (1992:261). Ewing points to Dwyer's *Moroccan Dialogues* (1982) as one of the earliest attempts to avoid the privileged position as author, which he does by presenting what are essentially transcripts of dialogue. By doing so he hopes to set right the imbalance of power between ethnographer and field subject. What he failed to realize was that he not only still controlled the selection of dialogue but more to the point, that he made "the erroneous assumption that meaning resides in words that can be captured and transcribed."[2] The anthropologist cannot write in a way that absolves her from her writerly power. It is her interpretation of the pauses, the inflections, the body language, as well as the words, in the context of her relation with the field subject, that enables her to respond sensibly to a comment.[3] Power imbalance enters inescapably into a relationship in which two people are talking, and one of them is writing a book about the other.[4] The clarity with which recent anthropological writing has made this transparent has led some anthropologists into a nihilist stance, that because the ethnographer cannot avoid his authority, ethnography is impossible: but that hopeless stance is misguided. It has led others into a vulgar Foucauldianism through which the anthropologist identifies with the subject as the victim of larger social forces which neither anthropologist nor subject can control. These are good projects and we learn from them, but they must be seen as attempts to deny a power asymmetry that is irreducibly there.

I suspect that one reason the colonialist critique of anthropology's past seems so damning in the present is that the profession has only recently begun openly to publish and to teach about the fieldwork-and-writing-up experience, and the cultural weirdness of that experience hangs around its practitioners' ears like a guilty cloud. Undiscussed and unexamined, this weirdness should indeed make practitioners feel remarkably uneasy, particularly when they are already primed to identify and to resist asymmetrical relationships. The source of the present uneasiness, then, lies in part in the consequences of the over-drinks-and-pretzels folklore which anthropologists have developed about fieldwork. The profession is remarkable not only in having a methodology which is unusually physically and emotionally taxing, but in rarely preparing its students to cope with its demands.[5]

Anthropologists are often given remarkably little training about the complexities of ethnographic relationships. Nobody really tells you in graduate school how to do your fieldwork. At Cambridge (where I took my doctorate) the faculty offered occasional seminars on mosquito netting and footwear—tennis sneakers for Africa, as Bohannan remarked, because they were sturdy and dried easily after you wandered through the frequent streams—and we were told that when we left the field we must always carry our field notebooks as hand luggage. But nobody talked to us about how to do an interview, or what it was like to dump yourself into the lap of someone's life, although this was certainly the indirect topic of our endless reading of ethnographies and field reports. And I still remember the shocked moment at a conference when my supervisor muttered, after one of the papers, that he didn't believe the ethnography; it suddenly dawned on me that despite my sophisticated epistemological theorizing, I had nevertheless imagined the ethnographer as an uncomplicated reporter-of-facts.

At Cambridge there was a romance of fieldwork, and as a romantic, like most anthropologists, I accepted it happily. In the romance of fieldwork, you are not a distanced, objective journalist (as anthropologists unkindly configure journalists) but you go native, you lose yourself in the other world, and then you return to write your dissertation. Abu-Lughod, in an exemplary moment of this merging, writes (as others do, but less eloquently):

> As we set off, I realized how proud I was that I finally had the proper items . . . I knew that my new sweater (worn *under* my dress), brightly coloured and interwoven with metallic threads, would be much admired, as would my gaudy new bead necklace, a gift from my friend the seamstress. I was able to see myself as I would be seen by others, and I took pleasure in knowing that I was finally suitably attired for a festive occasion. I was also prepared to cover my face with my shawl . . . By this time I would have felt uncomfortable had I not been able to veil. (1986:19–20)

This is what the romance is about: to lose yourself, to leave this dreary world of grant applications and diet Coke, and to become, for a little while, daughter to a warrior of the desert. That the immersion involves heartbreak is also part of the romance, and at Cambridge, at any rate, returned-fieldworkers told trauma stories of illness and desire, the desperate longing to return home when in the field and to the field when home and the fear (and hope) that the experience had altered them forever. The romance, admittedly, had grown somewhat more assimilative than it was in the days between the wars, when anthropologists wore western safari dress and paid their informants for their informing. My generation's ethnographer-models took native drugs, wore native dress, and occasionally married natives, whom we were no longer comfortable calling informants; and by then "native" had become an ironic trope. Even the more assimilative romance was short on methodological guidelines, but if you lived with a family or in a small village the implications were clear: you became a daughter—in tribal Africa (which Cambridge had favored ethnographically) you literally were defined with a kin term—and you learned what it was like to live and transgress that role. You became a member of the village, and in some measure, your dissertation was the knowledge you acquired in order to understand the village gossip.

The consequence of this romantic immersion—and the immersion is crucial; it is our naive response upon return that is less helpful—is the powerful unwritten rule that the anthropologist sees only the good in the societies she studies. This is, I believe, one of the ways in which we most commonly deal with our unacknowledged anxiety over the power asymmetry. Because we become part of the world we study, become accepted in some small measure as legitimate members of that world, we are often acutely conscious of the transition from outsider to insider, deeply grateful to those who have accepted us, and embarrassed, I suspect, of the power of our wealth, our nationality, and our pen. Because of this we tend to look for the worthiness of our newfound friends. And so the anthropologist, in the same essay that he passes from "gust of wind" stage to "acceptance" stage, compares a village cockfight to the greatest masterpieces of English drama. The anthropologist learns to take pleasure in the gaudy plastic trinkets worn by the Bedouin and writes not of their poverty but their poetry. The anthropologist goes on pilgrimage in South India and finds feces in his hair after the common bath and writes without cynicism about the profundity of religious collectivity. The anthropologist becomes an apprentice to a Nepali healer and writes about the aesthetics of healing in a mountain village rather than about the pathetic inadequacy of medical care. This is appropriate; we learn more from the attempt to see experience from another perspective than we do from the relentless cynical critique of the west's failure to ameliorate the suffering of the third world. Nevertheless, the discipline sets these expectations of happy identification rigidly. An anthropologist who violates the implicit code is excoriated, as was Colin Turnbull after the publication of a book in which he claimed that poverty made people mean and desperate, or for that matter Nancy Scheper-Hughes, a gifted scholar sometimes criticized for her insistent recognition of suffering in the cultures where she has worked.

It should not follow from the attempt to understand that the anthropologist should describe only the good. And yet it seems to. Behind the laudable enthusiasm lies a complex mixture of loneliness, guilt, and greed. One of the central tenets of friendship in Euro-American society is that you do not exploit your friend. Yet this exploitation is (admittedly by accident) the basis of anthropology as a profession. We arrive in a world that never asked us to visit it, and then we wait, sometimes intensely lonely, until we are accepted into it. Particularly in the last twenty or thirty years, acceptance has meant acceptance as a friend; and one makes friends, often very close ones, in the world which one has set out to study. To take notes upon that friendship, to go home and treat the notes as data and have the friends serve at least in one's mind as exemplars of the culture one describes is, I suspect, unsettling for many anthropologists. To write kindly about people who have befriended you and taken you in and cared for you during your dysentery, hepatitis, typhoid, or the other ravages one experiences in India but not in California—this return for generous hospitality seems the least you can do. This is a problem endemic to writing about people who will read your book, particularly when you hope (as many anthropologists do) to revisit the community of your first book for your second. Historians, who are often much more critical, do not suffer from these anxieties, nor perhaps do journalists who will visit a subject once and move on. For anthropologists the problem of kindness looms large.

But all the kindness in the world cannot deny the basic asymmetry of the undertaking. So the charges of colonial exploitation seem real in a world in which you turn your friend into field notes and reify them forever in a bound document in which you, the author, control and manage the representation of your friend, the subject. This turning-people-into-data is a real feature of anthropological life. Yet even that guilt-inducing problem might pass unnoticed if anthropology's larger intellectual purpose remained untroubled. If it were clear and straightforward what good we did as a profession, if it were transparently obvious that we added regularly to a mound of knowledge that the world would not have unless we created it, or that we had a real, measurable, practical impact upon daily human life—that we were a responsible, effective profession—we would be able to see that fieldwork relationships are usually based on respect and trust, and we would be able to help fieldworkers avoid the guilty insecurity which leads them to derogate their enterprise. Unfortunately, none of these things seem particularly obvious right now.

This is the therapist's dilemma: how to be equal, intimate, and effective within a relationship of unavoidable inequality. In therapy this inequality is straightforward: one person is the doctor, the other the patient; one is the helper, the other the helped; one is paid, the other pays; one says little of his life while the other has come to talk in detail about hers. But in the therapy relationship, the asymmetry becomes a tool, a projective screen, to understand the ways in which patients deal with and recreate powerful others. Intense transference feelings about the silent but powerful analyst are seen as clues about the way in which the patient constructs the present out of the history of the past. The asymmetry, then, becomes a route to the knowledge that the less powerful person sought, within a relationship of trust and respect. More to the point: the power asymmetry in the therapy relationship (when it is healthy) is a goal-oriented relationship with the aim of enabling the less powerful person to experience a greater degree of self-mastery and self-respect, a greater degree of power. The asymmetry is time-limited, appropriate only to that relationship, and the relationship fulfills the goals of both parties to it. The real question for anthropologists, the question on which the future of this discipline hangs, is whether anthropologists in the late twentieth century, when the political rules of the game have changed forever, can use this asymmetry productively, as a means to achieve an intellectually valuable and morally desirable good, without violating their sense of the integrity of appropriate human relations. And the real problem is that the goals of the discipline are currently up for grabs.

It is not at all surprising that this discipline of social meaning now experiences a crisis. The world in which anthropology was born has changed profoundly. We live now in the aftermath of the great historical continental drift of the end of empire, and we sense the world shifting under our feet. When England gave up India and the French, Algeria, they destabilized three hundred years of history in which Western people had assumed themselves to be morally, politically, and economically superior to all others. In an intellectual climate in which European and its derivative American culture seemed fundamentally desirable and good, the political, scientific, and emotional validity of anthropology was obvious, for the discipline sought to disrupt these calm complacencies. Margaret Mead attained her prominence in a world which could be shocked into change by tales from elsewhere. Fifty years after the end of the Second World War, in a society acutely aware of multicultural diversity, the urgency of the discipline seems very different. Anthropologists no longer write for all America, and small-town rural Americans who feel the urge for tales from elsewhere easily satisfy their yearnings through the popular media and visual images which carry more pungent force than mere words.

Anthropology is not entirely clear what it is about at present, as the discipline repositions itself within the radical transformations of the recent decades. Grimshaw and Hart point out that the accelerated integration of the world has severely embarrassed a project that once rested on its authority to explain unknown others to people back at home (1993:8–9). Nor, they continue, do the tools we once used always seem compelling now. "In a world of television, credit cards and mass travel, the idea that genealogical charts offer a sure guide to social structure is, to say the least, unconvincing" (1993:9).[6] Anthropology is a discipline of commonplace experience—you go and live as they do, and report back to those who have not been there—which developed as part of a political relationship that most intellectuals now find deeply troubling, and its initial aim—to chart constants and variations in social structure—seem to many deeply compromised by the then concomitant political need to establish difference as the justification for domination.

So whence will come our authority and our purpose? What anthropologists do has changed, and amidst the waves of self-critique it is salutary to see how oddly the charges of colonialist exploitation ring. Anthropologists now study geneticists, moviemakers, architects, urban centers, physicists, philanthropists, an automechanic in upstate New York. This change was the real point of Marcus and Fischer's tour de force: that anthropology has begun to attend to the sources of our own local culture, to the cultural contradictions within European and American life; it has begun to look for difference within the complexity of global urban-impacted culture rather than looking from outside at the isolated, illiterate other and his bullock cart. Anthropologists have already moved from the village to the city, to the Brazilian *favela* of people crowded in once unmentionable poverty (Scheper-Hughes) and to its opposite, Brazil's architectural utopia intended to recreate a noble and wholesome modernity (Holston); to the high-tech complexities of the medical school (B. and M-J. Good) and the Stanford Linear Accelerator (Traweek); to the grimy glories of the modern Greek city and its intrusions into the rural village (Herzfeld); to the horrors of genocide and ethnic violence (Tambiah); to the meaning of kinship—categories from Fortes—as elements of citizenship in the modern European state (Borneman); to conjuring magic in India through the lenses of gurus in Las Vegas (Siegel); to the quasi-anthropological conceptions, laden with political assumptions, of a beloved scientific journal and the workings of its editorial staff (Lutz and Collins); even when the anthropologist travels to the inaccessible Indonesian margins, as Tsing and Steadly did separately, she finds them in relation to the city and beyond. All of these recent ethnographies place the fieldwork site in relation: in relation to the local, the global, to the fantasies, expectations, and realities of state, rural, and international behavior.

This repositioning within the discipline becomes a way to think complexly about human relations constituted by their culture and also manipulating agents of them. As in the therapeutic relationship, the asymmetry—here, the fact that one person writes about others—could become integral to the ultimate goal of the relationship, if that were to further the relationship by understanding the perspectives of the different people within it, including the various changes provoked by the writing of the text. This is ultimately the point of Michael Herzfeld's provocative project, which compares the culture of modern Greece to the discourse of anthropology, a bold move which encouraged me to explore a similarly hubristic strategy here. He argues that anthropology teaches us not only about the societies we study, but about the identities and aspirations of those who study them. In fact that was always the point, that in studying the peculiarities of other cultures we were meant somehow to be studying ourselves. Yet in broad terms that project always fails, for human communication provides no clean mirrors but rather a knotted dialogic web. "Why should anthropologists expect to *resolve* in their own practices the very problem that constitutes the object of their study of 'others?'"[7] To catch the subtle intricacies of confused relationships without ascribed categories of empirical object and theoretical interpretation is enough, he argues: that is an anthropology of success, not loaded failure. He diagnoses the direction in which some anthropologists have moved.

Tsing, for instance, in a remarkable text which destabilizes the very idea of a bounded community, argues that the intellectual worth of the anthropological project is ultimately tied to the use of the writing project in clarifying and transposing the relationships of the partners to it. The power of anthropological work, she suggests, is to "stimulate culturally sensitive global histories in which cultural critiques are forced to position their own analytic vantage points . . . [Comparisons can lead to] a situating of analyses in the joined, divergent, and asymmetrical personal and institutional histories of both anthropologist and informant" (1993:297). The anthropological work, in this vision, is a challenge to the field subject because that work represents an attempt to hear what he or she had to say; the work helps field subjects to understand how they are heard, the anthropologist to hear more clearly, and the reader to understand better the structure and sensibility required for these partially successful communications (1993:300).

For a number of years Fischer has experimented with and argued for the use of this writing relationship as intrinsic to the discipline's intellectual goals. In "Ethnicity and the Postmodern Arts of Memory," he uses his understanding of his own relationship to the material to develop an analytic approach to contemporary ethnicity in pluralist, postindustrial society. In his reading of recent autobiographical works he notes: "what the newer work brings home forcefully is, *first,* the paradoxical sense that ethnicity is something invented and reinterpreted in each generation by each individual and that it is often puzzling to the individual, something over which he or she lacks control."[8] He sees this ethnicity, with its "feeling welling up out of mysterious depths" (in Clifford and Marcus 1986:197), as consequent to the general late-twentieth-century experience of the apparent globalization of culture and the seeming fragmentation of cultural tradition into elements of personal style. What is compelling is that he arrives at this conception of experiential tesselation, the fear that one's selfhood is like a scaly covering over something consciously not understood, through identifying transference (the perception of others through patterns established in the subject's personal past), through locating experiencing that has been denied because it is too painful but cannot be forgotten (Fischer calls this the return of the repressed in new forms), and through recognizing distorted repetitions of historical reeactments by means of these processes. In other words, he explores ethnicity as an individual's relationship to her understanding of her self.

Fischer deliberately moves away from the simple categories—us and them, urban and rural—towards a complex alignment of ethnographer and ethnographic subject, in which each is, as it were, implicated in each other, sharing a past or a political ambition or more often a chaotic social present. *Debating Muslims,* written jointly by an Iranian (Abedi) and an American (Fischer), is a text which engages at least two different audiences and explicitly rejects the idea of a single, bounded Iranian culture. Abedi describes his early life in a village, and Fischer uses his fieldworker's eye and his historian's subtlety to describe the death of a Baha'i martyr. But the two together describe Bombay talkies and Salman Rushdie, explicating the earnest satire for both sides of the heated debate—an account which vividly underscores both the need for an ethnographic sensibility while simultaneously illustrating the implausibility of older models of simple communities in the global traffic of modernity. And they describe, together, the surprising concatenations of Iranian culture in Houston, which is inseparable from Houston's cultural impact in Iran. This is a "psychocultural space" constructed through the differing perspectives of exiles and immigrants, a black comedy film playing off Iranian constructs of American constructs of Iranians, cross-fertilized literature and music, television, video, carpet stores, marriage ceremonies, memoirs of emigration—including Fischer's template, the familial origins of his listening ear—and reflections on experience abroad. In this world events take place throughout the city and across the country, history is complex and multistranded, and there is no single or unified narrator. The project adumbrates the problems and opportunities of anthropological accounts of modernity: the problems being the difficulty of describing these complex, poorly delimited communities well, and the opportunities being to develop the anthropological vocabulary to do so, not because the old vocabulary was wrong, but because it was not elaborated with these weirdly porous social environments in mind.

These are anthropological projects in which the concept of relationship is central: the relationship between people of different cultures, the relationship of those on the margins to those in the center, the relationship of individuals to their own past, all mediated through the anthropologist's sharpened awareness of people who are quite different from her but whom she tries to understand, and they her. The recent ethnographies describe patterns of interaction whose causal chains they then explain: how it is possible for a mother to reject her baby, or for one human being to hate another on no other grounds but religious affiliation, and for that hatred

to spiral into war; how human beings live with the fetid consequences of that war. They describe the manner in which prejudice
is formed and projected and the contexts out of which presumption
springs. They deliberately work in communities where human interaction has a bitter, baffling legacy: South Africa, Argentina,
independent nations with a recent colonial past. And as ethnogra-
phers they are motivated not only by a yen for knowledge but
also—as in all sciences—by its use, which for most of them is to
ease the tense relationships of an often unhappily intertwined sociality.

This does not yet add up to a new paradigm. But it is clear to
me that the literary turn which led anthropologists to conceive of
their work not as a kind of clear-cut science (although much of the
science-talk seemed to depend upon an idealization unrelated to
the messy laboratory) but as an interpretation, has done its work
in enabling anthropologists to see culture as a densely complex
interactive process. The comparison has taught anthropologists a
great deal and has inspired them to move into the analysis of
complex cultures which no one could dream of laying out in little
clear boxes. It would be a terrible cost if the comparison were taken
to an extreme that gave to anthropology a resonance of mere
fiction-writing and story-spinning, a discipline for uncreative nov-
elists. This resonance was hardly intended by those who pointed
to anthropology's fictive character, and to the fact that anthropological data is not something collected like peas but woven like
blankets. Still the resonance surrounds the field as the metaphor
has taken hold and developed. "Tell me," I was once asked at
dinner, "what would you say to a provost who wanted to move
your collegaues into the English department?"

Only if anthropology can reposition itself effectively, as an inter-
preter of a changed and radically reconstituted collection of global
polities in which the act of interpretation is not an exploitation but
a tool for responsible and effective cross-cultural understanding,
can the discipline survive and flourish into the next century. And
in this way the discipline is not unlike the Parsis. There are real but
unavoidable embarrassments in the discipline's practice—its traditional claim to knowledge is weakening, the unknown world has
shrunk markedly, its methodology is distinctively peculiar. These
real embarrassments are caught up in a fearful response to change,
in which the discipline is critiqued as incapable but which is a

displacement from anxiety about change itself. The rapid historical shifts of the current period have led many anthropologists to challenge the very merits of the discipline, for reasons which are not rooted in realities but in emotionally charged misreadings. Like the Parsis, if anthropology survives it will do so in a form very different from its nineteenth-century conception. But this is exciting. It is not clear what form Parsi culture will take in the diaspora, but it is obvious that if the community survives it will be through a different conception of the way in which its uniqueness is defined and its culture is taught. That could be remarkably interesting for Parsis.

For anthropology, a repositioning would be tremendous. This discipline has a unique methodology which through its very engagement—as messy and subjective as it is—can teach us something about people that archives, statistics and scheduled interviews cannot, because it can reach more deeply into the empirical stuff of human experience than any other discipline. Fieldwork teaches us real things about the world which we cannot learn otherwise and which can help large groups of people make sense of each other with insights they might not otherwise have. More than any other discipline, anthropology must teach across boundaries—teach the Americans about Turkish intellectuals, about Nepali healers, about Malagasy anxieties, and even about psychiatric perplexities—and our commitment to going native, going across, means that we can teach with empathy and vividness. We still go to the heart of darkness and return, even if the darkness is on 59th Street. We have a responsibility to teach about it well and wisely. And if we can own our power, but see it in service to a humanistic end, we may be able to see our field more directly, more appropriately, and with less of the public spectacle of anthropological self-flagellation that has recently confronted the scholarly world.

With all its oddities this discipline is very much worth preserving. Anthropology lacks the narrowly therapeutic goal that renders the therapist's power acceptable (even if only marginally, for some). Yet the discipline is, I would suggest, within the band of knowledge that from a broader perspective I would call therapeutic.[9] Understanding the grand spectrum of human nature helps us to be more tolerant, more insightful, ultimately more kind and responsible in the raising of children and the treatment of adults. Knowledge of others should help us better to tolerate the behavior of others, and to modify our own. These were the goals of Franz Boas and Margaret Mead, and they are good goals. And they have at their core the thesis which is both anthropological and therapeutic: that an outsider can see things which an insider cannot, that the attempt to communicate across boundaries depends on the capacity to hear as well as to say, and that the project of talking about human experience to an audience of troubled, awkward humans is a helpful one. Anthropologists look at the world in a way no other discipline does, for more than any other discipline we are acutely aware of the complexity of human relationships; our instinct, when we examine an event, is to contextualize it within local idioms of personal connections and their broken threads. Should the discipline choose to turn this basic skill—which is the heart of the fieldwork process—into the foundation for a new paradigm, this would be no bad thing. The confusions of global interaction demand some expertise in sorting through issues of appropriate and misunderstood relationships.

Beyond all this lies a more general point. Anthropology is a discipline of wonder and engagement, of (as Shweder reminds us) astonishment.[10] Most of us entered the field because we craved the imaginative riches of difference—the world of travellers' tales and magical fantasy, of camels, veiled women, feathered natives, of different clothes, food, and ways of being, beginning with the children's books that introduced us to little Pedro and his donkey, Micco the Seminole Indian boy, Grey Wolf and her Sioux family, like and unlike ours. For me New York's American Museum of Natural History, with its great, dark halls of dioramas and staring masks, carries as much responsibility as any book for my vocation. As I stood in front of the miniature villages of Northwest Coast salmon fishers and weaving Plains Indians and, for that matter, the glass-eyed otter whose fish has just been stolen by a greedy bear, I imagined myself in different worlds, and I loved it.

There is an angry sense in contemporary academia that the strident emphasis on difference and domination will save us from easy political complicities. In a review of a book which borrows that irritated sensibility, a study of the *National Geographic,* Stephen Greenblatt decries this stance as being too comfortable: "But why should we believe any of this? How can the dream of redemptive historical difference survive the end of the Cold War and linger on in the murderous age of ethnic hatreds? Why should we imagine that if we grasp more firmly the 'historical' roots of conflict we will then choose the morally preferable alternative? And how can we have any viable notion of human rights if we do not believe precisely that 'people who are hungry and oppressed have meaningful lives?'" (1993:119–120). As he points out, and the authors agree, the half-truths and blind sweetness of the images in *National Geographic* are not a palatable alternative. But surely anthropology is not asking that from us. Surely there is a route between the angry insistence on insufficiently engaged difference and the kindly platitudes of a bourgeois romance with poverty. Surely there is a way in which the nuanced recognitions, shocks, disengagements, and desires inherent in the long slog of intensive fieldwork can help us to speak to the political complexities that trouble us without implying our unthinking cooptation into a larger political structure of oppression. These conflicted moments in the field, in which we pull up sharply in the sudden awareness of radical otherness or in the embarrassed realization of fantasied merging, become good-to-think arenas for the relationship of different worlds and different people, and of the cuttlefish-like elusiveness of culture. And this, after all, is what we mean by "wonder": to doubt and yet to be curious; to want to know; to be surprised and awestruck and excited by something that we do not understand. To hold doubt, curiosity, and awe in tension is the engagement of fieldwork, and if we can stick to the honest description of the fieldwork, we may do a powerful lot of good.

NOTES

BIBLIOGRAPHY

ACKNOWLEDGMENTS

INDEX

◆ ◆ ◆ NOTES ◆ ◆ ◆

Prologue: Fateful Embraces

1. *Scotsman* review of *Plain Tales from the Raj,* ed. Allen 1987.
2. Ibid.
3. Lady Strachey (1898) in Karkaria 1915:107.
4. It is work on the popular edges of scholarship—work of historical accuracy, but also of personal nostalgia—that conveys most movingly the complex emotional dynamics of the British experience in India: Moorhouse 1983, Trevelyan 1987, Allen 1975, Woolf 1961; in fiction, Forster 1924, and above all Kipling, whose shifting, twisting, illusionist stance, crudely imperialist and cynically pro-Indian by turns, always profoundly enmeshed, reveals more than anything else the knotted history of the tortured British love affair with the Indian subcontinent.
5. A *durbar* was a court-reception by a prince; or, in the manner that the term was used in British India, a reception or exhibition by the government, in the course of which the subjects would pledge their loyalty. See Nuckolls 1990.
6. Moorhouse 1983:154–157. The centerpiece to this celebration, Edward VII, was, of course, not present; he was governing his primary kingdom in Great Britain.
7. The view of an ex-hand in Allen 1975:209.
8. Count von Koenigsmarck (1910) in Karkaria 1915:86.
9. The Marquis of Dufferin (1905) in Karkaria 1915:110.
10. These images appear in Trevelyan 1987 and Moorhouse 1983.
11. Tagore 1991; Mehta 1989; Ghosh 1988. One of the most powerful nonwestern, postcolonial elaborations of this metaphorical terrain is

Tayeb Salih's *Season of Migration to the North,* a harsh, violent imagining of an westernized Egyptian man's surreally powerful sexual attraction for westerners in London, and the suppressed rage against them that leads him to kill after passion, so that the passionate intimacy in itself becomes figuratively and literally a murderous act.

12. One of the most interesting features of this literature is the hesitant blurring of metaphor and historical factuality. Ballhatchet (1980) gives vivid accounts of the real encounter and is often cited in support of the metaphor; in a single edited volume one finds sexual relations as political resistance and political resistance expressed in sexual imagery (Haynes and Prakash 1991).

13. See for example Nandy 1983, esp 35–37; McClure 1980; Wurgaft 1983; also Said 1992. Conrad is the other exemplary novelist who arguably developed his views with complexity and depth. While Kipling is often treated more as scribe, an innocent informant (this is a little unfair), Conrad is considered to be more thoughtful.

14. One can find versions of this story in Said 1978, 1992; Ballhatchet 1980; Wurgaft 1983; McClure 1981; Mani 1987; Das 1986; O'Hanlon 1991; Stoler 1991, 1992; Callaway 1987; Inden 1990; Nandy 1983; and others.

15. Other classics of colonialism and oppression are Cesaire 1972 and Baldwin 1955. My goal here is to focus directly on the relationship inherent to colonialism, and the two texts I have chosen center squarely on those themes.

16. Memmi 1965:140. Hartsock (1987) uses Memmi's colonized other to set feminism in sharp opposition to a vulgar Foucauldianism. Hartsock takes from Memmi the argument that colonialism destroys both parties to the bargain, and that the colonized person is a projection of the colonizer's negative qualities—hence lazy, wicked, backward, and not entirely human. More to the point, to the colonizer all the colonized look alike. "Feminist readers of de Beauvoir's *Second Sex* cannot avoid a sense of familiarity. We recognize a great deal of this description." Hartsock's point is that in the construction of theory, *he* theorizes. Both the universalizing and totalizing voice of Enlightenment thinking, and the postmodernism which denounces it, are creations of the dominant power. From this perspective, Foucault is "a figure who fails to provide an epistemology which is usable for the task of revolutionizing, creating and constructing." His history is "parodic, dissociative, and satirical." It shows how to take things apart, but not how to put them together. He is, she says, in the position of the colonizer who refuses.

17. See Atalas (1977).

18. See for example Guha 1982; Guha and Spivak 1988, Sarkar 1989, Hardiman 1987—and others, notably Adas 1991 and 1992, Scott 1985, and

Raphael 1988. See O'Hanlon 1988 for a sophisticated critique of this line of analysis.

19. One reviewer acidly described this approach as "the vigorous genre explicating colonial invention of Indian 'tradition'" (Henning 1992:197). This is a somewhat unfair characterization of the subtleties of Dirks 1987, Prakash 1990 and 1992, Inden 1990, even Haynes and Prakash 1991. Nevertheless the point of this focus on Foucauldian representation has been to explore the limitations of agency; individuals are shown as caught up in larger power structures where independent thought and action are difficult.

20. The history-and-structure school is exemplified by Kelly 1991, Comaroff 1985, and more recently J. and J. Comaroff 1992. Nandy (1983) writes from within this perspective (but impelled by psychodynamic complexities) as do (for different reasons) O'Hanlon (1988 and 1991) and Stoler (1991).

21. There is a substantial literature in anthropology and sociology on elites; see Broomfield 1968 and Stonequist 1937. Although the current discussion centers in the colonial dilemma, it should also be placed within the larger frame of upwardly mobile social groups within complex societies.

22. It is dangerous to assert that humans are quite free to choose—any historical awareness gives a sense of the limitations within which people live and yet believe themselves to be free agents. I am trying to use the concept of choice here in a relative and not absolute sense. What I mean to emphasize is that the Parsis were not constrained by virtue of working with the British to internalize British style. The Gujarati *banias*, for example, whose commercial relationship with the British was if anything closer in seventeenth- and eighteenth-century Surat, did not do so. It is particularly the striking and self-conscious nature of the Parsis' identification with the British, and the fact that it seems to be self-consciously tied to self-advancement, that makes it possible for us to conceive of this cultural direction as a choice.

23. See Spitzer 1974, Cohen 1981, Wyse 1989; also Fyfe 1962; Peterson 1969; Wilson 1976; Last and Richards 1987.

24. Spitzer 1974:109.

25. This movement introduced a blend of African and European dress for men, encouraged the development of a specifically non-European Krio history, and cast doubts about the degree to which Europeanization was useful (see Spitzer 1974:111f).

26. The Krio press, however, would criticize this approach, admonishing the Krio to remember that Britain had freed their ancestors from slavery (see Spitzer 1974:193).

27. Wyse 1989: 89, 95, 105.

28. There are many examples of communities acting out new relationships with old semiotics in the rapidly changing political economy of colonial and postcolonial India. The semiotics of group identity often involved a hierarchical relationship to other groups, which could backfire economically when power relations shifted. Barnett provides an excellent description of this process for a South Indian caste (the Kontaikkatti Velalar-s) in a village near Madras. In the 1960s this landowning caste refused to take advantage of new industrial opportunities in Madras even though it was losing its land, because the refusal "to work at command," was a central attribute of group self-description. As the wealth of other castes increased through new networks of economic activity, the Kontaikkatti Velalar-s became impoverished. Barnett describes this as "a 'transformational' change in which the basic cultural system persists while codes for conduct alter" (1973:201). Price (1983) describes the way in which the conflict between the behavior appropriate for a "just raja" (distributing largess) and that of the gentlemanly *zamindar* (acting as a westernized capitalist) brought economic ruin to a late-nineteenth-century South Indian landholder. Fox (1984) describes how colonial political economy in nineteenth-century Punjab created a large urban lower middle class which developed a communal identity that sharply inhibited its ability to work with other Punjabi communities. This profoundly limited the political effectiveness of that class in the changing economy of the early twentieth century. As the *zamindari* system failed and the regional land-based groups rose in political power, elites created by colonial rule, reluctant to give up their acquired signs of status, were forced by their hesitancy into the experience of loss and decline.

29. Quoted in Tindall 1982:94. The burying place referred to is actually the Tower of Silence on Malabar Hill.

30. In Karaka 1884 II:116.

31. Ibid. I:329.

32. Ibid. II:295.

33. Cited in Hinnells n.d.:6.

34. Earl of Lytton to Queen Victoria, 1906. In Karkaria 1915:112.

35. Pithawalla 1932:19. Included in the volume is an article entitled "Iranian Character," which has attributed to Persians the role of intermediary which Parsis believed themselves to play: "Persia was, and must still be, a link between the old Oriental civilization and the new Occidental culture" (1932:13).

36. Markham 1932:xi.

37. Desai 1940:4, 49.

38. Dastoor 1944:28–9.

39. Dastoor 1948: foreword.
40. Wadia 1949:138–39
41. A fifty-eight-year-old housewife in *Parsiana* November 1974:26.
42. Mehta in *Parsiana* January 1989:6.
43. M. Pestonji, "And They Think They're Modern?" *The Daily* 16 August 1991.

1. The Current Community

1. Lord Harris, "Bombay," in *India, Ceylon, Straits Settlements, British North Borneo, Hong Kong.* The British Empire Series 1899. 1:68–69.
2. Moraes 1979:5. Moraes is also a poet and author of a minor classic, *My Son's Father* (1968).
3. This is an official figure from the 1981 Census of India.
4. Shobda De's *Socialite Evenings* (1988) tries to capture the feel of this world, and the peculiarities of its mix of sophistication and conservativism.
5. J. Ovington, "A Voyage to Suratt," (1689), in Karkaria 1915:485–6.
6. The *Times* 1911, in Karkaria 1915:169.
7. Sir Henry Craik, *Impressions of India* (1908) in Karkaria 1915:138–9.
8. One observer depicts her first intimate encounter with the Falklands Road area, where she went to find actors for a movie *(Salaam Bombay),* as follows: "The day we arrived a 25-yr-old Nepalese girl had died from withdrawal from brown sugar [heroin] overdose. There's a real brown sugar epidemic now in Bombay. It was an emotional moment, when all the girls were numb with shock, and yet there was the feeling that this was just one of the number gone, that others would fill the gap in a matter of a day.

   Visually the street was incredibly particular, lively, filled with the strangest juxtapositions. The brothels themselves were tiny little rooms, painted the inimitable peacock green-blue, lined with bright handpainted colour lithographs of the girls (each one more startling than the next, plus always a picture of Indira Gandhi). Outside, life is teeming. Women of all shapes and sizes are cooking chappatis on the ground, the white flour in stark contrast to the filth of their surroundings. There are mixed Nepali-Indian children everywhere, a lot of screaming and shouting. At least five vendours pass by, selling brightly coloured barettes and buckets and hairpins. In the far corner, a La Strada-type character sits smoking, guarding his turquoise painted ferris wheel on which two young prostitutes—barely sixteen—whirl about in glee. . . . [at Grant Road we met] a gang of five movie-crazy kids, all of whom have run away from their villages and families to find a life for themselves in Bombay. They're scrap collectors, scavengers, waiters at weddings, drug-peddlers, also bet-carriers for gamblers. . . . they tore their clothes off their backs and plunged into the filthy ocean. It was quite an image: these bodies flinging about in water littered with marigolds, coconut husks, fruits, straw, cloth" (Nair in Nair and Taraporevala 1990:9).

9. These figures are taken from the 1991 Census. The exact numbers are closer to 76,382 in India, with 53,794 based in Greater Bombay.

10. Kosambi (1986:160) argues that in 1930 the basis for residential grouping in Bombay changes from ethnic to socioeconomic/ethnic, when the clustering of Parsis (for instance) gives way to a clustering of Parsis and Christians, and that this may indicate the rise of a new professional class.

11. The Gujarati word *baag* actually means "garden," but among Parsis it is often used to refer to the complex of buildings which house Parsis and in this context is best translated as "colony."

12. Karaka 1947:5–6. This is a memoir of India written around the time of Independence. The author is not the same Karaka as the author of the nineteenth-century classic.

13. This is sometimes said to celebrate the changing of the *gahs,* the periods of the day. I saw it also done in Udwada, as I sat in a small bar until the afternoon grew dim and the proprietor similarly greeted the fluorescent light he switched on.

14. The Parsis have a religious calendar with thirty names days presided over by various spiritual forces or entities. Certain of them, like the twentieth day, Behram Roj, the *yazad,* or angel of victory, are deemed to be particularly important, and observant Parsis are likely to intensify their religious activities on such days.

15. In the fire temples the laity may observe some liturgical ceremonies across the *pavi,* or little water channels that mark off the sanctified space of ritual performance.

16. A recent survey revealed that 52% of Indian Parsi youth said that they thought in English, compared to 8% who declared they thought in Parsi-Gujarati; 44% of the elders said that they thought in English and 11% in Gujarati; the rest asserted that they thought in a combination of both languages (102 Parsis were surveyed in India). Writer 1994:253.

17. Parsis in rural Gujarat speak a less corrupted Gujarati than those in Bombay because they speak it as their dominant language, and use Gujarati with non-Parsi Gujarati speakers. For a linguistic analysis of Parsi-Gujarati see Gajendragadkar 1974. On the demise of Parsi Gujarati see Modi 1989.

18. The numbers include 2,900 in Pakistan, 5,000 in Europe, 9,700 in North

America, and 900 in Australia. The official Iranian census estimates around 90,000, but a Zoroastrian Iranian reported that the actual figures, which accord far better with figures in the past, are closer to 18,000. Reported in Khurody, "Parsis in America: The Pluralism Project at Harvard University," Saturday, October 30, 1993.

19. The survey was carried out by a well-respected and thorough demographer, Marlini Karkal. From a total of Parsi households of 17,024 in Greater Bombay she selected 2,000 households from the seven wards in Bombay which held 75% of the Bombay Parsi population; 1,937 households were ultimately interviewed with success. I trust most of the statistics but question those concerning household or individual income, for reasons reported later.

20. Fifty-four percent of the community was not employed (17% were students, 29% either housewives or unemployed, 9% retired).

21. It is very strange to have 2,000 rupees listed as the highest category: it is comparable to carrying out a similar survey of Jews in America, and establishing the highest possible category of annual income at more than $25,000. In this system, 1,455 rupees a month was the reported median income, but the figure is not very useful, as presumably 2,000 was factored in for the individuals of a higher bracket. These figures must also be taken with caution; it is very, very common to underreport income in India.

22. This information is taken from 1990 fieldwork and newspaper data, and I have not returned to India since; some of the offices may well have changed hands.

23. The young are also achieving. In the first half of 1990 the *Parsiana* reported as follows: winner of the women's first individual Indian triathlon (Khushnaaz Subedar); the 7th consecutive winner of the national judo competition and Asian Games medalist (Cawas Billimoria); holder of the Asian women's record for the 100-meter sprint (Zenia Ayrton); and copywriter award of the year (Freddy Birdy).

24. Consider, for example, a comparison between Parsis and Brahmins in 1872. The major occupations of the Parsis, who numbered 44,091 in Bombay, were: civil service (239), priests or associated functionaries (844), domestic servants employed in the house (2,088), other domestic servants (420), railway (102), keeping or using wheeled conveniences for hire (107), general merchants (638), brokers (189), clerks and accountants (1,883), contractors and builders (142), carpenters (1,187), nonagricultural laborers (118), printers (138), persons employed on newspapers and periodicals (158), distillers of wine and liquors (349), rentiers (419), men (3,336) and women (13,998) without income, and 14,702 children.

The Brahmins, proportionately, had significantly more civil servants, about the same percentage of servants, and more brokers and clerks. In 1872 Brahmins numbered 25,757: civil servants (356), religious function-aries (494), domestics in the house (1,397), other domestic servants (952), washermen (407), merchants (141), general retail-dealers and shopkeep-ers (120), brokers (282), clerks (1,787), nonagricultural laborers (669), milkmen (134), unemployed men (6,879) and women (5,340), and chil-dren (4,573). Parsis do not stand out dramatically in comparison with this group.

Also in 1872 a greater percentage of the Parsis were educated than any other community—21% of the men (this figure is attributed to "Parsis, Jews and others") and 11% of the women are under instruction, while this is true for only 7% of the Christian men and 6% of the women, 5% of the Buddhist men and 1% of the women, 4% of the Hindu men and 1% of the women, and 3% of the Muslim men and 1% of the women.

Compared to the Parsi community in 1982, the 1872 community looks somewhat similar. Twice as many in the community are employed in clerical work in 1872 as in 1982, but the proportional change is minor (1872=4.3%, 1982=8.3%); 39% are unemployed in 1872 as compared to 35% in 1982 (including the retired); 4% of the community describes itself as professional in 1872, 8% in 1982. The census categories may have changed significantly in the course of these hundred years and it is not clear what they tell us, but they do suggest that the composition of the Parsi community has not changed dramatically over the period.

25. Authors include Bulsara 1935, Desai 1940, 1945, Sidhwa 1955, 1956, Pithawalla and Rustomji 1945, Markham 1932. A fuller discussion of the problem of charity will be found later.

26. Certainly members of other communities beg outside the fire temple in Udwada, home to the holiest Parsi fire, where the Hindus are relatively prosperous. On an auspicious day five or six beggars line the path along which Parsis approach the temple.

27. See Bhaya 1988 for her survey of rural South Gujarat Parsis; drawing from 209 villages in the Bharuch-Surat-Valsad area, she surveyed 687 families. Of these 172 lived in what she describes as inadequate houses (*kutcha* as compared to *pucca*) and 34 in hutments—buildings patched together out of cardboard, iron, and thatch. Another 179 families had an annual income of 2,000–6,000 rupees. Kharas 1984 describes truly hor-rifying conditions for the elderly community priests.

28. It is standard to underreport income, and although the survey-maker promised anonymity, most people seem to assume that these figures are incorrect. I myself had great difficulties persuading people to give me

receipts: they feared that somehow the sum they earned would be reported to the Indian taxation authorities, and when they thought that their reported income would have an impact on their eligibility for charity, the figures cited would be far lower than the actual figure.

29. S. Taraporevala 1981:47. She also remarks that Zubin Mehta "represents the apotheosis of Parsi acculturation; the civilizing process which enabled an Indian to become a 'world famous' conductor of Western music." He is also, she remarks, the community's ideal representative to an outside world of German, Japanese, and American audiences. (1981:47).

30. In George Orwell, *Burmese Days*, quoted in Allen 1975:116.

31. *Parsiana* July 1981:8.

32. The Time and Talents Club is a charitable organization. Its membership tends to be elite, and its activities considerable. They sponsor mostly western music, often musicians passing through India, and dance and film events; they also sponsor Adi Marzban (described below) and other Parsi comedy.

33. His estate forbids the publication or translation of his work, so I am unable to provide more examples of it here.

34. When I spoke about this with a well-known humorist, he proceeded to explain that in Parsi-Gujarati certain body parts have names that can be proper names as well: *mancherji, pestonji* (bustline), *behramji* (buttocks), *adarji* (testicles), *shapurji* (penis). No one else had mentioned this to me.

35. These passages have been translated and glossed by Shehnaz Munshi; I translated (with her help) the passages above.

36. A survey of North American Zoroastrians revealed that 78% of a forty-person sample identified honesty as among the common positive characteristics of Parsis, and 65% identified argumentativeness as among the common negative ones. No other traits were identified by as much as 50% of the sample (Dastoor 1988:18).

37. Cited in Pangborn 1983:151–153. "Most of the Zoroastrians' problems, whether social, economic, ethical, or religious, bear similarities to those which have confronted (or presently confront) other communities possessing the national, ethnic, or religious homogeneity essential to identity. What lends distinction to them, however, is the fact that they trouble a community which has shrunk in size to a critical point. . . . The very real possibility of their extinction is always in their consciousness, heightening the poignancy and urgency of each individual concern. Given the ultimacy and finality of what is feared, the question arises as to why every resource is not marshalled in support of active, concerted attacks on every subsidiary problem. . . . The name of that authority [the reason more approaches are not taken] is tradition . . . Finally, the way of those most

obligated and yet least responsible—i.e. the way of the Parsis in India—is to talk."

38. This attitude exists even in published literature, although the feeling is more muted: "A Parsi needs to be a better Parsi first before he can vauntingly address himself as a worthy son of Mother India or even a citizen of the world" (Jhabvala 1946:i). The sentence clearly suggests that the Parsi is intended to be a citizen of India, and expresses a sentiment that most now accept. But there remains this sense that one is a Parsi, who happens also to be in India: a feeling very different from the political communal struggles to control a particular Indian identity and its power.

39. Pestonji, *The Daily* 16 August 1991.

40. Some of these themes—in particular, insecurity and ambivalence about belonging—are discussed in two essays by a psychiatrist and a psychologist, both Parsis: K. J. Sethna "The Psychology and Psychopathology of Parsis" (1984) and D. Dastoor, "Psychological Profile of North American Zoroastrians" (1988), which actually focuses more on the Bombay experience than on North American Parsis.

41. I am scarcely the first to notice an identity confusion within the community. Parsis talk about this freely, and among previous scholars Kulke has been among the most forceful in articulating the point. As he concludes, "[the Parsis'] cultural and national frame of reference became divided into three socio-cultural and political dimensions: India, Iran and England. This psychological identity conflict characterizes the Parsee's search for group identity as well as their political behavior since about 1900. The result was a permanent identity crisis, a permanent loyalty crisis, even if it was not always consciously felt" (1974:144).

42. Cf. Daniel 1984, Marriott 1990.

43. The novels and stories with which I am familiar tend to explore the movement from the traditional to the modern and its consequences for family ties, gender relations, the envisioning of the new polity, the carnage of Partition, and so forth. This of course is only a broad generalization: the novels of Anita Desai and the films of Satyajit Ray are pervaded by a sense of loss, decay, nostalgia, abortive longing. But those are not the dominant moods of K. P. Balanji, *Abhimanyu* (1978), S. R. Rao, *Children of God* (1976), Shobda De, *Socialite Evenings* (1988), Chaman Nahal, *Azadi* (1979), Shiva Kumar, *Nude Before God* (1983), Rama Mehta, *Inside the Haveli* (1977), Shashi Despande, *The Long Silence* (1988), as well as the many translated novels about Independence, the novels of R. K. Narayan, and the autobiographical accounts of Ved Mehta. See also Lutze 1985 and his claim that writers in Hindi take as their central focus the political stance of the writer and of writing.

44. Published in America as *Swimming Lessons,* it attracted favorable international reviews when it first appeared. *Such a Long Journey,* wonderful and profoundly depressing, appeared in 1991. While its characters are Parsi, the novel deals with the broader, weightier themes of governmental corruption and the nature of friendship.
45. The play won the Sultan Padamsee playwriting competition in 1978; Nandini Bhaskaran reviews the production (its first) in the Sunday *Times of India,* 1 July 1990. The playwright is Cyrus Mistry.
46. R. Writer, whose survey of 326 Parsis from around the world has just been published, argued that "the Indianization of the Parsis is perhaps the most striking feature for those whose knowledge of the subcontinent and the community is renewed through frequent contact with both. It is what strikes this author most forcibly" (1994:162).

2. In the Beginning

1. This was in the late 1970s. She was then in her teens.
2. This is a colloquial phrase used to refer to Parsis, in a sometimes affectionate, sometimes disparaging fashion.
3. The *sudreh* is a special shirt which devout Parsis wear under their outer garments, tied by the sacred thread of the *kusti.* The *kusti* is, in theory, untied and retied for prayers frequently throughout the day.
4. The text has been edited slightly to maintain continuity of personal pronoun and tense. The woman was in her late twenties in 1988, and comes from the upper middle class but not quite the community elite.
5. For example, Rosaldo 1980, Parmentier 1989. The anthropological interest in history has grown considerably in recent years, in part through the influence of the University of Chicago department, notably under the influence of Cohn, Singer, and Sahlins. When there is a discussion of the uses of history as applied to culturally specific history, Hobsbawm and Ranger's "invention of tradition" (1983) is sometimes invoked. The Parsis certainly are not inventing their history. They are, however, choosing to present a particular vision of it to themselves.
6. Most elements of Zarathustra's life, but especially his dates, have been hotly debated. Some western scholars held that Zarathustra lived in the sixth century B.C., an argument which seems to have arisen from a Middle Persian tradition which mistook a reference to Cyrus' conquest of Babylon for Zarathustra's birth (these scholars include Zaehner 1961 and Gersevitch 1964). On the other hand, some Parsi scholars, relying on Greek sources, have asserted a date of 7000 B.C., which most Parsis no longer accept, although those influenced by an esoteric version of the

religion continue to do so. ("How can an historian know anything of religion?" I was told by several such *kshnoomists*.) More contemporary discussions include Humbach 1984, Eduljee 1980, Henning 1951, and Herzfeld 1947. Here and throughout this book I treat Boyce as the scholarly authority of the current generation on the texts and early history of the religion. She points out that while it is impossible to determine Zarathustra's dates precisely, the evidence suggests two possible dates: surmising from the content of the Gathas that he lived when the Iranian Stone Age gave way to the Bronze Age, his dates would be around 1400–1200 B.C. (1979:2); extrapolating from the linguistic similarity of the Rig Veda (roughly composed from 1700 B.C. onwards), the appropriate dates would be 1700–1500 BC (1979:18); see 1975:3.

7. Boyce 1979:3, translating from the Avesta Yt. 13.67. I am using the word "heroic" here loosely, as Boyce uses it, to indicate a period like that of the *Iliad,* which predates state formation and in which individual warriors command power and may have been worshipped by their society. The classic description of a heroic age is Chadwick 1912.

8. The use of the Veda in this manner can be quite contentious, for the theological content of the Gathas is open to debate. Taraporewala, for instance, uses Vedic Sanskrit to argue that the concept of reincarnation is present in the Gathas. Taraporewala 1951:167, 729–30; the key passage for Taraporewala is Yasna 49.11.

9. In the Gathas he refers to himself as a "zaotar" a term used to describe a fully qualified priest (Boyce 1979:18). Zoroastrians argue that he is the only prophet of a major world religion to have been so trained.

10. The association with science grows powerful in the nineteenth century, as the next chapter details. By now the importance of natural law is well incorporated into the religion. A teaching course for North American Zoroastrians includes an article that begins as follows: "*Asha* denotes righteousness, justice and the divine\natural law that governs the universe" ("Asha," Farhang Mehr in McIntyre 1990).

11. Boyce 1975:27. Zaehner and others have tended to translate the word as simply, or primarily, "truth" (see Zaehner 1961:34ff).

12. There is something of a debate over what sort of plant this was, and whether it is the same as the *soma* mentioned in the Vedas (the Avestan word is *haoma*). It is likely to have been the ephedra plant, which seems to be mildly hallucinogenic; in Tadjikistan, where the influence of Zoroastrianism still remains, the word for ephedra is *homa* (personal communication by Sarah Stewart). See Zaehner 1961:88ff, Boyce 1975:157ff; also Kashikar 1990. As does Boyce, Kashikar challenges the argument (presented by R. G. Wasson 1969) that *soma* was a hallucinogenic mushroom,

the fly agaric *(amanita muscaria)*. Kashikar also supports the ephedra plant theory.

13. Much of our knowledge comes from texts composed later than Zarathustra's utterances, but probably referring to early practice. These texts are also found in the Avesta, but their linguistic structure suggests an earlier composition than the Gathas.

14. This may be a paraphrase from a Koranic text. J. Russell, personal communication.

15. Zadspram 14.17. The Zadspram is a Pahlavi or Middle Persian text dating from the ninth century, A.D., and it is one of the primary sources for legends of the prophet. The translations are taken from Mistree 1982, a fairly widely read book written for the community; Mistree was a student of Boyce's and specialized in Pahlavi.

16. Zadspram 16.49

17. This account of Zarathustra's murder makes an intriguing parallel with Freud's account of the murder of Moses. Freud argues that the murder of a great prophet of monotheism both symbolizes the revenge of the earlier (pre-oedipal) religious period upon the father of the monotheistic religion and immortalizes the murdered father, as guilt for his slaying comes to haunt those who have inherited the tradition.

18. Until recent years this book was one of the very few to introduce the religion to children. In 1988 Zoroastrian Studies published a colorful children's book (Mehta 1987) which is far more extensive in its treatment of the religion.

19. Zadspram 20.7. See both Mistree 1982 and Muller 1987 (the latter is a reprinting of the nineteenth-century *Sacred Books of the East* translations of the texts).

20. Zadspram 21.8; see n. 18.

21. Passage paraphrased and last bit quoted from Boyce 1979:19; it is also from the Zadspram.

22. Long passages of the Gathas refer to cattle herding. This also causes debate, as it is not clear how Zarathustra intends these passages to be interpreted. At least, it is not clear to many Parsis, who are unfamiliar with the scholarly literature of the topic. One of the appeals of an occult interpretation of the Gathas is that it presents much of the text as an elaborate metaphor. One Parsi, for example, explained to me at some length that he found no solace in the Gathas until he encountered Ilm-e-kshnoom, an occult Zoroastrian interpretation that enabled him to understand the cow as a metaphor for the soul and thus to understand Zarathustra's descriptions as a concern for the well-being—the pasturage—of the individual soul. A more orthodox interpretation is that the

cow represents the Good Mind, an aspect of Ahura Mazda (of what are called his Amesha Spentas) which is also part of the human mind. It is, however, important to note that much of the community does not grapple with these problems. To the extent that Parsis pray, they pray in the original Avestan, which they do not understand, and although they might dip into the English translation of the Avesta in times of trouble, they are more likely to become frustrated and turn to the Bible (or Sai Baba—at any rate, some other source) than to grapple with problems of metaphor.

23. This is Boyce's translation of Yasna 30.3 (Boyce 1979:20). Other translations differ somewhat, for example, Insler 1975:33 and Taraporewala 1951:136.

24. The finest western scholars of Zoroastrianism support the interpretation that the early religion is dualistic. As an anthropologist, not an Iranist, I cannot baldly assert the western view, particularly when many of the Parsis reject it. Despite my considerable respect for Boyce's work, then, I think it appropriate to present the work as one plausible interpretation amongst others.

25. This later text is a Pahlavi, or Middle Persian work, the sixth-century Bundahishn, which is the creation story.

26. Vimadalal 1979:73–74.

27. Discussions of theology by scholars of Zoroastrianism include Zaehner 1955, 1956, 1961, Henning 1951, Taraporewala 1965 [1926], 1951, Herzfeld 1947, Irani 1984, Mistree 1982, Chiniwalla 1942, Willams 1985a, 1985b, 1985c Russell 1984, 1985, 1987a, 1988, Dhalla 1930, Dabu 1976, Masani 1917, Insler 1975 and Boyce, as indicated. The *Catechism on Zoroastrianism* (Motafram 1986) is not, to my knowledge, read frequently by Parsis. One of the most recent scholarly texts is an important work by a young Parsi scholar (Choksky 1989), primarily focusing on the purity code.

28. Boyce 1979:29; Hinnells 1976; Russell 1987b. Russell (1986) makes a similar claim about Aristotle's conception of the good.

29. Boyce (1979:62ff.) suggests that the fire temple may have emerged as a tactical response to the importation of the Mesopotamian Anahita cult.

30. These figures are taken from Kharas 1984.

31. The fire for an Atash Behram, the most sacred of fires, is drawn from (1) fire used in the burning of a corpse; (2) fire used by a dyer; (3) fire from the house of a king or a ruling authority; (4) from a potter; (5) a brickmaker; (6) a fakir or an ascetic; (7) a goldsmith; (8) a silversmith; (9) an ironsmith; (10) an armorer; (11) a baker; (12) a brewer or distiller or idol-worshipper; (13) a soldier or traveler; (14) a shepherd; (15) fire produced by lightning; (16) a household fire from the house of a Zoroas-

trian. Each fire is purified 91 times: it is put downwind from a pile of sandalwood, frankincense, and other ignitable items. The fire then jumps to this new pile, and then a new pile of frankincense and so forth is made. The details of the consecration ceremony, as well as of nearly all Parsi religious rituals, can be found in Modi 1986 [1922]; a more contemporary version is Choksy 1989.

32. The *gahs* are the division of the day into different periods: midnight to sunrise, sunrise to noon (although this is determined to be roughly 12:45 in local Indian time); noon to 3 P.M., again 3:45 in local time; three until sunset; sunset until midnight.

33. Yt 13.95. Boyce 1979:30.

34. Daboo 1979:14. I am not sure how common this volume is. It is printed and presented as if it were an inexpensive household item, but I only saw it in one house.

35. Described allusively in Denkart DK VII 4.70; see also the Zardusht Nama. See Mistree 1982, Muller 1987 for sources.

36. The letter to the Central Board of Film Censors expressed these sentiments: "If the film is allowed to be shown, it will be a deliberate and malicious outrage to the Parsi Zoroastrian community, whose religious feelings are bound to be violently hurt by insulting . . . its religion and\or its religious beliefs." Quoted in *Parsiana* May 1985:17.

37. These are both late-ninth-century Pahlavi texts.

38. *The Parsee Voice* 2 (10)–11 1–15, 16–31 (March 1985). The *doongerwadi* is the place surrounding and including the Towers of Silence, where funeral services are held before bodies are left for the vultures behind stone walls, the traditional Zoroastrian custom for the disposal of the dead.

39. These are Assyrian records of military expeditions to the Iranian plateau. Boyce 1982:7.

40. For further detail see Olmstead 1948 and Frye 1962.

41. But see Sanjana 1906:41.

42. Boyce 1979:49; see also Humbach 1984.

43. Herodotus Bk. I:131–139.

44. This empire, like the Achaemenian empire, tolerated not only variations within Zoroastrian practice but also different religions. Many of the cities were Greek and Iranian, and on the eastern borders of the empire Buddhism emerged as a new and vital rival.

45. There is some dispute abut this date; some Parsis place it earlier. Here, as in the rest of the chapter, I take Boyce as my scholarly authority.

46. Desai 1988:23–24. This story is an old chestnut. Many Parsis told it to me on hearing of my work; non-Parsis, too, often told me of it. There is even a book about the community, proceedings of a conference intended

to determine how so small a community could be so successful, entitled *The Sugar in the Milk* (ed. N. and R. Singh, 1986). The story has a somewhat different form in Katrak 1959:109.

47. It is true that Zoroastrianism in Iran tends to be endogamous, but that is because of the violent Muslim reaction to apostasy. See Fischer 1973, esp. 67ff, for an anthropological discussion of Zoroastrianism in Iran and the differing approaches to exclusion.

48. Streysham Master, for example, writing in 1672, describes the community as mostly weavers (in Karkaria 1915:466). The movement from Gujarat to Bombay in the nineteenth century matches the pattern of caste-based migration in other European ports; it parallels that of the weaver castes in Madras and Calcutta, who were encouraged to migrate in order to staff textile mills. Axelrod 1974:29, Cohn 1971, and Hodivala 1920.

49. See also Fischer 1973:79ff. He points out that the core romantic story of the collective flight and acceptance thanks to Jadhav Rana has some weaknesses; notably, there is evidence for the existence of Parsis in India before the Arab conquest and their trickling in thereafter, and some reasons for skepticism about the historical source of the story (1973:81).

50. Jordanus; quoted in Firby 1984.

51. It is usually assumed that exposure of the dead is a comparatively recent phenomenon. Herodotus, for instance, does not report it. In I:140 Herodotus remarks: "There is another custom which is spoken of with reserve, and not openly, concerning the dead. It is said that the body of a male Parsi is never buried, until it has been torn either by a dog or a bird or prey. That the Magi have this custom is beyond a doubt, for they practice it without any concealment. The dead bodies are covered with wax, and then buried in the ground." The rationale for this practice arises from the repugnance of thrusting a body understood to be defiled by death into a medium understood to be sacred: earth, fire, water, or air.

52. This is a widely told story. In the single copy owned by a Parsi library the photographs of the pallbearers are indeed blackened, along with parts of the text which discuss the growing trend towards cremation. However, a friend owns an uncensored copy.

53. Namely, the eyes, palms, soles of the feet, and solar plexus. It is not clear to me whether this claim is accurate. In any event an elderly gentleman came up to me afterwards and explained that in London, where there were no vultures, two needs could be met by feeding Parsis to the hyenas at the London zoo. He seemed to be quite sincere.

54. Dubash 1906:ii. The *Zoroastrian Sanitary Code* (Bombay: Rahmanae Mazdayyasnan Sabha, 1906).

55. Fischer finds a similar tension on this issue in Yazd, Iran, and adds an

additional argument he heard in favor of the procedure: that it can speed the progress of the soul in the other world (1973:63).

56. Vakil in *Parsiana* 15 November–15 December 1973:7, 9–10. When I met Vakil in Bombay, he was still bitter at what he took to be the community's complete denial of the facts.

57. The Towers of Silence were a British tourist attraction at the turn of the century—at least, they were visited by many, although of course neither Englishman nor Parsi was allowed inside the *dokhma* itself (see the *Bombay Gazette* 1886). A typical account is in *A Descriptive Guide to the City of Bombay:* "A short distance beyond the reservoir we come to the Towers of Silence. Here the Parsees deposit their dead, to be devoured by vultures. On the trees and on the walls that surround the towers these hideous birds can be seen in dozens. Suddenly they rise in the air. A corpse is being brought." (Bombay: the *Times of India Press* 1887:33–34). Parsi compilers of non-Zoroastrian commentary on their faith (Bilimoria and Alpaivala 1898) cite numerous positive remarks made about the sanitary nature of the practice, but the growing enthusiasm for cremation and the public defense of the practice indicate growing community unease. See, for example, "Is the Burning of the Dead Body of a Parsi Zoroastrian in a Crematorium Allowed by the Zoroastrian Religion?" by Dastur Peshotan Sanjana, in the *Bombay Samachar* 19 July 1905, makes an impassioned defense of the practice, which suggests that it was under attack. And it is clear that not all the British responded positively to the practice. "If the Parsi method of selpuchre is rather ghastly, their wedding ceremonies, on the other hand, are a scene of brightness and animation unequalled" (*Old and New Bombay* 1911:64). And from an earlier traveler: "The burying place for the Parsees is an object the most dreadful, and of the most horrid prospect in the world, and much more frightful than a field of slaughter'd men" (Ovington, "A Voyage to Surratt (1689)," typescript p. 4). More description—along with pages of quoted comments from non-Parsis—can be found in *Towers of Silence* 1984; see also Rustomjee, 1978.

58. The Hanging Gardens at Malabar Hill, where the Towers of Silence are located, is a prime real estate area in Bombay. High rise apartment buildings have recent been built which overlook the *dokhmas*. Because the land is extremely valuable, Bombay-dwellers occasionally voice resentment over the small community's ownership of so much prime city land.

59. Daruwalla 1971:13–14.

60. Hinnells, *Parsiana* February 1977:18ff.

61. Modi 1905:29–30. He translates part of the Kisseh-i Sanjan (the history of Sanjan), a poem written around 1600 A.D. which purported to describe

the arrival of the Parsis in the India as the author, a *dastur,* heard it from another *dastur.* "One day he told me this story, having pierced the pearl of news with goodness" ([1905]:5).

62. For this period and the following see Karaka 1884; Modi 1905; Murzban 1917:50ff; Katrak 1959:107ff; Mirza 1987:30ff; Fischer 1973:84ff. Murzban's book has a frontispiece showing a photograph of Queen Victoria and carrying this caption: "Victoria the Good: The Great Queen of England and Empress of India, under whose sovereignty the Parsis attained the zenith of their prosperity and freedom—religious, social and educational."

63. This is a commonly estimated figure for the number of Parsis before the British. The actual number may have been very different.

64. Subramanian (1985, 1991), for instance, writes of the "Anglo-Bania" order in which Hindu-Jaina merchants dominated the commercial activity, "virtually monopolized" (1985:207) the brokerage, were prominent as bankers and moneylenders, and were important intermediaries in trade. From this perspective, Parsis were engaged in more or less the same activity but were far less important, and the fact that Parsis were the target of Muslim riots of 1788—Muslims were the real financial losers in the emerging European-based trade—was more or less incidental. Torri (1987, 1991) puts more emphasis on the importance of the Parsis and argues that the term "bania" in the historical records refers generally to native communities engaged in brokerage. The argument seems to hinge on the question of how to read the particular documents involved. Subramanian's own work contains evidence that Parsis distinguished themselves from *banias* but that the British did not set them apart (1991:337 and n.). Torri (1991) also conducts an extensive argument against treating all merchant-bankers as a single group.

65. Cf. Kulke 1974; also Hinnells 1978.

66. Cf. A. Guha 1982. For a detailed account of business practices in eighteenth-century Surat, see White 1979; also Eduljee 1987.

67. At some point Gujarati Parsis took control of the palm wine (toddy) production in Gujarat. The local *adivasis* (tribal people) then became indebted to, and exploited by, the Parsis. It is clear that this was occurring in the early twentieth century, and there is a lovely account by Hardiman (1987) of an attempt to halt the indebtedness. The practice may, however, have begun centuries earlier.

68. Rustomji Manok Dalal (d. 1719) and Dhanji Bairamji of Surat were both shipowning traders. Dorabji Nanabhai Patel (d. 1689) and his son Rustomji Patel (1667–1763) (the founders of the Dadyseth and Cama families) established trading houses in Bombay. Banaji Limji (d. 1734) and his

son Bairamji Banaji (1681–1753) carried on trade with Pegu (Burma) in the first part of the eighteenth century. These facts are all mentioned in A. Guha 1982:9.

69. These figures reported in A. Guha 1982:9–20.

70. Quoted in Tindall 1982:94. The "burying place" referred to is actually the Tower of Silence on Malabar Hill. But there are also less glowing accounts. Here is one from W. Geleyassen de Jongh *Gujarat Report* (c. 1630s), quoted in Firby 1984:130: "They may not lie in business matters, or say that their wares have cost more than is actually case; if they were to be dishonest in such matters, their sin would be 99 times greater than for an ordinary lie, nevertheless they cannot refrain from this in business, and they lie repeatedly for the sake of profit, as the other merchants do, without giving any thought to the great sin they thus commit."

71. The Kolis still remain at Bombay's southern tip, almost as if oblivious to the city which has grown up around them.

72. See the discussion in Wadia 1983 [1955]:183ff.

73. This was carved c. 1801 on the *Marquess of Cornwall* (a ship) (Tindall 1982:99). For a detailed history of the Bombay dockyard and its Parsi shipbuilders, see Wadia 1983.

74. Torri (1991:n.3) remarks that these records may well have been underestimates.

75. Karaka 1884. David also makes this point, but Karaka appears to be his source.

76. *Old and New Bombay* 1911:56.

77. *Description of a View of the Island and Harbour of Bombay.* Painted by R. Burford (London: T. Brettell, 1831:12).

78. *Tourist's Handbook to Bombay and India* 1900:91.

79. This figure constitutes some 6% of the total population of 816,562 (Kulke 1974:51). In 1813, half of Bombay's Fort residents—the Europeans lived in the Fort area—were Parsi (Kulke 1974:37) and some 10,000 Parsis lived within the city limits (Axelrod 1974:28). A native chronicler of 1863 cites the number of Parsis in 1854 as 110,544. Madgoakar, cited in *Ushta* June 1989:7.

80. Kulke 1974:54. Despite the central importance of weaving in seventeenth-century Parsi life, not a single Parsi is listed as a weaver. And Axelrod provides these figures for the occupations of Bombay Parsis from the 1881 Census (1974:28):

tradesmen:	1940 men and 59 women
servants:	2079 men and 416 women
merchants:	3317 men and 2 women
agriculturalists:	67 men and 2 women

manufacturers:	3610 men and 87 women
not classified:	565 men and 139 women

81. To quote one of the most famous of the Parsi entrepreneurs: "We cannot give up business and remain in a state of monotonous lethargy. Our habits and our early education have been such that the bustle of commerce and the excitement of business are essential to us." In Kulke 1974:130. From Sir Jamsetjee Jeejeebhoy Papers Notebook No. II:182, Letter from Jeejeebhoy to George Forbes (London, 28 August 1845). The 1931 Census listed the traditional occupation of the Parsis as trade (Kulke 1974:123).

82. Mangoakar, in *Ushta* June 1989:7.

83. Sir James Ferguson, introducing J. J. Modi's speech on "The Religious System of the Parsis," on January 12, 1885 (Modi 1885:ii). Ferguson makes errors in his enthusiasm—Parsi religious reformers, for instance, had by this point long been calling attention to the Hindu influence in the current practices of the religion—but it is his tone which is important.

84. *Imperial Gazetteer of India* Vol. VIII (Oxford: Clarendon, 1908:412).

85. Rutnagar 1927; Kulke 1974:56.

86. The Bombay spinning mill was founded by Cowasjee Nanabhai Davar and the iron foundry by Shapurji Sorabji. Other entrepreneurs included D. A. Hormasjee Wadia, a successful mill agent who left one million rupees for Parsi charities. Cowasjee Dinsha built one of the great business houses of the East in Aden, opened a private coaling depot, and operated a line of steamers between Aden, Red Sea ports, and the Somali coast. Cowasjee Naoroji Chhoi, a pioneer of the silk industry in Bombay, and Ardesar Barjorjee Godrej, founded the Indian safe- and soap-manufacturing industries: even today most middle class people in Bombay have Godrej locks on their steel cupboards. For short biographies of these and others, see Darukhanawalla 1939.

87. *Bombay Illustrated* 1904:63.

88. Kulke (1974:56) cites the Viccajee family as an example.

89. Chaudhuri in *Bombay Gazette* 1986:365 and 366; the reference is to the Cama family.

90. Sir Shapurjee Bharucha was the guiding light of the Stock Exchange. Well-known financiers included Sir Hormusjee Pirojsha Mody (Homi Mody). In the early twentieth century he held the posts of Chairman of the Bombay Millowners' Association, President of the Indian Merchants' Chamber, President of the Employers' Federation of India, Member of the Legislative Assembly of India, of the Round Table Conference, of the Reserve Bank of India, and Director of Tata Sons Ltd—an important man. Sir Sorabjee Pochkhanavala, the "Father of Indian Banking," established

with Phrezeshah Mehta the first Indian Bank in London (the Central Bank of India, 1911) and the Central Exchange Bank of India. The list could be extended. Again, short biographies of these men can be found in Darukhanawalla 1939.

91. Shortly after finishing his education he joined his father's company, and while the company suffered from speculation during the cotton boom bubble, he was not ruined.

92. "Tout Bombay" is Tindall's phrase (1982:27). There is another story about the hotel having been built the wrong way round, with the grand entrance facing the town and not the sea. When the architect saw the finished edifice, the story goes, he committed suicide in despair. This story is almost certainly false, as Tindall points out—the way the entrance faced is appropriate to its Oriental style—but I was told it many times. In any event, the fashion has now changed, and one enters the Taj from behind.

93. Kulke 1974:131. From the Hamilton Papers Vol. I, Letter No. 6. Hamilton to Curzon, 26 January 1900.

94. To cite a 1889 Parsi newspaper, the only way that India could operate as a single entity was through the "indomitable will and energy of a superior race [the British] which has but to relax its hold to see these different fragments of humanity waging a war to exterminate each other. It would be pure fiction to say that there is any other bond of sympathy or unity between them." *Rast Goftar*—a paper which Naoroji actually founded but which fell rapidly out of sympathy with his views—17 November 1889. Quoted in Kulke 1974:184. More detailed information, particularly on Naoroji's life in England, can be found in Mello 1985; and on Parsi involvement in moderate nationalist politics, in Monk 1985. On Naoroji's political life see Masani 1939 and Naoroji's numerous writings.

95. Chaudhuri 1986 makes frequent reference to Mehta in his history of Bombay; also see Mody [1963] 1921.

96. See "Madame Cama" by Khorshed Adi Sethna in the program for the 5th World Zoroastrian Congress Bombay 1990. In 1989 some of the young adults in the Bombay community produced a popular play about her life.

97. For example, in an 1884 personal letter to Lord Harris (India Office Library), M. M. Bhownagree, later Conservative M.P., expressed his hopes (which were fulfilled) for a political future thus: "Everyone of note and influence and most of all Parsees, who have seen me, wonder why I haven't yet stood for a Conservative Constituency. They all think it was time [sic] the Congress fad of Radicalism was laid bare, and the nonsense talked to the English public unchallenged in the name of India was exposed." And an unpublished novel by Phiroshaw Jamsetjee Chevalier

266 · Notes to Pages 93–94

(Chaiwala), internally dated as 1927, contains this piece of dialogue: (Young man:) "But the Parsis remain stubbornly loyal to the British crown, in spite of the various intimidations and inducements all around, is that so, governor?" (Older man:) "It scarcely needs any denying, my boy. During the present critical crisis of the tremendously huge anti-British Gandhi movement in that vast peninsula, the Parsi loyalty to our king is proverbial." (*The Tower of Silence* by Phiroshaw Jamsetjee Chevalier [Chaiwala]. Unpublished ms., India Office Library.

98. 1911 Census of India. The method of accounting changed by 1921, so that only 21% were reported to live in one room. The change is particularly remarkable because the method of counting was altered to make fewer divisions count as rooms. The 1921 Census reports some confusion as to the method employed by the 1911 Census. The challenge of using the Indian census material has been reported with some irony by an eminent historian, who remarks: "consistency is not one of the enduring virtues of the Census of India" (Conlon 1981:105). Census data on occupation is not helpful in establishing economic status, as categories combine workers of different levels. Shipowners and dockyard laborers, for instance, are entered in the same category.

99. In Dhobi Talao they were 8,619 out of 38,683, in Fort North 9,692 out of 25,400, in Khetwadi 7,326 out of 31,937. Census of India Bombay Pt. II Chap. 5, p. 25. To give some sense of the relevance of these figures, 55% of the Fort North tenements were one room, one of the lowest percentages in turn-of-the-century Bombay; 68% of the dwellings in Dhobi Talao and 81% in Khetwadi were one room. The Dongri and Mandevi areas, however, listed closer to 90% of the dwellings as one-room tenements. However, even a real definition was not always a clear guide to class. The 1909 *Gazetteer of Bombay City and Island* reported that middle class Parsis resided in the western section of Khetwadi, whereas the middle and lower class Parsis resided in northeastern Dhobi Talao and Fort North. The *Gazetteer* also remarks that "Parsis are ubiquitous in every branch of trade" (p. 293).

100. These figures are taken from the *Gazetteer of Bombay City and Island* Vol.3:200. The report of a 1850s gang of thugs is found in Vol.2:244: "At a time when public safety was quite insecure, when the city was infested by desperate gangs of thieves and other malefactors, he [Forgett, appointed as command of the police in 1855] had to use all his wonderful energy and acuteness to break their power . . . There was a notorious band of athletic ruffians in Bazaar Gate Street, consisting chiefly of Parsis. They used to occupy some rising ground, from which they swooped down on their prey. Their daily acts of crime and violence were committed with

impunity, and their names were whispered by mothers to hush their children to silence."

101. See, for instance, the remarks of the members of the Missionary Settlement for University Women, described later.

102. Jeejeebhoy in Darukhanawalla 1938:37–8.

3. The Power and the Glory

1. Frontispiece, Karaka 1884.

2. Karaka 1884 II:243; 245–46. The "first city" in the British Empire was London.

3. Chaudhuri 1986:646. I believe that the entry was written many years ago by a Parsi who is unattributed in the text; Chaudhuri is the general editor.

4. For example, Karaka 1884 II:264–65; 291.

5. Karaka 1884 I:97. He reports also that the proportion of children to full-grown women is also highest amongst the Parsis.

6. Parsis sent considerable material aid and gave political help to the remaining Persian Zoroastrians in the late nineteenth century.

7. Karaka 1884 II:295. The paragraph ends: "Can it then be wondered at that loyalty—consistent, deep and abiding loyalty—coupled with a touching reverence and affection for the royal family, has become a part of the Parsi nature, almost a part of the Parsi religion? so that with one consent the whole community daily prays 'God bless the Queen!'"

8. Taraporevala 1981:5. This is taken from an unpublished manuscript entitled "Paradise Lost: Acculturation and Historical Consciousness Among the Parsis of India." She borrows the term "civilizing process" from Norbert Elias.

9. Axelrod 1974:31. This figure is based on census data.

10. The word also carries the connotation of duty, understood now at least as including the notion of hard work. The texts frequently mention duty; see Modi 1932:149–154 and Modi 1914: esp. 21–23. Some western scholars have argued that the religious centrality of truthfulness, righteousness, and hard work is responsible at least in part for the Parsis' remarkable success (Whitehurst 1969, Kennedy 1962, Kulke 1974). The alternative argument is that it was the status of Parsis as minorities which enabled them to identify with the British so quickly and take advantage of the changing economic climate. Kulke ultimately adheres to this view. My point is that the Parsis probably used their religious concepts strategically to curry favor with the British. See also Brown 1972: 252–268.

11. Taraporewala 1965:18, 21. In his words, "The best description of *Asha* can be only given in the inspired words of Tennyson." It is notable that

a mid-twentieth-century priest would explain this central Zoroastrian concept through the words of a British poet.

12. For example, the biography of Jeejeebhoy and others in Darakhanawalla 1939.

13. Michael Fischer told me once that these rural Zoroastrians conceptualized evil as something almost tangible. The *druj* of impurity around a corpse was understood as demonic.

14. The shirt is tied round at the waist with a special cord, the *kusti;* its 72 threads represent the 72 verses of the *yasna,* a long and centrally important liturgy which includes the Gathas. In theory, the *kusti* is tied and retied many times a day: five times before sun or fire at certain subdivisions in the day and after using the lavatory. Before the *kusti* ceremony the ritualist first washes his face, hands, and if possible his feet. Then, as he unties the cord, he recites the Kemna Mazda. The translation of the original tongue (Avestan) reads thus (translation and source detail Boyce 1984:58). "Protect us from the foe, O Mazda and Spenta Armaiti! Begone, daevic Drug! Begone, the one of Daeva-origin, begone the one of Daeva-Shaping, begone the one of Daeva-begetting! Begone, O Drug, crawl away O Drug, disappear O Drug! In the north you shall disappear. You shall not destroy the material world of Asha! Reverence with which there is devotion and sacrifice." The cord is retied with the following Pahlavi and Avestan prayer, the Ohrmazd Khoday, and other short prayers. How much of the prayers a contemporary Zoroastrian understands is not clear, but she will know that the prayer is meant to protect her, and she will recognize the name Ahriman as she flicks the end of her *kusti,* to shake the evil from her.

15. Widely followed in the previous generation but less so today, the purity rules required households to have a small room, with iron furniture, in which the woman would live for the duration of her period. There she was allowed to touch nothing from her nonmenstruating life lest she defile it utterly. See the discussion in Choksy 1989:102. Hindu women are usually considered unclean for the first three days of their period, while the traditional Zoroastrian restrictions applied to the entire length of the bleeding time. One Parsi woman of my acquaintance remembered calling her mother to turn the pages of her school books as she studied during her menstrual period, the schoolbook propped on an iron bookstand.

In my first visit I stayed in a hostel for working women in the city. The warden told me that the Parsi residents were most peculiarly upset about trivial things. One of the girls, she said, had once left her *kusti* to dry in the bathroom, and telephoned the warden from work to put it in her room before one of the cleaning women touched it. Then, the warden continued, when they come back from a funeral, they refuse to enter the hostel until they have washed with water outside. So ridiculous, the warden said; one could wash perfectly well inside, but they would not.

16. Williams 1987:1. See also Choksy 1989 ; also the description of the major prefatory ceremony for the *yasna* and other high liturgical rituals, given in Kotwal and Boyd 1977. The primary purity laws for Zoroastrian are enjoined in the Vendidad, an elaborate ritual text which details regulations for all aspects of Zoroastrian life.

17. *The Parsi* 3:132.

18. Famous names include: Dastur Peshotan Sanjana, Kavasji Kanga, J. J. Modi, G. K. Narriman, S. K. Hodivala, M. N. Dhalla, S. Bharucha, T. Anklesaria, and so forth.

19. For instance, the Rahnumae Mazdayasanan Sabha, with Dadabhai Naoroji as its first secretary, was formed to encourage reform; it is now considered somewhat orthodox. See Bharucha 1979 [1903]:46ff.

20. Fischer 1973:97ff describes in some detail the citadel-storming style of Hataria's enterprise: he built (or rebuilt) fire temples, *dokhmas,* schools, and other community buildings, recruited students, and rather elegantly harassed the government about the Iranian Zoroastrians.

21. Most of this history is abstracted from Kulke's more detailed account (1974:142ff). The Iran League is still extant, but it is not (according to the August 1990 newsletter) in healthy shape. It continues to hold meetings, publish a newsletter, and—what seems to be its major activity—sponsor competitions, particularly for children. In 1990 these included a Shahnameh recitation competition (40 competitors), an elocution competition (47 competitors), a musical talent competition (86 competitors), an essay writing competition (26 competitors), a drawing competition (107 competitors), and a *rangoli* competition (22 competitors). Apart from the Shahnameh, the competitions are Parsi-oriented, but not particularly Iran-oriented.

22. Kulke 1974:142. Fischer 1973:106ff also indicates a rise in Iranian financial prosperity at the turn of the nineteenth into the twentieth century; this may have added to the allure. James Russell points out (personal communication) that the link with Iran was never fully broken, and that one should not overemphasize the importance of this turn to Iranian ancestry.

23. Such scholars included Comte, Spencer, Frazer, Tylor, etc. A review of the intellectual history of the period can be gained from Burrow 1966.

24. F. C. Cook 1884:lv. Excerpted in Bilimoria and Alpaivala 1898:79.

25. R. Brown c. 1880s. Not all scholars shared this view, but most described

the religion as ethically superior to most other faiths. See A. Franck and J. Oppert 1868. Also see the remarkable quotations gathered in Bilimoria and Alpaivala 1898 on this theme from Emile Burnouf, *The Science of Religions* (1888); *Chambers Encyclopedia* (1865); Frances Power Cobbe, *Studies of Ethical and Social Subjects* (1865); Marie, Countess of Caithness, Duchess de Pomar, *The Mystery of the Ages* (1887); *Select Writings of the Most Rev. Dr. Leo Meurin, S.J.* (1891); Ernest de Bunsen, *The Hidden Wisdom of Christ* (1865).

26. Zoroastrianism also became central for Europeans who turned to theosophy in their own quest to cope with the cold threat of science. The Renaissance cabalistic texts—theosophists read them for seeds of spiritual scientific wisdom—had presented Zoroaster as an ancient sage. In the nineteenth century his name returned as at least emblematic of this early ancient wisdom, and Zoroastrianism emerged as a core element in theosophical philosophy. (See not only Nietzsche, but the Golden Dawn's Sapere Aude, *The Chaldean Oracles of Zoroaster,* 1895). When Madame Blavatsky and Colonel Olcott arrived in India in the late nineteenth century, they discovered the Parsis with great fanfare and promptly recruited them. In Europe, meanwhile, Zoroastrianism became for theosophists and their ilk a mystic embodiment of wisdom and a mythic representation of faith.

27. These figures appear in Hinnells 1985.

28. A useful general account is Hinnells 1985. See also Lala 1981 and Lala 1984 for further examples.

29. Jehangir Cowasjee Jehangir Papers, Indian Office Library, London.

30. Hindu widows had low status and could not remarry, and the custom of child marriage placed many women in these unfortunate circumstances.

31. Quoted in Kulke 1974:112n; from Malabari 1894. Gidumal's 1982 biography portrays Malabari as an outsider to the faith he wanted to reform. The biographer describes the Englishness of Malabari's literary aspirations—he considered himself preeminently a poet, at least at the start of his career—and points to his use of English models in his printed poems, *Indian Muse in English Garb.* The biography has a flattering introduction by Florence Nightingale. See also Karkaria 1896.

32. Sir J. C. Coyajee, *The Future of Zoroastrianism,* n.d.:9. (By internal dating, at least 1925 and probably not much later).

33. See Shroff 1923:title page; Anklesaria 1936:7; Patel n.d. (prob. early 1920s):2.

34. Laing 1887:198; also quoted in Hinnells n.d.:4.

35. Carnegie, source not given, in Laing 1887:219–220. This kind of remark

is frequently made. For example, "There is no pleasanter sight in Bombay than the group of pious Parsis praying at sunset along the shores of Back Bay" (W. S. Caine, *Picturesque India* 1891:13–14; cited in Bilimoria and Alpaivala 1898:62); or the even more romantic description by Zenaide A. Ragozin: "Few forms of worship appeal more to our imagination and our sense of reverent awe than the homage paid to this purest of symbols [fire, or the sun] on the stainless mountain tops, by white-robed Athravans, raising their voice in song amid the silence of a wild and undesecrated nature" (from *Media*; cited in Bilimoria and Alpaivala 1898:186).

36. Cf. Comaroff and Comaroff 1992.

37. Naoroji 1890:14.

38. Postan 1870:19.

39. Karaka says that "In former years Parsi ladies of the upper and middle classes had, like the Mahomedans and Hindus, an objection to appear in public . . . This prejudice has now almost entirely worn away. Parsi ladies of all classes may be seen in public just like the ladies of the Western world" (1884 I:130–131).

40. These comments are taken from a Parsi compilation of European descriptions of Bombay (Karkaria 1915). Not all of his selections speak of Parsis, but many of those that refer to the island's social life mention these prominent citizens. Those from whose remarks I have abstracted this paragraph include Mrs. Postans 1839 (Karkaria 1915:287); J. H. Stocqueler 1844 (1915:295); Balcarres Ramsay 1882 (1915:303); Mrs. Guthrie 1877 (1915:314); Emma Roberts 1841 (1915:319); Mrs. Elwood 1830 (1915:321–2); William Shepard 1857 (1915:326); Baron von Huber 1886 (1915:333).

41. This argument is made most clearly in the literature concerning *sati*. Mani, for instance, argues that "women become emblematic of tradition" (1987:121); Das argues that the colonial construction of womanhood as traditional provided legitimate grounds to protect the women: "Whereas the fixation of the categories of case and tribe was related to the technology of governance, the knowledge about women was organized and interpreted in a manner permitting such claims of legitimacy to be defended" (1986:60). These are very general categories, but they are sufficient to indicate the possible political salience to the sophistication of the Parsi women. Chatterjee (1989,1993) further describes the way that Bengali women became a ground on which struggles over colonialism were fought. See also Sabin 1991 and Nandy 1980.

42. Briggs 1852:19, 21.

43. *Album of Men and Women of India* 1906:449

44. *Minister's Magazine* June 1899:616

45. *Album of Men and Women of India* 1906:447.
46. Sir John Crawford Burns. Tape recording, India Office Library, London.
47. *Old and New Bombay* 1911:141.
48. *Album of Men and Women in India* 1906:469.
49. Missionary Settlement for University Women, papers, India Office Library (see also Mary Dobson, papers). The pamphlet goes on to say that "as a community they are enormously wealthy . . . the younger generation speak English, some being more at home in it than in Gujarati."
50. "The Real Meaning of Work Among the Parsees," a lecture delivered by Frank Anderson in 1899 to the Annual meeting of the Missionary Society for University Women, India Office Library.
51. Invitation sent out in 1893 for the Women Students' Missionary Union, Missionary Society for University Women, India Office Library.
52. *The Parsi* 1905 1:8–9. The quotations reproduced here appear to be the work of multiple authors, not all of whom are identified.
53. *The Parsi* 1905 2:62.
54. Ibid. *1905 4:176.*
55. Ibid. 1905 8:324.
56. Ibid. 1905 8:325.
57. Ibid. 1905 4:190.
58. Ibid. 1905 6:209.
59. Kookadaru was a nineteenth-century Parsi priest, who is ascribed magical spiritual power. A contemporary Bombay priest, he practiced essentially as an intermediary in the late 1880s, and during this time a newly opened fire temple was dedicated in his honor.
60. One of the best accounts of muscular Christianity and its surrounding ethical penumbra is Girouard 1981. Caplan (1991) has written a fascinating article on the British representation of Gurkha manliness; one of the significant differences between the British depiction of manly martial Indians and the Parsis' self-description is the British emphasis on the child-like qualities of the Gurkha and the Parsis' emphasis on their own rationality. The anxiety about *not* being regarded as a martial race may account for the insistent wish, in the early twentieth century, that Parsis could be made military officers alongside the British.
61. The book, a remarkable insight into the enmeshment between Parsis and the British, is entitled *Stray Thoughts on Indian Cricket*. Patel 1905:70.
62. Patel quoted in Nandy 1989:135.
63. In Nandy 1988:52; quoting Mukherjee, *Between Indian Wickets* 1976:49–50.
64. Wurgaft 1983:53. See also Mannoni 1990 [1956]).
65. Callaway 1987:40. Callaway is writing about Africa rather than India,

but the general frame she describes seems not dissimilar from the Indian, for the straightforward reason that the colonizers in both cases are British. She quotes from Ruskin's 1864 lectures, "Of Queen's Gardens," to convey the new Victorian sensibility of gender: "The man's power is active, progressive, defensive. He is eminently the doer, the creator, the discoverer, the defender. His intellect is for speculation and invention; his energy for adventure, for war and for conquest, wherever war is just, wherever conquest necessary." In Callaway 1987:40. On this theme also see Girouard 1981 and Das 1986.

66. Mani 1987, O'Hanlon 1991, Engels 1983, Chatterjee 1989,1993; see also Sabin 1991, Nandy 1980.

67. See Ballhatchet 1980, Kelly 1991, Stoler 1991, 1992; Oldenburg (1991) describes a seemingly remarkable resistance against this regulation.

68. One of the most compelling recent documents along these lines is Malek Alloula's *The Colonial Harem* (1986). Alloula presents a series of postcards, used in casual correspondence, which feature Algerian women. With their drooping breasts, seductive poses, exotic outfits, poised posed difference, they embody the colonial ideology in which they were portrayed as alluring but elusive possessions.

69. Cama was one of the century's more energetic Parsi scholars, eager to learn more about the faith in order to shake off its "superstitious" Hindu accretions. The society was called the Rahnumai Mazdayasnan Sabha (Society for Religious Reform); this group was also involved in another society, the Dnyan Prasarak Mandli (Society for the Diffusion of Knowledge).

70. For example, Naoroji urges in his 1886 presidential address to the Indian National Congress to "Let us speak out like men and proclaim that we are loyal to the backbone" (Kulke 1974:175).

71. Mankekar 1968:41–2. There were also riots between Parsis and Muslims in 1874, after Rustomjee Hormusjee Jalbhoy (a Parsi) published a book in Gujarati on the life of Mohammed in which he referred to the mother of the Prophet's children as a kept woman *(rakheli rand)*. At least one Parsi was killed when, eight months later, the Muslim community noticed the book, and at least a hundred Parsis moved into the Fort area during the period for protection. See "The Memorial of the Parsee Inhabitants of the City of Bombay in the East Indies," a petition addressed to the government to ask for its protection. (K. R. Cama Oriental Institute document. The primary author is Jamsetjee Jeejeebhoy; eleven others are listed and an asserted 8,438 more have joined in the petition.)

72. Keki Daruwalla, "Father-in-Law," in *Parsiana,* January 1978:7.

4. We Are Not What We Were

1. Naoroji, for instance, sharply criticizes the state of religious knowledge in the community in 1905: "the whole religious education of a Parsi child consists in preparing by rote a certain number of prayers in Zend, without understanding a word of them; the knowledge of the doctrines of their religion being left to be picked up in casual conversation" [speech read before the Liverpool Literary and Philosophical Society: 1905:2]. Olcott, when he visited Bombay, makes similar remarks in 1882, and the main objective of orthodox writing throughout the end of the nineteenth and early twentieth century is to fight secularism (e.g. Sanjana 1906;1929).

2. In America, as a later chapter details, Parsis seem less harshly critical of themselves.

3. Blood is a powerful idiom in South Asian kinship, as indeed throughout the world. See Trawick 1990:131ff; Daniel 1984; Dundes 1991.

4. The Iranis are usually considered to be a subgroup of Parsis unless there is some need to distinguish them from Parsis. Irani is the "marked" term, like the traditional "she"; Parsi includes both Irani and Parsi, the way "he" traditionally includes both genders, unless the term "Irani" is specifically employed. However, in America, where there are many Zoroastrians who emigrated directly from Iran, the term "Irani" is usually used to describe them, and the people who in India would be called Irani are here consolidated with Indian Parsis as Parsi.

5. The best sociological study of Iranian Zoroastrianism in Iran is Fischer 1973. It has a rich and complex sense of the rural villages in which the Zoroastrian community lives cheek by jowl with two other faiths, Islam and Judaism. The thesis demonstrates the interdependency of religious ideology and practice on the one hand, and social and political structure on the other. The author argues that tightly knit organizations are correlated with socioeconomic mobility and strikingly illustrates how deeply religion is a thing of social organization, political desire, and sociological happenstance. Yet that knowledge of the sociological realities ought not to diminish the importance of understanding belief and faith. Boyce (1977) has also produced an analysis of an Iranian community, which is more focused on the ritual elements of the religion.

6. Many of these restaurants, I am told, have now been sold to non-Zoroastrians.

7. One of the favorites was the Texas Chicken Dance, called the birdie dance in India, which was performed with much discretion. In the dance one imitates a chicken which squawks, flaps its wings, and lays eggs.

8. The tension persists in the United States, though for curiously inverted reasons. The Iranian Zoroastrians who emigrated directly from Iran to

America have included some very wealthy people, often with liberal views regarding conversion and intermarriage. This in itself has been a source of tension, as events and buildings are funded and operated with assumptions that may be in conflict with Parsi orientations. In addition, Iranian Zoroastrians tend to think of themselves as Iranian first and Zoroastrian second, and the cultural divide between the two groups is considerable— not the least, Iranian Zoroastrians are often more comfortable in Farsi, whereas Parsis tend even to think in English, or at least in a mixture of languages (see "The 'Root' Cause" by Parinaz Gandhi in an interview with R. Writer, *Parsiana* August 1989:40, 43).

9. These are often located in southern Gujarat; Dahanu, for instance, is an Irani stronghold. I was friendly with an Irani businessman who owned a restaurant, a laundry, a wine shop, a fruit business, and several other businesses. He has travelled to Spain, New York, Canada and Amsterdam. But he sent his son to agricultural school, not college, and married off his daughters when they were in their early twenties.

10. This is from "Petition": "Send to us power and light, a sovereign's touch / Curing the intolerable neural itch / The exhaustion of meaning, the liar's quinsy [tonsillitis] / And the distortions of ingrown virginity."

11. Suntook n.d., published pamphlet, publication information not offered. The dedication reads: "Let us at this hour weave out a network of power to restore ourselves back to light and lustre: back to a radiant resurgence of ourselves."

12. The survey (Karkal 1984) reported that in the 25–29-year-old range, 80% of the Parsi men worked and 71.78% of the women; in the 30–39-year-old range, 93.03% of the Parsi men worked and 54.37% of the women. Comparable urban Indian figures were, for 25–29-year-olds, 86.78% of the men but only 12.17% of the women; in the 30–39-year-old range, 94.93% of the men and 15.14% of the women. Of Parsi men in the 20–39-year-old range, 35.08% had graduated from university but held no higher degree, while 8.93% had also taken a higher degree; 37.27% of the 20–39-year-old Parsi women had graduated from college but held no higher degree, but 7.61% had higher degrees. While 23% of the men 30–39-years-old reported an income over 2,000 rupees a month, only 7.8% of the women did (as with most Indian survey statistics on income, these figures may be underreported).

13. Translated by Shehnaz Munshi, Bombay.

14. *Parsiana* November 1974:26.

15. The letter is by Gulistan Engineer, *Parsiana* August 1990:15–16. *Peston-jee* also had a weak central male character who is Parsi, but the film did not particularly attempt to portray the Parsi community. Another film,

which did explicitly attempt to describe the community is, *On Wings of Fire;* it has none of the characteristics derided in the letter.

16. Review of the film by Prochi Badshah in the *Afternoon Despatch and Courier* 16 April 1990, entitled "Anyone Heard about Autonomy Lately?"

17. Cyrus Mistry, "Percy," 1985:40–56.

18. This last figure was based on a somewhat inaccurate tabulation and looks like a faulty statistic.

19. Kotwal 1937:13, 20. Firdausi is the author of the Shahnameh, the Iranian epic which takes place at least in part in pre-Islamic Iran, and is adopted by Parsis as a national epic. Its hero is Rustom. The second remark, admittedly, occurs in the context where the author is describing the failure of Parsi bee-keepers. This charming collection of essays is edited by N. B. R. Kotwal, the author of the quoted remarks, under the title *A Discourse/The Naked Truth.* He attributes most of what is wrong with the community to what he calls at one point the "apish fashion of mimicking a western practice" (1937:14).

20. H. P Mody in Desai 1948:xi.

21. Dastoor 1944:28–29. Italics mine.

22. L. Cama, *Parsiana* June 1977:32.

23. Jain businessmen often take a religious vow during their lives that requires them to be honest. The government is explicitly exempted from this requirement in the oath. If it were not, I was told, the gem industry would collapse. James Laidlaw, personal communication.

24. They also told me a story about a very eminent Parsi industrialist who, when his son married, told the inlaws that they could give inherited jewelry to the bride only if they legally declared it. Following the letter of the Indian tax law is not a common practice in India.

25. Another way of seeing the Parsi attitude is from a Hindu perspective—at least from the perspective of a friend of mine, a Hindu psychoanalyst. He remarked that Parsis had a literal conception of law which was inappropriate in India. When he, for instance, was importing some clothes from abroad for a theater production, the law demanded that he treat those garments as merchandise. He explained to the customs officials, however, that he was not going to sell the clothes, that they would be flown out when the production was finished, and convinced the officials to pass the items without the elaborate clearance forms and their associated charges. You must work in the spirit of the law, my friend explained, but Parsis, he said, think that they are doing something special by acting according to the letter of the law, and that is simply foolish. They do this to satisfy themselves, not the law.

26. Both of these stories—the bank-teller and the used car ad—are common Parsi yardsticks of community decline. But I was told by a non-Parsi that if you saw such an ad, it should give you confidence that the car has been cared for well.

27. The *jashan* is essentially a thanksgiving ritual, a presentation of fruits with prayers.

28. Pithawalla 1932:19. He includes an article entitled "Iranian Character," which has attributed to Persians the role of intermediary that Parsis believed themselves to play: "Persia was, and must still be, a link between the old Oriental civilization and the new Occidental culture" (1932:13).

29. Report in *Parsiana* February 1985:1–3.

30. Rohintan P. Peer in *Parsiana* January 1984:6.

31. Colley Dastur in *Parsiana* May 1983:3.

32. The arguments were directed to the Minority Commission, arguing that the Parsi community should be excluded from the 1980 Adoption of Children Bill, in which adopted children were to be considered of the religion of the adoptive parents regardless of their birth.

33. *Parsiana* April 1982:14, "The High Priests of Adoption." A response to this assertion was published in *Parsiana* the following October. The author of the letter, E. P. Bharucha, announced himself as opposed to conversion, but he expressed dismay at the arguments the priests employed. "The desire to preserve the 'racial gene' runs close to the Nazi philosophy. Further, the statements relating to wavelengths, their disturbance or their being embedded in genes does not appear to have been supported by any of the early Zoroastrian scriptural writings; nor is the same supported by experimental evidence or rational reasoning. The grafting of such an unsubstantiated wavelength theory to the scientifically established concept of genes is not even fair argument" (1982 October).

34. For instance, *Parsiana* November 1981:7 reprinted two articles from the *Guardian* [a major English daily paper] about Judaism. One described the decision of the Union of American Hebrew Congregations (a Reform movement) to welcome converts into the religion. In the other, the author argued that the Jews are an educated, sophisticated, financially and intellectually successful community who have retained their racial purity and ethnic identity despite great persecution—and perhaps they achieved as a group because of that very purity.

35. First-cousin marriages were exceedingly common in earlier Parsi days; it is said that in Gujarat a family rarely looked outside the parent's siblings for a child's match (Undevia 1984:26. Also see Undevia 1973).

36. A *Parsiana* interview-on-the street elicited this comment: "we need fresh blood because inbreeding has resulted in a poor mutation of the species."

Aspy Rana, age 44, Chairman, Department of Government and Politics, University of Baroda, September 1976:32.

37. For example, "Bombay," in Jhabvala 1987.

38. Vakil p. 6. He is citing Marfatia's study. The study is not in fact all that revealing because the percentages are taken from an analysis of the patients in Marfatia's practice, and it is not clear that his is a particularly representative practice—or indeed that the percentage of mental illness in different communities can be determined on the basis of numbers of expensive visits to private physicians. The other article cited, "Observations in Cancer in the Parsi Community of Greater Bombay" (Jussawala 1972), does not make the claim that the community suffers cancer at a higher rate than any other community in the world.

39. Aspy Rona in *Parsiana* September 1976:32.

40. Letter, 16 September 1990 *Bombay Samachar.*

41. This is the central administrative unit for Parsis in Surat and surrounding areas.

42. Paper from the Third World Zoroastrian Conference of 1978 in Bombay, author unknown.

43. Bulsara 1935:336,339. Italics in the original.

44. Community *panchayats* were brought into existence by the British government in Bombay, as means to allow individual communities to discipline their members. See Desai 1977.

45. From "Regional Experiences of the Fourth Congress Recommendations—Experiences and Future Priorities" by R. K. Anklesaria, Chief Executive, Parsi Panchayat, Bombay, presented at the Fifth World Zoroastrian Congress, 3rd-7th January 1990, Bombay, India, p. 23. The exchange rate varies; in 1990 it was roughly 18 rupees to the dollar.

46. Mobedji 1990. Talk at the Fourth All India Zoroastrian Youth Festival of October 1990.

47. This is a prayer of repentance and the worship of the glory and power of the fire. It can be found in standard prayer books, e.g. Vimadalal 1984.

5. Uncomfortable Realities

1. This is a building used to house the body before being taken to the Towers. It is at the *doongerwadi.*

2. *Bombay Samachar* 2 September 1990.

3. At least in the *Bombay Samachar* and *Parsiana,* to much attention.

4. Rusi Sethna in *Bombay Samachar* 9 1990.

5. Pamphlet published and printed by Adi Doctor (Bombay, 1990), p. 4.

6. Veera Doongriwalla, referring to a liberal *Parsiana* article in the November 1990 issue, p. 3.
7. H. S. Adenwalla, in *Parsiana* November 1990:3.
8. They are the most likely to send their children abroad and—because Parsis are hypergamous [their women marry "up"]—the group with the most numerically limited options for their daughters. The lower the class status of the daughter, the more men in principle who are eligible to marry her in the community.
9. The letter, directed to the Bombay Parsi Panchayat, was published in the *JameJamshed* (in Gujarati) on 4 November 1990.
10. For example, "those who do not respect Parsi customs or religious practices or who interfere with their working, such people cannot ask for any benefits from the community." Noshir Khorshed Dabu, son of the previous high priest at Wadia Atash Behram, in *JameJamshed* 23 September 1990:23.
11. Dinyar Vajifdar, with other priests. In *JameJamshed* 23 September 1990:14.
12. *Bombay Samachar* 2 September 1990.
13. This argument is reinforced in an important conservative pamphlet, published and printed by Adi Doctor, Bombay 1990: "Like our Atash-Behrams and Agiaries, the Dakhmas, with their *pavis,* their *taanas,* and the magnetic circuit operating in each *pavi* (because of the plethora of Baaj, Yasna, and Vendidad ceremonies performed during their construction) are fully CONSECRATED religious institutions of the Zoroastrians. Even the corpse of the most devout and pious Zoroastrian cannot be consigned to a Dakhma unless two very vital ceremonies, namely the Sachkar and the Geh Sarna, are performed on it. On account of these two indispensable prerequisites which only the dead body of a Zoroastrian is entitled to benefit from, the putrefaction called 'Druj-e-Nasu' that emanates from a corpse is confined and limited to a very limited area around the body, and its force and potency are considerably reduced. It is only then that the consecrated Dakhmas are ready to received the dead bodies of the Zoroastrians, and the talismanic circuits start operating. Since the erstwhile Parsee girl, who has married an alien, automatically ceases to be a Zoroastrian, no eschatological rites can be performed on her dead body, which, in turn, cannot be consigned to the Tower of Silence" (p. 4).
14. An editorial response to Kotwal's letter in *Bombay Samachar* 2 September 1990.
15. Manek Davar in *JameJamshed* 24 August 1990.
16. *Bombay Samachar* 11 November 1990.

17. On 12 October 1990.

18. This information came from a reliable source, but it has no firmer foundation than that.

19. Essentially, the initiation into the religion required for all Zoroastrians, usually performed when the child is about seven.

20. The marriage, at least, was in 1903; the *navjote* was some six months before. Around the same time, in 1904, a Rajput woman decided to have a *navjote* done as she reportedly wanted to be disposed of according to Zoroastrian rites.

21. Sir Dinshaw Maneckji Petit, Bt; Sir Jehangir Cowasji Jehangir, Kt; Rustomji Behramji Jijibhoy; Ratanji Jamshedji Tata; Bapooji Sorabji Patel; R. D. Sethna; Dr. D. N. Katrak; and Ranaji Dadabhoy Tata (the groom).

22. See the discussion in Desai 1977.

23. Sir Dinshaw Petit, Bt; Sir Cowasji Jehangir, Kt; Mr. Rustomji Behramji Jeejeebhoy, Mr. Ratanji J. Tata, Mr. Bapuji Sorabji Patel, Mr. Ratanji Dadabhoy Tata (the groom) and Nanbhoy Naoroji Ka:rak.

24. "I come to the conclusion that even if a complete alien—a *juddin*—is duly admitted into the Zoroastrian religion after satisfying all conditions and undergoing all necessary ceremonies, he or she would not, as a matter of right, be entitled to the use and benefits of the funds and Institutions now under the Defendents' management and control; that these were founded and endowed only for members of the Parsi community; and that the Parsi community consists of Parsis who are descended from the original Persian emigrants, and who are born of two Zoroastrian parents, and who profess the Zoroastrian religion, the Iranis from Persia professing the Zoroastrian religion, who come to India, either temporarily or permanently, and the children of Parsi fathers by alien mothers, who have been duly and properly admitted into the religion." Desai 1977:25–26; also *Parsiana* April 1982:6, 7.

25. Davar believed children of Parsi fathers and non-Parsi mothers ought to be admitted into the faith and so become Parsis. This seems to be because the Panchayat tolerated it (*Parsiana* April 1982:14). He described opposition to the acceptance of children born to Parsi fathers and non-Parsi mothers, usually kept women, but seems to have accepted such children when properly inducted into the religion. It is assumed in the community now, whether as cause or consequence of this judgment one cannot be entirely sure, that the religious lineage descends through the male. This is sometimes taken to absurd lengths. I was in a lecture once when a member of the audience rose to explain that science had proved that a father gave 90% of the genetic material to a child, and thus it was appropriate that the religion of the father should determine the religion of the child.

26. Davar in *Parsiana* February 1982:35.
27. Ibid.:37.
28. Ibid.:38.
29. Ibid.:39. The practice, however, seems to have been reasonably common at this period.
30. These remarks have been rearranged somewhat to make them more orderly for the reader; they were all part of the same conversation.
31. The actual figures are: 1881—85,314; 1891—89,808; 1901—93,637; 1911—99,412; 1921—101,075; 1931—108,988; 1941—114,890; 1951—111,791 [part of this drop is due to the number of Parsis in Pakistan]; 1961—106,184; 1971—96,735; 1981—71,630. The figures are reported in the Indian Census and in Nargolwala 1991:2.

    This calculation does not take into account the number of Iranian Zoroastrians living in Iran, estimated at around 25,000 in the late 1970s but reported as around 90,000 in a 1986 census (Oshidari and Kushesh 1990:3). Nor does it include the possibility of Zoroastrians living in mountainous Armenia and Iraq. Some Parsis hope that these "lost tribes" will number over a million. These figures are viewed with considerable suspicion by most Parsis (see Khullar 1990).

32. Axelrod 1974:147. Nargolwala, an expert in Parsi demographics, estimates that the community loses 120–150 people per year due to outmigration; 80–100 people per year due to students going abroad per year and not returning; and 40–50 people per year due to mixed marriages. If these figures are valid (they are, he says, "highly approximate," but he is working with all the statistics the Bombay Parsi Panchayat can offer and has Bombay Parsi Panchayat support), they account for no more than 3,000 people a decade. This is actually more like a third to a sixth of the decline. Nargolwala 1990:4.

    The estimate of Parsi and Iranian Zoroastrians living abroad is tracked only by their own communities. The "guesstimate" of North American Zoroastrians is 9,700, of whom 850 in Australia and 5,000 in Europe and the United Kingdom. Most of these individuals have migrated in the last thirty years, and in particular in recent years, often after receiving their university degrees abroad. Khullar 1990; also see Minocher-Homji 1990. Others estimate that even more Parsis live abroad.

33. Statistics indicate that 25% of the community is aged between 50 and 64, but only 12% between 0 and 14, giving the community profile a very top-heavy appearance; Karkal 1984:38. Other important figures: 36% of the men and women between 20 and 39 were college graduates, a remarkable figure in India; 98% of the community above the age of four was literate; 8.14% of the community described itself as professional, techni-

cal, or related workers; 9.35% as administrative, executive, and managerial workers; 8.32% as clerical and related workers; 9.63% as sales workers; 17.35% as students; 28.55% as unemployed or housewives, a remarkably low figure; 9.31% describe themselves as retired. Of those who work, the average income for men was 1,455 rupees a month, and for women, 1,117 rupees per month. This is comfortably within the middle class.

34. There seems to have been a significant shift in marriage patterns between 1890 and 1920. The mean age at marriage around 1871 was around 14–15 years; between 1891 and 1906 it moved up to 18–20 years; by 1932 it reached 25 years. See Patel 1891; also Axelrod 1974:131; Karkal 1984. There are odd years: in 1938 the average age is 34.9, and in 1949 it is 29.2. Karkal's average age for marriage is about 25, but higher rates are cited in Axelrod 1974 and Gould 1987.

35. In 1901, 3.33% of the Parsi women between 40 and 49 had never married.

36. According to the 1990 American Census, white married women 18–34, with five or more years of college education—in other words, extremely well educated women—expect an average of 2.88 lifetime births and had, when interviewed, already produced an average 1.2 children. For married women of all races 18–34, with five or more years of education, each woman had already produced 2.5 children and had a lifetime expectation of 4.3 (p. 43).

37. Axelrod 1974:141. Of course, these issues are notoriously difficult to assess in India, even in a westernized community.

38. Axelrod 1974; but see also Undevia 1973, 1984; Gould 1987; Billimoria 1988; and the many articles in *Parsiana*.

39. Roughly 53% of the marriages of both communities are neolocal. See table 15, Axelrod 1974:112.

40. See table 8, Axelrod 1974:100. Moreover—and this is an interesting finding—in none of the three communities studied is household composition significantly related to the level of the wife's education. See table 9, Axelrod 1974:101.

41. Axelrod 1974:126, table 17. As we have seen, despite the emphasis on love marriages, Parsis will still advertise for a marriage partner in the papers.

42. S. Desai, "The Will to Live" in *Parsiana* September 1980:27.

43. Gould, *Parsiana* March 1987:44, 51. "An aging, dwindling community."

44. G. Irani, "Women and Marriage," *Parsiana* March 1989:51, quoting *Attitudes of Parsi Youth (Females) Towards Marriage* by H. Billiomoria, commissioned by the Federation of Parsi Zoroastrian Anjumans of India and the Bombay Parsi Panchayat.

45. Summary of the Billimoria report, unpublished typescript available through the Parsi Panchayat. "Abstract of Research on Attitudes of Parsi Youth (Females) Towards Marriage" (p. 4).

46. There is also the ugly specter of biological deficiency, the possibility that once married, the couple will experience low fertility. The Parsi surveyor states:

"A discussion that needs further research concerns the biological change in the community. The data collected in the 1982 survey indicate that fetal miscarriage (stillbirths and miscarriages) among Parsi females is much higher than observed in the general population. It is known that the outcome of pregnancy is related to age and order of pregnancy. Females below the age of 19 and those in higher ages (over 40) experience higher wastage. Similarly, wastage is reported to be higher for higher orders of pregnancy. Even when allowances are made for the fact that Parsi females marry late, it is observed that the wastage of pregnancies for Parsi females is higher when compared to the females of the same ages in the general population, and this happens in spite of the fact that they are better nourished and receive better medical attention." Karkal 1984:23.

Some argue that inbreeding contributes to infertility. Before the 1910s, consanguineous marriages were the norm for Parsis, and marriage partners were drawn from a considerably smaller area than that available to the Hindu population. Parsis tended to marry immediately within the family: one biologist tells the story of three brothers, one of whom had seven sons, another two daughters and the third four daughters. Only one son went outside the family for a marriage partner. And he quotes an old lady in Navsari, Gujarat: "If a child had a cousin of the opposite sex, whose age matched hers (his) one didn't even think of looking elsewhere. If there was an appropriate match in the family, we went to our neighbors on the same side of the street. If no match was to be found even there, we looked on the other side of the Parsi *wad* [locality]. But if one violated this social practice and directly sought outside matches, a match would be hard to come by because the question would invariably be asked: why did she or he not marry inside the family? If there were no cousins of matching age, a second or distant cousin would generally be considered" (Undevia 1984:26. Also see Undevia 1973). It is possible, though at the moment there is no good evidence to support the claim, that the low fertility of the community has a biological cause.

47. Kanga 1990:8 [a novel]. The author is deliberately trying to make a point about the Parsi mother's power, control, and involvement by comparing the two.

48. This account is taken from Shirin's edited version of an interview we did in 1988 (it was one of many). The literary structure of the sentences has

been very slightly altered; also, I have deleted some of the identifying references.

49. Sheera Dastoor, "When Families Break Up" in *Parsiana* March 1986:31–34.

50. Ibid.

51. *Parsiana* April 1989

52. Jamsetjee Jeejeebhoy, President. *Parsiana* December 1983:3.

53. Noshir Vajifdar, letter to the editor, in ibid.

54. Shari Merabi, reporting on Peterson's presence at the inauguration of the Arbad Rustam Guiv Darbe Mehr Zoroastrian Center in Chicago, *Parsiana* February 1984:8.

55. Jehangir Shroff, Trustee of the Athornan Mandal, reported in *Parsiana* May 1983:17.

56. Homi B. Michocher Homji, *Parsiana* August 1983:5.

57. *Zoroastrian Studies Newsletter* May 1983; *Parsiana* August 1983:49.

58. Ibid.:67.

59. Ibid.:67–69.

60. The Persian Rivayats are documents of a correspondence between Irani and Parsi priests concerning matters of religious observance. The Irani response, taken as the voice of authority and guidance, is preserved as the Rivayats.

61. *Parsiana* August 1983:73.

62. Ibid.

63. The principal officiating priest involved in the *navjote* was a Chicago priest, and Chicago's organization is one of the largest in the United States; this response is thus noteworthy in the exchange.

64. *Parsiana* August 1983:75.

65. And appended also, under the title "Religious Boycott," was a statement from twelve American-based Zoroastrian priests: "This is to inform you that we, the following priests from New York, New Jersey, Connecticut and Pennsylvania area, have decided *not* to participate and/or associate in the performance of any Zoroastrian ceremony . . . either individually or jointly with [the two priests who performed the Peterson *navjote*]. . . . The *navjote* (by whatever name you may call it) has done untold and totally irreversible damage to the community and to our religion." *Parsiana* August 1983:79.

66. There are, not surprisingly, numerous rejoinders to Antia's 1985 booklet: Khojeste Mistree wrote a reply (one version of his argument can be found in "Conversion: A Mandate for Disunity," in *Parsiana* August 1983:53–57). One of the more eminent scholars of the community, Faribourz

Nariman, described Antia in print as a "reversed cripple" (quoting Nietzsche's *Thus Spake Zarathustra*) and attacked his arguments and sources, and "contradictions, inaccuracies, instabilities, irrelevance and inanities. . . . Some of the dangers underlying the catastrophic pro-conversion movement have been frankly and powerfully pointed out and the conclusion arrived at is that Antia's *Argument for Acceptance* is no argument at all" (*Parsiana* August 1986:95).

67. At the end Antia is quoting *Reader's Digest* (April 1963:248–252); the rest is from Antia 1985:5–6.

68. See also Hormazdiyar's reply, "My Dear Uncle Farli" (*Parsiana* October 1984:24) and also a supporting letter from 101 members of the Zoroastrian Organization of Greater New York (*Parsiana* October 1984:25).

69. For example, Peterson's navjote is described as a suicidal act in *Parsiana*, August 1983:63; the refusal to allow mixed marriages is described as suicidal in *Parsiana* April 1983:3.

70. *Parsiana* October 1990:44. This phenomenon is of course not limited to the Parsi community. Indeed, Parsis make less use of this custom than other Asian communities.

71. Ibid.:41.

72. Tarapore, *Parsiana* October 1983:3. (Letter to the editor.)

6. On Postcolonial Identity

1. I spent nine months of 1993 in Boston, working mostly on another project. I met Roshan on a library foray and then spent some time with her over the autumn. I wrote this chapter (but not the others) in Boston, and met with her and other Parsis throughout its composition.

2. There was, of course, a significant strain of rebellion in this desire. There have never been female Zoroastrian priests, and the thought that a woman—in all her menstruating impurity—might even attempt it is wildly idiosyncratic.

3. Roland (1988) argues this point, although he tends to underestimate the degree of the woman's dependence upon her in-laws' permission.

4. Both these characterizations are found in West, in Ferguson et al. 1990:28. West's essay is one of the most thoughtful discussions of this dilemma that I have seen. It also includes a telling description of Matthew Arnold and empire, and quotes the poet's sense of "wandering between two worlds, one dead / the other powerless to be born." In Ferguson et al. 1990:21.

5. "Writing Post-Orientalist Histories of the Third World: Indian Historiog-

raphy Is Good to Think," in *Comparative Studies in Society and History* 1990 32(2):383–408. The essay was reprinted in Dirks 1992.

6. O'Hanlon and Washbrook, "After Orientalism: Culture, Criticism and Politics in the Third World," in *Comparative Studies in Society and History* 1992 34(1):141–167.

7. "Can the 'Subaltern' Ride? A Reply to O'Hanlon and Washbrook" In *Comparative Studies in Society and History* 1992 34 (1):168–184.

8. Bhabha 1990.

9. Obeyesekere (1990) powerfully argues that accurate insight is not essential to transformation, because culture works through progressive representations of emotional conflict created through the process of human experience within sociality. It is a deeply interesting book.

10. The "lesser heat" may be a hangover from an imperialist idiom in which those who went abroad (the England-returned) were expected to be less tolerant of spicy food, and it may be that mildness became, to some of these immigrant communities, associated with high status. Of course, some Indian communities prefer mild food.

11. Adams House at Harvard University is part of a campus housing complex that has some features of the English university college system. It is known at Harvard for its encouragement of the arts.

12. Gergen (1991) captures some of the complexities of these new selves well, with his notions of the individual bombarded by an overflow of information, interactions, and transactional relationships.

13. This is a mode of speaking wherein the speaker remains the active agent of his experience. The speaker does not say, "the dreams stayed with me all day," but rather learns to say, "all day I continued to think about what I had dreamed"; instead of saying, "the sadistic fantasy came between me and my climax," the speaker says, "I delayed and attenuated my climax by imagining sadistic situations" (Schafer 1983:246–47).

14. It is also a direct attack on self-psychology, which Schafer understands to conflate agency and content. "We seem to end up [in Kohutian self-psychology] with a mind that is located both *within* and outside its boundaries, and that contains numerous little minds that are both *within* itself and at the same time *are* itself. This odd turn in self-theory is a sign that it is in deep trouble" (1992:25).

15. The types are: actual self, ideal self, self as place, self as agent or subject, self as object. The selves are: analysand self, social self (talking to friend), bombarding self, derogated self, exaggerating self, conciliatory advisor self, advisory self, and the defended self with redeeming features.

16. The anthropological text which has discussed the problems of internali-

zation in greatest detail is perhaps *Medusa's Hair,* which starts with a powerful cultural symbol and asks how individuals come to choose and identify with it. Obeyesekere 1981.

17. His point is that what Charles Taylor calls the "expressive individualism" of modern western identity, the originality of the autonomous Romantic artist, is culturally distinctive. He is attacked, however, by critics who misunderstand him to be arguing that only westerners have body and ego boundaries.

18. Kondo 1990; McHugh 1989. McHugh is targeting neither Lutz nor (clearly) Kondo directly, but rather the enthusiastically argued position that the Asian self and the western self as radically different. She sees difference, but also similarity. Both the singularity of the individual and the complexity of the individual's reflexive awareness have rich intellectual legacies. *The Category of the Person* (Carrithers, Collins, Lukes 1985) has done more than any other to lay out distinctions between the person (social being), the individual (body), the moi (self-awareness), and so forth.

19. See his analytically careful essay "Is the Western Conception of the Self 'Peculiar' within the Context of World Cultures?" (1993).

20. "'Self'-theories, whether Kohut's or Mead's, must result in too radical an appropriation of other minds into Anglo-American language games and life forms." Obeyesekere (1990:xx).

21. It seems to me that an approach like this, in which culture is not reified but treated as highly complex, deals with some of Abu-Lughod's (1991) quite legitimate concerns about the homogenizing effect of older concepts of culture without her more drastic solution, which is to write "against" culture, as a humanist.

22. *Fezana* 1993 6 (4):2.

23. Unpublished dialogue between a young man (quoted) and his non-Parsi mother, Seventh North American Zoroastrian Congress, August 1990, Houston.

24. Most of the participants were Parsi, but because the Parsis in North America are making strong efforts to ally with Iranian Zoroastrians, the emphasis was upon what it was to be Zoroastrian rather than Parsi. The problem of alliance is, as mentioned earlier, sizable. One of the several Iranian speakers almost claimed that Parsis were not Zoroastrians, her anger stemming from being told repeatedly by the London Parsis that she practiced her religion incorrectly, and from what she perceived to be the blind orthodoxy of much Parsi practice.

25. Mistree, in *Fezana* February 1993 6 (1):21.

26. Ibid., 1:23.

27. The transcript has been mildly doctored, to remove repetition and indiscretion. The humor was there from the start.

28. People can laugh under all circumstances, depending on their characters and culture. I am using the term here with the communicative valence it has in this interpretive community.

7. Anthropological Repositionings

1. Clearly this is a rhetorical exaggeration. However, the pressure to have a cultural tradition taught only by a member of that tradition is strong.

2. Ewing 1992:261.

3. Spence's 1982 critique of the attempt to create scientific data in psychoanalysis has some of the same resonance.

4. The degree to which this is evident in the field has much to do with the field-subjects' new awareness of writing and publishing. These dilemmas were perhaps less salient for early anthropologists. In a project dealing with contemporary psychiatry and psychiatric residents, the fact that I was writing a book was the single most important feature about me for most of my subjects. One resident went so far as to record the interview I was recording of him, not (he said) to check that I quoted him correctly, but (it transpired) so that he could interview me on my experience and feel that he was not so much in my power.

5. Not all fieldwork has to be difficult, but much of it is. For instance, one of the stunning features of Tsing's (1993) recent ethnography is not only the grace of its intellectual vision, but the personal danger, physical exhaustion, and wrenching loneliness—at least at the beginning of the author's work. Few disciplines insist on this level of personal risk from their members.

6. Grimshaw and Hart 1993:9.

7. Herzfeld 1987:204. In this passage he contrasts theory and ethnography, but the "studying ourselves" is cast as the universalizing theory for which anthropology ideally aims.

8. Fischer in Clifford and Marcus 1986:195; italics in the original.

9. Stephen Tyler also sees this potentially therapeutic feature of the fieldwork process, but he rejects the idea that it may be of advantage to any but the immediate participants in the discussion. See Tyler in Clifford and Marcus 1986.

10. Shweder 1991.

◆ ◆ ◆ BIBLIOGRAPHY ◆ ◆ ◆

A Descriptive Guide to the City of Bombay. 1887. Bombay: The *Times of India* Press.

A. U. 1873. *Overland, Inland and Upland: A Lady's Notes of Personal Observation and Adventure.* London: Seeley, Jackson and Halliday.

Abu-Lughod, L. 1986. *Veiled Sentiments.* Berkeley: University of California Press.

———— 1991. "Writing against Culture," in *Recapturing Anthropology,* ed. R. Fox. Santa Fe, N.M.: School of American Research Press, pp. 137–162.

Adas, M. 1991. "South Asian Resistance in Comparative Perspective," in *Contesting Power: Resistance and Everyday Social Relations in South Asia,* eds. D. Haynes and G. Prakash. Berkeley: University of California Press.

———— 1992. "From Avoidance to Confrontation: Peasant Protest in Precolonial and Colonial South Asia," in *Colonialism and Culture,* ed. N. Dirks. Ann Arbor: University of Michigan Press.

Album of Men and Women of India. 1906. Bombay: Rutnagar.

Allen, C., ed. 1975. *Plain Tales from the Raj.* London: Futura.

Alloula, M. 1986. *The Colonial Harem.* Minneapolis: University of Minnesota Press.

Anderson, B. 1992 [1983]. *Imagined Communities.* London: Verso.

Anklesaria, R. K. 1990. "Regional Experience of the Fourth Congress Recommendations—Experiences and Future Priorities." Unpublished ms. presented at the Fifth World Zoroastrian Congress, 1990, Bombay.

Antia, K. 1985. *The Argument for Acceptance.* Bombay: Parsiana Publications.

✳ Appadurai, A. 1993. "The Heart of Whiteness." *Callaloo* 16(4):196–207.

Appiah, A. 1992. *In My Father's House*. New York: Oxford.

Asad, T., ed. 1973. *Anthropology and the Colonial Encounter*. New York: Humanities Press.

Atalas, H. S. 1977. *The Myth of the Lazy Native: A Study of the Image of the Malays, Filipinos, and Javanese from the 16th to the 20th Century and Its Function in the Ideology of Colonial Capitalism*. London: F. Cass.

Atlas of the Bombay Presidency. 1887. Bombay: The *Times of India* Press.

Axelrod, P. 1974. "A Social and Demographic Comparison of Parsis, Saraswat Brahmins and Jains in Bombay." Ph.D. diss., The University of North Carolina at Chapel Hill.

—— 1990. "Cultural and Historical Factors in the Population Decline of the Parsis of India." *Population Studies* 44:401–419.

Badshah, P. 1990. "Anyone Heard about Autonomy Lately?" Review of *Percy*, in *The Afternoon Dispatch and Courier* 16 April. Bombay.

Bailey, F. G. 1960. *Tribe, Caste and Nation*. Manchester: Manchester University Press.

Balanji, K. P. 1978. *Abhimanyu*. Madras: Longman.

Baldwin, J. 1955. *Notes of a Native Son*. Boston: Beacon.

Ballhatchet, K. 1980. *Race, Sex and Class under the Raj*. London: Weidenfeld and Nicolson.

Barnett, S. A. 1973. "The Process of Withdrawal in a South Indian Caste," in *Entrepreneurship and Modernization of occupational cultures in South Asia*, ed. M. Singer. Durham, N.C.: Duke University Press.

Barth, F. 1993. *Balinese Worlds*. Chicago: University of Chicago Press.

Bayly, C. A. 1988. "Indian Society and the Making of the British Empire." *The New Cambridge History of India*. Cambridge: Cambridge University Press.

—— 1989. *Imperial Meridian*. New York: Longman.

Bayly, S. 1989. *Saints, Goddesses, and Kings*. Cambridge: Cambridge University Press.

Bengalee, N. S. n.d. *The life of Sorabjee Shapoorjee Bengalee, C.I.E.* Bombay: Bengalee.

Berry, M. E. "Introduction: Giving in Asia." *Journal of Asian Studies* 46 (2):305–308.

Berque, J. 1967. *French North Africa*. London: Faber and Faber.

Bhabha, H., ed. 1990. *Nation and Narration*. London: Routledge. 1994. *The Location of Culture* London: Routledge.

Bharucha, P. 1968. *The Fire Worshippers*. Bombay: Strand.

Bharucha, S. D. 1979. [1903,1893] *Zoroastrian Religion and Customs*. Bombay: Taraporevala.

Bhaya, C. P. 1988. *Report of the Socioeconomic Survey of Rural South-Gujarat Parsis.* Bombay: Bhaya.

Bhownagree, M. M. Papers. India Office Library, London.

Bilimoria, A. N. and D. D. Alpaivala, eds. 1898. *The Excellence of Zoroastrianism.* Bombay: Jamsetjee Nusserwanjee Petit Parsi Orphanage Captain Printing Works.

Billimoria, H. 1988. "Attitudes of Parsi Youth (Females) towards Marriage." Unpublished typescript (substantial survey). Bombay: Bombay Parsi Panchayat.

Birdwood, Sir George. Letters. India Office Library, London.

Bloch, M. 1990. "Foreword," in *Prospero and Caliban* by O. Mannoni. Ann Arbor: University of Michigan Press.

Boman-Behram, B. K. and A. N. Confectioner. 1969. *The Decline of Bombay.* Bombay: Boman-Behram.

The Bombay Gazette. 1886. Bombay.

The Bombay Gazetteer. 1899. Vol. IX. Part I. Bombay.

Bombay: The Gateway of India. c. 1942. Bombay: The Rotary Club.

The Bombay Guide. 1938. Bombay: Contractor.

Bombay Illustrated: Her Resources, Industries and Commerce. 1904. Bombay: The *Times of India* Press.

Bombay Marches on. . . . 1957. Bombay: The Directorate of Publicity.

Borneman, J. 1992. *Belonging in Two Berlins: Kin, State and Nation.* Cambridge: Cambridge University Press.

Boyce, M. 1975. *History of Zoroastrianism.* Vol. I. Leiden: E. J. Brill.

———— 1977. *A Persian Stronghold of Zoroastrianism.* Oxford: Clarendon.

———— 1979. *Zoroastrians: Their Religious Beliefs and Practices.* London: Routledge, Kegan Paul.

———— 1982. *History of Zoroastrianism.* Vol. II. Leiden: E. J. Brill.

————, ed. 1984. *Textual Sources for the study of Zoroastrianism.* Manchester: Manchester University Press.

Briggs, H. G. 1852. *The Parsis or, Modern Zerdusthians.* Edinburgh: Oliver and Boyd.

Broomfield, J. H. 1968. *Elite Conflict in a Plural Society.* Berkeley: California.

Brown, D. N. 1972. "Duty as Truth in Ancient India." *Proceedings of the American Philosophical Society 1972* pp. 252–268.

Brown, J. 1985. *Modern India.* Delhi: Oxford.

Brown, R. 1880s. *The Religion of Zoroaster Considered in Connection with Archaic Monotheism.* London: D. Bogue.

Buch, M. 1919. *Zoroastrian Ethics.* Baroda: Buch.

Bulsara, J. F. 1935. *Parsi Charity Relief and Community Amelioration.* Bombay: Bulsara.

—— 1938. *Mass and Adult Education in India*. Bombay: Bulsara.

—— 1948. *Bombay: A City in the Making*. Bombay: National Information and Publications.

Burns, Sir J. C. Tape recording of a businessman's memories of Bombay before Independence. India Office Library, London.

Burrow, J. 1966. *Evolution and Society*. Cambridge: Cambridge University Press.

Callaway, H. 1987. *Gender, Culture and Empire*. Chicago: University of Illinois Press.

Cannadine, D. 1990. *The Decline and Fall of the British Aristocracy*. New York: Anchor.

Caplan, L. 1991. "'Bravest of the Brave': Representations of 'the Gurhka' in British Military Writings." *Modern Asian Studies* 25 (3):571–597.

Carrithers, M., S. Collins, S. Lukes, eds. 1985. *The Category of the Person: Anthropology, Philosophy, History*. Cambridge: Cambridge University Press.

Cavalier, Z. S. 1899. "Parsee Women." *India, Ceyon, Straits Settlements, British North Borneo and Hong Kong. British Empire Survey*. Vol. 1. London: Kegan Paul, Trench, Tribner.

Census of India 1981. Greater Bombay. Bombay: Maharashtra Census Directory.

Census of India 1911; 1921; 1961; 1981. Government of India.

Cesaire, A. 1972. *Discourse on Colonialism*. Trans. by Joan Pinkham. New York: Monthly Review Press.

Chadwick, H. M. 1912. *The Heroic Age*. Cambridge: Cambridge University Press.

Chatterjee, P. 1989. "Colonialism, Nationalism, and Colonized Women: The Context in India." *American Ethnologist* 16(4):622–633.

—— 1993. *The Nation and Its Fragments*. Princeton: Princeton University Press.

Chaudhuri, K. K., ed. *Gazetteer of India. Maharashtra State: Greater Bombay District*. Vols. 1 (1986); 2 (1987); 3 (1986); History of Bombay (1987). Bombay: Government of Maharashtra.

Chaudhuri, N. C. 1951. *The Autobiography of an Unknown Indian*. London: Hogarth.

Chevalier, P. J. (Chaiwalla). "The Tower of Silence." Unpublished novel, internally dated 1927. India Office Library, London.

Chiniwalla, F. S. 1942. *Essential Origins of Zoroastrianism*. Bombay: The Parsi Vegetarian and Temperance Society.

Choksy, J. 1989. *Purity and Pollution in Zoroastrianism*. Austin: University of Texas Press.

Clifford, J. and G. Marcus, eds. 1986. *Writing Culture*. Berkeley: California.

Clifford, J. 1988. *The Predicament of Culture*. Cambridge: Harvard University Press.

Cohen, A. 1981. *The Politics of Elite Culture*. Berkeley: California.

Cohn, B. S. 1971. *India: The Social Anthropology of a Civilization*. Englewood Cliffs, N.J.: Prentice Hall.

———— 1984. "The Census, Social Structure, and Objectification in South Asia." *Folk* 26:25–49.

———— 1987. *An Anthropologist among the Historians and Other Essays*. Oxford: Oxford University Press.

Comaroff, J. 1985. *Body of Power, Spirit of Resistance*. Chicago: University of Chicago Press.

Comaroff, J. and J. Comaroff. 1992. *Ethnography and the Historical Imagination*. Boulder: Westview.

Cox, E. C. 1887. *A Short History of the Bombay Presidency*. Bombay: Thacker.

Coyajee, J. C. c.1925. *The Future of Zoroastrianism*. Bombay: M. J. Karani.

Crapanzano, V. 1980. *Tuhami*. Chicago: University of Chicago Press.

———— 1985. *Waiting*. New York: Random House.

———— 1990. "On Self Characterization," in *Cultural Psychology,* ed. J. Stigler, R. Shweder, G. Herdt. Cambridge: Cambridge University Press. pp. 401–426.

D'Andrade, R. and C. Strauss, eds. 1992. *Human Motives and Cultural Models*. Cambridge: Cambridge University Press.

Daboo, E. D. 1979. *Pictorial Gatha*. Bombay: Shah.

Dabu, K. S. 1976. *Handbook of Information on Zoroastrianism*. Bombay: Ranji.

Dadachanji, F. K. 1941. *Philosophy of Zoroastrianism and Comparative Study of Ethics*. Bombay: The *Times of India* Press.

———— 1980. *Parsis: Ancient and Modern*. Karachi: Dadachanji.

Daniel, E. V. 1984. *Fluid Signs*. Berkeley: University of California Press.

Darton, F. J. H. 1931. *From Surtees to Sassoon*. London: Morley and Mitchell.

Darukhanawala, H. D. 1939. *Parsi Lustre on Indian Soil*. Bombay: G. Claridge.

———— 1935. *Parsis and Sports*. Bombay: Darukhanawala.

Daruwalla, K. N. 1971. *Apparitions in April*. Calcutta: Writers Workshop.

————, ed. 1980. *Two Decades of Indian Poetry*. Sahibabad: Vikas.

———— 1982. *The Keeper of the Dead*. Delhi: Oxford University Press.

———— 1987. *Landscapes*. Delhi: Oxford University Press.

Das, V. 1986. "Gender Studies, Cross-cultural Comparison and the Colonial Organization of Knowledge." *Berkshire Review* 21: 58–79.

Dastoor, H. R. H. 1944. *Parsi Problems*. Nagpur: Albert Press.

Dastoor, D. 1988. "Psychological Profile of North American Zoroastrianism." Unpublished ms. presented at the 6th North American Zoroastrian Congress in Toronto.

Dastur, K. N. n.d. "Translations and Interpretations of Chiniwalla's Writings." Unpublished ms.

David, M. D. 1975. *John Wilson and His Institution*. Bombay: John Wilson Education Society.

—— 1973. *History of Bombay*. Bombay: Bombay University.

De, S. 1988. *Socialite Evenings*. Delhi: Penguin.

Deboo, B. S. 1990. *Parsis and Inbreeding*. Lynnwood, Wash.: Deboo.

Desai, A. 1965. *Voices in the City*. Bombay: Orient Paperbacks.

Desai, B. 1988. *The Memory of Elephants*. London: Sceptre.

Desai, S. F. 1940. *Parsis and Eugenics*. Bombay: Desai.

—— 1945. *A Changing Social Structure*. Bombay: Bombay Parsi Panchayat.

—— 1948. *A Community at the Crossroad*. Bombay: New Book.

—— 1977. *History of the Bombay Parsi Panchayat*. Bombay: Bombay Parsi Panchayat.

Description of a View of the Island and Harbour of Bombay. 1831. Painted by Mr. R. Burford. London: T. Brettel.

Deshpande, G., ed. n.d. *An Anthology of Indo-English Poetry*. Delhi: Hindi Pocket Books.

Deshpande, S. 1988. *That Long Silence*. New Delhi: Penguin.

De Sousa, A. and D. A. De Sousa., eds. 1984. *Psychiatry in India*. Bombay: Bhalani.

Dhalla, M. N. 1930. *Our Perfecting World*. New York: Oxford.

—— 1975 [1942]. *Aek atmakatha [An Autobiography]* Trans. E. T. Gool and B. Rustomji. Karachi.

Di Leonardo, M., ed. 1991. *Gender at the Crossroads of Knowledge*. Berkeley: University of California Press.

Dirks, N. 1987. *The Hollow Crown*. Cambridge: Cambridge University Press.

—— Ed. 1992. *Colonialism and Culture*. Introduction: 1–26. Ann Arbor: University of Michigan Press.

Dobson, Mary, and the Missionary Settlement for University Women. Papers in the India Office Library, London.

Doctor, A. F. 1990. *Dakmas out of Bounds for Zoroastrians Marrying Non-Zoroastrians*. Bombay: Doctor.

Douglas, J. 1883. *A Book of Bombay*. Bombay: *Bombay Gazette* Steam Press.

Driver, D. E. 1987. *Handy Booklet on Zoroastrianism*. Bombay: Rumar Publications.

Dubash, 1906. *The Zoroastrian Sanitary Code*. Bombay: Rahmanae Mazdayyasnan Sabha.

Dubois, A. 1985 [1906]. *Hindu Manners, Customs and Ceremonies*. Delhi: Oxford University Press.

Dundes, A., ed. 1991. *The Blood Libel Legend: A Casebook in Anti-Semitic Folklore*. Madison: University of Wisconsin Press.

Eddy, Mary Baker. 1971 [1875]. *Science and Health with a Key to the Scriptures*. Boston: First Church of Christ Scientist.

Eduljee, H. E. 1980. "The date of Zoroaster." *Journal of the K.R. Cama Oriental Institute* 48.

——— 1982. "Reincarnation and Zoroastrianism." *Ushta* suppl. 3(1).

——— 1987. "Parsis and the Portuguese in 17th Century Gujarat." *Journal of the K.R. Cama Oriental Institute* 54:22–44.

Engineer, B. A. 1918. *Advancement of Religion: An Article contributed to the Dastur Hoshung Memorial*. Bombay.

Engels, D. 1983. "The Age of Consent Act of 1891: Colonial Ideology in Bengal." *South Asia Research* 3(2):115–134.

Erikson, E. 1968. *Identity, Youth, and Crisis*. New York: Norton.

Ewing, K. 1992. "Is Psychoanalysis Relevant for Anthropology?" In *New Directions in Psychological Anthropology*, eds. T. Schwartz, G. White, C. Lutz. Cambridge: Cambridge University Press. pp. 251–268.

Ezekiel, N. and M. Mukherjee, eds. 1989. *Another India*. Delhi: Penguin.

Fanon, F. 1967. *Black Skin, White Masks*. New York: Grove.

Ferguson, R. and M. Gever, T. Minh-ha, C. West, eds. 1990. *Out There: Marginalization and Contemporary Cultures*. Cambridge: M.I.T. Press.

Fifth World Zoroastrian Congress Souvenir Volume. 1990. Bombay: World Zoroastrian Organization.

Firby, N. K. 1984. *European Travellers and Their Perceptions of Zoroastrians in the 17th and 18th Centuries*. Berlin: von Dietrich Reimer.

Fischer, M. J. 1973. "Zoroastrian Iran between Myth and Praxis." Ph.D. diss., University of Chicago.

——— 1980. *Iran: From Religious Dispute to Revolution*. Cambridge: Harvard University Press.

Fischer, M. J. and M. Abedi. 1990. *Debating Muslims: Cultural Dialogues in Postmodernity and Tradition*. Madison: University of Wisconsin Press.

Forster, E. M. 1924. *A Passage to India*. Harmondsworth: Penguin.

Fourth World Zoroastrian Congress Souvenir Volume. 1985. Bombay: World Zoroastrian Organization.

Fox, R. G. 1984. "Urban Class and Communal Consciousness in Colonial Punjab: The Genesis of India's Intermediate Regime." *Modern Asian Studies* 18(3):459–489.

Framjee, D. [Karaka] 1858. *The Parsees: Their History, Manners, Customs and Religion*. London: Smith, Elder.

Franck, A. and J. Oppert. 1868. *French Views on Zoroastrianism.* Bombay: Education Society's Press.

Freud, S. 1967 [1939]. *Moses and Monotheism.* Trans. Katherine Jones. New York: Vintage.

Freud, S. 1957. *A General Selection.* Ed. by J. Rickman. New York: Doubleday.

Frye, R. 1962. *The Heritage of Persia.* London: Weidenfeld and Nicolson.

Fyfe, C. 1962. *A History of Sierra Leone.* Oxford: Oxford University Press.

Gajendragadkar, S. N. 1974. *Parsi-Gujarati.* Bombay: University of Bombay Press.

The Gazetteer of Bombay City and Island. 1909. 3 vols. Bombay: The *Times of India* Press.

Geertz, C. 1973. *The Interpretation of Cultures.* New York: Basic Books.

—— 1983. *Local Knowledge* New York: Basic Books.

Gergen, K. 1991. *The Saturated Self.* New York: Basic Books.

Gershevitch, I. 1964. "Zoroaster's Own Contribution." *Journal of Near Eastern Studies* 23(1):12–38.

—— 1975. "Die Sonne das Beste." *Mithraic Studies,* ed. J. R. Hinnells, pp. 68–89.

Ghosh, A. 1988. *The Shadow Lines.* New York: Penguin.

Gidumal, D. 1892. *Behramji Malabari.* London: T. Fisher Unwin.

Gilroy, P. 1992. *The Black Atlantic.* Cambridge: Harvard University Press.

Girouard, M. 1981. *The Return to Camelot: Chivalry and the English Gentleman.* New Haven: Yale University Press.

Gould, K. 1987. "An Aging, Dwindling Community." *Parsiana,* March, pp. 44–51.

Good, B. 1994. *Medicine, Rationality and Experience.* Cambridge: Cambridge University Press.

Good, B. and M-J. Good. 1980. "The Meaning of Symptoms: A Cultural Hermeneutic Model for Clinical Practice," in L. Eisenberg and A. Kleinman, eds., *The Relevance of Social Science for Medicine,* pp. 165–196. Dordrecht: D. Reidel Publishing.

Greenberger, A. 1969. *The British Image of India.* New York: Oxford University Press.

Greenblatt, S. J. 1991. *Marvelous Possessions.* Chicago: University of Chicago Press.

—— 1993. "Kindly Visions": A review of *Reading National Geographic,* by C. Lutz and J. Collins. *The New Yorker,* October 11, pp. 112–120.

Greenstein, G. 1992. "A Gentleman of the Old School: Homi Bhabha and the Development of Science in India." *Daedalus,* Summer 1992:409–419.

Grimshaw, A. and K. Hart. 1993. *Anthropology and the Crisis of the Intellectuals.* Cambridge: The Prickly Pear Press.

Grossberg, L. and C. Nelson, P. Treichler, eds. 1992. *Cultural Studies.* London: Routledge.

Guha, A. 1982. *More about the Parsi Seths: Their Roots, Entrepreneurship, and Comprador Role 1650–1918.* Occasional paper no. 50. Calcutta: Center for Studies in the Social Sciences.

Guha, R., ed. 1982. *Writings on South Asian History and Society.* Delhi: Oxford University Press.

Guha, R. and G. Spivak, eds. 1988. *Selected Subaltern Studies.* New York: Oxford University Press.

Gupta, A. K. *Between a Tory and a Liberal: Bombay under Sir James Ferguson 1880–1885.* Calcutta: Bagchi.

Handbook of Basic Statistics of Maharashtra State. 1988. Bombay: Directorate of Economics and Statistics, Government of Maharashtra.

Hardiman, D. 1987. *The Coming of the Devi.* Delhi: Oxford University Press.

Harrell-Bond, B. 1975. *Modern Marriage in Sierra Leone.* Paris: Mouton.

Harris, F. 1958 [1925]. *Jamsetjee Nusserwanjee Tata.* London: Blackie and Sons.

Hartsock, N. 1987. "Rethinking Modernism: Minority vs. Majority Theories." *Cultural Critique,* Fall, 7:187–206.

Haug, M. 1861. *Lecture on the Origin of the Parsee Religion.* Poona: Deccan Herald Press.

——— 1865. *A Lecture on an Original Speech of Zoroaster.* Bombay: Education Society's Press.

——— 1978 [1878]. *The Parsis.* Delhi: Cosmo.

Haynes, D. 1987. "From Tribute to Philanthropy: The Politics of Gift-Giving in a Western Indian City." *The Journal of Asian Studies* 46 (2):339–360.

Haynes, D. and G. Prakash, eds. 1991. *Contesting Power: Resistance and Everyday Social Relations in South Asia.* Berkeley: University of California Press.

Haynes, E. 1990. "Rajput Ceremonial Interactions as a Mirror of a Dying Indian State System, 1820–1947." *Modern Asian Studies* 24(3):459–492.

Hazen, W. and M. Mughisudden, eds. 1975. *Middle Eastern Subcultures.* Lexington: Lexington Books.

Henning, R. J. 1992. Review of G. Prakash, *Bonded Histories. Journal of Asian Studies* 51(1):197–8.

Henning, W. B. 1951. *Zoroaster: Politician or Witch-Doctor?* London: Oxford.

Herodotus. 1910. *The History of Herodotus.* Trans. G. Rawlinson. New York: E. P. Dutton.

Herzfeld, E. 1947. *Zoroaster and His World*. Princeton: Princeton University Press.

Herzfeld, M. 1987. *Anthropology through the Looking-Glass*. Cambridge: Cambridge University Press.

Hinnells, J. R. "Social Change and Religious Transformation among Bombay Parsis in the Early Twentieth Century." Unpublished ms., n.d.

——— 1976. "Zoroastrian Influence on the Judaeo-Christian Tradition." *Journal of the K. R. Cama Oriental Institute* 45: 1–23.

——— 1978a. "Anglo-Parsi commercial relations in Bombay prior to 1847": *Parsis and the British. Journal of the K. R. Cama Oriental Institute* no. 46.

——— 1978b. *Spanning East and West*. Milton Keynes: Open University.

——— 1980. "The Parsis: A Bibliographical Survey." *Journal of Mithraic Studies*, 3:100–149.

——— 1985. "The Flowering of Zoroastrian Benevolence." *Papers in Honour of Professor Mary Boyce. Hommages et Opera Minora*. Vol. X. Leiden: E. J. Brill, pp. 261–326.

——— 1987. "Parsi Attitudes to Religious Pluralism." *Indian Attitudes to Religious Pluralism*, ed. H. Coward. Albany: State University of New York Press, pp. 195–233.

Hobsbawm, E. and T. Ranger, eds. 1983. *The Invention of Tradition*. Cambridge: Cambridge University Press.

Hodivala, S. K. 1920. *The Parsis of Ancient India*. Bombay: Hodivala.

——— 1925. *Indo-Iranian Religion*. Bombay: British India Press.

Holland, D. and N. Quinn, eds. 1987. *Cultural Models in Language and Thought*. Cambridge: Cambridge University Press.

Holston, J. 1989. *The Modernist City*. Chicago: University of Chicago Press.

Hopkinson, T. and D. 1975. *Much Silence: Meher Baba: His Life and Work*. Bombay: B.I. Publications.

Humbach, H. 1984. "A Western Approach to Zarathustra." *Journal of the K. R. Cama Oriental Institute* no. 51.

Imperial Gazetteer of India. Vol. VIII: *Berhampore to Bombay*. 1908. Oxford: Clarendon.

Inden, R. 1990. *Imagining India*. Oxford: Blackwell.

India, Ceylon, Straits Settlements, British North Borneo and Hong Kong. 1899. The British Empire Series Vol. 1. London: Kegan Paul, Trench, Tribner.

The Indian Masonic Journal Vol.1. January-December 1947. Bombay: *Times of India* Press.

Insler, S. 1975. *The Gathas of Zarathustra. Acta Iranica 8*. Leiden: E. J. Brill.

Irani, G. 1984. "Philosophy of Religion and Zoroastrian Thought." *Journal of the K. R. Cama Oriental Institute* no. 53.
——— 1985. "The Relevance of Zoroastrianism in the Modern World." Unpublished ms. presented at the 4th World Zoroastrian Congress, Bombay.
Irani, R. A. 1985. *Conversion in Zoroastrianism: A Myth Exploded.* Pune: Irani.
Ishiguro, K. 1986. *An Artist of the Floating World.* London: Faber and Faber.
Jackson, A. V. 1928. *Zoroastrian Studies.* New York: Columbia University Press.
Jalbhoy, R. H. 1886. *The Portrait Gallery in Western India.* Bombay: Education Society's Press.
Jehangir, Jehangir Cowsjee. Papers. India Office Library, London.
Jeejeebhoy, J. 1866. *The First Parsi Baronet.* Bombay: Union Press.
Jeejeebhoy, J., et al. 1874. *A Memorial of the Parsee Inhabitants of the City of Bombay in the East Indies.* Document, K. R. Cama Oriental Institute. Bombay.
Jeejeebhoy, J., ed. 1918. *Some Unpublished and Later Speeches and Writings of the Hon. Sir Pherozeshah Mehta.* Bombay: Commercial Press.
Jhabvala, R. P. 1973. *Travellers.* New York: Simon and Schuster.
——— 1975. *Heat and Dust,* New York: Simon and Schuster.
——— 1987. *Out of India.* New York: Simon and Schuster.
Jhabvala, S. H. 1946. *A Catechism on Zoroastrianism.* Bombay: Jhabvala.
Jussawalla, A. 1975. *Missing Person.* Bombay: Clearing House.
Jussawala, D. J. 1972. "Observations in [sic] Cancer in the Parsi Community of Greater Bombay," in *B. D. Petit Parsee General Hospital Diamond Jubilee Year 1972.* Bombay: Parsee General Hospital. pp. 88–89.
Kakar, S. 1981. *The Inner World.* Delhi: Oxford University Press.
——— 1989. *Intimate Relations.* Delhi: Viking.
Kanga, F. 1990. *Trying to Grow.* Delhi: Ravi Dayal.
Karaka, D. F. 1884. *History of the Parsis.* Vols. I and II. London: Macmillan.
Karaka, D. F. 1947. *I've Shed My Tears: A Candid View of Resurgent India.* London: Appleton-Century.
Karanjia, B. K. 1970a. *More of an Indian.* Bombay: Sindhu Publications.
——— 1970b. *Rustom Masani: Portrait of a Citizen.* Bombay: Popular Prakashan.
Karkal, M. 1984a. *Survey of the Parsi Population of Greater Bombay.* Bombay: Bombay Parsi Panchayat.
——— 1984b. "Pale Fire." *Science Age.* September, pp. 18–24.
Karkaria, R. P. 1896. *India: Forty Years of Progress and Reform: A Sketch of the Life and Times of Behramji M. Malabari.* London: Henry Frowde.

———, ed. 1915. *The Charm of Bombay.* Bombay: Taraporevala.

Kashikar, C. G. 1990. "Apropos of the Soma-Haoma." *Proceedings of the 1989 K. R. Cama Oriental Institute International Congress.* Bombay: K. R. Cama Oriental Institute.

Katrak, S. K. H. 1959. *Who Are the Parsees?.* Karachi: Pakistan Herald Press.

Kaye, J. W. 1856. *The Life and Correspondence of Sir John Malcolm CCB (Late Envoy to Persia and Governor of Bombay).* London: Smith Elder.

Keesing, R. 1992. *Custom and Confrontation.* Chicago: University of Chicago Press.

Kelly, J. 1991. *The Politics of Virtue.* Chicago: University of Chicago Press.

Kennedy, R. 1962. "The Protestant Ethic and the Parsis." *The American Journal of Sociology* 68:16–20.

Kharas, H. 1984. "A Socio-economic Survey of the Priestly Class (Mobeds) of the Zoroastrian Community in Bombay Extending to Thana." M.A. thesis, Bombay University College of Social Work.

Kharshedji Rustomji Cama 1831–1909. Oxford: Oxford University Press.

Khullar, A. 1990. "Demographic Trends of the Community and Future Implications for Zoroastrian Institutions." Unpublished ms presented at the 5th World Zoroastrian Congress, Bombay.

Khurody, K. 1993. "The Parsis in America: The Pluralism Project at Harvard University." Unpublished ms.

Kincaid, C. A. 1922. *Our Parsi Friends.* Bombay: The *Times of India* Press.

Kipling, R. 1987a [1890]. *Plain Tales from the Hills.* Harmondsworth: Penguin.

——— 1987b [1891]. *Life's Handicap.* Harmondsworth: Penguin.

——— [1900]. *Kim.* New York: Modern Library.

Klein, I. 1986. "Urban Development and Death: Bombay City, 1870–1914." *Modern Asian Studies* 20(4):725–754.

Kondo, D. 1990. *Crafting Selves.* Chicago: University of Chicago Press.

Kosambi, M. 1986. *Bombay in Transition: The Growth and Ecology of a Colonial City 1880–1980.* Stockholm: Almquist and Wiskell.

Kotwal, F. M. and J. W. Boyd. 1977. "The Zoroastrian *Paragna* Ritual." *Journal of Mithraic Studies* 2(1):18–52.

Kotwal, N. B. R. 1937. *A Discourse/The Naked Truth/etc.* Bombay: Kotwal.

Kulke, E. 1974. *The Parsees in India.* Munchen: Weltforum Verlag.

Kumar, R. 1968. *Western India in the 19th century.* London: Routledge and Kegan Paul.

Kumar, S. 1983. *Nude before God.* Delhi: Penguin.

Lal, P., ed. 1969. *Modern Indian Poetry in English.* Calcutta: Writers Workshop Books.

Lala, R. M. 1981. *The Creation of Wealth*. Bombay: Jamsetji Tata Trust.
———— 1984. *The Heartbeat of a Trust*. Delhi: Tata McGraw-Hill.
Lalkaka, P. 1987. *Zarathustra and Me: Our Religion—Activity Book One*. New Delhi: Delhi Parsi Anjuman.
———— 1988. *The Navjote and Me: Our Religion—Activity Book Two*. New Delhi: Delhi Parsi Anjuman.
———— 1989. *The Kusti Prayers and Me: Our Religion—Activity Book Three*. New Delhi: Delhi Parsi Anjuman.
Langstaff, H. 1983. "The Impact of Western Education and Political Changes upon the Religious Changes of Indian Parsis in the Twentieth Century." Ph.D. diss., University of Manchester.
Last, M. and P. Richards, eds. 1987. *Sierra Leone 1787–1987*. Manchester: Manchester University Press.
Leach, E. and S. N. Mukherjee, eds. 1970. *Elites in South Asia*. Cambridge: Cambridge University Press.
Lebra, T. S. 1993. *Above the Clouds: Status Culture of the Modern Japanese Nobility*. Berkeley: University of California Press.
Levi, P. 1989. *The drowned and the saved*. New York: Vintage.
Levy, R. 1973. *Tahitians*. Chicago: University of Chicago Press.
———— 1990. With Kedar Raj Rajopadhyaya. *Mesocosm*. Berkeley: University of California Press.
Levy, R., trans. 1967. *The Epic of the Kings (Shah-Nama)* London: Routledge and Kegan Paul.
Lopate, P. 1987. *The Rug Merchant*. Harmondsworth: Penguin.
Lord, H. 1630. *A Display of Two Forraigne Sects in the East Indies*. London: Fra Constable.
Low, D. 1991. *Eclipse of empire*. Cambridge: Cambridge University Press.
Lutz, C. 1988. *Unnatural Emotions*. Chicago: University of Chicago Press.
———— and J. Collins. 1993. *Reading National Geographic*. Chicago: University of Chicago Press.
Lutze, L. 1985. *Hindi Writing in Postcolonial India*. Delhi: Manohar.
Mahood, M. M. 1977. *The Colonial Encounter*. London: Rex Collings.
Malabari, B. M. 1894. *The Indian Problem*. Bombay.
———— 1887. *Infant Marriage and Enforced Widowhood in India*. Bombay: the *Voice of India* Printing Press.
Mani, L. 1987. "Contentious Traditions: The Debate on Sati in Colonial India." *Cultural Critique*, Fall, pp. 119–156.
Mankekar, D. R. 1968. *Homi Mody*. Bombay: Popular Prakashan.
Mannoni, O. 1990 [1956]. *Prospero and Caliban*. Introduction by Maurice Bloch. Ann Arbor: University of Michigan Press.

Marcus, G. 1992. *Lives in Trust.* Boulder: Westview.

Marcus, G. and M. Fischer. 1986. *Anthropology as Cultural Critique.* Chicago: University of Chicago Press.

Marfatia, J. C. 1972. "Parsis and Mental Health." *Parsee General Hospital Diamond Jubilee Year 1972.* Bombay: Parsee General Hospital, pp. 62–66.

Mariani, P., ed. 1991. *Critical Fictions.* Seattle: Bay Press.

Markham, S. F. 1932. *A Report to the Sir Ratan Tata Trustees on Problems Affecting the Parsee Community.* Bombay: Sir Ratan Tata Trust.

Marriott, M., ed. 1990. *India through Hindu Categories.* New Delhi: Sage.

Masani, P. S. 1917. *Zoroastrianism Ancient and Modern.* Bombay: Masani.

Masani, R. P. 1938. *The Religion of the Good Life.* London: George Allen and Unwin.

—— 1939. *Dadabhai Naoroji: The Grand Old Man of India.* London: George Allen and Unwin.

Masani, Z. 1987. *Indian Tales of the Raj.* Berkeley: University of California Press.

Maushardt, C., ed. 1930. *Bombay: Today and Tomorrow.* Bombay: Taraporevala.

——, ed. 1940. *Some Social Services.* Bombay: Taraporevala.

McClure, J. 1981. *Kipling and Conrad: The Colonial Fiction.* Cambridge: Harvard University Press.

—— 1991. "Late Imperial Romance." *Raritan* 10(4):111–130.

McGuire, J. 1983. *The Making of a Colonial Mind.* Canberra: Australian National University Press.

McHugh, E. 1989. "Concepts of the Person among the Gurungs of Nepal." *American Ethnologist* 16:75–86.

McIntyre, D., ed. 1990. *An Introduction to the Gathas of Zarathustra.* Pittsburgh: McIntyre.

Medhora, D. J. 1886., ed. *The Zoroastrian and Some Other Ancient Systems.* Bombay: Indian Printing Press.

—— 1887. *Ancient Iranian and Zoroastrian Morals.* Bombay: Ripon Printing Press.

Mehta, A. 1987. *The Story of Our Religion: Zoroastrianism.* Bombay: Zoroastrian Studies.

Mehta, G. 1980. *Karma-Cola.* London: Minerva.

—— 1989. *Raj.* New York: Fawcett.

Mehta, P. D. 1985. *Zarathustra.* Longmead, Dorset: Element Books.

Mehta, R. 1977. *Inside the Haveli.* New Delhi: Mayfair Press.

Mello, D. C. 1985. "The Parliamentary Life of Dadabhai Naoroji." *Journal of the K. R. Cama Oriental Institute* no. 52.

Memmi, A. 1965. *The Colonizer and the Colonized*. Boston: Beacon.

Miller, B. S. 1991. "Presidential Address: Contending Narratives—The Political Life of the Indian Epics." *Journal of Asian Studies* 50(4):783–792.

Minocher-Homji, H. 1990. "Demographic Trends of the Community and Future Implications for Zoroastrian Institutions." Unpublished ms. presented at the 5th World Zoroastrian Congress, Bombay.

Minocher-Homji, N. 1988. "Ahura Mazda and Ahriman." *Bombay Samachar*, June 26.

Minister's Magazine. Missionary Settlement for University Women. Papers. India Office Library, London.

Minutes by His Excellency Sir Richard Temple, Bart, Governor of Bombay. 1878; 1879; 1880. Bombay: Government Central Press.

Mirza, H. K. 1987 [1974]. *Outlines of Parsi History*. Bombay: Mirza.

Missionary Settlement for University Women. Papers. India Office Library, London.

Mistree, K. P. 1982. *Zoroastrianism: An Ethnic Perspective*. Bombay:

——— 1985. "The Relevance of Zoroastrianism in the Modern World." Presented at the 4th World Zoroastrian Congress, Bombay.

Mistry, C. n.d. "Doongaji House." Unpublished play performed Bombay 1990.

——— 1985. "Percy." *Bombay*, March 7–21, pp. 40–56.

Mistry, R. 1987. *Tales from Firozsha Baag*. Harmondsworth: Penguin.

——— 1991. *Such a Long Journey*. New York: Vintage.

Mobedji, M. 1987. "A Research Study of Charitable Trusts Founded by Parsis in Bombay and Their Social Welfare Objects, Activities and Administration Process." M.A. thesis, Bombay University College of Social Work.

——— 1990. Unpublished manuscript on charity in the Parsi community. Bombay. Fourth All India Zoroastrian Youth Festival.

Moddie, A. D. 1987. *India in Search of Values*. Bombay: Allied Publishers.

——— 1968. *The Brahmanical Culture and Modernity*. Bombay: Asia Publishing House.

Modi, B. 1989. "Parsi-Gujarati: A Dying Dialect." *International Congress*. Bombay: K. R. Cama Oriental Institute.

Modi, J. J. 1885. *The Religious System of the Parsis*. Bombay: Modi.

——— 1905. *A Few Events in the Early History of the Parsis and Their Dates*. Bombay: Fort Printing Press.

———, ed. 1907. *The K. R. Cama Masonic Jubilee Volume*. Bombay: Fort Printing Press.

——— 1914. *Moral Extracts from Zoroastrian Books for the Use of Teachers in Schools*. Bombay: British India Press.

—— 1921. *The Marriage Ceremony of the Parsees.* Bombay: Fort Printing Press.

—— 1986 [1922]. *The Religious Ceremonies and Customs of the Parsis.* Bombay: Society for the Promotion of Zoroastrian Religious Knowledge and Education.

—— 1932. *Oriental Conference Papers.* Bombay: the Fort Printing Press.

Mody, H. 1963 [1921]. *Sir Pherozeshah Mehta.* Bombay: Asia Publishing House.

Mody, J. R. P. 1959. *Jamsetjee Jeejeebhoy: The First Indian Knight and Baronet.* Bombay: Mody.

Mohanti, P. 1985. *Through Brown Eyes.* Delhi: Penguin.

Monk, C. 1985. "The Parsis and the Emergence of the Indian National Conference." *Journal of the K. R. Cama Oriental Institute.*

Moorhouse, G. 1983. *India Britannica.* London: Paladin.

Moraes, D. 1968. *My Son's Father.* Harmondsworth: Penguin.

—— 1979. *Bombay.* Amsterdam: TimeLife Books.

—— 1987. *Collected Poems 1957–1987.* Delhi: Penguin.

Motafram, R. R. 1986. *Cathecism on Zoroastrianism.* Bombay: Motafram.

Muller, M., general ed. 1987. *Pahlavi Texts.* Trans. E. W. West. Part 1, 1880; part 2, 1882; part 3, 1885; part 4, 1892; part 5, 1897. *Sacred Books of the East.* Delhi: Motilal Banarsidass.

Murzban, M. M., ed. 1917. *The Parsees in India: being an enlarged and copiously annotated, up to date, English version of Delphine Menant's Les Parsis.* Bombay.

Nahal, C. 1979. *Azadi.* New Delhi: Orient Paperbacks.

Naipaul, V. S. 1976. *India: A Wounded Civilization.* New York: Vintage.

—— 1990. *India: A Million Mutinies Now.* New York: Viking.

—— 1994. *A Way in the World.* New York: Knopf.

Nair, M. and S. Taraporevala. 1990. *Salaam Bombay.* Delhi: Penguin.

Nanavutty, P. n.d. [modern pamphlet]. *Atar: A Vision.* Calcutta: Nanavutty.

—— 1977. *The Parsis.* Delhi: National Book Trust.

—— 1979. *The Navjote.* Delhi: Delhi Parsi Anjuman.

—— 1980. *The Kusti Prayers.* Delhi: Delhi Parsi Anjuman.

—— 1981. *Ahura Mazda and the Creation.* Delhi: Delhi Parsi Anjuman.

—— 1987. *Fravarane (I Believe).* Delhi: Delhi Parsi Anjuman.

Nandy, A. 1980. *At the Edge of Psychology.* Delhi: Oxford University Press.

—— 1983. *The Intimate Enemy.* Delhi: Oxford University Press.

—— 1988. *The Tao of Cricket.* Harmondsworth: Penguin.

Naoroji, D. (Dhanjibhai). 1890. *A short account of the Parsis.* London: Nisbet.

Naoroji, D. 1901. *Poverty and Un-British Rule in India.* London.

—— 1905. *The Parsee Religion.* Bombay: Oriental Review.

Narayan, K. 1989. *Storytellers, Saints and Scoundrels.* Philadelphia: University of Pennsylvania Press.

Nargolwala, P. 1990. "Demographic Trends of the Community and Future Implications for Zoroastrian Institutions." Unpublished ms. presented at the 5th World Zoroastrian Congress, Bombay.

Nateson, G. A. 1930. *Famous Parsis.* Madras: Nateson.

Newell, H. A. c. 1914. *Bombay (the Gate of India).* London: Harrison and Sons.

Newspaper cuttings 1921–1922. India Office Library, London.

Nuckolls, C. W. 1990. "The Durbar Incident." *Modern Asian Studies* 24(3):529–559.

Obeyesekere, G. 1981. *Medusa's Hair.* Chicago: University of Chicago Press.

—— 1990. *The Work of Culture.* Chicago: University of Chicago Press.

O'Hanlon, R. 1988. "Recovering the Subject: Subaltern Studies and Histories of Resistance in Colonial South Asia." *Modern Asian Studies* 22(1):189–224.

—— 1991. "Issues of Widowhood: Gender and Resistance in Colonial Western India." In *Contesting Power: Resistance and Everyday Social Relations in South Asia,* eds. D. Haynes and G. Prakash, pp. 62–108.

O'Hanlon, R. and D. Washbrook. 1992. "After Orientalism: Culture, Criticism and Politics in the Third World." *Comparative Studies of Society and History* 34(1):141–167.

Old and New Bombay. 1911. Bombay: G. Claridge.

Oldenburg, V. T. 1991. "Lifestyle as Resistance: The Case of the Courtesans of Lucknow," in *Contesting Power: Resistance and Everyday Social Relations in South Asia,* eds. D. Haynes and G. Prakash, pp. 23–61.

Olmstead, A. T. 1948. *History of the Persian Empire.* Chicago: University of Chicago Press.

Ong, A. 1993. "On the Edges of Empires: Flexible Citizenship among Chinese in Diaspora." *Positions* 1(3):745–778.

Oshidari, J. and M. Kushesh. 1990. "Demographic Trends of the Community and Future Implications for Zoroastrian Institutions." Unpublished ms. presented at the 5th World Zoroastrian Congress, Bombay.

Pangborn, C. R. 1983. *Zoroastrianism: A Beleaguered Faith.* New York: Advent Books.

Papers in Honour of Professor Mary Boyce. 1985. Acta Iranica 24. Leiden: E. J. Brill.

Parekh, C., ed. 1892. *Eminent Indians on Indian Politics.* Bombay: Education Society's Steam Press.

Parmentier, R. 1987. *The Sacred Remains.* Chicago: University of Chicago Press.

The Parsi: The English Journal of the Parsis and a High Class Illustrated Monthly. 1905–6. 1(1–12). Bombay: The Parsi.

Parthasarathy, R., ed. 1976. *Ten Twentieth Century Indian Poets.* Delhi: Oxford University Press.

Patel, B. B. 1891. "Statistics of Births, Deaths, and Marriages among the Parsis of Bombay during the Last Ten Years." *Journal of the Anthropological Society of Bombay* 2: 448–458.

Patel, G. 1966. *Poems.* Bombay: Nissim Ezekiel.

—— 1976. *How Do You Withstand, Body.* Bombay: Clearing House.

—— n.d. "Princes." Unpublished ms.; performed Bombay 1970.

—— n.d. "Savaksa." Unpublished ms.

—— 1988. *Mister Behram.* Bombay: Praxis.

Patel, J. M. Framjee. 1905. *Stray Thoughts on Indian Cricket.* Bombay: The Times of India Press.

Patel, J. P. c. 1920s. *Methods of Prayer and Ceremony.* Bombay: Sanj Vartaman Press.

Paymaster, R. B. 1917. *Navroziana, or, the Dawn of a New Era.* Bombay: Paymaster.

Peace of Mind towards Progress. 1978. Bombay: Behramji Lalkaka Education Trust.

Peel, R. 1987. *Spiritual Healing in a Scientific Age.* New York: Harper and Row.

Peterson, J. 1969. *Province of Freedom.* Evanston: Northwestern.

Petit, M. D., H. S. Mehta, and P. S. Jhabvala, eds. 1972. *B. D. Petit Parsee General Hospital Diamond Jubilee Year.* Bombay: B. D. Petit Parsee General Hospital.

Picturesque Bombay. 1917. Bombay: Taraporevala.

Pinder, D. A. 1906. *Visitor's Illustrated Guide to Bombay.* Bombay: G. Claridge.

Pithawalla, M. B. 1919. *If Zoroaster Went to Berlin; Or the Ladder of Perfection.* Poona: Pithawalla.

—— 1932. *The Parsee Heritage.* Bombay: The Young Zoroastrian Circle.

Pithawalla, M. B. and B. S. H. Rustomji. 1945. "Population Trends of Parsi Setlements on the West Coast of India." *Journal of the University of Bombay* 13.

Pocket Book of Labour Statistics. 1989. Chandigarh Shimla: Ministry of Labour.

The Polytheism of the Parsis. 1851. No. 4, Parsi Gujarati Series. Bombay: Bombay Book and Tract Society.

Postan, H. D. c.1870. *The Parsees.* London.

Pusalker, A. D. and V. G. Dighe. 1949. *Bombay: Story of the Island City.* Bombay: Popular Press.

Prakash, G. 1990. "Writing Post-Orientalist Histories of the Third World: Indian Historiography is Good to Think." *Comparative Studies in Society and History* 32(2):383–408. Reprinted 1992 in *Colonialism and Culture,* ed. N. Dirks.

———— 1992b. "Can the 'Subaltern' Ride? A Reply to O'Hanlon and Washbrook." *Comparative Studies in Society and History* 31(1):168–184.

Price, P. 1983. "Warrior Caste 'Raja' and Gentleman 'Zamindar': One Person's Experience in the Late Nineteenth Century." *Modern Asian Studies* 17(4):563–590.

Price, R. and S. Price. 1992. *Equatoria.* London: Routledge.

Quigley, D. Review of R. Inden, *Imagining India. Modern Asian Studies* 25(2):403–406.

Rabinow, P. 1977. *Reflections on Fieldwork in Morocco.* Berkeley: University of California Press.

Raheja, G. 1988. *The Poison in the Gift.* Chicago: University of Chicago Press.

Rao, R. 1989. *An Indian Idyll and Other Stories.* Bombay: Orient Longman.

Rao, S. R. 1976. *Children of God.* Bombay: Orient Longman.

Raphael, V. 1988. *Contracting Colonialism.* Durham: Duke University Press.

Ray, R. 1987. "The Changing Fortunes of the Bengali Gentry under Colonial Rule: Pal Chaudhuris of Mahesganj, 1800–1950." *Modern Asian Studies.* 21 (3):511–519.

Reid, A. 1988. "Female Roles in Pre-colonial Southeast Asia." *Modern Asian Studies* 22(3):629–645.

Reviews of Administration in the Bombay Presidency. 1933. Bombay: Bombay Central Press.

Roberts, J. 1971. "The Movement of Elites in Western India under Early British Rule." *The Historical Journal* 14(2):241–262.

Roland, A. 1988. *In Search of Self in India and Japan.* Princeton: Princeton University Press.

Rosaldo, R. 1980. *Ilongot Headhunting 1883–1974.* Stanford: Stanford University Press.

———— 1989. *Culture and Truth.* Boston: Beacon.

Rudner, D. 1987. "Religious Gifting and Inland Commerce in Seventeenth-Century South India." *The Journal of Asian Studies* 46(2):361–379.

Rushdie, S. 1988. *Satanic Verses.* New York: Viking.

Russell, J. R. 1984. "Zoroastrianism as the State Religion of Ancient Iran." *Journal of the K. R. Cama Oriental Institute* no. 53.

—— 1985. "On the Necessity of Dualism." Unpublished ms. presented at the 4th World Zoroastrian Congress, Bombay.

—— 1986. "Aristotle and the Ashem Vohu." *Ushta* 7(2)13–14.

—— 1987a. *Zoroastrianism in Armenia*. Cambridge: Harvard Iranian Series 5.

—— 1988. "The Rite of Muskil Asan Behram Yazad amongst the Parsis of Navsari, India." *Acta Iranica* 28:521–534.

—— 1989. "Parsi Zoroastrian Garbas and Monajats." *Journal of the Royal Asiatic Society.* 1:51–63.

Rustomjee, F. 1978. *Zoroastrian Ceremonies for the Disposal of the Dead.* Calcutta: Rustomjee.

—— 1984. *The Life of Holy Zarathustra*. Bombay: Kotwal.

Rutnagar, S. M. 1927. *Bombay Industries: The Cotton Mill*. Bombay: Rutnagar.

Sabin, M. 1991. "The Suttee Romance." *Raritan. 11* (2):1–24.

Said, E. 1978. *Orientalism*. New York: Pantheon.

—— 1991. "The Politics of Knowledge." *Raritan 11*(1):17–32.

—— 1993. *Orientalism and Culture*. New York: Knopf.

Salih, T. 1969. *Season of Migration to the North*. Trans. D. Johnson-Davis. London: Heineman.

Sanford, A. 1949. *The Healing Light*. Evesham: Arthur James.

Sanjana, R. 1906. *Zarathustra and Zarathustrianism in the Avesta*. Leipzig: Otto Harrosowitz.

—— 1929. *Spiritualism through Zoroastrian Eyes*. Bombay: Sanjana.

Sapere Aude. 1895. *The Chaldean Oracles of Zoroaster*. As set down by Julianus, the Theurgist. Gilette, N.J.: Heptangle Books.

Sarkar, S. 1989. *Modern India 1885–1947*. London: Macmillan.

Schaeffer, E. N. 1936. *Pictorial Bombay*. Bombay: New Book Co.

Schafer, R. 1983. *The Analytic Attitude*. New York: Basic Books.

—— 1992. *Retelling a Life*. New York: Basic Books.

Schechner, R. 1987. "A 'Vedic Ritual' in Quotation Marks." *Journal of Asian Studies* 46(1):108–110.

Scheper-Hughes, N. 1992. *Death without Weeping*. Berkeley: University of California Press.

Scott, J. 1985. *Weapons of the Weak: Everyday Forms of Peasant Resistance*. New Haven: Yale University Press.

Scott, P. 1976. *The Raj Quartet*. New York: Morrow.

—— 1977. *Staying On*. New York: William and Morrow.

Seervai, K. N. 1899. "The Parsis." *Gazetteer of the Bombay Presidency* Vol. IX Part 2. Bombay: Government Central Press.

Sethna, K. A. 1990. "Madame Cama." Presented at the 5th World Zoroastrian Congress, Bombay.

Sethna, K. J. 1984. "The Psychology and Psychopathology of Parsis," in De Sousa and De Sousa, eds., *Psychiatry in India*. Bombay: Bhalani, pp. 79–96.

Shroff, J. D. 1923. *My Religion: Some Reflections*. Bombay: Taraporewala and Sons.

Shweder, R. 1991. *Thinking through Cultures*. Cambridge: Harvard University Press.

Sidhwa, B. 1978. *The Crow Eaters*. New Delhi: Penguin Books.

Sidwa, R. K. 1955. *Scheme to Remove Poverty and Unemployment from the Parsi Community*. Bombay: Sidwa.

———— 1956. *A Statistical and Socio-economic Study of Poverty, Unemployment and Some Pressing Problems among Parsis of Bombay*. Bombay.

Singer, M. R. 1964. *The Emerging Elite*. Cambridge: M.I.T. Press.

Singh, N. and R. 1986. *The Sugar in the Milk*. Delhi: Institute for Development Education.

Smith, K. 1982. "A Study of the Treatment of Myth and Traditional Values in Contemporary Indian Drama Written in English." M.A. thesis, Flinders University of South Australia.

———— n.d. "Interview with Gieve Patel, Bombay, January 20, 1981." Unpublished ms.

Sorabji, Cornelia. Papers. India Office Library, London.

Spence, D. 1982. *Narrative Truth and Historical Truth*. New York: Norton.

Spiro, M. 1993. "Is the Western Conception of the Self 'Peculiar' within the Context of World Cultures?" *Ethos* 21(2):107–153.

Spitzer, L. 1974. *The Creoles of Sierra Leone*. Madison: University of Wisconsin Press.

Spivak, G. C. 1987. *In Other Worlds*. London: Routledge.

Staal, F. 1987. "Professor Schechner's Passion for Goats." *Journal of Asian Studies* 46(1):105–108.

Steadly, M. 1993. *Hanging without a Rope*. Princeton: Princeton University Press.

Stoler, A. 1985. *Capitalism and Confrontation in Sumatra's Plantation Belt 1870–1979*. New Haven: Yale University Press.

———— 1991. "Carnal Knowledge and Imperial Power: Gender, Race, and Morality in Colonial Asia," in *Gender at the Crossroads of Knowledge*, ed. Di Leonardo, pp. 51–101.

———— 1992. "Rethinking Colonial Categories: European Communities and the Boundaries of Rule," in *Colonialism and Culture*, ed. N. Dirks, pp. 319–352.

Stoller, P. 1989. *The Taste of Ethnographic Things*. Philadelphia: University of Pennsylvania Press.

Stonequist, E. V. 1937. *The Marginal Man*. New York: Scribner's Sons.

Strizower, S. 1971. *The Children of Israel: The Bene Israel of Bombay.* Delhi: Oxford University Press.

Subramanian, L. 1985. "Capital and Crowd in a Declining Asian Port City: The Anglo-Bania Order and the Surat Riots of 1795." *Modern Asian Studies.* 19(2):205–237.

——— 1991. "The Eighteenth-century Social Order in Surat: A Reply and an Excursus on the Riots of 1788 and 1795." *Modern Asian Studies* 25(2):321–365.

Suleri, S. 1992. *The Rhetoric of English India.* Chicago: University of Chicago Press.

Suntook, R. n.d. *Immediate Urgency for the Formation of a World's Zoroastrian Organization to Combat against Our Dwindling Numbers, and to Ensure Our Survival and Our Revival.* Bombay: G. Claridge.

Tagore, R. 1991. *Selected Short Stories.* Trans. and intro. W. Radice. New York: Penguin.

Talati, K. M. 1953. *Light on the Zoroaastrians Mazdayasnian Religion.* Bombay: Bombay University Press.

Tambiah, S. J. 1992. *Buddhism Betrayed? Religion, Politics and Violence in Sri Lanka.* Chicago: University of Chicago Press.

Taraporewala, I. J. S. 1965 [1926]. *The Religion of Zarathustra.* Bombay: B.I. Taraporewala.

——— n.d. [after 1947]. *Zoroastrian Philosophy.* Bombay: The *Bombay Chronicle* Press.

——— 1951. *The Divine Songs of Zarathustra: A Philological Study of the Gathas of Zarathustra.* Bombay: Taraporewalla and Sons.

Taraporevala, S. 1981. "Paradise Lost: Acculturation and Historical Consciousness among the Parsis of India." Unpublished ms.

Taraporevala, S. M. 1987. "Religiosity in an Urban Setting: A Study of Parsi College Students in the City of Bombay." Ph.D. diss. University of Bombay.

Tavaria, P. N. 1971 [n.d]. *A Manual of "Kshnoom": The Zoroastrian Occult Knowledge.* Bombay: Masani.

Tata, J. R. D. 1986. *Keynote.* Bombay: Tata Press.

Taylor, C. 1989. *Sources of the Self.* Cambridge: Harvard University Press.

——— 1991. *The Ethics of Authenticity.* Cambridge: Harvard University Press.

Theosophy in Zoroastrianism. 1975. Bombay: Bombay Theosophical Federation.

Third World Zoroastrian Conference Papers. 1978. Bombay.

Thornton, D. 1898. *Parsi, Jaina and Sikh.* Cambridge: The Religious Tract Society.

Tindall, G. 1982. *City of Gold.* London: Temple Smith.

Torri, M. 1987. "Surat during the Second Half of the Eighteenth Century: What Kind of Social Order?" *Modern Asian Studies* 21(4):679–710.

———— 1991. "Trapped inside the Colonial Order: The Hindu Bankers of the Surat and Their Business World during the Second Half of the Eighteenth Century." *Modern Asian Studies* 25(2):367–410.

Tourist's Handbook to Bombay and India. 1900. Bombay: Watson's Esplanade Hotel.

Towers of Silence. 1984 [1899]. Bombay: Bombay Parsi Panchayat.

Traweek, S. 1988. *Beamtimes and Lifetimes.* Cambridge: Harvard University Press.

Trawick, M. 1990. *Notes on Love in a Tamil Family.* Berkeley: University of California Press.

Trevelyan, R. 1987. *The Golden Oriole.* New York: Simon and Schuster.

Trilling, L. 1971. *Sincerity and Authenticity.* Cambridge: Harvard University Press.

Tsing, A. 1993. *In the Realm of the Diamond Queen.* Princeton: Princeton University Press.

Undevia, J. V. 1973. *Population Genetics of the Parsis.* Miami: Field Research Projects.

———— 1984. "The Genes that Tell the Parsi Story." *Science Age:*25–27.

U.S. Bureau of the Census, Current Population Reports, Series P-20, no. 454. *Fertility of American Woman: June 1990.* Washington, D.C.: U.S. Government Printing Office.

Vajifdar, N. 1973. *Let us pray.* Bombay: Vajifdar.

Vakil, S. R. n.d. *Parsi and Conversion: An Objective Study.* Bombay: Vakil.

Vimadalal, J. R. 1979. *What a Parsee Should Know.* Bombay: Vimadalal.

———— 1979. *Who is a Parsee-Zoroastrian?.* Bombay: Vimadalal.

———— 1984. *The Sacred Khordeh Avesta.* Bombay: Bombay Zoroastrian Jashan Committee.

———— 1984b. "Zoroastrianism and the Problem of Evil." *The Bombay Parsi Panchayat Quarterly Review* 3(4):1–3.

———— 1985. *Seven discourses.* Bombay: Vimadalal.

Visitor's Guide to Bombay. 1862. Bombay: Caxton Printing Works.

Vittachi, V. T. 1987. *The Brown Sahib (revisited).* Harmondsworth: Penguin.

Wacha, D. E. 1914. *The Life and Life Work of J. N. Tata.* Madras: Ganesh.

Wadia, J. H. 1950. *Sir Jamsetjee Jeejeebhoy Parsi Benevolent Institution Centenary Volume.* Bombay: Wadia.

Wadia, Nowrazjee Noshirwanji. Papers (the Wadia Masoleum). India Office Library, London.

Wadia, P. A. 1949. *Parsis ere the Shadows Thicken.* Bombay: Wadia.

Wadia, R. A. 1983. *The Bombay Dockyard and the Wadia Master Builders.* Bombay: Wadia.

Wasson, R. G. 1968. *Soma: The Divine Mushroom of Immortality.* New York: Harper, Brace, and World.

Weil, S. 1952. *Gravity and Grace.* London: Routledge and Kegan Paul.

White, D. L. 1979. "Parsis as Entrepreneurs in Eighteenth-century Western India: The Rustom Manock Family and the Parsi Community of Surat and Bombay." Ph.D. diss., University of Virginia.

—— 1991. "From Crisis to Philanthropy: The Dynamics of Eighteenth Century Parsi Philanthropy." *Modern Asian Studies* 25(2):303–320.

Whitehurst, J. E. 1969. "The Zoroastrian Response to Westernization: A Case Study of the Parsis of Bombay." *Journal of the American Academy of Religion* 37(3):224–236.

Williams, B. 1981. *Moral Luck.* Cambridge: Cambridge University Press.

Williams, A. V. 1985. "The Concept of Evil in Zoroastrianism." Supplement to the Newsletter. *Ushta* 5(4).

—— 1985b. "A Strange Account of the World's Origin: PRDd. XLVI." *Papers in Honour of Professor Mary Boyce. Hommages et opera minora.* Vol. XI. Leiden: E. J. Brill. pp. 683–697.

—— 1985c. "The Meaning and Place of Ancient Zoroastrian Doctrines in the Modern Multi-faith World." Unpublished ms. presented at the 4th World Zoroastrian Congress, Bombay.

—— 1987. "The Body and the Boundaries of Zoroastrian Spirituality." *Religion* 19(3):227–240.

Wilson, E. G. 1976. *The Loyal Blacks.* New York: Putnam.

Woolf, L. 1961. *Growing: An Autobiography of the Years 1904–1911.* London: Hogarth Press.

World Zoroastrians Souvenir Issue. 1984. First World Conference on Zoroastrian Religion, Culture and History. London: World Zoroastrian Organization.

Writer, R. 1994. *Contemporary Zoroastrians: An Unstructured Nation.* Lanham, Maryland. University Press of America.

Wurgaft, L. 1983. *The Imperial Imagination.* Middletown: Wesleyan University Press.

Wyse, A. 1989. *The Krio of Sierra Leone.* London: C. Hurst.

Zaehner, R. C. 1955 *Zurvan: A Zoroastrian Dilemma.* Oxford: Clarendon.

—— 1956 *The Teachings of the Magi.* London: Allen and Unwin.

—— 1961. *The Dawn and Twilight of Zoroastrianism.* New York: Putnam.

Zahar, R. 1974. *Franz Fanon; Colonialism and Alienation.* New York: Monthly Review Press.

‹ ‹ ‹   A C K N O W L E D G M E N T S   › › ›

From the early imaginings of this project to this more polished form, many
people have been very helpful, and it gives me great pleasure to thank them
here. The Fulbright Foundation, the British Academy, the Nuffield Foundation, Rotary International, and the University of California San Diego funded
different portions of the work. Michael Fischer has been a singularly tolerant
and astute friend. His was one of the first scholarly works I read on Iranian
Zoroastrians, and ever since he (and his work) have both encouraged and
challenged me. He patiently commented on two quite different drafts of this
book. Amartya Sen also read the manuscript and made gentle and insightful
remarks. Jennifer Cole read it at a crucial stage, and gave me effective, usable
comments. I am grateful to Nathan and Lochi Glazer who read the final
version of the manuscript and helped me to improve it, as did James Russell,
a remarkable scholar who is both technically brilliant and intellectually broad-
minded. Akhil Gupta, Gerry Graff, and Gary Alan Fine were most helpful
readers. Nazneen Cooper and Noshir Khurody read the manuscript not as
scholars of the Parsis but as Parsis, and were courteous, incisive, and very
useful. At the University of California, San Diego, my colleagues have been
unfailingly generous with their time. Freddy Bailey, Roy D'Andrade, Jason
James, Michael Mccker, and Mel Spiro read all or parts of the manuscript at
various stages, and repeatedly asked the difficult questions that propelled it
further. Conversations with Suzanne Brenner, Charis Cussins, Jim Holston,
and Marcelo Suarez-Orozco enabled me to see the project from different
perspectives. Kit Woolard asked me whether I was ready to make public some
of my private concerns about the profession. Lisa Rosen produced the title for
the first chapter. Shelley Burtt was, as usual, the best of friends and readers.

Conversations with Vincent Crapanzano, Michael Herzfeld, Rick Shweder, David Rudner, James Laidlaw, Susan and Chris Bayly, and Carrie Humphrey have all had important consequences for the direction of this work. Hastings Donnan made me see what was really interesting in the story. John Hinnells introduced me to my first Parsis and gave generously of his time, as did Alan Williams and Mary Boyce. Polly O'Hanlon had a powerful influence on my thinking years after we had a series of conversations I didn't fully understand at the time.

Parsis have been unfailingly hospitable. The K. R. Cama Oriental Institute under the direction of Dastur JamaspAsa was kind beyond the demands of hospitality. Khojeste Mistree, Shehnaz Munshi, and the rest of the Zoroastrian Studies group included me in many activities and were very kind to a lonely, confused American. Adi Doctor, Homai Bode, Meher Master-Moos, the Dubashes, the Shroffs, the Bankers, the Khurodys, the Pestonjis, the Daruwallas—many Parsis took time to speak with me and to guide me, and in the process I gained some important and enduring friends.

Lastly let me thank Lindsay Waters, who is exactly what every editor should be: he gauges the writer/scholar's skills, believes in them, and thereby helps to make more out of them than the writers themselves thought possible.

INDEX

Abu-Lughod, L., 231
ambivalent attachment, 22–24
anthropology, 2, 223f
Appadurai, A., 191, 194–195, 203
Appiah, A., 191, 194–195, 203
Asad, T., 225
asha, 65, 100
authenticity, 200–201
Axelrod, P., 169–171

Berry, M. E., 106
Bhabha, H., 191, 195–196, 197
Bharucha, P., 167
Billimoria, H., 172
Bombay, 27–31, 46
Borneman, J., 236
business success, 105

Cannadine, D., 20
charity, 96, 97, 105–107, 126, 150–152
Chaudhuri, N., 6, 49
Christian Science, 48
Clifford, J., 191–192, 226
colonialism, 2f
Comaroff, J., 227
community complaints, 126f
conversion, 158f
Council of Vigilant Parsis, 73–75
Crapanzano, V., 207–208
cricket, 117, 119–120
Cusrow Baag, 32–33

D'Andrade, R., 208–209
Daruwalla, K., 52, 82–83, 125
Davar decision, 164–165, 280
decay, trope of, 130
Desai, B., 35, 52, 78–79, 117–118, 173
Desai, S. F., 25, 141, 142–143
Dina and Richard, 218–221
Dirks, N., 194
dokhmenashini, 80–83, 86, 158f, 260, 261
dualism, 68–69

effeminacy, 132f
English language use, 37–38, 113
Erikson, E., 199–200, 211
Ewing, K., 229

Fanon, F., 10, 12–13, 14
fertility, 133, 282, 283
Fezana, 214
Fischer, M., 237–238, 260, 268, 269, 274
Freud, S., 23

Gatha Studies Trust, 213–214
Geertz, C., 209
gender, 5–6, 88–9, 98, 112–113, 117f, 132f, 174f, 271
Gilligan, C., 203
Gilroy, P., 203
Good, B. and M-J., 235

Gould, K., 172
Grimshaw, A., and K. Hart, 235

haoma, 256–257
Hartsock, N., 246
Haynes, D., 100–101
Herzfeld, M., 2, 235, 236
Holston, J., 235
humor, 221

identity, 191–194, 197–203, 254;
  semiotics of group identity, 248
Inden, R., 9
intermarriage, 160f
Iran, 51, 102–104
Iranis, 130,131, 274
Ishiguro, K., 17

Jeejeebhoy, J. J., 1, 105
Jussawalla, A., 53–56

Karaka, D. F., 24, 96–99
Karanjia, B. K., 70–72, 167
Keesing, R., 225
Kipling, R., 7–8, 245, 246
Kondo, D., 209
Krios (Creoles), 18–19

Lebra, T., 19
Lutz, C., and J. Collins, 236, 241–242

Mani, L., 191, 196, 210
manliness, 117–122, 126, 130, 272;
  unmanliness, 132f
marginality, 191f
marriage statistics, 168
Marzban, A., 43–44
McClure, J., 7, 196
McHugh, E., 209
Memmi, A., 10–12, 13, 14
Mercer, K., 193
Mistry, C., 60–62
Mistry, R., 56–60
moral concepts, 96f, 127f
Mukherjee, B., 192

Nandy, A., 6, 8, 14, 119–120
Naoroji, D., 92–93, 123, 274
Navsari, 35, 38

O'Hanlon, R., and D. Washbrook, 193–
  194
Obeyesekere, G., 209
Ong, A., 204
Orwell, G., 4

Parsis, 4–5, 14–17, 31–38 passim;
  British relationship with, 84–86,
  104, 111–116; ethos, 41–62; in
  Gujarat, 38–39; history of, 78f;
  humor, 43–45; monuments, 46;
  resistance to the British, 92–93, 123–
  124; standard of living, 39–41, 93–
  94, 252
Patel, G., 52–53
Percy, 139–141
Persian qualities, 97, 102–104
Peterson, J., 179–183
postcolonial identities, 186f
Prakash, G., 193–194, 225–226
Price, R. and S., 224–225
progressiveness, 96, 107–109, 126, 130,
  148–149, 158f
purity, 96, 101–104, 126, 130, 146–148

Quinn, N., 208–209

Rabinow, P., 227–228
Ripon Club, 43
Roshan, 186f
Rudner, D., 106

Said, E., 226
Salih, T., 246
Sanjan, 38, 78–79, 83
Schafer, R., 203–206, 210
Scheper-Hughes, N., 232, 235
Scott, P., 5, 19–20
Shah, Roxan Darshan, 158f
Shirin, 633–64, 66, 174–176
Shweder, R., 212, 241
Sidhwa, B., 88–89
Siegel, L., 236
Silko, L. M., 227
Spiro, M., 209
Spivak, G., 191, 210, 226–227
Strauss, C., 208–209
Suleri, S., 6, 191, 194, 197, 203
Surat, 38

Tambiah, S. J., 236
Tata, J. N., 91–92
Tata, R. N., 163
Taylor, C., 211–212
tradition, debates over, 158f
Traweek, S., 235
Trilling, L., 200–201
truthfulness, 96, 97, 100–101, 126, 130, 144–146
Tsing, A., 236–237
Turnbull, C., 232

Udwada, 38–39

Wadia, P. A., 25–26, 141–142

West, C., 192, 197, 203
westernization, 110-0116, 135–137, 171
White, D. L., 107
Williams, B., 16
Willingdon Club, 42–43
women, role of, 133–135, 174–179
Wurgaft, L., 7

Yasmin, 50–51

Zarathustra, 65–69, 72–76, 255, 256, 257
Zoroastrian Studies, 62
Zoroastrianism: as practiced, 36–37; history, 65–78